My Father's Love

Portrait of the Poet as a Young Girl

Also by Sharon Doubiago

poetry
Chinatown
Hymn to the Cosmic Clothesline
Visions of a Daughter of Albion
Hard Country
Oedipus Drowned
Psyche Drives the Coast
South America Mi Hija
The Husband Arcane.   The Arcane of O
Body and Soul
Greatest Hits
Love on the Streets

stories
The Book of Seeing With One's Own Eyes
El Niño

editor
*Wood, Water, Air and Fire, The Anthology of Mendocino Women
        Poets* with Devreaux Baker and Susan Maeder
Western Edge: 33 Poets, with Bill Bradd and Duane BigEagle
The Dalmo'ma Anthologies and Empty Bowl Press with Michael
        Daley and the Ohode Collective, 1980-1987

My Father's Love

Portrait of the Poet as a Young Girl

A Memoir

VOLUME ONE

Sharon Doubiago

Wild Ocean Press
San Francisco

Lines quoted from *Hard Country,* West End Press, 1982, 1999; *Body and Soul,* Cedar Hill Publications, 2000; *Psyche Drives The Coast,* Empty Bowl, 1990; *The Book of Seeing With One's Own Eyes,* Graywolf, 1988; *Love on the Streets, Selected and New Poems,* University of Pittsburgh, 2008.

Grateful acknowledgement is made to the editors of publications in which earlier versions of sections of this book first appeared:

"California Daughter/1950," by "D.S.", *Aphra,* New York, Spring Summer, 1976. (Listed in *Martha Foley's 100 Distinguished Short Stories:1976*).

"California Daughter/1950," *I Never Told Anyone: Writing by Women Survivors of Child Sexual Abuse,* by "Jean Monroe," eds. Ellen Bass and Louise Thornton, Harper & Row, 1983; Harper Perennial, 1991.

"Raquel, First Grade," *The Mendocino Grapevine,* Ukiah, 1978.

"The Word with Wings," *LCQ (Literary Center Quarterly),* Seattle, WA., Fall 1990.

"The Word with Wings," *The American Voice,* Lewisville, KY, No. 24, Fall 1991.

"Fragments from the Sacred Text: The Writer's Life as a Subject." *Left Bank Review,* Blue Heron Publishing Inc., Hillsboro, Oregon, Winter 1991. Also, *Writer's Northwest Handbook,* 4th Edition, Media Weavers Press, Hillsboro, OR, 1991. Also, *Rain City Review,* Portland Oregon, Fall/Winter 1995-96.

from Chapter 1, "My Father's Love," *The Nevada City Poetry Series Anthology.* Fall 2001.

from Chapter 1, "My Father's Love," *New College Review,* online, Spring 2006. http://www.newcollege.edu/ncr/doubiago.htm.

from Chapter 8, "Santa and The Black Dahlia Reading Lessons," *The Santa Monica Review,* Spring 2005.

Chapters 11-12, *Ensemble, (online),* July 2006. Chapters 13-14, *Ensemble Antholozine* (print), July, 2006. Chapters 15-16, *Ensemble. (online),* Oct 2006. Chapters 17-19, *Ensemble Antholozine* (print), October, 2006. www.ensemblejourine.com.

from Chapter16, *Cadence of Hooves, A Celebration of Horses, An Anthology of Poetry,* Yarroway Mountain Press, 2008.

Chapter 34, "Let the Images Rise: My First Poem," The Poets' Encyclopeadia.com. www.poetsencyclopedia.com/doubiago.shtml.

*

For information please contact Wild Ocean Press, www.wildoceanpress.com or www.sharondoubiago.com or http://members.authorsguild.net/sdoubiago

Doubiago, Sharon,
My father's love, Portrait of the poet as a young girl, volume 1, a memoir-1st ed. Fathers and daughters, childhood and youth, incest, trauma, memory studies, poetry, women studies, feminism, Southern California studies (Ramona), American history, Tennessee, North Carolina, Virginia. The Civil War, The 1898 White Supremacist Race Riots of Wilmington, North Carolina, the Brown Lung Tuberculosis Epidemic, the Danville Cotton Mill, Virginia, 1920s, The Ducktown Copper Mine Strikes, 1930s

Includes biographical/genealogical references: John Hancock, Jesse Corn, Mary Sharp, the Edens, the Clarkes, the Swains, Simmons, Chitwoods, the Doubiagos

ISBN: 978-0-9841304-0-5

Printed in the United States of America

Wild Ocean Press
1371 21st Avenue
San Francisco, CA 94122
www.wildoceanpress.com

for **Gae**- *"a place in the river where one must swim to cross."*
for **Penny**- *"There are two losses, Hilde* (Penny) *and Beverly."*

Mama, April, 1997.

for **Chelli Dawn-** *my brother and Beverly's daughter, who, if I had told in adulthood, would have been spared the same fate.*

for mi hijos, Shawn and Danny and Ryan

PARA TODOS LOS NIÑOS

Some of their names have been changed.

Table of Contents

Author's Note 1

Book I: Mama and Daddy

Chapter 1: Conception, Birth 9
Chapter 2: Hollydale, Mozelle 26
Chapter 3: Bridget Colleen 40
Chapter 4: Clarke Frederick 53
Chapter 5: Penny, World War II 68
Chapter 6: Mozelle, Strick, Sambo, Grandpa 80
Chapter 7: Five years old, genealogy and stories......... 94
Chapter 8: Kindergarten 113
Chapter 9: First Grade, Grandpa Avon Marion Edens ..128
Chapter 10: Second Grade....................................139

Book II: Gae

Chapter 11: Second Grade 151
Chapter 12: Second Grade 163
Chapter 13: Summer 180
Chapter 14: Third Grade 194
Chapter 15: Summer. 217
Chapter 16: Summer...236
Chapter 17: Fourth Grade 244
Chapter 18: Summer 262
Chapter 19: Fifth Grade 268
Chapter 20: Fifth Grade 276
Chapter 21: Summer 295
Chapter 22: Sixth Grade 301
Chapter 23: Sixth Grade......................................314

Book III: Mama

Chapter 24: Sixth Grade 331
Chapter 25: Summer 340
Chapter 26: Summer 348
Chapter 27: Seventh Grade 351
Chapter 28: Seventh Grade 360
Chapter 29: Seventh Grade 369

Book IV: Ramona

Chapter 30: Seventh-Eleventh Grades 375
Chapter 31: Eleventh-Twelfth Grades 396
Chapter 32: Twelfth Grade 403

Book V: Poet
Chapter 33: Palomar 411
Chapter 34: Topanga 424

Notes 435
The Families 436
A Note on Sources 445
Acknowledgements 446
About the Author 448

"and down they forget as up they grow" e.e. cummings

"I hadn't so much forgot as I couldn't bring myself to remember." Maya Angelou

"There is no agony like bearing an untold story inside you." Zora Neale Hurston

"Until the missing story of ourselves is told, nothing besides told can suffice us: we shall go on quietly craving it." Laura Riding Jackson

"Memory is accomplishment." William Carlos Williams

"All that I was taught at home or in school was colored by denial, and thus it became so familiar to me that I did not see it. Only now have I begun to recognize that there were many closely guarded family secrets that I kept, and many that were kept from me.... How old is the habit of denial? We keep secrets from ourselves that all along we know.... I am beginning to believe that we know everything, that all history including of each family, is part of us, such that, when we hear any secret revealed, a secret about a grandfather, or an uncle, or a secret about the battle of Dresden in 1945, our lives are made suddenly clearer to us, as the unnatural heaviness of unspoken truth is dispersed." Susan Griffin

"Who shall measure the heat and violence of the poet's heart when caught and tangled in a woman's body?" Virginia Woolf

Author's Note

"Your secrets will wear the faces of your children." Rainer Maria Rilke

When I was seven I was raped by my father, climaxing the sexual relationship he'd had with me from birth. He continued non-penetrative—at least as I remember—sex until I was twelve when I told my mother. In 1969, with an Incomplete in Creative Writing preventing me from receiving the Master's Degree in English, I wrote under the pressure of a five day deadline, *California Daughter.* This story quickly brought me the offers of two Ph.D. Creative Writing Fellowships (University of Iowa and University of California, Irvine) and a nine month fellowship residency at the Fine Arts Work Center in Provincetown, Massachusetts, all of which I turned down out of the shock of what I had written and of my professors seemingly too-eager appropriation. Nobody was writing or telling this kind of story then. I couldn't help but feel that its "brilliance" was its sensational subject matter, not my writing talent, that "they" were just interested in working with a girl who'd had sex with her father and dared to write of it. I took a vow which lasted five years never to be a creative writer. I dropped out, became a hippie, a countercultural mother, a private Joycean scholar, and an anti-war activist.

But over the next twenty years the story took on a life very much its own. It was published by the early, influential New York feminist magazine, *Aphra,* under the initials, D.S., becoming one of the first stories in the new incest awareness movement. It was chosen for Martha Foley's *One Hundred Distinguished American Short Stories of 1976,* read in consciousness-raising groups and workshops, and republished under the pen name Jean Monroe in the first major anthology on the subject, Ellen Bass and Louise Thornton's *I Never Told Anyone: Writings by Women Survivors of Child Sexual Abuse.*

When my father was dying he confessed the rape. Minutes before her death, my mother, who had mostly maintained that she didn't believe me, divorced my father "spiritually forever," acknowledging, at least, his betrayal of her. I was the caretaker of both in their long dyings.

My Father's Love is an in-depth, Proustian expansion of the sixteen page 1969 story that I'd always refused to develop, sometimes against great pressure, both personal and professional. It includes the "normal," happy, and inspired parts of my childhood too, and much of what I've always known of my parents' difficult histories—these being essential to grasping the full story. (And essential to alleviating my lifelong fear of our story being sensationalized or exploited.)

Observing me writing in my journal during my father's final illness a family friend asked what I was doing. "She's writing it all down for when we croak," he quipped from out of his coma. Yes, Daddy. This is finally my story which I sacrificed for you and Mama, and which I realize only now you both fully anticipated, in fear and dread, and waged lifelong psychological warfare against me to suppress and prevent it.

My Father's Love is the story of a girl labeled beautiful. "The ideal of physical beauty," Toni Morrison says, "is the most destructive idea in the history of human thought." *My Father's Love* is about this most destructive idea—how it destroyed not just a father's love, but a mother's and a sister's too.

It is about memory, language, truth, lies, deception, manipulation, and denial. It's about remembering and forgetting. About not knowing in the first place. It was written remembering and reliving. And then forgetting again. Then, in reading the writing, having to realize what the writing said, having to be as smart as any potential reader—this anticipated reciprocity is reason in itself for writing memoir. It was written in the awareness of the "memory wars" of the past decade and the subsequent publishing censorship on the subjects of incest and sexual molestation.[1] It was written in awareness of the controversies of memoir writing.

When I wrote *California Daughter* in 1969 I did not remember the rape itself. *California Daughter* is about "the lesser molestations" from age nine. Volume Two of *My Father's Love* tells the story of the shock of my father's confession. From 1969 until then, 1987, through the profound feminist-incest, parental-abuse consciousness era, I meditated regularly on our relationship, but I never "imagined" the rape (except in nightmare). I would have never allowed the memory if he hadn't told me. I was in denial. Denial in our culture is at least as common as lying. And though I tried to digest the fact in the years after his death and before I began the writing I still had not emotionally, or psychically. I certainly never saw my mother's and sister's parts in maintaining my Philomela's cut-out tongue.

When I say that *My Father's Love* is directed towards the controversies of the memory wars and memoir writing I am referring mainly to its not being traditionally shaped by the narrator. That traditional shaping, the author's voice over the material (and the reader) is what leads to fiction. If I had written *My Father's Love* by the prevailing rules I would not have gotten to the real story. If I had written the story of my childhood as I consciously carried it all my life, until this six year process, if I had spoken from the "clear," and "organized" stance of the How-to-Write-Memoir books, I would have written a very different book. I would have written, for one thing, a much less damning one of my parents; that is, I would have remained in and written from the delusional spell cast upon me by them and our situation. And, to quote the poet Laura Riding, I would be still quietly craving my story. My survival instinct, my love for my family, and a literary reputation for "seeing with one's own eyes" had always prevented me from seeing what actually happened, which became blatantly clear in writing it out in the method that I used.

It is also not written by another standard: that the emotional truth is the truth, more important than the factual or being true to the facts. I suppose this standard is in behalf of the "creative," but I wanted the facts which helped to create my emotional truth and the creative in me, many of which had always been denied, or denied me. I wanted to know what happened, the true story. Every mistake, untruth, wrong year or wrong assumption took me down a road further from what I was seeking. (No doubt there are still wrong roads here but not from lack of my trying to find the right ones.) No fictional story or myth can match the emotional root power of factual truth. And making art of facts, and of one's life, are not contradictions.

I want the truth, as close as it is possible to get to it, and I want it in books called "memoir." If the story is the emotional truth over factual truth then the writer has a moral obligation to call it fiction (or fictional memoir, etc.), from both the reader's perspective and from all the persons, dead or alive, in the real life story. The prevailing approach now falls right into the notions of the False Memory Syndrome advocates, that memoirists, especially incest tellers, are just telling their emotional truth—their memories are false, they are lying, their motives are sensationalism, profit and revenge.

I began keeping memory lists years ago. I discovered my story by putting remembering before telling, and never telling anything I was unsure of, unless apparent or stated in that context, and verifying as much as I could—with family albums and other photographs, baby books, diaries, journals, testimonies, interviews, letters, films, tapes, history dates, formal research—and then having to deal with what the words said, and what putting the memories in sequence summed up, as their non-verbal, non-linear, free-floating reality inside me didn't. Probably nothing was more advantageous and undeniable than the simple method of chronology. I dismantled much good writing on discovering I had the sequence wrong, only to discover, almost invariably, a deeper, more profound story.

"Surely all art," Carolyn Forché says, "begins in a wound." The artist is our modern day shaman. In ancient worlds the shaman was the one who, torn apart, put herself back together again for the community in order to tell the community how. How to survive. This is also the Psyche myth, her search, and work, for the human soul. My book is about the evolution of a poet, in survival of family and society—and prose, if you will. From my beginning there was an issue with, a difficulty about, an entanglement with, language. The fragmented nightmare images rooted in actual occurrences, and the waves of emotional terror, love, and faith turned into images, sound, rhythm and meaning of poetry, to language communicated as fragments, as in the linebreaks of poetry—that is, language fragmenting prevailing consciousness—sometimes into prayer, and even paranormal seeing and prophecy.

Sexually abused children learn to leave the body during the ordeal; they develop out-of-body consciousness. The brain compartmentalizes. Trauma memories are stored in different parts of the brain than normal memories; they are often not remembered at all, then something happens and there they are—Freud's "the return of the repressed"—flashbacks, nightmares, and cryptonesia which are memories recalled not as memories. You can be in one reality one moment, another the next, without making the connections.

Psychology conferences have recently been engaging poets as keynote speakers because we deal with much the same material as psychologists and therapists, but have found a different way into this realm—through art. This is not to pathologize art, particularly poetry, or to diminish the therapeutic of formal psychoanalysis. Writing is therapeutic, but as art it is much more than that, it is a gift to the world, and in that shamanic work and giving it is potentially more therapeutic than the sole self-involvement of therapy.

My Father's Love is an effort to understand how my father, a sensitive young man of moral integrity and religious training could have been so blighted as to make, and continue to make, a soul-destroying, daughter-and-family-obliterating mistake. Indirectly, it is about the negative effect of our legal/criminal codes. My father, as a man, was sexually empowered by the culture, while simultaneously required by it to lie, deceive and hide this sexuality—psychic blackmail, if ever there was such. Let me be clear:

I would do today what I did at seven—I would protect him, and us, from the State, even for all the damage subsequently incurred. My whole family was condemned to secrecy, and therefore, helplessness, in part for fear of the "justice system." I am not advocating such, I am simply stating another psychic reality, which is fairly universal.

The complexity may seem overwhelming, but this is Psyche's task. The legal system will never eradicate this sin. The root of sexual and psychological abuse is in culture's fascism, its anti-humanness, its soullessness. Other realities and ethical systems have to be found, starting with much greater consciousness in raising children. "No one taught me how to be a father!" my father bemoaned repeatedly at the end. "Why wasn't Fathering taught me in high school?" The current popularity and importance of memoir is part of an evolution toward greater consciousness.

The last paragraphs of Volume Two take place on my last day in my mother's Ashland, Oregon home after her death. During the night a neighbor's house burned to the ground. Only with the newspaper story did I learn that Vladimir Nabokov completed *Lolita* in this house in 1953. *Lolita* is listed as fourth on Modern Library's 100 Best Novels of the 20th Century.

I was Lolita in June 1953, the month he moved here. That's when I told my mother.

Fourth!

It's fifty years later in America but it's still taboo for Lolita to tell her own story.

"Mama and Daddy, is it you? Did you burn his house down for me?"

§

Book I
Mama and Daddy

Honor thy father and thy mother. Exodus 20:12

Jealousy is an unnatural lust. Ovid

One

I am the tiny space between my parents facing each other. This is my earliest memory. We are in the sun-yellow kitchen. I am exactly between them. He is accusing her of something and she is sobbing back at him, trying to protest. There's the smell of feces and blood, something terrible between them, some terrible misunderstanding. Whoever is the self?

The soul is created from a sexual union, a poet said.

I was conceived on Redondo Beach in Southern California, on the north side of the pier, beside the creosoted, barnacled piling, a bed of sand washed by the high tide every twelve hours. She was a waitress at the Japanese café at the end of the pier. He had ridden the rails north to catch the wheat harvest in Washington. In their letters they'd talked of having a baby, made the decision, though everyone protested, how can you bring a child into this world? When she got off work at eight that night he was there. They couldn't wait to get back to the apartment. They didn't need to, she wasn't going to use her diaphragm. I guess you could say I couldn't wait.

My parents came to California in a getaway car. Four men and Mama, the driver having shot and killed a friend in a legal midnight duel on the McCaysville bridge over the Ocoee-Toccoa River, the border between Tennessee and Georgia. Legal: midnight, mid river, mid states. But now the dead man's brothers would be out for him. *They chewed bubble gum all the way/to plug the holes in the radiator,/to quiet the hunger pains.*[2] Cecil Frederick Edens and Audrey Garnet Clarke shared one profound fact: both were from families who came to the New World over a hundred years before the Revolution, original members on both sides arriving in the 1620-30s. The Edens' side from England—the Hancocks, Corns, Chitwoods, Winns, Martins, Overbys, Goodloes, Stovals—were "original aristocrats" of Virginia. (My fifth great-grandparents were anti-slavery neighbors of Thomas Jefferson—the John Hancock land survey bordering Monticello was done by Peter Jefferson, Thomas' father.) They were founders (Edenton, North Carolina; Patrick County, Virginia; Estill Springs, Tennessee), land breakers, ferry and bridge builders, educators, college founders and endowers, justices of the peace, church leaders and preachers, diarists, emancipators and abolitionists, women's rights advocates, Indian and Revolutionary War fatalities and decorated heroes, and a few, starting late, twenty years into the nineteenth century as if in fall, plantation slave owners. John Hancock, Daddy's fourth great-grandfather, was the first signer of the Declaration of Independence.

The Clarkes—the Swains, Reynolds, Jacksons, Simmons—from England also, and Scotland and Ireland, tended to mate with the Cherokee, Choctaw, Seminole and Lumbee, thus rooting the family in the most ancient American tree, and some in extreme victimization. Mama's paternal grandfather's great-grandfather was William Rogers Clark of the Lewis and Clark Expedition and brother of George Rogers Clark, "Revolutionary general and conqueror of the old Northwest;" her paternal grandmother's great-grandfather was Saloli, the Cherokee son of Ga-tal-sta Catalst, born in 1791, who took the last name Jackson for his Commander in Chief, Andrew, in the Battle of Horseshoe Bend against the Creeks. Her maternal grandmother's grandfather's brother was R.J. Reynolds of tobacco infamy.

Or so I was always told. Most of the records bear out what I was repeatedly ordered to never forget. In fact they reveal a significant number of illustrious ancestors of the early American roll call that were forgotten—Benjamin Franklin, Richard Swain, first "white" male born on Nantucket Island, Francis Scot Key, and others.

Everyone fought in the Civil War. Both genders, all the sides (though by then all were Southerners), all the races.

They were so poor when they first got to California in May, they survived by night raids on the cornfields in Torrance and Long Beach. Mama and my Aunt Alice, to whose house on Cade Street they arrived, wore the men's overalls
> *to stuff the golden-haired ears.*
> *Daddy and Uncle K.D. drove along the outside*
> *of the tall rows in the getaway car.*
> *Mama always laughed when she told me*
> *of the farmer on Rosecrans*
> *who shot at her.*

And so soon after their arrival Daddy jumped the train to Walla Walla, Washington to make some money, just as he'd done in Tennessee as a teenage boy.

They were certain I was a boy. They named me Clarke Frederick Edens, set a place for Clarke at the table each night.

"My maternal instinct was so great I wouldn't put anything in my body that might harm you."

Though there was barely enough to eat, soon she had nothing that fit. She dreaded the idea of being seen in a second-hand clothes shop, kept putting it off. Finally, with Daddy's encouragement and accompaniment, she dared the Long Beach Salvation Army Thrift Store, picked out some nice maternity clothes. But up at the cash register she was so mortified she couldn't go through with it. She fled, leaving the hours of selection on the counter.

She found a doctor in Long Beach. The first thing he said in looking at her on the table was "You were made to have babies, weren't you, Mrs. Edens?" Though long and small through the waist her hips were wide-set. He could not have said a more endearing thing. Even as a little girl, she, motherless, had played at being a mother. Her plan was to be a perfect mother. That was why she waited until she was twenty. She'd read that a teenager's body isn't mature enough to make a healthy baby.

Daddy finally got on as the Good Humor Ice Cream man for the Hollywood Hills. He always told us this when we licked our ice cream cones. Julie London was one of his customers. One day she came out of her house and stopped his tingle-lingle tingle-lingle truck. Then in the telling he would sing *"My heart belongs to Daddy."* When I grow up and live in those same hills, a little to the east, people will tell me I look just like Julie London. Once a door-to-door salesman exclaimed when I opened it, Julie London! Julie London, older than my mother, also sang *Round Midnight, I'm in the Mood for Love, Easy Street, Daddy* (another Daddy song), and *The Thrill is Gone.* Those songs have always played inside me.

On the Sunday before I was born, "the day you were scheduled to be born," they were at the beach at Point Fermin, San Pedro, the southern tip of the Los Angeles Basin. They were in the rocks with Annabelle, a little white mutt with a black ring around her left eye. Two guys were out in a small boat, cutting up, just having a good time.

"I was getting a kick out of them, but I said something awful. 'Serve them right if one of them drowned.' Then it happened, maybe a wave turned them over. They were calling for help. Your father ran for help and I stood on the rocks, calling to them to hold on, help is coming. It went on all afternoon, it was terrible, terrifying. Then one let go. The other kept going under after him, kept trying to pull the drowned body out. I was depressed for days. You were born six days later, on Saturday."

All my life I'd seen the photographs of Daddy and Annabelle in the Point Fermin rocks six days before I was born (though none of Mama with me inside her), but I didn't hear this story until September 20, 1987, on the third day after his death. We were walking through the Oregon dunes, my sister, brother, and I, with our mother, near the north mouth of the Siuslaw River, when, as we leaped a puddle, she just let this story out.

A missing piece fell into place like a grain of sand to the dune we were walking. My life shifted slightly.

My first spontaneous poem, *I Was Born Coming To The Sea,* written for her on her fifty-eighth birthday tells of the boy out in the ocean I have always sensed.

They told me the sound was a boy out there
telling boats how to come in through the fog.
I listened to the waves slapping him around.
I heard his crying, his lonely orphanage in the sea.
When we fished, I cast my line to him, I was coming
to the sea when I was born,
the buoy I heard through water and storm
was a boy calling me.

Because they were Southerners they pronounced buoy as boy. Many of my drowning experiences—in dream, writing, and reality—had seemed until that moment paranormal, of inexplicable coincidences, of extrasensory perception. I pull up to a beach and, as if called, become part of a drowning. I camped on a beach near Chappaquiddick the night of the infamous Mary Jo Kopechne drowning, was tormented all night by a waking nightmare of a woman trapped in a leaking air container out under the ocean, calling me to rescue her. Now with my mother's new story I realized my experiences are of the sensory, of the body itself. How do the grunion know the highest tide? The salmon their natal creek mouth? We reenact, often unconsciously, our childhood dramas as adults; inexplicably, until that moment in the dunes, I had reenacted, or at least reexperienced my prenatal experience all my life. Déjà vu. I had "already seen" him: I was born coming to him drowning in the sea.

But it took even longer to realize another part of the story. April 20, 1941 was the seventeenth anniversary of her mother's death.[3] The depression I swam in the last six days I was inside her was connected to the body she had been in her first nine months. But not even our father's death allowed her to make that connection, at least to us.

It was also Adolph Hitler's 52nd birthday.

When she woke that morning she knew I was coming. She took a laxative. She'd been told this would help. They were the renters now of Aunt Alice's little white house on Cade Street. They walked the several miles to the hospital. On every corner last night's headlines blasted **London Mother, Baby, Go on Shopping Trip.** The photo was grotesque, more a monster from nightmare than a young mother in her gas mask and iron helmet. The metal and rubber-hosed bundle in her arms was the baby, not weaponry for the purpose of mass destruction. *"This is what motherhood in London means these days. This young mother, with basket* (hanging off her elbow under the entombed infant, a surreal remnant from the Old World), *went shopping during a gas mask drill. Note the elaborate protection for infants against the deadly weapon Britain fears Hitler will not hesitate to use when he thinks it is necessary...."* Masks will be a constant in my first six weeks of life. All humans will wear them.

They walked to the wrong hospital, the Catholic hospital.

"You're to go to Seaside Hospital."

So then they set out for Seaside, on the other side of town. At Seaside they examined her and sent her out to walk some more. You're way too tight for anything to be born.

They walked—me inside her coming—the hilly streets of Long Beach all day. Now on every corner, next to the masked mother and baby, were the evening headlines

WARFARE IN GREECE RAPIDLY NEARS END. Nazi Force Within 30 Miles of Athens: British Are Cut Off. Berlin Says Hundreds Are Captive. London Pins Hopes Upon Aid of U.S. Thebes Falls Before Drive of Panzers.

She avoided the papers as best she could. She regarded herself an orphan of The Great War. World War II will rarely be in her endless stories to her children. Maybe not even in the stories to herself, though how conscious my mother was of her omissions and denials is one of my big questions.

"All that walking, plus the laxative, must have been the reason you came so fast."

The doctor examined her at eight, declared I wouldn't be born for twenty-four hours. It was Saturday night and he left for a party. I was born forty minutes later.

She was rushed into the delivery room. Frantic calls were made, kept being made for the doctor. She was strapped around the ankles and the table turned vertical with her head down to keep me from coming.

"They kept giving me cans of ether trying to hold you off till they could get ahold of him on his way to his party. You were coming so fast they hung me upside down."

She screamed so loud Daddy burst into the room. It was against all the rules of Seaside Hospital, and all the rules of society then, but my father was present at my birth. My mother told this story as much as any other. How fantastic, how exceptional my father was. How much he loved her. How all men should be this way.

"They'd put him out the door, it was against the rules, I was screaming my head off, he'd come through the other door. Finally, they gave up, gave him a gown and mask."

A woman delivered me. (Perhaps this had something to do with why or how "they" gave up, allowed my father to be present.) Her name is not on my birth certificate. The line for M.D., Midwife or Other is blank. On the line Attendant's Own Signature is C.R. Pentz, M.D. The name Doctor Pentz is as familiar to me as Long Beach, Cade Street, Artesia, Bellflower, Rio Hondo, Pico Rivera, Rancho Los Amigos, Florence, Firestone, Bell Gardens, Paramount, Norwalk, Hynes and other names in my mother's repertoire of stories from that era, but I'm surprised to find his name on my birth certificate. She spoke of Dr. Pentz in telling of the births of my sister and brother but not, as I recall, of mine. My doctor was always just the doctor. I guess she was being faithful to the facts. He did not deliver me.

But when I finally got out she saw the heavens open up, the angels singing, and her father, Guy Clarke, who had died five years before when she was fifteen, smiling down. My mother will tell me this, or write some version of this for my every birthday. "I really did see the angels, Sharon, and my father when you were born."

Mark tells that when Jesus was baptized, "*straight way, coming up out of the water, He saw the heavens opened, and the Spirit like a dove descending upon him.*" I do think my birth was a baptism for my mother, the miraculous beginning of a new family for her, the rebirth of so many she had lost.

At 8:40 p.m. on April 26, 1941, in the heavens over Long Beach California, the Sun, Venus, Moon, Saturn, Jupiter and Uranus were all in the constellation of Taurus and had just set on the ocean horizon with Mercury at the tail of Aries leading them down. (Uranus on the horizon was still visible). This was the astronomy. Astrologers interpreted this rare line-up of five planets with the sun and moon, in or conjunct to, the earth sign Taurus, at Hitler's fifty-second birthday, as ominous. Opposite that descent over Long Beach the cusp of Sagittarius was ascending. The Scorpio-Sagittarius cusp, the massive explosion of stars between the scorpion's tail and the horse's raised front hooves, is the origin/past of our galaxy in Science's Big Bang theory, and the origin/past also in universal myth. For instance the ancient Tibetan name for this cusp is *The Linga Sharira*, which is also the name for the whole galaxy we call *The Milky Way*. The Native Southern California name is *The Puchipa*. The meaning of the ancient names—*The Long Body of the Dream, The Long Body of the Tongue, The Long Body of God, The Long Road Souls Travel*—embodies a stunningly sophisticated comprehension of the structure of our long galaxy and our solar system's placement within it. The annual, astronomical moment when the solar system moves into a right angle to the galaxy's outer ends, to the Scorpio/Sagittarius cusp on the one—the past from which the solar system explodes—and the Taurus/Gemini cusp on the other—the future/extragalactic space to which the solar system sails—was recognized and celebrated. This right angle creates the crossroads of the ecliptic, and in myth the Crossroads of Time and the Universe when the Music of the Spheres can be heard, when the Gods call for us, when the Dead of the year can depart the Earth—that is, step off. The exact moment of this event occurs now every November 22, but the Linga Sharira is the original Halloween, All Souls Day, before the wobbling of the poles caused the earth to be out of wack with Western Civilization's calendar. The Sagittarius cusp also rises on the Earth's horizon every forty-eight hours, a wheels-within-wheels Linga Sharira pattern that, seemingly, will make itself known throughout my life.

I was born on my father's mother's sixty-first birthday. My father so loved his mother my middle name comes from her—Maude Lura or Lura Maude (as she recorded it in her Bible under Marriages). (Sometimes she spelled it Maud.) Lura means moonlight.

My first name comes from the novel, *The Grapes of Wrath,* by John Steinbeck, the nation's best selling book for the two years prior to my birth. *The Grapes of Wrath* is about the Great Depression, about the migration to California by the Okies—people fleeing the Dust Bowl of Oklahoma and the Midwest. Long Beach was known as the Okie Town. The majority of the Okies—Okla is Cherokee for red and homa means people—were former displaced Scots-Irish/Native Americans once again forced on a trail of tears. Rose of Sharon is the main female character in the book. Her name is from Solomon's Song in the Old Testament. *"I am the rose of Sharon and the lily of the valleys."* Her baby dies, but she breast feeds a starving man back to life. Rose and Sharon are the same name in Hebrew as in Rasharon, meaning the Line to God, as in the spiraling, ever-opening line of the rose petals from the bud center. There were always at least three other Sharons at my grade level in every school I attended—once there were six.

Her first memory of me was my voice. "It was so... like singing. Not harsh like the other babies. You could hear you in the nursery under all the other babies. It was ... beautiful."

She got an infection. She always put it "in the eleven days we were in the hospital," implying that the infection came from the hospital. "For your first eleven days I wasn't allowed to hold or nurse you. But I made the nurses pump my breasts so I wouldn't dry up."

She listened to me crying down the hall. "You had the softest lowest sweetest voice in the nursery. I always knew it from all the other babies. Kind of husky. I'd send your Daddy down to bring back descriptions of you, what you were doing."

"In the nursery," he will write in his last birthday card to me, "everybody matched or paired us, you looked that much like me. You had a very sexy cry, you know Wa, Wa in a low husky voice. Your crib mates were a screaming howling mob but you just wa wa'ed in a type of Come up and see me sometime, Mae West type of voice."

After visiting us the first time, Daddy went to Knott's Berry Farm to have his photograph taken professionally. To catch the moment in time he became a father. I never understood why it was significant that he went there, but it was; the little fact was never dropped, it was as important as the date. Maybe, with Mama in the hospital, it was an opportunity to do a little tourism. Perhaps he was taken there by a buddy, or buddies. Maybe the Knotts were from Tennessee. Maybe he knew them.

Dr. Pentz brought her the U. S. Government's pamphlet, *Infant Care,* saying she had to study it before she could go home with me. The government's philosophy was that holding, fondling, or cuddling the infant was to be avoided so as not to spoil the child. Physical contact between the mother and child was to be avoided as much as possible. Mothers were not to pick up their babies and comfort them. Feeding had to be done by schedule, for twenty minutes every four hours. Play was scheduled for ten minutes a day. The practice of separating the baby from the mother so that she could rest and recover from the delivery was especially emphasized. She was urged not to use the old fashion rocking cradle but to obtain a stationary crib instead.

The government's pamphlet, based on Luther Emmett Holt's 1894 *The Care and Feeding of Children*—with fifteen editions to 1935 it was the Dr. Spock book of the era—and the fact that I was kept from my mother my first eleven days will always be her main explanation as to why I turned out as I did. "I know what's wrong with you Sharon," she'll say to the very end, "you weren't held enough as a baby."

I wasn't born a thumb sucker, but on my tenth day, according to my Baby Book, I found it.

"We brought you home from the hospital in a '30 Roadster Ford, 'Margie.' Margie had a rumble seat." On every corner was the headline: **Hitler, Master of Europe!**

She was so weak she couldn't walk. Daddy had to carry her in his arms. Then he had to carry me in.

The old woman living across the street just marches in and takes over, we need help. Garnet Phiffer boils my diapers and bottles and cleans house and fixes meals for them. She sits on Mama's bed and reads to us from *Daily Word.* She believes I'm her son reincarnated. Who was your son? She whispers his name in my ear. Was he the one who drowned?

Garnet Phiffer, actually our Cade Street landlady, is the one who introduced my mother, Audrey Garnet, to the Unity Church. "Unity, you understand, is rooted in the writings of Ralph Waldo Emerson," Mama will tell me when I become an English major.

"Isn't it interesting that you had two Garnets in the beginning. I can't remember how her son died. She was a member too of The Great I Am, which I didn't understand, but the *Daily Word* writings were exactly how I felt about God and life. It fills my life."

Finally she's able to put me to her breasts. The clouds open up and my grandfather, Guy Clarke, that redheaded Irish Cherokee, is smiling down while she sings *tura lura lura. Tura lura lie.* Milk is still my favorite food.

But in a week the milk is mixed with something bitter, sour. Tura Lura is now a song of sobbing. Her big red nipple pulling out. "Look what you've done to me," she groans. "I'm just a mass of blood from nursing you."

I loved her too much, I sucked too hard. I sucked her nipples raw to the point they bled. Unfortunately she doesn't have her Daddy's red hair—

she was a blonde until the pregnancy—but she has the thin, sensitive skin
of a redhead.

Blood and tears, my mother's dread of me. My dread of myself. My
too great love.

It's his job to give me the 2:00 a.m. feeding so that she can get some rest.
"Oh, it's a full time job just trying to feed you." Before sleep she pumps
her milk into a bottle. She makes him promise to wear a mask.

In the night he lifts me from the buggy, naked but for his face. There's
nothing he hates more than to wear clothes in bed. His skin has a slight
sour smell, so different than hers. He changes my wet diaper, wipes and
vaselines me, puts the heated bottle in my mouth, holds me.

They both wear masks when holding or just being near me the first six
weeks of my life. She's terrified of the germs that wiped out her whole
family. He's afraid of germs too, maybe especially of hers. I love his
laughing and joking. Sometimes he loves me, maybe rolls me around his
Little Cecil. Sometimes, when the mood hits, he doesn't love me. It's so
hard for him to get back to sleep and they can't have sex yet.

He was jealous of me. I took her from him. He used to have her all to
himself but now when he came home she was in love with me. I was at the
breasts that had once been all his. They were even bigger than before. One
day as she nursed me "he got so mad he put his fist through the window,
shattering the glass. Glass flew everywhere."

She will compulsively tell fragments of this all my life. Sometimes it
happened before I was born and "he cut his hand all up," so evidently it
happened more than once. He was jealous of me even then, growing
slowly but steadily inside her, possessing her in a way he could never,
even though I was his planted seed. She will look at me, say "that did
happen to you, whether you remember or not," and as compulsively clam
up when I ask for the details. She will look at me as if to say, if I confess
to you this awful thing about your father will you then be okay? And
maybe, will you still believe I was a good mother?

"It's just that your father was so unhappy in the first years. Those
moods would strike him."

"Was he unhappy about being married?" I practiced asking that.

"Oh, no. Oh, no, he was very happy to be married to me. But ... well,
he was jealous. There was a man I went with just before I met your dad, a
baseball player, who had a little boy. I was sixteen. He wanted to marry

me, the attraction was sexual. I ran away from Virginia partly to get away from him. If I had stayed it would definitely have become sexual. He was constantly trying to get me to have sex, coercing and tricking me. Once we were sledding. He jumped on top of me as we came down the hill. I knew it could lead to sex, conception. I just knew I was going to be trapped into marrying him. I liked his three year old boy but I felt I was too young to marry, to be the mother of that little boy, I had a whole life ahead of me.

"He even found me."

He found her the week after she was married. He knocked on their hotel door in Charlotte, North Carolina.

"And I made the mistake of telling your father about us. I confessed that yes it was sexual but we did not go all the way. That this is why I ran away from Danville and now I loved him, I married him. Well, he could never forget this, he would get in those moods. There was one time when you were a baby ... " and she would tell again of the time he got so angry he put his fist through the window, shattering glass everywhere.

"The biggest shock of all was that he was jealous of you."

Then my mother would add, reassuringly, that my father had a special love for me, a love deeper than even daughter love.

Every day from two to four I lie in the buggy outside under the tree, naked. Annabelle with her half mask is under me, guarding me. It's hot. Mama is so proud that I am out here naked soaking up the sun. All this vitamin D. There is a white gauze veil to keep the flies off, another mask between me and the tree and the sky and the clouds and the birds. She is across the grass and though I am crying for her she is saying "I can't Sharon Lura. Not yet. Oh, Heaven knows how much I surely wish I could, but it would not be good for you, the government says so."

This yearning for my mother, her yearning for me. My little knees, east and west, my insides open to the world. The birds in the tree, the gulls flying over. Crying and crying. Her milk gushes out like a Pacific storm to hear me crying and her own crying "I can't pick you up, Sharon Lura, not till ten minutes to four, this is because I love you." I wa wa harder. "*Rock a bye baby*" gushes from her "*in the tree top.*" Mama's dilemma is waves of the ocean, the tree whooshing in the wind from the sea above me. "*And down will come baby, cradle and all.*"

Then from way across the sea I hear her singing "*Tura lura lura. Tura lura lie.*

T'is an Irish melody."

"When you were six weeks old your father taught me to drive. He'd already shown me how the gears and clutch work, out on Paramount Boulevard. It was a '26 Buick. It had reverse gears. We brought you home from the hospital in a '30 Roadster Ford, it had a rumble seat. But then we had a chance to get this two-seated luxury Buick.

"That Sunday we went to the top of Mt. Wilson. There's photos of this day. Coming back down, on Atlantic, Sunday bumper-to-bumper traffic, he handed the car over to me. You were in a basket in the back seat. Before we got home I was passing cars up, whipping in and out. He was scared, but kept his mouth shut.

"The next day I took you to your first doctor's examination. I drove alone, just you and me all the way down Cherry to Long Beach. I figured I knew how to drive now. The doctor couldn't believe I was still nursing you."

The doctor. Doctor C.R. Pentz.

Over the Fourth of July weekend, when I'm ten weeks old, more pictures are taken of me and Daddy. We're both on our stomachs on the quilt outside and we've raised our heads to the camera. (On the back in my grandmother's hand is written: *This is the one I like best.*) In another we're on our backs and he's holding a dark weird-looking bottle to my mouth, and we're eyeing each other. The blissful bedroomy expression on his face is from his wonderful side. In still another I'm sprawled naked on my back in the buggy, a string of big beads in my mouth, my pudendum exposed. My long oval tummy, my kicking legs, my open mouth, my mounds of Venus and my open rows of labia. My look is of joyous triumph—here I am, world! so happy I made it! A Mae West look saying "Come up and see me sometime." Perhaps I am mirroring my photographer.

Everywhere we went people exclaimed "My what a handsome boy!"

We would be coming down Long Beach Boulevard, me on my back in the buggy, the beads in my mouth, Mama with her figure back proudly pushing me. Cars honking. Pedestrians stopping her to see the baby.

"Oh!" They'd gasp peeking beneath the white veil. "That girl has no clothes on!"

But dressed, for the first fifteen months of my life, until the mass of blonde curls came in, everyone just assumed I was a boy. I was that handsome, she always said. Bald, you could see my intelligence. The way I looked right back at everyone, so seriously.

"You looked like your father. You had a ... strange look..." She shapes the fingers of both hands around her eyes like a Halloween mask and moves them across her face and out into her hair. "Through here."

There's a 1916 post card photograph of my father as an infant. He is truly handsome but as a "baby" he is strange. He looks old. He looks too knowing. He looks too smart. There's a look across his big bald head on his little baby shoulders that would make you believe in the Soul if you didn't. He's wearing a white lace dress but he looks so masculine you could almost believe the current pop concept that men are from Mars.

Actually, my father was from Uranus.

My Aunt Giny, Mozelle Virginia Clarke, Mama's baby sister, graduated from Hughes School in Danville Virginia that June and turned nineteen in September.

"*I was so stupid I didn't know I was supposed to leave,*" she wrote me three weeks before she died in April 1999.

"*There seemed to have been a policy to leave when you graduated. I was just so confused.*" Hughes School had been her home since she was five. It had been Mama's too, from age eight, but she got kicked out at fifteen for repeatedly running away.

The School called my mother in Los Angeles and wanted to know what to do with Mozelle.

"*They put me on a train out there. There was nowhere else for me to go.*"

She arrived in October. I was almost six months old. I had said my first words "*ma-ma-ma*" and "*pa-pa-pa.*" Mama wrote in my Baby Book: "*she definitely distinguishes between the two.*"

"*I am completely void of understanding so many things about that time. Everything was so completely foreign to me. Fred [Cecil] could never believe I had never even been in a grocery store when Garnet wanted me to go get some oranges. I was terrified and had no idea about getting the right change. I remember how Garnet taught me. And she got the job for me at the Pentz's. I worked for them as a maid for two years...*"

Now my father was jealous of Mozelle, of my mother's love and attention to her sister. He resented her intrusion on their privacy. He married an orphan, not a mother, not a sister. He was the starving man who needed her milk-of-kindness breasts all to himself. "You don't know how to make change?" he sneered. His contempt! His questioning her veracity.

He was sexually turned on by her too and of course that was her fault. In writing this book I have come to see that most likely he made advances—in the least, advances—to my aunt, my mother's sister.

There's a photo of Mozelle sunbathing in a one-piece on Cade Street. Her pearl white skin shines. So do her wide-set sky-blue eyes, her mile-wide mountain cheekbones, her red river mouth. Her breasts are even larger than Mama's, wonderfully round shapes like pies cooling on her narrow rib cage. Her reddish black hair falls in shiny waves over them and down to her waist. She is tall, taller than Mama, long limbed and very thin. She is more beautiful than a movie star. More beautiful than Loretta Young who everyone says she looks like. Physically, Mozelle's quarter Cherokee and quarter Lumbee-Seminole prevail. She's asked by strangers the name of her tribe. She's what I want to look like when I grow up.

I'm lying naked in my buggy which is getting too small for me, under the shade tree. There's gasping, sobbing, screaming and shouting, and sirens, and the sky full of metal.

The Japs have bombed Pearl Harbor and are on their way to bomb our naval fleet here in Long Beach next. Kamikazes are zooming through the sky. Mozelle can't stop crying. I can sit up now but hands are holding me down, fingers are probing inside my legs. Something bursts in my groin. Now I can't stop screaming either. Who was present that day? Is this when I rupture, get my hernia? Is this memory or just a psychic metaphor? All my life I will nightmare myself as a baby, an ugly, freakish, deformed baby about seven to eight months old with a huge Third Eye in the middle of my forehead, exploding from my bed straight up to the sky, then screaming as I crash back to Earth, "NO!"

A week later, the next Sunday, I stand up by myself.

Uncle Lawrence arrives, just back from chasing the Sandinistas through the jungles of Nicaragua, to be shipped out next to the Pacific Theater. The oldest of the three orphans, he too was kicked out of Hughes at fifteen, for dyslexia. He doesn't stay with us long. Daddy fumes that the whole family is here, but Mama kicks her brother out because "of his messing with the married woman next door." The woman next door is an intolerable issue to her what with Daddy's constant accusations and insults about her trashy illegitimate family. She will prove herself to him. Marriage is the sacrament of human society, more important than one's birth family. One is to cleave from one's family, cleave onto the husband, the head. She told this story of Lawrence late and outside the context of his orders for the new war. The war for my mother was about her reputation, her escape from her birth family's astoundingly tragic history of illegitimate races, classes, pregnancies, diasporas, homelessness, and early deaths.

But surely she worried some about her brother going off to war, about kicking him out.

I'm not fully weaned when she goes back to work for fifteen weeks to earn the money for the down payment on the house in Hollydale, which costs $3,450, already a hundred dollars more than last month.

Now I spend four hours alone with Daddy each evening. He's working at the furniture store with Odie, his best friend. He comes home about four. She takes off. She works in a café on Artesia Boulevard in Bell-flower. About two miles. She walks back home at ten each night. There are air raids, blackouts. One night Japanese planes fly over Inglewood. She isn't afraid, she doesn't think anything of it. She makes ten dollars a week for fifteen weeks to make the ninety-nine down, then works a little longer to buy some used furniture.

I suck my thumb I miss her so much. I love my thumb so much he hates me.

December 15-21, 1941: Sharon had diarrhea due to her mother working.

For my first Christmas dinner we went to the cafe where Mama was working. I met my Aunt Alice and cousins Billie and Shirlie and we celebrated their fifth and fourth birthdays. Uncle K.D., Daddy's older brother, was already at the war. Billie Jean stood around not talking, just sucking her thumb and staring.

I was the most unbaby baby Aunt Alice had ever met. She tried to baby talk me. I wouldn't smile at her. I just stared at her like she was silly.

"You were eight months old when I first laid eyes on you. You were sitting in a high chair without any hair. My first thought was what a shame she's not a boy. She's too handsome to be a girl. Then I cooed to you, baby talked you, made faces, carried on. But you just stared at me. You weren't a normal baby. Finally I got embarrassed. You stared at me so hard I felt like I was acting like a fool."

It's cold and dark and I feel alone like in the beginning. My thumb is red like fire. To put it in my mouth burns and makes tears gush from my eyes, makes sobs explode from my throat. At first I can't believe it, I forget. But every time flames burn in my mouth. Searing pain like Pearl Harbor on the Day of Infamy.

She lifts me, cooing baby shush. Carries me to the front room where the light hurts my eyes.

Sharon has never been able to sleep since we coated her thumb to keep her from sucking it.

It was always soothing to hear my mother acknowledge my sleeplessness even if she was too certain of the reason, too anxious to take the blame herself. She never expressed regret about coating my thumb. "Thank goodness you don't still suck your thumb," she'd sigh. "Look at five year old Billie Jean still sucking hers. Aunt Alice had better coat it, her teeth are going to come in bucked like mine." I remember falling into the shock, feeling double-crossed about my thumb, that I could no longer comfort myself in the long boring hours alone. But I remember knowing no, Mama, that's not the reason I can't sleep.

I'm eight and a half months old and though I have twelve teeth I'm still nursing. Once again I make my mother bleed. This devilish look comes over my face and she just knows it's coming. Suddenly, without warning, I clamp down, bite her.

"How could you?"

I don't know. I'm sorry.

The eruption of my teeth with the pain of your wanting free of me.

The tension's alleviated by biting.

You're looking for an excuse to wean me.

That's my devilish look. If you want to quit, ma-ma-ma, just say so. Just quit.

My mother will always make excuses, tell little white lies rather than be direct and honest. She doesn't dream she can be direct and honest and still be loved. Or safe. Pa-pa-pa would really have her then.

But she isn't safe in her excuses either. You want to bite her.

On January 20, 1942, when I'm almost nine months old, Reinhard Heydrich, head of Adolph Hitler's security police, assembled fourteen high ranking Nazis and bureaucrats for a breakfast with a view of the Havel River. Heydrich laid out detailed programs for the "Final Solution"—the extermination of all eleven million European Jews—which in fact was already under way.

All my life, even to this morning's San Francisco Chronicle, it's been publicly debated as to just exactly when we knew what Hitler was doing to the Jews. It must have been in the early Sixties when I first drove home to ask my mother if she knew back then. And again in the Eighties when Mozelle, by then a Mormon fundamentalist, first declared the Holocaust a fiction. "We knew," my mother said, sternly, but quietly. She always answered that question that way, up until her death. "Oh yes. We always knew."

§

Two

Something happened to my father in September of either his freshman or sophomore year at Tusculum College in East Tennessee. He was asked to leave and never return. My father hated Septembers. Everything bad that ever happened to him happened in September, Mama will say when he dies in September.

He was twenty-two when he met her, March 30, 1938, in Charlotte, North Carolina. Whenever I asked him about his youth, even when I was very young, he always snapped, "I don't remember." What was his life between 1935 when he graduated from Ducktown High School at the height of the Depression and 1938?

He started catching the rails for work in California, then Washington, the summer of 1932 when he was sixteen. This was one fact told unto myth. There are pale Post Office post cards to his mother in his beautiful, immaculate hand, assuring her in pencil that he is fine. The earliest one tells of his being picked up hitchhiking out of Ducktown by a woman from their church, Mine City Baptist, and his first night in the YMCA in Chattanooga.

On March 30, 1998, the sixtieth anniversary of their meeting, and four and a half months before her death, my mother, very ill, told the story again. I never grew tired of my mother's stories, no matter how many times they were repeated. Daddy came into the Charlotte Public Library looking for the want-ads. She had that section, was working the crossword. *"His hand came from across the table, pointed to the word"* as I quoted her in an early poem, *They Met in a Library*. The crossword puzzle was about the American Constitution. He walked her to work at the department store lunch counter on the corner.

"He was there when I got off work eight hours later. He walked me home. We came to a courtyard, I think the City Hall. He nudged me into it. He kissed me and put his hands on my breasts. Of course I pulled back, no. He apologized. He apologized by explaining that he was living with a man, a male lover, and was desperate to be turned on by a woman."

I riveted to attention while remaining unmoving, nonchalant. I knew that he met her after work, walked her home. They'd almost met three days before, on her eighteenth birthday, when they were both on the same corner in a crowd watching a parade. But I had never, not ever heard this. Nor for all my thinking on him and our relationship had I ever dreamed such a notion.

Why did I feel it was imperative not to show any reaction, to remain unsurprised? Why didn't I gasp *"Daddy had a male lover? Mama!?"* I said nothing. It only occurs to me writing this that I could have responded, that she expected me to respond.

I think now that she'd tried to tell me about his homosexuality or bisexuality for the last ten years of her life.

They—that's how Mama always put it, but probably it was her—picked out 5903 Roosevelt Avenue in Hollydale before the house was built.

"What I'm going to say now I do not mean to be derogatory or nasty in any way," Mozelle writes in the first of the letters she wrote me just before she unexpectedly died eight months after Mama.

"When I went to visit Garnet on my usual Wednesday afternoon off she took me with her to show off the lots where some houses were going to be built there in Hollydale. They wanted that corner lot but Garnet didn't have the $5.00 to get their name down on the list. I gave her the five to sign the list."

I am surprised to hear this little fact, one I don't remember my mother ever telling in the many tellings of how they managed to get the house in Hollydale. Mozelle may not have meant to be derogatory or nasty but she was still trying, for some reason, in virtually her last breath, to set the story straight. *"I'm not sure,"* she began, *"if I should be angry with you or hug you. Your letter took me back a number of years but also made me lose a few too. I have hardly done a thing but cry. I can't talk to anyone without the tears flowing. Don't ask WHY - I have no answer - but some of the things you asked brought great pain to my mind of some of the remembrances. I thought I had forgotten."*

Hollydale is a part of South Gate, but on the east side of the Los Angeles River. In those days it had its own post office. Twelve miles north of Long Beach, twelve miles south of downtown Los Angeles, sixteen miles east of Redondo Beach, and twelve miles west of the La Puente/Whittier Hills, Hollydale is at the heart of the LA Basin. 5903 Roosevelt is on the corner of Roosevelt and Industrial Avenues.

But I grew up there. I know the place the way I first knew English. From inside. You don't learn to talk from a book. You don't learn your first place from a map. There are holes in my knowledge of Hollydale, holes that would be the first things covered in my adult learning processes. To me the Los Angeles River is second only to the Pacific Ocean as an entity of water but only in this writing have I finally fully grasped that we were on its east bank. I have tried to get this straight before but even so it has always felt like we were on the west bank. East was old and backwards, as in Back East. This attempted correction of my childhood geographical dyslexia has been almost as difficult as some of the information that has come through recently about my parents. *"My wound is geography,"* Pat Conroy says. *"It is also my anchorage, my port of call."*

There are pictures of me, ten months old, in my little red riding hood outfit Mama knitted, wandering through the frames before the walls and roof are on. She got a discount by agreeing to do the painting and loan work herself.

Mama loved the sun. She loved yellow flowers, yellow anything. She painted the kitchen bright yellow. She was a genius at doing loan work; when I'm grown it will be her career in real estate. We moved in on April 3, 1942, twenty-three days before my first birthday.

"That picture of Mozelle standing, holding you on the porch, is on your first birthday."

Daddy and Aunt Mozelle took baby Sharon to the beach, while mother worked—my Baby Book reports how my First Birthday was celebrated. *Baby Sharon seemed to enjoy the trip very much.* I weighed twenty-nine pounds.

On the surface my mother was prim and proper. Excessively so, I thought as a girl and practiced growing into the rhythmic slink and slouch of my father. I have a reserve, she'd say. I am not like other people. This was true. But underneath, my mother was soulful and deep. She was orgasmic. She could be quieter than a bedbug being so but you couldn't help but feel it all through the house, her orgasms sweeping through like tsunamis. My mother was happiest, most fulfilled, when making love with my father.

I'm lying in my new blue iron crib in the new room. My mother's long face appears over the crib. The mirror behind her is oval, and has bronze-colored curlicues that come together at the top like waves meeting in riptide. She found it in a second hand store. In this mirror I watch the light going down in the west as night and rising again over the mountains in the east as morning.

Now my father's wide face is there too, above me, the back of his head in the mirror. He comes up behind her, laughing. He puts his giant head on her left shoulder, he looks down at me, puts one hand beneath her butt and one under mine, and he nibbles at her ear, making goosebumps on her arms. Then they make love standing there.

That night, or at least that month, our second month in the house, the first important event at 5903 Roosevelt Avenue, Hollydale, California occurs. We conceive my sister. This was the plan. My mother the orphan has a home now for the family she will make.

Daddy puts in a garden. He makes a plow that he pushes through the soil. Corn comes up and grows way over my head. He grows tomatoes, Mama's favorite food, bigger, more delicious than any in the store.

Mama and I catch the P.E. Red Car on the tracks up behind the church. We go to Huntington Park, we go Downtown, oh, we go all over. We love to be in the open caboose going to town with all the other people, my mother so happy, so thrilled with beautiful Los Angeles, sun year-round and yellow flowers, the air blowing in our faces, the smell of geraniums and eucalyptus everywhere, my little white shoes out in front of me, the lace on my white socks cuffing the crisscrossed shoelaces, looking up in ecstasy to my mother's sun-illuminated, cheek-mountain-bone face, bigger than the purple mountains' majesty.

Walking tiny between them afraid of falling through the cracks. We walk out all the piers. Boards bigger than me. The ocean waves splashing up between the cracks, both of them whisking me up, laughing. All three of us.

Following Mama's big behind, her scrumptious rump Daddy calls it, up the new lawn. Her rump like the billowing clouds speeding overhead, my wide entry. The entry to open again soon for my brother or my sister.

The world opens up when we go for a ride. Opens all the way to Mexico, to Santa Barbara, up the snow-capped mountains and beyond them to the desert where the wildflowers bloom. To the west, to Japan, China, and patty cake, patty cake, around to here again. To Tijuana—I'm on a white donkey wearing a big sombrero, Uncle K.D. holding me—up to Ramona, to Julian, down to the Salton Sea. To the laughing gulls, to the date palms. To the earth quaking underneath to the old mission bells ringing above. Most of all I love the ocean. Long Beach. Seal Beach. Tin Can Beach.

Coming back from that trip to San Diego and Tijuana to see Uncle K.D. and Aunt Alice and Billie and Shirlie, the transmission went out in Laguna Beach, hit the pavement on El Camino Real, clunk! We drove it for another six months, clunking all the time. I was mortified. When we got the '39 Chevy right after moving to Hollydale I wouldn't go near the old one, even when they got into it to fool me. This was always told to illustrate that I was a born snob.

The feeling when accused of something I didn't do. The feeling when they've got it wrong about what I did do. The feeling inside like a huge mass of something blocked. Wanting to explain, to protest, but unable to. Even when I learn to talk, even now at times, I'm unable to get past the block, I'm unable to talk.

They're in their favorite pine tree out over the Basin, up on Mt. Wilson. Mama in slacks is showing. Her face is of sorrow, grief, deep seriousness, maybe fear. My mother loved people who smiled and laughed to the point of prejudice against those who didn't, but—did any of us ever realize this?—she rarely did either. She had her reserve and was proud of it. She knew who she was. (And we knew we had to be happy, she couldn't take any more grief.) Her pale hair is pulled back in barrettes and Daddy holds the two of them. I am blessed to behold the three of them.

A baby. A baby is growing inside her tummy. She reads to me, holding me to it, and we grow it together. She tells me stories about it. Sometimes she is very tired growing the baby, she gets very serious and Mozelle begins to cry. When Daddy comes home, poor boy from work, he storms through. They cry for their Daddy dead in Virginia. They don't say their father Guy Clarke is my grandfather—my mother, I realize only now, never referred to him as my grandfather, he was hers, all she ever really had—but once in awhile the clouds open and I see him smiling down.

She keeps telling me about miraculous love, about my brother or sister who is coming.

Marilyn Ripp lives up Roosevelt beyond the lot where they're laying the foundation for a new house. All day there is the sound of grinding from the whirling cement truck and men yelling and laughing at each other and at me walking out of the house and down the sidewalk without my diapers.

I am as big as Marilyn, definitely plumper, bigger boned, but she is older than me, way over two. Marilyn can talk. There is no photograph of this moment, but I've waited all my life to write it:

We are sitting on the enclosed back porch, the stucco smelling, dampish place between the kitchen and garage walls, just before the dark entrance to under the house. Staring at her mouth I try to make my lips into the shape of hers. Then I try to make my lips move the way her lips are moving. I want to make the words she makes, to duplicate the magical way she talks. The way her whole mouth forms words from the rush of her inside. Then it happens. I fall into Marilyn Ripp's face. I fall into waves, like falling into the ocean and the sky beyond. Suddenly the world is twice as large, I remember what infinite is. I fall into the pores of Marilyn's soft golden-shadowed skin, her gold dark pool round eyes where her soul floats and flecks. I fall through her hair, the soft glowing bouncy brown curls around her wondrous face. I explode with miraculous love. The more I look into her face, her whole being, the more I explode the way Mama explodes with Daddy. Oh, I love you. I love you. Yes! Those are the words. I love you.

Then another miracle. An earthquake! It cracks across the top cement step on the front porch ripping the foundation like paper. I lie in my blue iron crib and watch the railing billow like the sea. And down will come baby, cradle and all. Mama worries about the house she bought, but she's not afraid, Southern California is Paradise and negative thoughts never cross her mind. Mozelle, however, becomes hysterical and we all have to calm her down, me with the laughter bubbling up. Oh! The earth moving under us feels wonderful. The bubbles keep coming up with each earth wave, then recede like the waves at the beach.

There is a photograph of Marilyn Ripp and me sitting on the front porch. *Sharon Edens & Marilyn Ripp. SLE age 20 months. Dec 1942.* I sit properly, with my legs together, soled in my white laced-up shoes and red socks, but you can see that I am beside myself with the thrill. My left hand curls into my thigh, my right into the back of Panda held to my right breast in just the spastic way my hands curl now when I fall in love, or am deeply thrilled. In the olive complexioned, mature Marilyn, her hands together between her wide spread knees, a businessman's stance, you can almost see in her smile, the slight hint of self-consciousness, almost condescend-sion, of one who knows she is adored. Her feet are much bigger than mine. Under our tan calves, the ants and crabgrass are emerging from the earth-quake crack.

Mama worries about my loving too much, about the intensity of my feelings for Marilyn Ripp. Sharon sometimes you act more like Marilyn Ripp than Sharon Lura. You could lose yourself. You must never, not ever, forget who you are.

Sharon May Ritchie moves into the newly finished house three down from us, on the other side of Marilyn. Sharon May is six months younger than me, she just started walking. Her mother Peggy is Southern too, from an island off the coast of Alabama and she's expecting another baby too. Her father Johnny is a commercial artist who works for the Huntington Park Signal. And her name is Sharon too.

My father's parents arrived in downtown Los Angeles by train from Tennessee, Friday, November 13, 1942. Mama was five and a half months pregnant. It was probably her idea to bring them out, they had nowhere else to go. Uncle Marion had been helping them since the Ducktown copper mine strike was lost, despite his contempt for his father going out on strike six months before his guaranteed retirement pension and therefore losing it. Losing everything. He'd moved them from Ducktown, in the Southeast corner of Tennessee where they had lived since 1907, to Afton, near Greenville in Northeastern Tennessee where he'd gone to Tusculum College and was now a professor. But things had gone from bad to worse. Another war and now Marion was in Naval Officer training school. Still, with war, there was hope that Grandpa could get a job in California. Mama was thrilled to be the one to provide the place. Her mortification from having to go home to them in Ducktown when Daddy lost his job right after they married, with his mother's disapproval of her as being beneath the Edens, was something she would never get over. Now she could repay the debt. She'd look out the kitchen window and recite Ruth's words to her mother-in-law Naomi, whither thou goest I will go, for thy people shall be my people. And she knew what it was to be destitute.

We're waiting in the vast, gleaming white-tiled La Ciudad de Los Angeles Union Station. A few hobos are sleeping upright in the chairs. Mama keeps saying do you realize, Sharon, your grandfather lived in Arizona before it was a state? Do you realize your grandmother was a teacher, a poet, a newspaper reporter? Do you realize that Lura Maude is a Chitwood from the bluebloods of Virginia? Do you realize that her great-great-grandmother Nancy was John Hancock's daughter, that her great-great-grandfather Jesse Corn fought with George Washington at Valley Forge, that their daughter, her great-aunt Mary Corn Sharp freed her slaves and paid passage for eighty-three of them to Liberia Africa? Do you realize that her grandfather, your great-grandfather John Chitwood fought for the North, thereby losing everything? Do you realize, Sharon Lura, that you were born on your grandmother's birthday, April 26, and are named for her?

The train is pulling in, my grandparents are getting off, both wearing hats like in the movies of Back East people. She is tall, gray, stiff and stern, wearing a long dark blue coat with a glittering brooch on the lapel; her black hat has a wide brim dipping over her eyes and her black crocheted purse shaped like an envelope is tucked under her left arm. He is like Daddy, he has a dance in his walk when he hops off in his suspenders, his tie askew, his coat hanging off his arm, grinning big. Daddy is so happy to see them, especially her. He shouts Pa! and shakes his hand vigorously up and down. He moans Ma and encircles her frail bones in his. She is refusing to smile. She's acting mad.

It must have felt like the end of the world for my grandmother who had never been out of the state of Tennessee and never nightmared this ending. Everything was gone. Two of her sons were at war.

Everything was gone except for what she had managed to pack in the black trunk. We wait a long time at the end of the roaring train for it to be taken off, Grandpa telling Daddy what he saw out the window crossing the country. "We got off the train for awhile in El Paso, isn't that right, Ma?" Then Daddy and Grandpa and the railroad man are struggling with the trunk. Lura Maude stands there silently with her pointed chin raised in the air. Everything she could possibly save is in there, her diaries she's kept from 1889 when she was nine, photograph albums of her parents and grandparents, marriage records, family Bibles, newspapers, books of poems and her own poems, letters, land grant and tax receipts from before the Civil War, her teaching credentials and proof of our being descended from the Virginia Aristocracy, from John Hancock and the Founding Fathers, from Middle Tennessee pioneers, from Mary Sharp who, after liberating her plantation slaves at her husband's death in 1852, endowed Mary Sharp College, the first academic college for women in the United States.

First thing, they want to see the ocean. Imagine having never seen the ocean! Daddy drives straight down Alameda to Artesia to Atlantic to Ocean Boulevard and there it is.

"Gen-tle me-en...!" Grandpa whistles.

He grins huge and charmingly at the camera, into my mother's eyes who's taking the picture of their first sight of the Pacific Ocean. My mother is the only one who has ever understood him.

"He was so glad," Mama explained the photograph. "She was so mad. She didn't want to come to California, she's very unhappy. He's very happy having wanted to return to the west since the teens."

Now I sense the set-up, his winning my mother over from his wife, Daddy's mother. Mama winning him over from her too.

In the back seat of the car my grandmother gathers me, her first granddaughter, from Mama, sits me on her lap. Her hands go all over me. I look just like her sister Ida who died at twenty-two. Ida was her first sorrow. When she gets to my left knee she yelps "Ah, there it is!" What? "See this black dot?" I try not to see it, turn my head into the oval back window in which Cherry Avenue is receding narrower and narrower into a disappearing dot. "That's what we call in Tennessee a beauty mark. Ida had one on the same spot. Ida Mae Chitwood was a poet. There are poets in our family all the way back to King Edward the Fourth's Poet Laureate. And she was shy too, just like you."

The black mole becomes the longitude and latitude, the news of who I am. And where.

They stay in the big bedroom. Mama and Daddy move into mine. Mama begs Daddy to put on his pants to go to the bathroom. She knows better than to ask him to sleep in something. Did he go nude in his mother's house? Nights and mornings and sometimes in the middle of the day they are making love. I listen for my grandparents making love on the other side of the wall. I hate the screech of my iron slats being let down, announcing to everyone I'm in need, or at least that something is happening to me. I like to do some things without anyone knowing.

"It was harder on them than on us. It was all very hard for her. She wanted her own house."

When Mozelle comes she sleeps in the dining room on the army cot. I love the fold-up denim and crisscrossed wooden-legged thing. But sometimes she forgets to fold it up in the day time and put it out in the garage and Daddy yells at her.

Every Sunday we go for rides, way down the coast to Mexico. Grandpa sits in front with Daddy; Grandma, Mozelle and Mama sit with me in the back seat. Grandpa loves the rides, Grandma just tolerates them. He looks up to the houses on the Laguna hills and lets out a long sigh. "Gen-tle me-en...! How do those people make a living?"

We stop at a gas station. When they get out to stretch Mama hisses to Daddy she's so prim and prissy, so negative. How dare she think she's above me.

"He got on as night watchman at the large pottery place across the tracks, began saving his money to go back to Arizona, buy a place. That was his big dream. She wanted to go back to Tennessee of course.

"He bought his electric car he was so proud of. Mozelle came around then, lived with us too.

"'Gen-tle me-en,' he'd sigh, looking up to the houses hanging off the cliffs."

Mozelle would laugh and say she had the Arizona dream too, ever since she read Zane Grey.

I'm still not talking. "If you don't start talking pretty soon, Sharon Lura, Dr. Pentz says we're going to have to take you to a specialist."

Daddy huffs, "She's not even trying." He looks at me like he just knows I'm faking. "Isn't that right, Sharon Lu Lu?"

But when they were children, children were seen, not heard. They say this and say this, the whole circle of them on the couches and chairs in the six visible corners. What's to become of the world the way children are raised now?

The day before Thanksgiving Mama and I are holding hands, walking up Industrial past the church and she is explaining that we are too broke to buy a turkey. She says we never say the word poor, we say we are just broke. She feels so bad because my grandparents are here and her sister and Thanksgiving is Daddy's favorite holiday. It's his favorite because it's about family. We are thankful that we can provide a home for his parents but we are too broke for a turkey.

I point to the seagulls flying over the steeple and say my first sentence. "That's okay, Mama, Daddy can shoot an ea-gull."

The next day, Daddy's favorite day, our whole family, Grandma and Grandpa and Mozelle at the Thanksgiving table with our oven-roasted chicken and pumpkin and mincemeat pies, Mama announces "Sharon Lura finally said her first sentence yesterday."

Everyone puts their wings and legs down.

"She said 'That's okay, Mama, Daddy can shoot an ea-gull.'"

They laugh and laugh at me; they don't praise me. Before the meal's over the story is repeated again. It's like they forget I'm sitting here.

But I got high praise for my success in using the potty chair. That day I wanted so badly to contribute to the family, to show my thankfulness too.

"Sharon would bring out her potty chair," Mama would tell friends in the shock of some of my published writing. "So proud, set it down. I'd be so embarrassed I would die. Set it right down in front of company. She never did have any shame."

"Did I use it?" I thought to ask one of the times I was present.

"I'd shame you. I would be so embarrassed."

"Look at that sexy father of ours," I gasped to my sister, Bridget, stunned by the photograph she'd dug up from somewhere and enlarged. We were celebrating my return to Ashland, Oregon from Paris after my grandson's birth—Mama's first great-grandchild. I'd been gone four months. In the photograph our young parents are leaning against the driver's side of the Chevy. Daddy's arm is around Mama and he's looking down on her in bedroomy pleasure, his right leg bent up and back to the running board. She's grinning big if self-consciously, her bangs curled around a Forties coil looking more like a hat than hair, in perfect flat alignment with the telephone cross poles behind her. If she's pregnant with Bridget she's not showing yet. In the baggy folds of his pleated slacks, beneath the jauntily open jacket, the round rim of his penis shows.

"Oh, yes," our mother said, so casually. "He was always sexy."

Yes, maybe, but our mother never talked that way. Sexy is a word I had never heard her use before. And now I have to hear that she was affirming to my sister, oh yes, Sharon always saw her father as sexy, continuing the conversation I know now they were having in my absence. I wouldn't know until reading her diary for this book that during my absence she had been reading my journals.

On April 25, 1994 she told me she wasn't a virgin when she and Daddy married. She quickly added that she did lose her virginity with him.

"Something I didn't tell you the other day (about the guy from whom she fled Danville, who found her the week after she married Daddy). Your father and I did have sex before we were married. About three weeks before. Fourth of July, I think. He came over to see me, everyone else was gone. There were no chaperones to stop it. We ended up in bed."

"Was he loving?" I couldn't think of anything else to say to this staggering new story after a lifetime of stories about their three month courtship, her obsessive emphasis to me on the importance of maintaining my virginity, not to even think of their shamings and punishments for my indiscretions.

"Oh he was very loving."

"We went the next day to Myrtle Beach, this is why I've always remembered and told of that day. I'd lost my virginity."

It was an overcast day—my mother hated cloudy days—but even so they were badly sunburned. The danger of sunburns on foggy beaches was part of what she repeatedly told about Myrtle Beach that day as we were growing up, what she was warning us about. The sun reflects off the particles of moisture in the air like mirrors. They both got the chills, became very sick. While they were lying under the cool skies, not realizing they were burning, her fourteen-year-old double-first cousin Dewey Harold Clark, whom she hadn't seen since her Daddy's funeral in Danville, walked by with some friends. He whistled at her in her cotton one-piece that had no stays or supports or means of disguising the shape of her body—she always told this part in contempt of the tight elastic suits of the 50s and 60s—before he recognized that it was Audrey Garnet, daughter of his mother's sister, daughter of his father's brother, the one who had taken care of him as a baby and so was always called his first mother, though only four years older than he. Harold's parents, Myrtle and Walter, I know now, represented the dissolute character of her family that she had determined to escape. But now she had lost her virginity, an irreconcilable mistake. The mistake of all the Simmons' women. She burnt so badly she threw up.

"There was no blood. I've never understood this.

"But later, the week after we were married, when the man I'd fled found me—your father and I were in bed, he'd just lost his job and we didn't know how we were going to pay the night's rent—like a fool, I'd quit my job because I was married now, I was a wife, that's what you did in those days. We got married on Friday night, your father went to work at the shoe store Monday morning and was fired. We don't employ married men, they told him. There was a knock on the door, it was Paul. I'm married now, I said—and he went away, that was the last time I ever saw him—and I went back to your father in the bed. I told him that yes the relationship had been sexual, he wanted to know the details, I told him about the sledding incident, that that's why I fled Virginia for fear I'd do it with him, in which case I'd probably have married him, and this drove your father crazy. He became certain I had. His jealousy became insane.

"He had told me of his indiscretions. But he was a man. That's how I understood that. So finally I told him of mine. It was the biggest mistake I ever made. It changed forever our relationship. He wanted to possess me, not just own me, but possess every part of me."

Not even then, or maybe especially then, did I think that losing her virginity might have had anything to do with the fact of the marriage itself. To imagine that she had reservations in marrying my father, that she might have wanted her freedom, as she had said of Paul, that she felt trapped by Daddy, is more than blasphemous to all she maintained about their marriage.

"The School emphasized that a woman who wasn't a virgin would never have a family. Men married only virgins."

I'm still grasping just how traumatized my mother was by the virginity-at-marriage edict. She was an orphan who wanted a family more than anything else.

It's clear only now that in those last years in which I lived with her she was trying to tell me more of the story of their marriage, to explain her compromised situation, to even, at times, open to the truth of her husband and daughter. But I couldn't realize this. Partly because simultaneously she was doing the opposite—"Working both sides of the street!" Daddy's voice hisses from out of the Universe—boosting the marriage to the ideal and searching for anything to prove I was guilty of falsely accusing him, my anger just like his, terrible, inexplicable, unjustifiable, not her responsibility, so mean of me, still trying to win the argument against him, now a poor defenseless dead man. Or more compassionately: poor poor Sharon suffering from her overactive imagination, her twisted mind, her false memory. I told her only twice (but I didn't know she was reading my journals), once at twelve, and the other time when he confessed four months before his death and she demanded to know everything that he'd said. Both were such traumatic experiences for us I assumed she'd "forgotten." She had always been a story teller—an inveterate teller of the same stories. Now there were new stories, or rather, new details to the old ones. My ears would start ringing—I couldn't take up the hints she was dropping, couldn't enter the potential discussion for my fear of where it might lead and what it might do to her. To us. But I wrote down what she told me, in her presence, like dictation, the family stories she herself worked to preserve, somehow oblivious that this fueled her fear that I was planning a book about me and him. Much of this book is from that dictation.

I was being published. People were calling from all over, talking with her when I wasn't there, saying things like Sharon's a great poet. This clearly took her aback. My mother deeply revered books and writers from the many childhood years she spent in bed with rheumatic fever, reading. That professor said Sharon's a great poet, she'd mumble in dismay, right in my presence. Her goal in life was to be a great mother. She knew what her responsibility was now. One time a People magazine was left under my pillow, open to the page of the mother of Miss USA-1958 telling of her struggle to accept her daughter's sexual molestation charges against her father. And then Bridget, after years of being my main witness, confidante and healer, taken aback too, I guess, by my publications, taken back to her oldest jealousy—our father so in love with me he raped me, so oblivious of her it didn't even matter that she witnessed it—started mixing in the oldest charge, that I was a sick, deranged, evil, bad-seed child, as Daddy had always said. The magazine was put under my pillow the night our mother witnessed a ferocious fight between us which sent me flying from the house bleeding. My mother loved me anyway, she kept saying. It was in how I learned of her grandmother Elizabeth Reynolds Simmons' rape and murder that I first saw how nearly impossible it was for her to speak of things not within her power-of-positive-thinking, story-teller control.

I get in bed. In the great relief of going down suddenly my mother is here. As if I've entered her bed. Her realm. Not her arms. I was never fully in her arms. Even in the first days of my life I wasn't allowed there.

To describe her realm would be to describe her voice, something that is not possible to do in writing. *Sharon.* The sound of *Sharon* as it rang from her body only. She is the one who called me. *Sharon. Sharon Lura.*

The realm is lit by skyblue eyes. It's a good thing, my second husband said in meeting my mother, she's a good person with eyes like those.

It is her loving me even in incomprehension and hideous betrayal. Even as the other woman. *Sharon.*

My mother is a poem I will never be able to write
though everything I write is a poem to my mother

§

Three

It's my brother or my sister. Mama says it is mine as much as hers or Daddy's. I must not forget this. I must not be jealous. This is the greatest joy in life, to have a brother or a sister. They're having it for me so I won't ever be alone. She says Daddy planted it in her and now it's growing in the same room I was in, the room I made inside her, the room I made for it.

"My maternal instinct was so great I wouldn't put anything in my body that might harm you guys."

February 27, 1943- Audrey went to the hospital.
February 28, 1943- Sunday, Audrey is very sick today. We are so uneasy but praying and trusting all will be well. Cecil is so worried.[4]

It tears head first through her, then gets stuck. Her birth canal can't expand because I came so fast I ripped through it and it healed as scar tissue. The baby's stuck in the scar tissue of me. My mother wants to die and she almost does.

If Doctor Pentz had realized how much I had scarred my mother he would have cut it out of her. When he grasps the extent of the scar tissue it's too late. It has already started down the birth canal.

For it to get out the scars have to be broken down, they have to be stretched. She's in hard labor for twenty-three hours at Downey Community Hospital. It's the worst experience in her life of many life-threatening difficulties. Mozelle is at the hospital with her the whole time. Since she's working for the Pentz' this is not a problem. I don't know where my father is.

I'm in the living room looking out the window beyond the tall geraniums to the house being built next door. I like to watch how they're doing it but I don't like that it's about to block my view of Marilyn's. I'm trying to put my dress on. I've finally figured out that if I hold my hands on the front side of the hem of the dress's back side and put it up over my head the front side will come down right. I put my head up through the hole of the skirt and bodice, get it through the neck hole, then both arms through the smaller holes. It feels like I'm helping the baby through, that my coming through the dress helps the baby come through my mother. Like magic, my white dress with red hearts comes down and is on, is on right!

My grandparents are across the room and witness my feat. I'm jumping around elated, I'm a big girl now, I can dress myself, Mama won't have to do it anymore, she'll be free to take care of my little brother or sister.

Grandma is writing in her diary. Grandpa says come here Goldilocks. He takes off my dress, and like magic, I put it on again. And again. And again.

My sister, Bridget Colleen Edens, finally birthed at ten minutes to midnight on Sunday, February 28, 1943, twenty-two months after me. Nineteen forty-three was not a leap year but as little girls we pretended it was. Sometimes we told other kids that Bridget missed that fate by only ten minutes. Imagine, having a birthday only once every four years! Imagine, she'd be only one, not four—two not eight, three not twelve. My sister was so special this was a story almost cosmic enough to describe her.

For all the agony and danger she put Mama through, and the terrible distress she too experienced, the crushing contractions and Mama's screams begging God to let her die, she came out smiling. Our mother will always tell this: I swear Bridget came out smiling. Nothing could have made our mother happier. I tried until my face hurt but I never smiled enough. (Everyone wore masks when I was born; it was a long time before I learned about smiling.) Bridget Colleen, my new sister, is Sunday's child, full of the sun's great energy, joy and light. And no one's afraid now of germs, there are no masks.

March 2, 1943- Cecil worked late tonight. I am sorry for I wanted to hear from Audrey & baby.

M arch 9, 1943- A letter from Kermit in Africa. Audrey & baby came home today.

Ten days is a long time to be without your mother when you are twenty-two months old. It would have reminded me of my first eleven days. When she finally comes home with Bridget Colleen and I get to hold my new sister it feels like the heavens open and Love like a dove descends on me.

She's bald and has no eyelashes or brows. But her eyes are wide set. Oh I love wide-set eyes Mama says and quotes the wide-eyed blue-eyed girl song. She doesn't sing it because Daddy says she can't carry a tune, and so I don't sing it either, I just love her wide-set blue eyes. Grandma says the eyes are the windows of the soul. I stare for long minutes into my sister's soul.

Only twenty-two months later and involved in a big war, but the Government has completely reversed its policy on child-raising. Now the manual instructs the mother to pick up the baby whenever it cries, to feed it on demand, to hold it as much as possible, to love and play with it.

Mama will always say that this switch in the Government's policy is responsible for our opposite personalities. "Or maybe it was that by then I rebelled." When Aunt Alice met my sister, Bridget winked at her. We were in the restaurant where Mama used to work. I had stared at her from the same high chair when she tried to baby talk me, trying to comprehend what she was saying, trying to take her seriously, which made her feel like a fool.

A few months later Sharon May's mother births Susan. Then her milk dries up so Mama, with more than she knows what to do with, more than Bridget can consume, pumps her milk for Susan. Or maybe she actually nursed her, which was the word Mrs. Ritchie used in telling this at Mama's memorial. "We did that sort of thing in those days," she said. Daddy just goes out of his mind. Maybe Bridget resents sharing our mother too.

Grandma and Grandpa moved into a duplex on Comolette Street in Gloria Gardens, Downey about two miles away. Grandma was so happy to finally have her own place.

"Sharrr onnnn.... Oh Sharon Lura...?" They're calling me to come out to the garage.

I open the kitchen back door. I step down into the back porch corridor. I open the garage door, step down into the dark cool.

"Don't be afraid Sharon Lulu, we're in here too."

Then the lights come on.

A fantastic white swan perches in the middle of the garage, taller than me. He takes my breath away. (Now I know what that expression means.) Two new-moon wheels are his rockers. Between the two sides down in the middle is a seat and there are little handles in his ears. Daddy lifts me up and puts me in him. I can just barely reach the handles. He shows me how to rock back and forth. He and Mama are so excited for me. I rock and I rock and I rock. I love you, I love you, I love you Swan and Daddy. I love the whole wide world.

He shows me how he made him. He drew his sides on thin tracing paper making a pattern. Then he cut the plywood from the pattern. He shows me the special saw for the rockers. He sanded and sanded, then painted him white, the back, the feathers, the big arching wings. I am astounded that he can do this. I am astounded, moved to a gratitude I've never experienced before, that he made him for me.

When he was dying, before his confession, I underwent a trance in a writing workshop. We were on a giant white swan flying out over the blue Pacific, me a little girl behind him, holding around his middle. I came out of the trance in rare tears and remembered the swan he made for me. And of course, though astounded—where do the myths come from?—I remembered the myth of Leda and the Swan.

The second time our mother saw her father after he died, Bridget was about three months old.

"We were walking in Long Beach. I had your dad carry her so I could look at her. I walked behind. And I saw my dad again, just as clear, smiling so largely at me. I don't know whether I saw him looking at me looking at Bridget, or I saw him in Bridget, but I saw him."

I am almost there now, our family walking in Long Beach, our new baby so loved even Guy Clarke is there.

The house next door is finished and the Henkas are moving in. They're from North Dakota, they're Lutherans. They are different from us, especially in their bodies. But this is so strange I can't really think it, I just see it. And hear it. Their shrill voices, words out of their tight lips like spits. Norwegian must mean Northern, Mama says. Mr. Henka is tall, thin, gray, and balding with a big hump in his back. Mrs. Henka wears dark lace-up block high heels like Grandma's but with white socks even when she's vacuuming and it's a hundred. They seem like grandparents to me but they must be either pregnant with Sammy or about to make him. Imagine that! They have a daughter, too, about five or six, way too old to play with, named Marie. In all the years there, Marie Henka rarely played with the rest of us. I see now that she must have had a lonely childhood.

They fence their lot in a high cyclone chainlink to keep me out. Silver crisscrosses around and above my head for miles. Most astounding, they paint their front porch and three steps red enamel! Must be Norwegian, Mama says.

I'm running with a pencil in my hand around the post of the Henka's new chainlink fence, coming up the front yard when I stumble and fall on it. The lead breaks off and lodges deep in the skin behind my right cheek bone. When my wound heals, the pencil mark remains, a permanent tattoo on my face. Mama says it's like Indian war paint, it means something.

"I bet it means you're going to be a writer like your grandmother."

I can't say Mozelle. "Her middle name is Virginia," Mama says, "try Virginia." When Virginia finally comes out it comes out as Giny. Mozelle became for all of us kids Aunt Giny, though many times I tried to change back to Mozelle for the beauty and rarity of that name.

One night Mozelle's voice called down Industrial Avenue from Main Street. "Audrey!" she cried, waking Mama and Daddy. Daddy turned on the light, and again Mozelle called as if for help. "Audrey!"

It was two a.m. Daddy got out of bed, put on his pants, went outside looking for her. He walked all around the house several times, but Mozelle was nowhere to be found. Mystified, they tried to go back to sleep.

The phone rang, waking them again. It was the Long Beach police. Mozelle Virginia Clarke has been in an accident. She was in a crosswalk on Atlantic Boulevard in front of Jordan High School when she was hit by a car. Her front teeth were knocked out, she's unconscious, and it looks like some bones are broken.

"I remember calling for Garnet to pick me up. Then I heard the sirens... I remember crying for Garnet when I would come to and I have a very vague memory of her and Fred standing at the foot of my bed and Garnet crying. This was the Spring of 1943. I would have called her Audrey then and him Cecil."

I'm standing in their bedroom, they're both exclaiming to me from the bed that they both heard Mozelle calling Audrey. They will exclaim about this throughout their lives. Mama has many ESP experiences—mostly, she knows what's going to happen just before it does—but this one happened to Daddy too, happened to both of them together, at the exact moment Mozelle was hit. My father will always tell of this with as much wonder as my mother.

While she was still recovering from the accident Mozelle met and fell in love with Joe, a sailor in the U.S. Navy like Uncle K.D. They were married the night before he was shipped out to the war in Japan. But the following week when she applied for her Navy allotment she was informed that he had a wife who was already receiving it. Then she learned that the justice of the peace who "married" them was really his best friend who had shipped out on the same battleship. He had fooled her just so he could sleep with her. Then she discovered that she was pregnant.

"I left the Pentz's that summer," she tells in that last letter, giving me her version for the first time, only slightly different from the one Mama told back then, *"when I met Joe and fell head over heels in love with the heel. I lived with him for two weeks when he left for San Francisco to*

catch his ship and saying he needed the marriage license to get an allotment for me. This was so hard for Fred to believe. I was telling the truth."

Dr. Pentz examined her. He told Mama and Mama told her sister she was pregnant. He assured them he would arrange the adoption. They both gasped no. No. Meanwhile the placenta was at the mouth of the uterus. She had to go to bed immediately.

Daddy snarls Mozelle is a whore, just like Mama. Daddy's voice is hard. Mama is crying. And Aunt Giny too. And now Bridget is wailing.

"Fred just would not believe me. When we went to court for the Insurance settlement Fred took a day off from work to be my guardian. I wasn't 21. Garnet was there in court too, but Fred answered the questions." In November the insurance company deposited the money in a checking account in Mozelle's name. *"So when Garnet told me I was pregnant she and Fred found this convalescent home on Kingsley Avenue off Sunset Boulevard in LA where I could stay in touch with the doctor. They signed me up under his care."*

Daddy sneers and hisses all the way, turning the corners so fast I sling across the back seat into Aunt Giny's lap. She grabs me, holds me to her, sobbing. I feel the baby in there. Why do they have to go away, why is Daddy so mad? Mama says his mother wouldn't understand. She's so ashamed of Mozelle before her mother-in-law. She's sitting there in the front seat stewing in mortification and paralysis, holding Bridget now goo-gooing, smiling and winking at all of us. She's mortified by her unwed pregnant sister, paralyzed by her husband's self-righteous offense, by his kicking her pregnant sister out of our home, by her concern for the baby, by her concern for civilization, devastated by his accusations like his mother's against her uncivilized family, and not the least paranoid, probably devastated from actual knowledge of his sexual attraction to her, the way he flaunts it, about her sister being in the same house with them. Mozelle is whimpering, giant tears forming in her eyes and falling slow motion onto her lips, then onto my face looking up at her, whimpering, *Joe.* Oh Joe where are you?

The place on Kingsley Avenue is shiny silver, wax and glass under fat palms and surrounded by orange trees. At the front desk, after we've inspected the room that's smaller than our small bedroom, Mama shifting Bridget from hip to hip, reaching for me behind her left one, assuring her sister how it will all work out, out of every bad comes some good, like this money from your accident, whatever would we have done without it, Dr.

Pentz will be here for you, and of course we will too, Cecil's just in one of his moods, he'll get over it. Mozelle writes the check for the five months care, then she writes Daddy a check for testifying for her in court and losing a day's wage. Plus money for a better car. No! Mama protests, but Daddy takes it. After all, she got the money because of his testimony.

Then we leave her in that strange silver glass place. On the way out Daddy picks an orange to suck on the way home.

"To this day I can't ever remember being so ill or scared. Dr. Pentz confined me to bed the whole pregnancy. A very lonely time to think and realize what had happened to me. The ladies that took care of the home were paid for five months care but they barely fed me. I think I lived off of buttermilk and crackers the entire time there."

We return home and Mama, to win Daddy back, or in the martyr spirit that sometimes overcomes her, makes love to him without precautions.

We were all planned but Clarke came early. How often through the years this will be reiterated. "We didn't have spontaneous sex but for once and that was when Clarke was conceived."

Each Christmas Mama bought a new ornament ball for the tree to commemorate the year. This was Bridget's first Christmas, my third. But the mood in our house was not happy or festive. Mama realized she was pregnant. The thought of going through labor again seized her with a terror and dread like none she'd known before. For the first time she had morning sickness; later she will tell us through our pregnancies that morning sickness means it's most likely a boy. "From the beginning boys are weaker, harder to carry; most natural abortions are of boys." She dreaded telling Daddy, telling anyone. The gloomier and nastier things got, the happier Bridget became, trying to cheer us up. She would bring us the joy of the season, the joy of the baby born, the joy of life no matter what.

Dr. Pentz assured her it wouldn't be as bad this time. "I see, Audrey, that your cervix's stretched now, it'll be capable of contracting and expanding this time to push the baby out. You are so lovely, Audrey, even inside. And Mozelle, that poor thing, I know the perfect parents for Mozelle's baby. The Yates are rich, they are educated, they can give it everything. I hope you are talking to her, Audrey. How could Mozelle possibly condemn the child to the life it will have with her, an unwed mother and no father? How can she be so selfish?"

"Dr. Pentz," my mother responded to the face between her legs, "my sister is determined to keep her baby. She has never forgiven our mother for dying when she was a baby."

When she finally told Daddy she was pregnant he really went off the deep end. He left, and didn't come home that night. The next morning she phoned Mozelle and told her she was pregnant too, and that she couldn't possibly take care of four babies. Maybe she should give it up for adoption as Dr. Pentz is urging. There's this rich couple in Pasadena, the Yates. Maybe that would be the best thing for everyone after all, Mozelle, for you too.

Marilyn Ripp moved away. I never saw her again. A family with three big boys moved into her house.

Right after New Year's, though her care and rent was paid through May, Mozelle left the convalescent home on Kingsley, walked to the bank on Sunset, drew out what she had left and, with the few clothes she had in a bag, walked, though the placenta was at the mouth of the uterus, all the way downtown to Union Station and bought a ticket for Phoenix, Arizona.

"I was such a disgrace I thought no one wanted me around, that they wanted me to get lost." It killed her about Audrey. She had to get the baby away from Dr. Pentz, from everybody.

When she got to Phoenix, the only place she knew to go to was the Red Cross office. She told the lady about Joe and the phony marriage. The lady took her to the Florence Crittendon Home For Unwed Mothers on Adams Street. A doctor was called. Again she was confined to bed. Despite great pressure, even trickery, she refused to tell where she came from or who her closest relative was. She stayed in bed the whole time in Phoenix. Just as a child she read Zane Grey.

Mama doesn't know where her baby sister is. She's throwing up all the time. Sometimes a bolt of anger strikes like lightning—Daddy's to blame for her sister's disappearance. Then she feels shock for thinking such a thing. That's not how you hold a marriage together. No one said it would be easy. You must cleave from your family. In the exams Dr. Pentz wrenches around inside her like it's her fault her trampy sister has disappeared, stolen that baby right out from under him. He had the adoption arranged. Poor Mr. and Mrs. Yates. Mama loves the Irish poetry of William Yeats like her Irish daddy Guy Clarke who recited Yeats' poems that time she ran away to find him living in the slave shack in Chatham, and so got kicked out of the School. *Come away, O human child! To the Waters and the wild. With a fairy, hand in hand.* So it confused her when the sound of Yeats went through her in Dr. Pentz' melodious voice and hands saying in the same breath how she was made, unlike her sister, to make babies. *For the world's more full of weeping than you can understand.*

We manage to get home just in time. She runs to her petunia bed and throws up. Sometimes she's so ashamed, so angry at Mozelle she feels more distant from her than ever, wherever she is. After all, they never lived together after they were put in Hughes School, founded when the TB epidemic killed so many employees at the Dan River Cotton Mill. They were going to be divided among various relatives but their mother's last wish was that her children not be separated. But at Hughes Mama was put in the Middle Girl's Cottage and Mozelle was put in the Little Girl's Cottage and Lawrence was put in the Boy's Cottage, and that was that, they rarely ever saw each other. Mozelle still doesn't know about their father's troubles and if and when she's ever found she intends to protect her from that, no way would she be able to understand. And she will not allow the suspicion about her and Dr. Pentz and sometimes about her and Daddy that probe like fingers in her head. Maybe Joe the Sailor isn't the father.

My mother's whole life had always been in the hands of doctors, "the whitecoats" who could save her family, but who, in fact, almost always wreaked havoc upon it.

The professional photograph taken that winter of Bridget and me has become a sort of portent of what was then, of what will always be, about us. I'm scooted close to her—my fat, bald baby sister beaming in joy. Her fat hand holding her fat ankle: she's the glorious, grinning baby Buddha. My big head with its silky white curls hangs forward onto my narrow chest and shoulders in a sort of melancholy trance (the bad posture I still suffer when depressed), my big round dark eyes looking up from under the burden, the bangs cut straight across my wide forehead. It's true, we are complete opposites. For all my white curls I am as dark as my sister is light. Coming into Bridget's energy field of ever-expanding aura, mine ducks and, not so much hides as takes a back seat. This is allowance for her. She is my baby sister. This is love. There is nothing further from love than competition. I refuse to see that she's competing with me. Smile!

There is nothing harder for me than to obey orders to betray myself and my family. We are not happy.

Feb 2, 1944- Sharon Lura and Sharon May got lost or went to market when their mothers did not know it. They came back in about an hour.

We were searching for Mozelle. Along the way we kept our eyes out for Marilyn too. It was hard coming home without them, but the sense of accomplishment in just getting all the way to the Hollydale stores and back was worth all their tears, spankings, warnings and lectures.

There isn't a diary from February 9, 1944 to December 31, 1945. It seems unlikely that my grandmother didn't keep one then, given her lifelong recording. Perhaps it's simply gotten lost but I can't help but wonder if my mother destroyed it. Several things happen in this period that become family secrets.

When Mozelle was in labor they told her she was dying. And probably the baby too as the cord was around its neck. They were giving her last rites. You must tell us now who to notify. Her brother Lawrence is on the Bataan Death March, or is it Iwo Jima, or is it the Battle of the Bulge? No doubt he's dead like Joe. Maybe America is dead too. In the contraction that sent her over the blackest edge she gave them her sister's name and address.

Penelope Ann Clarke was born April 19, 1944.

When the Home for Unwed Mothers called Mama it was the twentieth anniversary of their mother's death.

I turned three one week later.

Sharon Lura Edens is a quiet, inclined to be serious child, she wrote in my Baby Book under Three Years Old. *She has deep thoughts and a definite mind of her own. She will always need a good deal of mother and father companionship or she may be inclined to draw into a shell. She is above average in health and ability, however slow in learning to talk- Not openly affectionate but very faithful and loyal to her loved ones....*

Sharon's first song is "Shu-Shu Baby." She asks the blessing - "Heavenly Father- Thank you for this food. Amen." Sharon started attending Sunday School- She takes Sharon May Ritchie who is only two and a half.

I had a birthday party. She carefully listed the presents and who they were from. The one that jumps out: *Aunt Giny: pr of cloth house shoes.*

I put them on and would not take them off. "Shu-shu my baby."

When Mozelle recovered she worked for the telephone company in Phoenix, leaving Penny in the Unwed Mother's nursery. Florence Crittendon's home felt a little like Hughes School, comfortable and familiar, but she would not sign any of the papers put forward for Penny's adoption though there was pressure on her to do so.

"I went back to Long Beach when I was told I had to take her or she would be placed with a family."

Penny! A teeny golden-copper round coin of a thing, a baby girl. I am three years old now and Bridget Colleen is walking and soon we'll have another brother or sister. Another Edens, Daddy shouts when he's in a good mood. The house is incredible with baby sounds and smells and milk and love, goo-goo talk, and "pee you!" Mama and I babysit Penny while Aunt Giny looks for work. Bridget and Penny on their backs side-by-side in the blue iron crib getting their diapers changed and Bridget winking at Penny and on the couches and flannel blanket-laid floors and over both of Mama's shoulders goo-gooing to each other. Sometimes Bridget pokes Penny in the eye to make her cry, then pretends she didn't. Oh, a boy would make your Daddy so happy, Mama sighs!

"I met a girlfriend, Joanie, who needed someone to take care of her three while she worked a shift. She'd take care of Penny while I worked another shift. This worked for awhile. Remember the pottery factory by the railroad tracks? That's where we worked."

It's the same place where Grandpa is night watchman. Sometimes she arrives just before her four-thirty shift, just before Daddy returns from Douglas, and has to leave Penny with us. Daddy will go berserk when he gets home but what can we do? She comes through the front door with her shiny black pompadour up over her magnificent facial bones, her cloud of perfume, and thrusts Penny onto Mama's huge stomach and races off for work over the tracks in her red, white and blue pumps. Bridget starts crying and Daddy comes home, takes one look at Mozelle's illegitimate kid, storms back out, back to Johnny's. Mama's stomach contracts so much she collapses in Daddy's easy chair, knowing this is nothing to what's coming. When Mozelle gets back at midnight, barefoot, her bad leg and feet are swollen and hurt so bad, her pumps are in her bag and the eyebrow pencil lines drawn up her long calves are smeared. Daddy is just getting home too and is so nasty she grabs Penny and all the things in the diaper bag Mama has gotten ready for her, including a snack, she's so worried, Mozelle you're too skinny, and tries to get out. Then Penny wakes up, is screaming and Mozelle is crying to her baby that soon the war will be over and her daddy will come home to them. Out they go, the screen door banging shut. Heaven only knows how they get back to Long Beach at that hour.

I come home from playing with Sharon May with her teeth marks down my back. Mama lectures me not to let Sharon May Ritchie bite me, but I keep on letting her because she wants to; it makes her feel good. First instinct for me will always be to let the other do as they want.

I keep coming home with new bites and Mama keeps lecturing me I must bite her back. But Mama remember how you cried when I bit you?

Finally one day when Sharon May is going at it, this force rises up inside me like heat rushing up from the floor heater, propelling my teeth into her upper right arm. Sharon screams and then so does her mother. I run as fast as I can, screaming "Mama! Mama!" Faster than I've ever run, all the way back down the cement block sidewalk of Roosevelt to our house, up the lawn, onto the porch, inside the screen door, to behind my mother who has run to the door in response to my screams.

We're at the door, me behind my mother's big thighs and mountain belly, peeping out from the flap of her cotton print smock. Mama locks the screen door. Mrs. Ritchie comes up the porch with Sharon May bawling hysterically in her arms. She demands that Mama send that little bitch Sharon Lura out here this very minute so Sharon May can bite her back.

I wait to see what my mother will do. Sometimes Daddy says I'm lying and she seems to believe him.

"I am sorry," my mother says. "But every day my Sharon Lura comes home from playing with your Sharon May with bite welts down her back. I'm sorry, but to tell you the truth I am a little relieved. I have lectured her, you understand, to bite your Sharon back."

"If," Mrs. Ritchie screams, "I ever catch Sharon Lura outside I promise you I am going to knock the shit out of her."

"Furthermore," my mother says, haughtily, "We do not use that kind of language in our house and I'd appreciate it if you didn't talk that way in front of my little girl."

Mrs. Ritchie did not speak to my mother for a year.

Every night after our bath I hang onto Mama's thick calves over the electric floor heater to feel the heat blowing up. Tonight I have come from the bath looking for my flannel nightgown, to stand over the heater like she does, to warm my bottom. Daddy is lying on the couch reading the newspaper and Mama is still in the bathroom with Bridget. The heat rushes up the back of me. I put my bottom out more to it and fall down. It hurts bad and then it hurts really bad. Daddy gets the Vaseline for Bridget 's bottom and lays me across his lap and soothes my burn with it, telling me not to be a crybaby.

I have three grill stripes down my fat pink bottom that hurts so much I can't sit down for a long time. Not in my Swan, not anywhere. This is awful but very very funny. Oh, that she might have scars there, Mama frets. Daddy laughs until tears fall down from his eyes onto the crimson stripes cupping my two buttocks and she looks at him sideways. He checks my hiney for months, laying me across his lap, rubbing and rubbing it with the Vaseline, and laughs that laugh. First they are crimson, then blistery, then brown, then pale pink, then white moons like the Swan's rockers across my rear. He keeps asking to see my bottom even after it's healed, to see if I've scarred, and is disappointed, close as he examines me, not to be able to see the stripes anymore. My face in the scratchy brown couch, my bottom in the air, Daddy taking forever to examine me. Sometimes Mama is standing in the kitchen doorway watching, her arms crossed in front like she's mad at us. I twist my head around, look back down on my bottom for the scars. I feel sorry not to have the thing anymore he so loved to see.

We're on the front lawn. I've just driven my trike down the cement curve of our white sidewalk. Daddy drops down to me. I feel the waves. His head, his giant forehead like the globe of the world, drops back both sides to the sky, his finger is God's shaking in my face, his wallpost knees engulf me. His whole body, everything in him shakes with anger and contempt. His face is too terrifying to be looked at.

"Don't you tell a story, Sharon Edens! Do you hear me? Don't you ever, ever, tell a story on me."

I won't Daddy, I won't. I won't, I promise.

§

Four

"You were a mama's girl," my mother would say. "Then suddenly you became a daddy's girl." Toward the end there was an emphatic quality to this declaration as if she was remembering a specific incident, defending her own behavior, or maybe even trying to break through some of my blindness regarding her and Bridget. As always, she was informing me of who I am: her betrayer, his seducer, though such words she would never utter, nor would I ever think until now.

He gets off from Douglas at four-thirty, has a quick beer at Johnny's. At five-thirty or six he comes in from the garage. I'm in the kitchen to greet him. My mother acts disgusted like there's something wrong with me. My father acts like he's proving something to her. I refuse to know what it is.

"Only if Mama says it's okay," he says looking at her, one long wide eyebrow like the drawbridge to Terminal Island rising up, sort of challenging her. He collapses in his easy chair, opens a beer, starts reading the paper. Mama's in the kitchen doorway, her arms crossed in front, the serious *for-shame-Sharon* look on her face. Lately he says that and lately she's been saying no.

"Okay," she says this time, reluctantly. To perform under her scrutiny makes me clumsy but in the spirit of my task I gallantly do so. It's a privilege and joy to clean my father's feet, he feels left out, unloved, and is so tired from working for every morsel of our food. I'm helping. I'm helping like she helps him. I'm a worker too.

Unlacing the boots, the long hard pulling to get them off, the clumps of mud and silvery specs dropping from the grooves of the soles, the release of the smell, the damp sweat of his wool socks, the new hole Grandma will darn—does darn-it come from darning?—his white damp feet like swan wings, with dark red hairs on the tops of each toe, sometimes a line of dirt under the big nail. His feet are unbelievably big, white and heavy. It is especially a privilege to clean out the jam from the deep hollows between each of his ten toes.

Where does toe jam come from and why is it shameful? Is it like the little white balls that accumulate in the folds of my labia? Smegma, Mama says, but I can't say that word. Daddy needs me to clean out his toe jam, someone has to do it, it's an honor. I'm proving I love everything about him. He giggles that giggle, what's a man to do with a daughter like Sharon? The setting sunlight coming through the kitchen shingles makes dark circles under their eyes. *Sharon!* How can you?

In time, her answer is always no. To think now, what I wouldn't then, that my three-year-old loyalty and innocent efforts for him, for our family, made her suspicious of me. Made her jealous of me. To see that he worked to make her jealous. To think what he was charging me with, to counter what she was charging him with, to see who I was between them, is still almost unbearable.

Many of my earliest memories have sexual undertones but I didn't see this until I put them in writing.

I'm coming through the living room from playing outside. It's really really hot. We have company. Odie and Eleanor are sitting together on the couch, they're from Tennessee too. My grandparents are also sitting here, and the Rupps too. And maybe Mozelle with Penny in her lap. And others, it seems, who are sitting around like ghosts. Daddy's in his armchair, and even Mama is sitting down, on a dining room chair she's pulled up.

"Lady Godiva!" Daddy shouts.

Everyone laughs.

"Now Sharon Lura, when you're through pottying don't you come traipsing out naked again, riding your high horse in front of company again."

I don't remember traipsing naked in front of company but Daddy always tells this to company so that must have been when I was really young, just barely walking.

"Sharon Lura just loves to be naked, don't you Sharon Lulu?"

They roar again.

"I dress her in a real cute sun suit," Mama says, throwing up her hands, shaking her head. "Iron and starch the ruffles, brush her hair, put bows and barrettes in it, send her out to play. But in a while, I'll be washing dishes at the kitchen window and here she comes back down Roosevelt stark naked, hair undone, twirling her sunsuit on her finger."

They roar and laugh and talk again like I'm not here. I must have been one when I did that.

"Goldilocks and I go for a walk around the block," Grandpa says. "Half way round I look down and she's pulling Audrey's silk drawers from her pocket, putting them on her head like a hat. By the end of the walk they've slipped plum down around her neck like a necklace." Grandpa laughs that laugh Daddy laughs.

That's back before Bridget was born. Before I could even dress myself. I was practicing.

"Why my lands, one time," Grandma says, "I looked up Roosevelt and here they come, Sharon Lura stark naked but for Audrey's silk panties up to her armpits like a movie star's strapless gown."

"Who's Lady Godiva?"

Their laughter dies down. I love to hear the story and maybe this time I'll understand it. Sometimes Grandpa recites it but mostly it's my father who tells of the beautiful blond Queen who pleaded to the King for mercy from his high taxation of the people. *"If they pay this tax they starve! And I would die."* The King said he'd repeal the tax if she'd ride his prize white stallion naked through the streets of Mercia at noon. Godiva agreed to do this, for Mercia and the people. She sent a herald through the town crying the hard condition, pleading to them not to look.

"Then she rode forth, clothed only with chastity," Grandpa recites.

"But thank goodness," Mama says, "Lady Godiva had long blond hair to her bottom that hid her nakedness."

"Rippled ringlets to her knees," Grandma corrects.

"Like you, Sharon Lura, you have long blond hair and you like being naked and this is why Daddy calls you Lady Godiva."

"Then she rode back, clothed only with chastity."

From a crack in a barn slat where he was hiding, Tom of Coventry peeped. The King kept his word, the tax was repealed, the people loved her, but poor Tom, in the moment he saw Godiva, was struck blind.

"Lady Godiva is where we get the expression Peeping Tom!" Daddy roars.

"This happened just before the Norman Conquest," Grandma says. "Do you realize the Edens have their line traced back to the Battle of Hastings in 1066?"

"Don't ever cut your hair," Mama says.

I sit beside him as he rides me in his new electric car
open to the high palms that line Paramount Boulevard
Mama says they'll cut down soon to widen the road.
He calls me Goldilocks.

I love the specialness of Grandpa's Autoette, so different from the other cars, the wind on our faces. Like a toy, a golf cart or something. Shiny dark blue with a black leather seat. It has a stick thing you move right and left that's the steering wheel. He plugs it in at night behind their house. We drive along the outside of the lane, between the poor gas-rationed cars and the very tall palm trees.

I'm unsure if the following really happened or is indeed a "false memory," a mistaken projection onto an innocent man who happens to have been my paternal grandfather, but the image is in me, it won't go away though I have tried to make it do so. We're in his new electric car in the back yard in Downey, we're about to set out for Hollydale, I'm being lifted up over his penis that's sticking up out of his fly into the air. I'm struggling to get free of it, of being set down on the wiggly jiggly thing. Grandpa is laughing, it's okay Goldilocks. It won't hurt you. Isn't it something?

It has always been easier to suspect my memories as false than to believe them. I never would have remembered the rape if my father hadn't confessed it.

I don't remember the following incident at all.

"I saw your dad looking at you once when you were real small," she blurted out near the end when she was waffling between proclaiming me guilty of falsely accusing him and admitting that it was true; weighing her hurt at his betrayal against her fear and guilt at having failed me, of this being apparent to the world in whatever I might write. "I pulled your dress down and shouted 'No! Don't you dare!' I threw my hands over his eyes, 'Don't you dare!' Do you remember that?"

And then it seemed she was accusing me of lying again. "You don't remember that? I screamed, 'Don't you dare, don't you dare!' Oh, Sharon, I don't believe you don't remember that."

She was my greatest love. Her mother died when she was four. We were her first and only lasting home. I always knew that one of her biggest fears was in being found a failure as a mother.

I'm standing before the dog, my head as high as his head. I love him. We are in our old Cade Street front yard visiting Billie and Shirlie who live here again, the white picket fence surrounding us. He's perfectly still before me, his long side as high as my shoulders. Usually in my mind he is tan, almost white, but sometimes he's black. I reach out, he's so magnificent, run my hand down his soft hairy neck then across his backbone toward his long curling-up tail. Suddenly, his giant head snaps around and his teeth clamp onto my right knee.

The pain of his betrayal is greater than the pain of his teeth sunk all the way to my bone. My feelings are so hurt! I meant him love. I could never hurt him. How could he not know I love him?

Daddy grabs me up, rushes me across the street to Garnet Phiffer's who believes I'm her son reincarnated.

Who was your son? I sob.

"A stray," Garnet says. "Been hanging around Cade Street the past few days."

"Dogs are afraid of children Sharon Lura," Mama soothes. "Children are so unpredictable. He couldn't help it."

In Dr. Pentz's office both my parents huddle around me seated on the high, white paper-covered brown leather table. I stare at the mole on top of my left knee, trying to stop crying. He sews the deep tooth hole shut with a needle and black thread just like Grandma darns Daddy's socks. Tears are watering Daddy's eyes, hanging in his gold lashes. Mama never cries but it's like tears are flooding inside her where the baby is. It is from this moment that I remember what Dr. Pentz looked like. He was in his early forties, he had straight dark hair combed and oiled straight back exposing a receding hair line. He was somewhat stocky and had a roundish face and sometimes wore glasses and always a white coat with a stethoscope hanging down.

He taps my wounded knee with his hammer. I'm staring at my mole. My leg springs up in his round stomach and they all laugh.

Word is sent through the neighborhood to find the stray, to be quarantined, tested for rabies.

"Rabies!" Mama is beside herself.

Don't hurt him! He didn't mean to bite me.

If they can't find him I'll have to have the ten days of rabies shots, more painful than childbirth.

"I don't know which would be worse," Mama says to Daddy in the car going home, "rabies or the shots."

They shoot you in your belly button with a long awful needle.

It is a long time, full of dread and fear, days and days, but my mouth doesn't start frothing and just in time they find the dog, quarantine him.

Don't hurt him, don't hurt him.

Then it is proven that the beautiful dog doesn't have rabies. He doesn't have to be killed and I don't have to have the shots, just the black stitches taken out, which hurts enough to make me cry again. I hate to cry.

I have the black mole on top of my left knee and now the white tooth circle mark on the inside of my right one. The permanent tooth mark will always be a reminder of the danger of love in the world, and my foolishness, but testimony, too, in the face of that—my greater feelings of

protectiveness rather than anger at one hurting me—of my greatest
fidelity: love.

She knew it would make the labor more difficult, but as much as she tried
to fight it, as much as she meditated, tried to think positively, tried to
relax, she remained seized by fear. She was going to die this time. She
would rather die than go through that again. Her own cries to God that
lasted hours birthing Bridget, almost a full twenty-four hours of hard
labor, woke her at night as if they had gone only a short way out into the
atmosphere, were circling back now over the LA Basin, a bad riptide.
Sometimes when she thought of how she had not protected her sister and
baby from her husband she wanted to die. She couldn't forget that it
was the third pregnancy that led to the decline and death of her mother.
She could remember her mother's realizing that she was pregnant with
Mozelle, how the dread and horror filled her and the whole house.
    Clarke Frederick Edens was born August 31, 1944, at 2:45 in the
afternoon, in Downey, California. Dr. Pentz was the delivering physician.
Mama was twenty-four and Daddy was twenty-eight.
    "I screamed so hard they could hear me clear to Chicago," I heard her
tell Clarke not very long ago. "But, then, you were the prettiest baby
they'd ever seen in the hospital."
    Dr. Pentz wanted to give her a hysterectomy while she was still in the
hospital. Against his warnings and consternation she refused. Even for the
paralyzing fear she planned to have a fourth child.

Bridget and I stayed the ten days with Aunt Alice and Billie and Shirlie on
Cade Street. Aunt Alice's sister Rema Mae and her two children, our
cousins Joal and Michael, were living there too. Their father, Shane from
Oklahoma, had disappeared. Uncle K.D. was at the war.
    More than being my first home, more than Garnet Phiffer who knew
me as her reincarnated son, more than Billie and Shirlie, and the dog that
bit me, Cade Street is Shane to me.
    I don't know why. I don't remember him, just Shane. Shane from
Oklahoma. Some deep voice admonishing: don't ever forget Shane.
    I feel so much mystery and confusion in regard to my sense of Shane I
sometimes wonder if he's the one who poked his finger in me on Pearl
Harbor Day, the one who lifted me in his chair over and down on his erect
penis. What is more dangerous? To allow such thoughts, or to not? Maybe
the mystery is simply that he disappeared like our dog Annabelle and Aunt

Giny and Joe and Marilyn and soon others from this period and everyone was looking for him, crying and wringing their hands why? Shane, why? Rema Mae and my cousins were heartbroken. All through the war Rema Mae was trying to recover from Shane. Maybe it's just that I feel bad about the loss for Joal and Michael of their father, black haired and handsome Shane, maybe my memory is the unrequited hope, the promise made that he will come back. Maybe I imagined his death in the war.

But I married his son on Cade Street while Mama was in the hospital with Clarke.

Michael is dark and quiet like his father and has eyes that I fall into like I did into Marilyn's. He asks me to marry him and I say yes. The day comes for the big wedding. My white table cloth veil sweeps the ground when I come down the weedy aisle between everybody. Joal is the preacher and Billie and Shirlie are the flower girls and Bridget is the ring bearer. Aunt Alice is our photographer and Michael the groom carries a broom. I mean every word of my vow to him and I can feel that he means every word of his too. Then we jump over the broom and our union's sealed. Aunt Alice says we are made for each other, we are both such serious, strange children, and though she calls us kissing cousins we're only cousins by marriage. We are not blood kin. This is not incest. This is when I first heard that word.

Then something happens that makes me feel very bad and confused. I can't remember what it was except: I want to go home. Besides, I'm worried about our father who's lonely without our mother and me and Bridget. When no one's looking I take my sister's hand and we start north across the pale yellow field of high grass, we just started walking north to Hollydale, the sun going down over the Pacific. I know the way. I know I can find it. We are ploughing through the high wavering clicking foxtails over our heads to get to our lonely father so he won't disappear like their father. We plough forward to our home, to our parents, to our new brother when Aunt Alice catches us. I was a child who hated to cry but I may have then.

"She knew exactly where she was going, how to get there." Laughter. Laughter and laughter forever. This becomes one of those defining stories about me, my Lewis and Clark side, my traveling gypsy, my dead reckoning, no one thinking that there may be reasons, even principles involved in my crazy undertakings.

When the war was over Rema Mae married Jerry and they moved back
to West Virginia and opened the movie theater in their town, and soon we
had a new cousin back there named Richard.

When Joal was thirteen it came out that from the time she was seven
Jerry had sexually molested her. For years in every gathering of the aunts,
the talk was of that rat Jerry who was sent to prison and now we could
understand what was wrong with Joal, why no doubt she'd grow up to be a
fat old maid. "At least it wasn't blood kin," Aunt Alice reassured us, "not
incest."

Clarke Frederick Edens was the most beautiful baby ever born. Everyone
who saw him said so. His face—his countenance, Dr. Pentz said—was
breathtaking. He was born with black hair, ivory white skin, purple eyes
and thick black lashes. As she had with all three of us, and Penny too, she
searched his head for signs of her father's red hair, saying maybe the new
hair will come in red, but she was thrilled that the Indian finally showed.

Aunt Alice and Mama are whispering at the kitchen table about something
that must be cut off of baby boys.

"What?" I'm coming through the door from the living room. I see them
contract.

"When you're old enough you will know," Mama says in her wise
tone.

But I heard enough to know it's something that sticks out of boys and
not girls. I certainly know of penises, they're not cut off. I see a wing. It
must be a wing. Boys are born with a wing that must be cut off to civilize
them. I heard something about a blade for the cutting which makes me see
the shoulder blade that sticks out like a wing left over from the prehistoric
times when man could fly, a thing that must be cut to make him civilized,
to make him a man.

My brother had to have the cord under his tongue cut too.

"I can still see him when they brought him to me the first time, blood
all over his mouth, all over his diaper. They did it at the same time, no
anesthesia. Sobbing, just sobbing. A little tear hanging in his thick curly
dark lashes."

This I was never too young to hear. Mama never got over the shock.

"The doctor said the stem was all the way out to the tip of his tongue,
he would have never been able to talk. I think you and I have a bit of
tongue-tiedness too."

At the beach I study my father's back and all the other men's, my groom Michael's whose face for some reason I can't look into now, trying to see where their shoulder blades were cut. I peer into the dark crevice when Daddy's arm folds back and I think oh, poor thing, to be a man, that that was cut. I have the sense that it was just one of the shoulder blades, not both, and this is part of the mystery too. When boys fold back their arms I think I do see the cut, but then in the bathroom mirror, holding my own back, my wings look cut too. I can't tell the difference.

When I hold my brother I am holding a cut creature. Cut wings will be characteristic of Clarke, who is ruled by winged Mercury. Cut boy trying to fit into civilization. The cut wing of his tongue.

Because he had three babies, two brothers in the war, and was building planes for the war, Daddy was exempted from the draft. Experimental Aircraft Mechanic was his title at Douglas. "He worked with measurement, plexiglass. Math was his weakness but measurement was his genius. He worked to one sixty-fourth of an inch, he was extremely precise which is partly why he kept getting deferred. But he hated Douglas."

And it was humiliating to be a healthy young man on the streets during World War II.

She thought she was pleasing Daddy by giving him a boy, but ... "with Clarke's birth your father's jealousy became insane."

Mama and our new baby brother are home from the hospital in the big bedroom. They are in the double bed with lots of pillows. Clarke's beautiful countenance lies beside Mama's big left nipple dripping bluewhite milk. But he's crying. He has colic. They are under the covers, this is good, they will be warm, they will be okay, the milk will make it better. We're all together now, our miraculous family. I'm so excited, so happy, so thrilled with our new brother I can hardly contain myself.

Bridget and I are on the living room couch trying to contain ourselves. Daddy wants it to lie down, to rest his weary bones, to read the paper. He has this great idea. "Sharon Lura, why don't you get Bridget and the two of you bang on the door till she lets you in."

I get her off the couch, lead her to the door, teach her how to knock. He lies down, laughing, cheering us on. Together we knock and knock on the bedroom door.

"Go away," Mama pleads from behind the door, thinking that we mean our brother harm, that we're bad for him.

"Keep it up girls," Daddy enthuses.

I'm so thrilled—by Daddy's joke too, he's such a teaser she always says with goosebumps—I bang harder so she'll know it's not true, laughing and yelling.

"We love you Clarke, we're glad you're born!"

"Keep on banging girls," Daddy laughs till the tears are coming and we do, it's so much fun, we're celebrating our brother's birth. We bang harder. We're pounding on the door to remind her just as she has always said he's our baby too, me and Bridget together pounding and laughing with both our fists, to our mother, let us in! let us in! He's our brother! We're getting carried away but it's pure Love so it's good. Grandma told me about the Primitive Baptists like Grandpa's sisters, how they writhe on the floor with the snakes and speak in tongues and the women wash the men's feet every Sunday just like I like to wash Daddy's and this is a way of knowing God. We're pounding on the door in thanksgiving that hallelujah, he is born! It is so much fun. To be making Daddy laugh so hard. I'm so happy to be telling my brother he doesn't have to cry, that he has me and Bridget for sisters.

My banging on the door, getting my baby sister to do it with me, causes Mama's milk to dry up, that's how jealous I was when Clarke was born. The milk sours in her breasts, gets compacted, turns to cheese. This causes Clarke not to have enough time at her breast which causes him to have life-threatening illnesses for the next few years.

I'm sorry, I feel awful, but that was not what I meant. My poor mother, in her exhaustion and weakened, wrung-out state—imagine, she has forgotten how to walk again—has forgotten about Daddy too, his moods. She will always tell of his insane jealousy at Clarke's birth, but she will also always tell of mine.

What does jealous mean?

You feel mean to your baby brother and sister because you are not the only child now.

No. I don't. I love that I'm not the only child now.

You want to be the only child.

No. That's not true. I'm not jealous. I love that I have a sister and a brother. They belong to me too, as I belong to them. This is the greatest joy, to have a brother or a sister. You had him for me and Bridget you said so we won't be alone. Now we know the joy, the happiness of a brother just as you said we would.

Sharon can't admit she's jealous, Daddy says. Sharon always ruins everything.

Peering into my mouth with his flashlight Dr. Pentz lifts my tongue with his wooden stick to see if my stem is too thick like Clarke's. It almost makes me throw up, but he says her cord is normal. A little on the thick side, she'll never be fluent. Audrey, I'm afraid what she really needs is a psychiatrist. He gives me the stick like an ice cream stick to add to my collection.

Why is it important to talk? In Sunday School we say *Lord, even before I say a word, you know.*

We're in the long silver-green car. It's pouring cats and dogs. I'm in the back seat, on the left side, behind Daddy. Mama is in the front passenger side, the most dangerous seat in an automobile. The mother's seat is called the suicide seat she says. Clarke is in her lap, the bottle in his cherry red angel's mouth, against the windshield.

"I have to go potty."

Mama and Daddy laugh, then get mad.

"Sharon always has to go potty."

"Dr. Pentz says we need to take her to a psychiatrist. The minute we get in the car to go anywhere Sharon has to wet. Isn't that right, Sharon Edens?"

But I do have to go.

"We'll have to bring a can when we go for rides," Daddy says. "A coffee can would work, right Mama? More effective than a psychiatrist."

"She was held only ten minutes a day," Mama says, looking at Daddy. "That darn Government pamphlet. That's what's wrong with her."

We pull into that old gas station. They're so mad at me. Clarke's colic acts up, he's screaming hysterically again. Bridget is still in diapers but she is gloating, no, I don't have to go.

"Go on, Sharon, let's see if you really have to."

The station is on the corner, up a cracked, black asphalt hill. The last time we were in there was with Aunt Alice, Billie and Shirlie, and Mama lectured us about never sitting on the toilet seat directly. She showed us how to sit on our hands if there aren't paper covers or toilet paper to make a cover, then how to scrub them afterwards. Billie Jean has VD because she sat on this toilet seat, unprotected. VD is germs that eat away at your bottom, germs picked up from filthy toilet seats, that crawl up the holes in your bottom, it's germs you can never be cured from, not even by penicillin, germs that take years to reach your brain to dissolve it so it runs out of your nose, your bottom, your ears, all the holes of your body.

I climb the hill. They are in the Chevy shaking their heads. I manage to get the filthy door open, and then get my bottom up on the toilet seat, the VD germs all over my hands, I can't get my bottom on right, I'm terrified I've got VD now, and what is going to happen to Billie Jean? and my mother's not even here to see how much I really did have to go. I don't flush it. I'm not strong enough and I don't want to touch anything else and no one's going to know anyway. I can't reach the soap powder that's like sand, like the soap she washes clothes in. I do get the water on but it barely trickles out and it's cold. You need hot water to kill germs. The sink is black with zillions of them.

Back in the car Daddy says "Sharon's sick. Sharon needs a psychiatrist."

He's teasing. We Edens don't believe in psychiatrists.

"She's just jealous because her brother has been born. Isn't that right Sharon Lura?"

Down Imperial we go. A hundred different waves are washing in.

"I am not jealous."

This really sends them into peals of laughter.

A hundred different waves will always wash in. I examine each one, trying to see what I'm doing wrong.

When I tried to tell my mother in the nineties that I wasn't jealous, she scoffed, "Well, why then did the doctor say you needed a psychiatrist?"

Mama assumes that everyone is jealous, it's human nature, look how unreasonable your otherwise perfect father is, he loves me so much he just can't stand sharing me, and no doubt Bridget doesn't get enough attention, though look how sunny that Sunday child is. She's not jealous. Everyone's jealous but Mama and Bridget.

When Clarke was three months old his black Indian hair fell out and came back in gold. For Christmas, Mama said. Luckily his eyelashes stayed black and his eyes purple and always she demonstrated how you can comb your fingers through his white hair and see the black and the red hairs. She did this with all of us, always looking for her father, that red-headed Irish Cherokee, Guy Clarke.

"Joanie's husband suddenly came home from the Navy. Suddenly I had to find other arrangements for us...."

Aunt Giny and Penny stayed with us again. There's a flash of Mama and Aunt Giny in their big flower dresses, reds and greens all around their big rumps, standing face to face in the living room, diapers on their shoulders to catch the spit-up, bouncing their babies to stop their crying. They're talking to each other, they're lucky to have each other, they're sisters. They draw the seams up the back of each other's calves with the eyebrow pencil.

Sometimes Mama isn't miserable about us. She plays peekaboo with us, all four of us in the bedroom. "How much do I love you four? This much? This much?" And she swings out her arms till her fingers touch in back and says "More than all the ocean and all the sun and moon and planets and stars put together!" The thrill of seeing and hearing her do this, just before turning out our light over Clarke's crib brings the explosion of joy inside I know is love.

But mostly she's exhausted, a nervous wreck from the four of us under three. From the seven of us counting Daddy and Mozelle. She's afraid she's going to land in the hospital.

"I went back to see Mrs. Pentz in Long Beach...."

Mama told her this would be good.

Mrs. Pentz couldn't possibly have a baby around but she knew this older couple who needed a housekeeper and wanted a child in their lives too. The job provided a little house in the back. The Yates wanted to adopt a child but they were unable to qualify for one because of their ages. Mozelle accepted the position, this way she could have Penny and make her living too, and be around caring people. Mr. Yates was the principal of a Pasadena elementary school, Mrs. Yates was a teacher, they were well-off, well-educated, just lonely for a child in their lives. They'd lost their only one, a son, to drowning, and they couldn't have any more. This arrangement would be good for everyone.

I have a memory of visiting a magical little house like a doll house that Aunt Giny and Penny were living in behind a big witch's gingerbread house in Pasadena. I remember order that made it hard to breathe, green mowed grass and big granite circles to walk on to get to their door, a red rose bush at the side of it. Maybe there was a gardener. We are bringing my Swan. I'm loaning it to Penny so she won't be lonely.

Dr. Pentz, in his great admiration of my mother—he couldn't help letting her know every time he laid his eyes on her or put his fingers inside her—kept telling her how the Yates could provide for Penny as Mozelle could not.

When I finally did start talking I must have had a Southern accent. Maybe that was partly why I was slow, I could hear the discrepancies, the way you're supposed to talk in Southern California and the way my family talked. I heard the little snickers and the constant miming, *where ya' all fru-om-uhh?* Though recently I've listened carefully to both sides of the family, those still in North Carolina, Virginia and Tennessee, and I can hardly detect the crude redneck Southerner of the mimics, the media, the clichés. I hear a soft, sensuous, careful enunciation, a pleasurable effort in the speaker in saying each and every syllable as a whole word unto itself. An intoxication with one's own voice put out into the warm southern clime, the thick corded ancestral tongue hanging mid-mouth, salivating erotically.

Maybe as a child I heard the discrepancies in the way my North Carolina (mountain and seashore), Southwestern Virginia, Scots-Irish Cherokee and Lumbee—oh, to consider the Cherokee influence—matron-raised (rich widows of Civil War generals) mother and Aunt talked—it was in high school that I trained my tongue to say *ant*—to the way my father and his parents, straight from Elizabethan England (the Rivers Avon and Eden), by way of Virginia, Alabama and Tennessee, talked. Maybe I heard the Chitwood-Edens' disapproval of the talkative Clarke sisters whose family had little schooling. My father's grammar was impeccable—his mother had been a school mistress and all his grandfathers all the way back had been school masters, ministers, justices of the peace, etc.—but he didn't carry on much, outside of orders and admonitions and teasing. ("Why don't you use proper commas in your poetry?" he cried at the end, from inside his steel head brace.) It was my mother who talked and talked and talked to me.

There was a brief moment in the mid-eighties when I took up the quip to my few confidants: "Well, when your father jams his penis into your mouth and ejaculates, it's hard then to talk."

I don't think this actually happened, though those words came out of me like regurgitation, like they possessed me. A little white lie maybe, like Mama taught us to make, to make the point.

But no, to answer a difficult friend. No. It is not like I blacked out and then the light came on. It's about language. I did not forget any of it, I just didn't have it in words. To have had it in words, to have used them, would have been life-threatening.

I would not give up Giny for the beautiful Mozelle, a river in France where the ladies wear no pants, because Giny rhymes with Penny. I was holding onto Penny with Aunt Giny. There are many forms of remembering.

Who is Lady Godiva?

That her body could be used to defeat the King

That her body like Christ's could be used
on behalf of the people suffering
That like God the Father
no man could look upon her body
and remain whole

Why did Tom's blindness
so tickle my father?

Why was I more worried about Tom
than Godiva?[5]

§

Five

I was born with a little hollow in the middle of my breastbone. My father has the same hollow. They are always telling me to show it to the company. "You were born to be a girl no matter what," Dee Rupp laughs.

"But Daddy has it too."

And then they really laugh.

Was Dee my father's lover?

A love once said the same thing of the slight heartshaped hollow in my sternum. God, you were meant to be a girl, you had cleavage even before you had breasts. But I think I have always had breasts. My father's hollow was deeper, wider with dark red curly hair circling it. Even now when I look down on my breasts I see my father. I see his fingers fingering my hollow. I smell him.

I was born with a hernia too, at least that's what was said, in my right mound of Venus. Where boys have it, Dr. Pentz explained. Inguinal. Girls are supposed to have hernias in their belly buttons. My mound swells when I overexert myself, like when I run hard. I could die if the wall closed and my insides got stuck on the outside. So everyone is always checking me for that too. Mama and Daddy, Grandma and Grandpa and the neighbors. When I am six I can have the operation, then I'll be okay, everything will be fine, my life won't be in danger and they won't have to keep checking on me.

Sometimes, looking down, I wonder if my breastbone, sucked in between my nipples, came out below in my right mound, the place boys have hernias.

Every night I stand in the white porcelain tub to be examined. "We would gather in the bathroom," my sister tells and tells again, "to look at Sharon. Her chest, her swollen hernia." In the bathtub. In the backyards and on the sidewalks when hard at play. Pull down your panties Sharon so we can check. The neighbors gather around. It could kill you if you keep running. It could kill you if we don't check. Looking down on it myself, my three year old, my four year old self, my white cotton panties obediently down around my dirty tan knees, all their eyes on it.

When Daddy falls asleep on the couch I sneak up and open an eye lid. Then I open the other. I have both his eyes pried open but he keeps sleeping. His face is so big, so white, so breathing. I show Bridget how to do this. We examine the inside of him. We search for his soul.

We beg him for toe rides. Mama's too tired. I love being on top of his feet, moving in his rhythm. But he doesn't like to do this, especially with me. "Sharon's too big," he complains, throwing me off, taking Bridget on board. I thought he was talking about weight but now it occurs to me that his complaints to Mama were about my head bobbing so near his groin.

I hear them discussing who I am again. The air, everything, changes, is weighted with their whispers in the kitchen. I run there to them from my bed. "What did you say? What did I do?"

"Sharon and her big ears," Daddy says. "Sharon can hear through walls. When she wants to."

Sometimes he says "Sharon hears only what she wants to hear."

I study my ears in the mirror. What does seduce mean?

"There was a little girl who had a little curl"—and Mama draws with her finger a curly question mark down my forehead—"right in the middle of her forehead. And when she was good she was very very good. But when she was bad"—and my mother's voice changes and her finger presses harder into my forehead—"she was horrid."

Sometimes she gives me an enema. She says it will make me feel so much better, she loves enemas. I hate enemas. I have to lie face down on a towel on the bathroom floor with no place to put my face, while my bottom and stomach are being blown up with hot water. "Hold it in, hold it in as long as you can," she says. It never makes me feel better, it makes me feel horrid, it gives me a stomach ache, I hate enemas, but more than anything I want to please my mother. I want what she wants.

I love the way all three of us fit in the bathtub, me, the biggest in the deepest part of the water, by the spigots, Bridget in the middle, and baby Clarke at the end. While Mama heats more water on the kitchen stove, Daddy washes us. He sings *"hey diddle diddle the cat in the fiddle"* and his hand makes arcs of water over each of our towheads and he laughs until tears stream his face and land in the bubbles. *"The boy did laugh to see such sport."* Then he sings the even more incredible Owl and the Pussy-cat. *"O lovely Pussy, O Pussy, my love, what a beautiful Pussy you are, you are, you are, what a beautiful Pussy you are."*

Suddenly Mama is in the door screaming at him, "Don't you dare! Don't…you… dare..!"

"Under hypnosis," Bridget has written me several times, *"I would so often see you and Daddy and how Daddy looked at you, how we'd all study your chest, your hernia."*

I have all my sister's letters, and all my mother's, and copies of all mine to them—forty-five years, thousands of pages. I've managed to hang on to these through all my moves and living on the road. I thought I was preserving our love, my mother and sister in writing, our stories, our passage through life, for the future, whatever it might be, for the future family even. I was always told my memory is faulty, this was to safeguard against that. I was trying to find what had happened to us, the story we were blind to or had forgotten, just like everyone forgets, just as Bridget was doing with her years of work with therapists, then becoming one herself, a New Age holistic body worker, a kinestheseologist, a practitioner of energy medicine. I didn't know that I was gathering evidence. I could never think that I would need evidence against them.

We're on the living room floor playing with Daddy. This is how she recently remembered that play in a letter to Clarke's daughter, Chelli, who was also molested by our father.

"As a toddler, crawling around on the floor, still too small to talk, I knew Daddy's obsessiveness toward Sharon was unnatural and weird. He did not treat her as a little girl, but as some grown woman he was pursuing. It was the ongoing theme in my childhood.

"I was the one among the three of us who 'watched.' Clarke hungered for Daddy to love him, tried in every way imaginable to get Daddy to play with him, approve of him. I ached for Clarke. He didn't know how to protect himself. He was tireless in trying with his little open heart.

"This one night Daddy was trying to get Sharon to play with him, teasing her, laughing with her. She was not laughing; it was serious. But I was watching Clarke, who as he had done over and over before, crawled over to Daddy, who pushed him away in disgust."

But in this very same letter she scolds Chelli for being *"hypnotized"* by me into believing that our father molested her too, shaming her about the damage she was doing to the whole family, and questioning her character, her integrity, her morality, memory, and mental state in the ways Daddy always did me and Chelli. She generously offers to be her healer, to *"work on her,"* to heal her body and soul.

When Chelli told me, at the height of the crisis with my sister and mother, barely a year before our mother died, she described sex acts identical to those he performed on me, descriptions of which I had never told, with the partial exception of my first story, *California Daughter*, which Chelli says she never saw.

"Aunt Sharon," she began, her infant daughter at her breast, "if ever you need someone to testify on your behalf, I will, because he did it to me, too."

I am still reeling from the shock of this. I know now that it's common for child victims of sexual abuse to believe they are the only ones, it is such an aberration it's inconceivable to consider others, but still it's just about unforgivable that I never considered the possibility of his molesting any of the seven grandchildren. This is how denial works. You expose your own children to the monster to prove everything's just fine, to prove you do love, trust and forgive. In the spirit of —in the fantasy of—the close, ideal, really great, loving family. And besides, as Mama and Bridget said constantly after his heart attack in 1971, his first serious encounter with mortality, "Daddy has changed." And all that was so, so long ago.

Chelli's coming to me was a collaborative effort with my daughter, Shawn, who, it turns out, knew about her Grandpa with both me and her cousin from the time she was twelve. Miserable and frightened, but empowered by coming of age at the height of the feminist movement, Chelli confided in Shawn. Shawn was miserable and frightened too. Her beloved stepfather, Max, had just left us, not in small part because of my first publication—that old college story, *California Daughter*, which she found in a box of the published copies under my desk. "I read that story about you and Grandpa so it was easy to believe it about Chelli. But then I saw it!" she tells. "One very specific incident in 1975 or 6. I saw him grope her breasts."

"The thing is, Mom, why didn't anyone else see it?" she has asked several times. And always follows this with, "The thing is, he never touched me."

I finally had to ask her what she meant by that. She understood the common tactic of familial molesters choosing one child to violate while encouraging the others to see that child as untrustworthy. "Remember Mom, how he always treated Chelli just like he treated you?"

No. I never quite realized that.

It was humiliating to be a healthy young man on the streets during World War II. Our father always said that. Near the end of the war he was finally "drafted." "*Clarke, I think everything would have been different had not your father been drafted into the Army when you were only seven or eight months old....*" Mama wrote in March 1987 to my brother when our father's cancer was diagnosed as terminal.

In his long dying, the storyteller came out. One day, near the end of the war, he was downtown LA and someone actually spit on him. He knew he could never kill anyone, he was chicken-hearted, but he marched right into the recruiter's office, which happened to be right there, and enlisted.

Now here is something illustrative. My father lied about me regularly, slandered me and cast aspersions on my character, so if I ever told what he was doing to me no one would believe me—I am able to say this only now—but he would not lie about such a thing as being drafted when actually he enlisted, as my mother would lie and did so quite freely. She called such discrepancies white lies. White lies are used for kindness, compassion, explanation or solace, or as positive thinking to help ease our lives into greater ease, or as good manners, or as simple shorthand or convenience so as not to detract from the point being made; in her mothering she actually instructed us in how to use them. But my father had contempt for white lies, especially hers, mine, and my sister's, contempt so great as to be terrifying—Daddy hates nothing more than a liar is one of those sentences about him—and only now do I finally see that his contempt was a blind to keep us from knowing that he in fact was not always a truth teller; that in fact his dishonesty was deep.

What was he doing downtown? He loved Pershing Square, the Biltmore Hotel, the Cecil, we often drove around there on our Sunday rides. Recently I learned that in the forties the Biltmore was the homosexual center of Los Angeles.

And yes, in this I may be guilty of reading too much into too little.

One day, in her last house on Jennifer Street in Ashland, Oregon, my mother came to me and said, very pointedly, it seemed, "Daddy left January 24, 1945. He was discharged from the Army March 3, 1946."

His Army records give April 6, 1945 as the date he entered (though one, the Honorable Discharge Record and Report gives May 3, 1945 as both his date of Induction and Date of Entry into Active Service). Conceivably this is an exceptional instance in which my mother confused her dates, after all she ended up in the hospital the morning after he left, as she always told, with a one hundred and four temperature caused by a strep infection and after all, January 24 was the day her father died nine years before (and after all even the US Army gives conflicting dates), but now I wonder if in fact he left us in January, two and a half months (at least) before he enlisted. Now I wonder if they had separated.

This is the period of which she always said that if they lived now, they wouldn't have made it. By that July they would have been married seven years. She always warned me about the seven year itch. If they were separated my mother would have had difficulty admitting it even at the end. But she knew how scrupulous I am with dates—as scrupulous as she. It is not inconceivable that she hoped I'd catch this if ever I turned to this writing.

There's a Long Beach studio photograph of the five of us the evening before he leaves. Mama's wearing her blue velvet-collared, camel-colored coat and Bridget and I are wearing matching linen coats that she made. Along with pictures of us earlier in the day riding on his back—I remember vividly the strange rhythm of his big lumbering body on all fours—it is clear that it is April or May. Clarke is at least seven months old, not less than five. I'm the big grinning one in this picture, the only one smiling. If it's April 5, it's twenty-one days before my fourth birthday. Bridget, who has close to a sneer on her face, is two years and thirty-six days old.

Though fidelity and service to one's country is always required to be greater than to one's family, the fact is, when Daddy joins up he is deserting us. But maybe he had already done so.

"I would have left your father, even during the war. I didn't. Having a home for you three kids was more important than myself. I even loved another man."

By the time she was saying this, a much stronger statement than the seven year itch one, and another instance of her seeming to be explaining herself, it was hard to take in.

"Why would you have left?"

"I couldn't have any friends. He was so jealous of even the women taking my attention. He hated the women on the block. He'd come home and want to know what I'd been doing all day. He'd see fingerprints on the woodwork and start screaming. I'd be exhausted with you three and the housework, making all your clothes, preparing meals, trying to keep the house up. I was supposed to pull weeds in my spare time. He'd accuse me of visiting with the neighbors. He was obsessed with the idea that I was having an affair. He'd lie awake at night trying to figure this.

"Once we were sitting on the couch with Odie and he accused me of deliberately trying to arouse his friend by wearing shorts. It was over a hundred degrees, but he insisted women wore shorts only to arouse men.

I'd be working in my flower beds in the backyard, my flowers were the one place of solace and escape for me, and he'd go into one of his tantrums because I was wearing shorts. Odie or Dee might stop by, even Johnny Ritchie might see me."

I like to think that my mother would have left my father for the way he treated my brother. I like to think she would have left my father for the way she caught him looking at me. I like to think she would have left him for the way he neglected my sister, never looking at her at all.

Why didn't I ask who the other man she loved was? Why didn't I assume that's why she would have left?

Partly because for most of my life she maintained that they had the ideal marriage. She loved him so much, she'd say, that if he died she'd die very soon afterwards.

Penny was given up at ten months. ("Given up" is the way it was always put but "stolen" is the more accurate term.) That's sometime between January 19 and February 19, 1945.

Maybe Daddy left the house blaming Mozelle and Penny. Maybe then our mother encouraged her sister to give up her baby in the effort to get Daddy back.

Maybe Mama sided with Mozelle and Penny and kicked him out. Then regretted, panicked. What she said again and again was that she just couldn't take care of another baby. She never blamed Daddy and what he couldn't take. What he couldn't take was because he was a man.

Maybe she suffered untold guilt, as perhaps Daddy did too, about the loss of this child.

Maybe he joined the Army out of spite anyway, even after Penny was given up, jealous of her feelings of loss and concern for Penny and Mozelle rather than for him, for whom now she was showing signs of resentment, anger, and blame. Maybe he joined the Army to be gone like Penny, to make her grieve for him. He could dominate her on some levels but when he realized it wasn't total domination, maybe he left in meanness and defeat. If he left after Penny was given up—and most likely he did—the doublecross would have been devastating.

Maybe he left because, as she always said, with Clarke's birth his jealousy became insanity. Maybe he left because she caught him with her sister. As soon as I write that I think it's true. Maybe he left us for a man. Maybe he left to get away from me. Maybe, if he was a pedophile—still, the shock of certain words, the classifications—he left to get away from his house full of children. Maybe he joined the Army to become a man.

Whatever, once she affirms the commitment to him, to the marriage, she deserts herself and us. Once she begins the downward spiral of complicity, the more lost we all become.

I have a haunting memory of looking for our father on the streets of Huntington Park and in Long Beach. Looking down the tracks both ways at all the railroad crossings.

Mozelle had continued to struggle against the Pentz-Yates pressure to give up her daughter. Then she got a really good job offer in the naval yards at San Pedro. She left Penny that day with Mrs. Yates to check it out. When she returned Mrs. Yates wouldn't let her back in the house, not even to see Penny, because, she said, she was a bad influence. She threatened to call the authorities.

There were no authorities my aunt could call. Who would defend her? She was unmarried, Penny was illegitimate. She was worn down. Even her sister was saying it might be for the best. Maybe Cecil would come home (if indeed he was already gone) if she gave up her baby and got out of our hair. And how could she justify denying her daughter all that the Yates had to offer her? They would send her to the best schools. War was raging all over the world, Joe was probably dead, she herself was taken from her mother when she was seven months. By the time she got to our house she was hysterical. Mama called the Yates. Mrs. Yates promised Mozelle she could have her baby back if she got married, if ever she could find a husband given her disgrace, and could provide the child with a decent home. For now Penny would be safe, in a good, secure home.

"And so the Pentz's arranged for Penny to be adopted by the Yates in Pasadena."

Once in the Jennifer Street house seemingly from out of the blue, Mama came down the stairs to me writing in my office, and as pointedly as she ever got, blurted out "Dr. Pentz wanted to have an affair with me."

She kept trying to tell me more of the story, to even open to what she might not know. But my lifelong habit of silence, then paralysis in responding to her sudden openings, and Bridget's rushing in to encourage her to believe I was guilty of false memory, that I was out to destroy his memory in order to become a famous writer—our mother so wanting to believe that, or rather so relieved to find an ally in the oldest family lie—she was then unable to continue the confrontation. She switched tactics.

She sided with Bridget. "Poor, poor Sharon," she begins her diary, very clearly addressed to me and the world. "I'm afraid she really does believe her father molested her."

Now I learn subtraction. Penny was here, now she is not. Take Penny away, now we are Pennyless. Subtract Marilyn, subtract Shane, subtract Daddy, subtract Penny. I couldn't say Mozelle but I knew the story of Moses, the baby boy hidden in the bulrushes because the Pharaoh decreed that all Hebrew baby boys had to be killed. Did my grandmother Susie know Mozelle is girl for Moses, did she name her Mozelle because she knew she was dying? Does a name give you your destiny? Put a penny in your shoe in case you ever get lost, Daddy would say as we rose up over the Hollydale railroad tracks. I will nightmare a missing baby girl all my life. Sometimes she's hidden in the back bedroom. I talk Mama into showing me. As we walk down the hallway to her I'm saying we love her Mama, don't we love her? But when she opens the door the baby girl explodes like a bomb from the crib and I see that her Third Eye is too big, too visible, is so dominant she's a monster and this is why we've had to hide her.

My sister experienced Penny's loss on an even more primal level. She becomes Penny, the given-up, lost little girl.

"Were you upset, Mama, when Daddy went in the Army?"

"I landed in the hospital the next day with a raging fever. I went and saw him off, on the bus in Long Beach. I went home, went to bed. The next day they had to get the Red Cross to get him back from Camp Roberts. It was a strep infection."

My mother always became ill after an initial crisis was over. As she put it, she used all her strength to get through the crisis, but then, when everything was seemingly okay, somewhat back to normal, there'd be no energy left. She would almost die.

Was Dr. Pentz still her doctor? His name, the stories about him, end sometime through here.

President Roosevelt suddenly died. "I loved that man!" Mama cried. She stood at the kitchen window on Roosevelt looking down Industrial quoting FDR. "The only thing we have to fear is fear itself." When she was a girl she hated that she couldn't vote for him. Then there was the war so the

Constitution was put aside. And so, amazingly enough, she got to vote for him in her first election.

It was April 1945, the final all-out effort, and because they weren't sure to which theatre they were sending Daddy, they vaccinated him for both places, Europe and Asia.

I know my father, like all soldiers in all wars, was affected in unaccountable ways. His huge sense of personal dignity, his sense of privilege from being the spoiled baby in his family would have been devastated by the rank and file system, by having to follow orders, by the officers' contempt for the enlisted men. But none of this would have been a match for what he would have begun to fear as his destiny, for the stories coming back of why they kept needing new recruitments.

But his bootcamp photo album which I've only just discovered in Mama's drawer of his saved things shows him happy. Shows him clowning around with all the guys. In one photo eleven of them are naked taking a shower on a hill under a wooden water tank. Maybe bootcamp felt a little like his Ducktown home with his father and three older brothers and all the miners. These photos are in stark contrast to the one of him in August on the Hollydale front lawn in his uniform in which he looks exceedingly unhappy.

He ranked high as a rifleman. (Measurement, to one sixty-fourth of an inch, was his genius.) But he could never kill anyone. He was chicken-hearted. He said this in shame of not being a man. Sometimes he said yellow-hearted.

She stands at the kitchen sink looking longingly down Industrial. Maybe the man she really loves is driving by up there on Main. Then she prays to forget him. She must close her mind to the negative. She will lift up her eyes unto the hills from whence cometh her help. She prays to think positively so as not to draw the negative to her. So as not to get sick again, so as not to die like everyone has, so as not to let them take her children. So as to rise above her station in life, the ruin of the tribes that runs through her genes. She prays to take care of what she can. (She just couldn't take care of Penny. She cannot love the other man.)

America has never lost a war are the words she says to the three of us sitting behind her at the little table eating our oatmeal and toast. America has never been bombed. There's never been a war fought on this continent. The army has never been brought out against the people. She is saying America is sacred, special, protected. She is saying we will be okay. She is praying. She, Cherokee and Southern, is telling little white lies.

Grandpa teaches me left and right. Three of his four sons are in the war now. In which direction lies the North Atlantic Sea, Africa, Japan, Camp Roberts? He must be worried, though it's no secret that he hates Kermit because he's Grandma's favorite, that my Daddy is his favorite, though he wouldn't breathe a word of this to me except in hillbilly yawp making fun. Maybe he smokes his pipe more, chews and spits more; he's got a bad cold, maybe he's afraid he's dying. We're standing on the cement driveway before the closed garage door when his big hands turn me by the shoulders to face the railroad tracks. He shows me the sun setting in the west. The church is on my left.

And he teaches me about the constellations. You just draw a line with your eyes and connect the stars and then the Big Dipper and even the Little Dipper are plain as day. What's a dipper? He carried a water dipper everywhere he went in Arizona, a place and time so long ago there were no water faucets, and no cars.

All my life I will turn on that cement driveway under my grandfather's big Tennessee hands to the tracks to know left and right.

And so why did I have Hollydale backwards? To write now "south down Industrial" from that position, rather than as I've always said it, "north up Industrial," is like swimming against the tide. Just this January when I was there I got lost again. For some reason I am always turned around in Hollydale.

Mama came to me another time and pointedly, almost angrily said "The Hollydale house faced south." In my first book, *Hard Country,* it says north. Her tone was: "See. You make mistakes, Sharon."

The war with Germany was over. The war with Japan was still going on.

She went up to Camp Roberts at the end of boot camp with three other women. Again, we were left with Aunt Alice. He still didn't know where he was going.

"So then we waved goodbye to our husbands." She said this the morning she came down the stairs to tell me the January date of his initial departure, in an ironic tone she rarely used.

"Daddy went up to Ft. Ord in Monterey. I went home. When I called back he was sick. Oh he was sick. He was so sick he had been given the last rites by a Catholic priest! It was in his tonsils. Malaria or something. They had given him so many shots in bootcamp they almost killed him. By August the vaccines combined in a life-threatening allergic reaction that went down on him. It went down on him."

Two weeks after their seventh anniversary we dropped the atom bomb on Hiroshima. Three days later we did it again, on Nagasaki.

Aunt Alice, Billie and Shirlie pull up outside, come running into the house. "The War is over! The War is over!"

They order us to crawl into the cupboards under the kitchen counter, to pull out all the pots and pans. This has always been prohibited. Then Billie and Shirlie pile the three of us sideways into my red wagon, fitting us just right like the Three Bears in the bathtub and on Daddy's back. They give us each a pot and a lid to bang together, urge us to scream "The War is over! The War is over!"

Big blond Billie Jean, sucking her thumb though she's eight now, pulls us around the wide corner of Roosevelt, up Industrial and down Wilson to Arizona, Shirlie bringing up the tow, sometimes pushing, making sure Clarke doesn't fall out, all five of us, screaming "The War is over! The War is over!" Cars are going by and honking and we meet others banging pots and pans too. Shirlie calls her big sister Me-Me. I love that. Billie has beauty but Shirlie has wit, Mama says.

"The war was over but he was sick. He was very sick for a very long time, from August to March. They wouldn't take out his tonsils for fear that would spread it, and they were afraid to give him any more shots, so they just hospitalized him.

"It was non-infectious VD. It says so on his Army Records: non-infectious VD."

§

Six

"Joanie helped me to move back to Long Beach and I roomed with Jeanie. We worked in San Pedro at the Navy where I first saw Strick. He was a guard and checked I.D. pictures. Next Jeanie and I were in Big Bear for a weekend. He came to have breakfast at the same restaurant. He was being transferred to Barstow and I agreed to go with him. This was in August '45. He got a 72 hour pass for the 16th of September 1945. We went to Las Vegas and got married. I told Strick all about Joe and Penny before I married him."

"Mozelle must find her baby," our new Uncle Strick says, "she will never be whole without her baby. The Yates promised they'd give her back if she found a husband. Well, she's got one now and we want our baby."

But the Yates go back on their word. They won't let Mozelle even see Penny who's almost eighteen months now and wouldn't remember her. She's not even Penny any more. They've changed her name and won't tell what it is.

We're in Uncle Strick's shiny jalopy driving to Huntington Park. It's really hot. Everyone's sweating. "Horses sweat," Mama corrects us, citing the School's lesson on the use of proper words. "People perspire." Uncle Strick who's two years younger than Mozelle is shirtless behind the wheel. On his giant perspiring back are the bullet holes from Guadalcanal.

We're searching for a parking place. He doesn't know if he can parallel park, he's still a little weak. Now Aunt Giny is up in the building searching the records. We're all out by the trunk of the blazing jalopy, which he's opening to find his medicine. He was born rich, Mama explained, but his family lost everything in the Crash. His grandfather jumped from a skyscraper. We don't have skyscrapers in Los Angeles because we have earthquakes. I love my Uncle Strick. I study the bullet holes beneath his cut wings as he rummages through the trunk. He says the Navajo Indians ran the radios because the Japs couldn't break their codes. Mama keeps looking up at the Hall of Records, which is not high enough to be a skyscraper, worried, so worried.

Now Aunt Giny is crying in our parents' bedroom. Crying so hard she can't stop. Sometimes Uncle Strick lies with her to comfort her. Mama makes her tea but still she can't get ahold of herself.

"Maybe it's for the better, Mozelle, it would hurt Penny now to lose Mrs. Yates. Remember how you thought Grandma was your mother? Penny might not even know you now, Mozelle."

When she finally comes out she's quoting King Solomon's judgment about cutting the baby in two so that both women who claim the child can have a half. Solomon knew the true mother would be the one who prevents this from happening. She lets Penny go. Mama says this is real love. They get in Strick's jalopy, Aunt Giny in a teary trance, and drive back to Milwaukee, Wisconsin where a good job with Schlitz Brewing Company is waiting for him.

Her tears, the bullet shrapnel in Uncle Strick's back, banging pots and pans to celebrate the dropping of the Bomb on Japan, the scary name Hirohito (scarier than Hitler), letting Penny go, Daddy sicker and sicker in his penis: that's the end of the war for me.

And Uncle Strick was right. Mozelle will never get over the loss of her first child, Penny Ann Clarke. Nor will anyone.

As soon as he could walk my brother started running away from home. One afternoon he came waddling back down Industrial in his diapers, his golden curls trailing in the Santa Ana Wind like a leash back to a little black dog at his heels.

"Little Black Sambo came to our house when Clarke was 14 months old," Mama wrote in his Baby Book. That would be Halloween, 1945. *"Sambo was about six or seven months old. He seemed to sense a responsibility for Clarke and followed him at all times when Clarke left the yard. Several times Clarke wandered away to Hollydale. Once the police picked him up at the County Farm about six blocks away. Ever-faithful Sambo was with him."*

I remember the panic, then the great joy of seeing Clarke and Sambo pull up in the police car.

"Daddy was very sick that Christmas, away at the Army."

According to his Army records I found in my mother's things, Private Cecil F. Edens of Fort MacArthur, Calif was admitted December 27, 1945 to the Pasadena ASF Regional Hospital and discharged January 9, 1946 with instructions to report to proper station without delay. *"Diagnosis: 1. Prostatitis, chronic, non venereal, non suppurative, severe, cause undetermined. 2. Epididymitis, chronic, non suppurative, non venereal, mild, left, cause undetermined. #1 and #2 cured."*

But he wasn't cured. Three days later, on January 12, he was readmitted with the same diagnosis. On February 7 he had a vasectomy. What did she mean by "non-infectious VD?" In her diary my grandmother says *"Cecil is very discouraged."* He was still very sick on his thirtieth birthday a week later on Valentine's Day. He was discharged from the hospital on February 28, Bridget's third birthday, and from the U.S. Army, on March 3. Forty years later when he suffers and dies from prostate cancer this earlier condition will haunt us.

I remember the daily drives up the Los Angeles River, then the Arroyo Seco to Pasadena. The ominous-looking, cream-colored Regional Hospital—yes, Mama said, you could call that a skyscraper—loomed over the Rose Bowl with hundreds of small windows reflecting the afternoon sun descending to the Pacific. A famous landmark resort hotel before it was seized by the government under the War Powers Act, we could see it long before we got there, the silver-blue San Gabriel Mountains wavering behind it, Daddy on the sixth floor in the shimmering window second from the northwest corner, watching us coming. He would come down to the lawn in his wheel chair so that we children could visit with him. His biggest complaint was that he couldn't sleep in the nude. For Mama it must have harked back to her childhood and visits to her father in various sanitariums, and her own home, Hughes School, the years she spent in bed. If they were separated perhaps this is when their reconciliation began.

It was a big joke, to him especially, that he was classified as a war casualty. On January 2, 1946, the *Times* and the *Examiner* ran front page photographs of the war wounded lined in wheelchairs along Colorado Boulevard for the Rose Parade. **HEROES!** You can see how handsome my father was in his uniform, and his jokey winsome smile, no sign of his condition except for the blanket on his legs.

Now he can't have any more babies. We can never have another brother or sister. Dr. Pentz had wanted to give Mama a hysterectomy after Clarke's birth but she wouldn't allow it. She planned to have one more. She'd sort of laughed, implying it was ordained or fated or in the stars just to have the three of us. She was proud to still have her uterus.

Soon after Daddy comes home we have Bootcamp Inspection.

He calls us out of the bedroom. We are ordered to sit on the couch. We are ordered to sit as still as possible. This is the test. Who can sit the stillest? He and Mama sit at the other end of the room. They inspect us.

It is extremely uncomfortable to be looked at this way.

"See how Sharon's scowling, Mama?" Daddy says. "Beauty is only skin deep, Sharon Lura."

Mama pierces me with her Third Eye trying to see if there's beauty inside me.

"Bridget has great personality. Pretty is as pretty does. See how she smiles all the time."

Clarke's the winner. He's only nineteen months but he's sitting the stillest.

I'm glad for Clarke, but it's surprising that Daddy chooses him as the winner, he always treats him so badly. Maybe this was Mama's condition for him to be able to come back. Maybe he's showing that he does too love Clarke.

Sitting the stillest, smiling big, is evidence of beauty inside. I come in last place. Maybe he's proving to Mama I'm not his favorite.

I'm coming down the S-curvy sidewalk carrying my birthday cake with five candles in it. Suddenly a voice, Daddy's voice, cracks though the joy and I'm terrified.

"Look at that Sharon Lulu on her high horse, would you? Puttin on the style, aren't you Gal?"

Clarke's first sentence, delivered emphatically, with hands on his hips, his long silver-gold curls shaking, was "I is not a girl." He was that beautiful Mama always said. I was so handsome at that age everyone thought I was a boy. Why, I puzzled, was my brother insulted to be taken as a girl while I had been thrilled to be mistaken for a boy?

"ZZZZZZZ-zzzzzzz." He stands at the screen door saying "Zzzzz-zzzzz."

"I think he's remembering the barbershop," Mama says. "He had the most beautiful curls."

He keeps running away with Black Sambo.

"I think he's looking for the barbershop," Mama laughs. "Must be the Clark in his blood."

I asked my brother recently for his earliest memory.

"I remember dropping a watermelon in Hollydale, coming in the back porch."

Instantly I remember the incident too, how the red chunks and black seeds splattered everywhere like guts, over the steps, into the muddy water bordering the cement, up the hard-to-clean stucco walls. And Daddy exploding too, calling him names like stupid! and clumsy! and girl!

because he dropped the watermelon he was so excitedly carrying into the house from the car.

I don't remember thinking of myself as a girl. By the time Sammy Henka shows us his thing to prove he's a boy, and Bridget and I show him our things to prove we're girls I am already very bored. I know. I know. All these silly, unimportant differences. His wrinkled white penis over the straggly pink geraniums. Our funny folds of glistening pink labia under them.

On both sides of our house are cement square curbs built out from the wall about two feet by three feet, about four inches high, marking the entrances to the crawl space under the house. The entrances are shut off by framed screens. Inside the screens it's thick with spiders and yucky webs. Probably black widows, we are constantly warned. Black widows like dark warm places and when they make love to the boy spider to make babies they kill him. They could kill us too.

When the three of us plan and then actually pull off pooping together inside the cement square on Sammy's side to see if there is a difference in girl poop and boy poop, well, this is interesting. All three of us have to hold our poops until two p.m. Thursday.

But try as we do to see it, as much as we scientifically inspect the evidence, we cannot detect the gender difference.

True, Sammy's demonstrations of how far he can arc his pee over the cement curb, through the chain link fence and into his own yard, almost to his mother's red roses, is a difference. I'll never be able to do that.

But Mama says never say never. If I really make up my mind I can do anything.

So then my mind spends time working on that.

We make another date to see if diet could have anything to do with the color and texture of poop but just as with the gender tests the results are inconclusive.

March 16, 46- I allowed Kermit [K.D.] to get his dad some liquor for his cold. I am sorry & ashamed.
March 19, 46- Avon working but sick with bronchial trouble.
March 25, 46- Avon went to work feeling a little better.
April 3, 1946- Avon continued to grow worse and we took him to Long Beach Community Hospital tonight, Kermit, Cecil & I.

March 25, 1946 was Grandpa's last day to ever work. Exactly one month after Daddy's discharge from the hospital Grandpa entered the hospital. He was there until April 29. He *"had some pus drawn from his left side." "Dr. Luff says Avon has virus pneumonia."* It's clear in the diary that Grandma, without saying it, is fearful of the worst. This must be the legendary period that Uncle K.D., who'd reenlisted, took a thirty day leave and visited his father's bedside every day. "They've always hated each other," Mama explained. "But now they're getting to know each other and K.D.'s beginning to understand why his father was so mean to him." For some reason Daddy's devotion is not legendary. For the next two years he shaves his father daily, gives him his medicine, charges his Autoette's battery, talks with his mother, is a devoted and loyal son. In May, Uncle K.D. *"goes to sea on the USS Lowry."* He sails for Bikini and the atomic bomb testing.

Johnny's Bar was across the tracks on Main Street at the corner of Garfield where the Hollydale shopping district began. Across from the bar, but facing west and parallel to the river, were the drugstore, the dime store, and McCay's Market. On the other side of Garfield, which widened there for the one block—up to the tracks where it changed to Cherry of Long Beach—were the post office, an insurance office, a sewing store, a dress store, a furniture store, and always an empty store or two, all with their backs to the river. Continuing up Main, a block beyond the light was the shoe repair store, the small Hollydale library, the VFW Hall, then three blocks of houses of the same development as ours, Utah, Oklahoma and Pennsylvania, then the Hollydale Stables, then the wide Los Angeles River bed. Mama explained that there was nothing wrong with Johnny's, it was good Daddy had a place to relax, to have a beer or two with the guys. She was working harder than ever now to preserve the marriage, to allow him what was so hard for him to allow her, a little space, love and trust. She was working from the Golden Rule, do unto others as you would have them do unto you. He would see her love and trust in him and then finally be able to give her the same. She was probably, also, siding with him against his mother's fierce Prohibitionism.

Sometimes I waited in the car outside the mysterious Johnny's, a little afraid in the dark, while Mama went in for him. A few times I got to go in and have Bit-O-Honeys displayed inside a neon-lit case. Once I had a Shirley Temple. Suddenly let into his big secret world, sitting on the barstool next to him, I saw that it was true, as Mama was always saying, my father was the most handsome man in Johnny's.

In the lot up on Industrial just before the church were piles of coal the train once dumped. "Must have been a shipping mistake," Mama said, "no one uses coal in Southern California." Hobos were living in the coal piles. Daddy called it a hobo jungle, told again of jumping the freights to Washington when he was a teenager, pointed out the black campfire circles where they heated their cans and ate straight out of them. He showed me how to open a can without a can opener. I wanted to grow up to be a hobo with my father. I saw us tramping along, catching the rails, living on the run, living in the hobo jungles, eating pork and beans straight from the can.

There's a bridge over the Los Angeles River somewhere near Long Beach that he helped build when I was a baby. It is of low white cement arches, only about three or four feet high, "modern," he said, but with curlicue doodles engraved in the cement. "Your father is a perfectionist," Mama exclaimed. Sometimes we were across this bridge before I recognized it. I begged them to always tell me when we were approaching it. I was trying to figure how a bridge is built over water. On our rides I sat in the back seat for miles contemplating this. My father knew.

"E-D-E-N-S." She's always spelling our last name to someone on the telephone. "Yes, with an S. As in the Garden of Eden, but many. The S was added during the Revolutionary War to distinguish us from the Edens who stayed loyal to England."

She doodles when she talks on the phone. That's what she calls it. Designs she makes with the pencil as she's listening. She doodles *Charles Eades* over and over on the little white pad. I'm trying to learn to read and write. I copy *Charles Eades,* double checking that she didn't write Charles Edens. I won't know until 1988 who Charles Eades was—the man who raped and murdered her sixty-three year old grandmother; Elizabeth Reynolds Simmons, when she was fifteen—but I never forgot this.

Grandpa's bad cold just gets worse and worse, even for the new miracle drug penicillin, one of the good things that came out of the war. That darn night guard job, it was so rainy last year. He has a hard time breathing.

June 30, 46- Dr. Kearns came today. Avon seems improving slowly. We listened to the Atom Bombing.

July 1, 46- ...Cecil gave his dad penicillin.

July 4, 46- Avon sat in yd a few minutes. Cecil gave his dad penicillin.
July 5, 46- Cecil gave last of penicillin.

The Clares lived across the street on the corner of Arizona. Judy Clare was tall, with long, golden brown curls made from sheet rags. I loved to look into her face which had lots of angles and interesting lines like she was an old person though she was only seven. It's Irish, Mama explains. I wanted my face to be like hers, I wanted Irish lines. Sometimes Mama accused me of coming home acting more like Judy Clare than myself.

Something awful is happening. All the kids who live on our side of Roosevelt are gathered in a huddle and are sneering, snarling and laughing at something about the Clare kids. "Sticks and stones may break my bones," Judy Clare is crying, "but words will never hurt me." Her head hangs down as she runs across the street from their attacks, she's sobbing as she disappears inside her house. Inside I'm screaming, how can you be so cruel? but nothing comes out of my mouth. I don't want their feelings hurt too. I want to run after her, to all the Clares and tell them I saw what happened. "Sharon's always for the underdog," Mama says. She says this of Daddy too. I'm just like him.

The three of us are in the Clare's house. The most astounding thing: they have glass candy dishes placed around the living room, full of jelly beans and little hard candies. Imagine having candy just sitting around in your house and not eating it. "It's for guests," Judy says. "That's us," I assure my brother and sister. "Help yourself."

That afternoon before Daddy gets home from work Mrs. Clare comes to our door and tells Mama that we ate all her candy. "Is this true, Sharon?" I hadn't realized that we'd eaten all of it. "Just wait till your father gets home."

Mama used to say that she didn't believe in spanking but Daddy does and maybe he's right. She's trying harder to include him in the family. He feels so left out. When he comes home he looks at us and says just wait till Saturday morning.

It's a long week. Everything about this seems unfair. Why was there candy put out if we weren't to eat it? Were we not guests? How can you not eat candy? To make us wait till Saturday is like premeditated murder which they both say is even worse than regular murder.

On Saturday morning the three of us are raised into the tree, told to select our switch. Because I'm the biggest I'm given the kitchen knife to cut them. Then Daddy brings out a dining room chair and sits under the tree. We line up in our stairstep line, first Clarke, then Bridget, then me.

Clarke doesn't even know what's coming. The branch he chose with all its little twigs comes hard across his bare thighs and he cries, and cries each time. Next it's Bridget's turn; she's hysterical even before Clarke's done. I don't cry. It stings like crazy but this isn't right. I will not give him the pleasure. The capillaries on the outside of my right thigh break into little red tree branches.

We are switched a few more times like that but then it stops. Maybe Mama stopped it. But the switches are permanently tattooed there so that I can never forget.

As always he gives the three of us our baths at night so Mama can get some rest. Now that Clarke is bigger we fit even more snugly in the white tub. Three peas in a pod. Our six white knees up to the edge, our eenie meanie miney moe thirty toes. Hey diddle diddle he laughs until he cries to see such sport, his hollow in my chest, yep, Sharon's the only one that's got it. I stand up so he can inspect my hollow, my hernia, my switch marks, and scrub my trunk. O lovely Pussy, O Pussy, my love, what a beautiful Pussy you are, you are, you are, what a beautiful Pussy you are.

The big boys on the block, mainly the three who now lived in Marilyn Ripp's house, and the Beaver brothers from around the block, dug a deep hole in the empty lot across the street from our house. This was their fort. They'd dug on it all through the war. The hole was as big as a room and had tunnels and caves carved into the sides.

One day they take me down there, lay me head first into one of the tunnels, leaving my legs out on the outside. "We're going to play doctor. We need to inspect your hernia." They push up my dress, pull off my panties, they examine me. Then they put sticks, tree twigs and little rocks up inside me. They say "Don't worry Sharon Lura we're not hurting you." They are pursuing their medical education. This happens several times before I fully realize I don't like it.

One day I'm coming down the sidewalk and when I get in front of the big boys' house, suddenly they are all around me, about four of them, maybe five, about twelve or thirteen years old. Then as suddenly Sambo passes between me and the blue levis and cowboy boots surrounding me, growling. Their hands, so big, dangle down, motion to Sambo to go home. "Go home Sambo!"

It hurts, I'm trying not to cry, they're looking for something way up inside me, they seem so interested, this is important to their education, I'm studying the earth ceiling of the cave when I hear Mama screaming "Sharon!" and Sambo barking. I see her on the far rim of the hole silhouetted against the blue sky, looking down on me naked from the waist down, the boys working on me. "Sharon!" Sambo is pacing back and forth beside her barking. "Sharon!" she screams, and the boys scramble up out of the hole and are gone.

She spanks and spanks me as she drags me home. She is so ashamed of me she can't tell me. How could I let boys do such a thing to me? Don't I have any shame?

Soon after that the three main boys move to Yucaipa out in the desert mountains. Mama would love to move to Yucaipa. The name Yucaipa will always mean to me the hole. When we visit, Mama so happy to see them in Yucaipa, I become paralyzed in the dust, the sun. I think Yucaipa was my first experience with pixelation, the seeing that everything is coming undone at the seams.

"I do have a haunting memory," Bridget writes in that same letter to Chelli, after urging her to consider that I've hypnotized her into believing that our father molested her too, *"about Daddy and the whole family when we were little and took a Sunday drive and had a picnic up in the mountains that were all brown and dusty. I got lost, looking for the path back to the car. The haunting part is that it never occurred to me that anyone would look for me. I knew none of them would. I imagined Mama would lament that I was lost, but would understand there was nothing anyone could do and all of them would drive away. When I saw Daddy walking down to find me, I was stunned. It's like that happened yesterday."*

We go up Mt. Wilson in search of snow. There's a caged grizzly bear, a roadside attraction. I'm standing at his cage, he's so big, much bigger than me. He has a hump like Mr. Henka and long front claws for tearing open his prey and digging honey out of bee hives. Once grizzlies roamed all over California, killing the settlers, even picnickers. That's why they're on the California flag. Right then a hairy black and yellow bumble bee that's gotten stuck in the sweater I'm trying to put on stings me on the arm. It hurts so bad I can't help but cry, and cry harder as it gets worse. Daddy goes bananas at me for making such a fuss in public, for being such a crybaby about such a tiny thing as a bee. This hurts even more than the sting. Now I'll always be afraid of bees, I'll always see grizzly bears and Daddy racing back to the car to leave me unless I quit crying.

In some places, coming around a corner on the road up Mt. Wilson, you can see the Observatory. We're all in our places, me behind Daddy, Bridget behind Mama, Clarke newly in the back between us. Everything feels awful from my bee sting. Beyond Bridget's head is a forest of waving white aspens in a mountain meadow. She's telling again how once upon a time she was a lost little girl in those woods. She goes on and on about what happened to her. Soon she's going to run away again. She's going to get her Little Red Riding Hood hobo stick and take off. I'm thinking about this, it helps not to think of my bee sting, I'm thinking about our lost little cousin Penny, about my sister who loves the fairy tale of being lost. Mama calls it a fairy tale, laughing how foolish. First my brother, now my sister.

Beyond the blue sky and white clouds is the black infinite Heaven with dots of light that are stars and planets and the Spirit like a dove descending.

Coming down, the movie searchlights are strafing the sky in search of the real lost little girls.

There is nothing he despises more than a bully. When he says no hitting below the belt, that's a cardinal rule from boxing, his voice is so full of righteous indignation and horror at such a thought as to send chills up my spine. When he says there is nothing worse than kicking a dog when he's down, you could not possibly nightmare he would ever do such a thing. I was a fairly smart child but my father was hard to get. I could not think, but Daddy you're a bully.

I'm standing behind him sitting on the step of the back porch. Standing up I am exactly Daddy's height sitting down. He's holding Sambo's muzzle shut with one hand and plugging the two nostrils with the fingers of his other, laughing as Sambo squirms more and more to breathe. Daddy's just teasing, there's nothing he despises more than a bully, but it's so funny to see Sambo struggle, to see the wild fear in his eyes. He says "Suffer, boy!"

I watch the shiver run up Daddy's long back curving over our Little Black Sambo. My heart pounds. I know I'm experiencing something important about humans. I think this. The fun and delight they get in causing pain, the way Daddy laughs with such glee. His glee in being the master of Sambo's breath. He does this a lot. Just like he saw his Pa do to the pit bulls he bred. Probably like something Grandpa saw his Pa, the Confederate soldier, do to his prize horses, so prized he disinherited his own son who hurt one. Never mind that he was hurt. Something important about humans is here. I determine to try it myself, to try and understand.

We're in the middle of the back yard, back by the swing set. I do it like Clarence Darrow for the defense, like a scientist in the spirit of a lab experiment. I hold the three holes of Sambo's muzzle and nostrils shut until he's squirming and whining and I feel the shiver and see my father and I understand. Then I collapse down on him into the tall crab grass, sobbing, apologizing. I vow in his flappy ear I will never do this again.

As a young woman I will nightmare having sex with famous men I can't stand and would not have sex with in waking life, in the same spot, on the back porch of the Hollydale house, the spot I first knew true, miraculous love with Marilyn and where my brother dropped the watermelon so that Daddy smashed his soul against the wall and where he tortured Little Black Sambo for the fun of it. I was trying to carve out a life of integrity and morality in the conviction that just one such tiny carving affects the world, tips the balance. So I'd awake devastated and even more perplexed as to how and why I could dream of fucking President Nixon or Frank Sinatra, devastated by what my nocturnal carving was doing to the world's psyche. I would never, could never, deny that it's the thought that counts.

Like Jesus, he is a carpenter and a fisherman, Mama points out. He's a perfectionist in everything he makes. She says he is a man of integrity and profound principles. She says he's a great man, he enjoys people of all walks, from the lowest to the highest and has a value of fairness greater than anyone she knows. She says people who belittle other people do so to make themselves feel big which is something Daddy would never do. He is a big teaser though, she says, he has a great sense of humor. She always says he's so handsome. She says these things in his presence as if he's not there. She says these things over and over to us making him a hero in our eyes no matter how contrary his ways are to her words. She will do this to the very end of her life. So that we can't see his cruelty and hypocrisies. She compares him to all the men in the neighborhood and I see that it's true, as she says, he's better than all of them in every way.

Most of all he loves to fish. I love to fish with him. I'm stunned and moved by the many photos of him fishing through the years.

We fished from the narrow rock ledge
that jettied the ocean at Seal Beach.
We crawled out to where crabs and unnameables crawled
out of dark seaweedy crevices, the dark holes

the ocean kept screaming up from.
We sat there, always on the dark side, for hours
days.

It takes patience and silence
to be a fisherman.

Perhaps that was the point of Inspection. To learn to be fishers with
him. I remember the three of us all day on the Seal Rock jetty fishing with
him, and as young as we were, only whispering.

He has quinsy.

"George Washington died of quinsy!" Grandma gasps.

The doctors finally take out his overly-vaccinated tonsils that contain
every disease under the sun. He's so sick again, again he may die.

He's on the couch. He's so sick he pays no attention to me. I'm looking
down on him from above his head. They cut out his tonsils which were
connected to what was cut out of his penis. It's terrifying to see your big
father weak and sick and lost so far inside himself. I'm looking down on
him the way the boys looked up inside me trying to understand life. I'm
terrified he's dead. I watch his hairy chest, the heartshaped valley to see if
it's going up and down. I don't open his eyelids. Come back alive, Daddy, I
love you. More than anything I don't want him to die.

When he's well again we're going down Cherry after it is no longer
Garfield and I'm deep in thought about how perfect my father is compared
to the other men, how right my mother is about this. Dee Rupp has straight
black hair. John Ritchie is too skinny and never utters a word. Bill Henka
has a hump in his back. Odie is just plain funny looking with long buck
teeth. Not even Uncle K.D. is as handsome as his baby brother, my father.

"Sharon's deep in thought," Daddy says behind the wheel. "Whatcha'
thinking Sharon Lura?"

"I'm worrying that I won't be able to find a husband as perfect as you."

Daddy and Mama look at each other and Daddy says, "See."

I see only now that my fidelity to him, in the spirit of every lesson my
mother and my Sunday School were teaching me about love and
forgiveness, and deepest, my own temperament, confused her and fed her
paranoia and was proof of his ongoing defense to her that I was in sexual
love with him, that I, a little girl, was trying to seduce her daddy, feelings
that she, survivor of the Dead, could herself have known for her dying

father. She could believe that I was in competition with her for his love. I am made to finally see that she herself suffered jealousy, and that he played this for all it was worth.

There was the opposite, in complete entrapping simultaneity, the accusation I did hear, repeatedly, that I didn't love him. Given my temperament, the denials, the Sunday School lessons, and the poor suffering world all around me—how is the world to be saved? Through Love. Let it start with me—it was this charge that I chose to be conscious of, to stake my life on, to prove that I do love my father.

§

Seven

I'm five, spinning cartwheels under the Los Angeles sky, to the rhythm of the mantra I've learned from Socrates: Know thyself!

The riches of my heritage, both sides—Grandma told me of Socrates—helped me to survive.

My survival was for my father whom I love to this day, and suffer for him as well as for myself, his trespasses against me.

But mainly my survival was for my mother who couldn't take another loss.

Mozelle, who worked on the genealogy of her dead family most of her life, found an immigration ship's log record that shows our Swains came from Orton-Cumberland, England to Southport, North Carolina at the Cape Fear River mouth in 1650. She also discovered that the Southport Swains and Reynolds who intermarried through the centuries were originally Quakers.

Mary Ann Swain Simmons had five sons. Moses, Christopher, Daniel, Alexander, and John. Moses was twenty-one, six foot seven and a half inches tall, "stark blue eyes and dark hair," when he enlisted May 25, 1861 five days after North Carolina seceded. He was wounded and taken prisoner May 12, 1864 at Spottsylvania, Virginia, transported to the infamous prison camp at Elmira, New York, where he died of pneumonia September 14, 1864. His grave number is 250.

Christopher, Daniel and Alexander Simmons were severely wounded at Gettysburg and taken prisoner, July 1, 1863. Christopher died of pneumonia at Aikens Landing, Virginia (date not given), the place on the James River where Civil War prisoners were exchanged; Daniel died of pneumonia October 1, 1864 (place not given). Alexander (Sandy) was released from the prison camp at Aikens Landing, May 12, 1865.

My great-great-grandfather, John Burrows Simmons, enlisted August 10, 1861, at the age of fifteen, not long after his big brother Moses, and was wounded at Chancellorsville, Virginia, May 3, 1863. He was paroled at Appomattox Court House April 9, 1865 when Lee surrendered. "Grandma Simmons always told us," Mozelle repeatedly said, "that he walked barefoot all the way home to Southport. All he had to eat was dried corn, a few raw peanuts, and opium for his wounds."

John Simmons' son, Christopher Columbus Simmons, my great-grandfather, born in 1868, was raised on a plantation at Town Creek, about thirty miles up the Cape Fear, that was lost to carpetbagger terrorism when he was thirty-four and raising his own children there. The murderous December 1898 white supremacist take-over of Wilmington, North Carolina, the only instance in U.S. history of an elected municipal government being violently overthrown—in this case elected black officials—had expanded through the surrounding area. Returning from an emergency town meeting of plantation owners, crossing Town Creek Swamp, he was shot at, the bullet passing through his vest; another bullet lodged in Myrtle's crib inches above her head. He said it's not worth it. He packed up his family and abandoned the homestead.

Christopher Columbus' wife, my great-grandmother, Elizabeth Reynolds of Southport—her grandfather's brother was R.J. Reynolds of Reynolds Tobacco Company—had a child, Olive, out of wedlock between the ages of thirteen and fifteen, by her German piano teacher. She married Christopher Columbus Simmons ten years later and had ten more children, seven of whom survived to adulthood—Ernest, Dewey, Sarah Susie, Myrtle, Maybelle, Luella and Bessie. Sarah Susie Simmons was my mother's mother.

Christopher Columbus maternal lineage is Native American but mostly unknown. Mozelle deduced that his birth mother was Eahnee, Cherokee/Lumbee, buried at Black Mountain, North Carolina. His younger sister Belle, of whom I have three photos, looked, according to my mother, "just like him;" she looks full-blooded Indian. Eahnee died at or soon after Belle's birth and John remarried Suzannah Willits who hated CC. There is an interesting, well-written and detailed Bicentennial account of CC by his next-to-youngest child, Luella Simmons Sperry, the only Simmons to reach old age, telling of an interesting but eventually tragic life of shrimping out of Southport after the plantation was lost, farming and bootlegging, running from the law with Elizabeth and their children, and finally, jails and starvation poverty, and the deaths of most of his children from tuberculosis before his own in 1927. The Lumbee, evidently the mixed-blood remnants of several genocided mid-Atlantic coastal tribes, African Americans—the tribe was known for sheltering runaway slaves in their swamps—and in legend, at least, English survivors of the Virginia Lost Colony—legally changed their name from Cherokee in 1952. The famous story of the Lumbee hero outlaw, Henry Berry Lowry, is like the "Indian Robin Hood" stories my mother always told of the family—that we are brave, proud, compassionate, self-sacrificing, not racist, dangerous when provoked and above all else, free. Lowry was last heard of in 1872 when he successfully robbed the Robeson County bank and disappeared with the fortune into the swamps. Christopher Columbus was four years old.

John Simmons, CC's father, remained addicted to opium for his "Soldier's Heart" up until opium was made illegal in the early part of the twentieth century. During CC's childhood and young fatherhood in Town Creek "he sat rocking in the corner with his opium for his wounds," and was prone to violent outbursts, mainly against CC. Eventually he was sent to Wilmington for the cure. Luella remembered him in both states, addicted and cured, tickled that in his last years he was a dapper and healthy "lady's man."

CC's third child, Susie Simmons (born June 12, 1899), married Guy Henry Clarke (born December 9, 1896) in 1915. They had three children, Lawrence, Garnet Audrey (my mother), and Mozelle Virginia. Susie died of TB on April 21, 1924 in Danville, Virginia, at the age of twenty-four. My mother was four years and three weeks old.

Guy Henry Clarke's mother was Nancy Jackson of Spartanburg, South Carolina, Roan Mountain and Asheville, North Carolina. Nancy, two sisters and her mother, Hester Andrews Clark, are listed on the Cherokee Rolls of 1896, and though the two sisters are on the 1924 Baker Rolls, "the final Roll of the Eastern Cherokee," my great-grandmother Nancy is not. However, her descendent records in my possession go back to 1793, with the first US census, in which Gatalsta Catalst and her son, Saloli (Fox Squirrel), born in Cherokee territory, 1791, are listed. The Jacksons (said to be traditional Cherokee) are still prominent on the North Carolina Cherokee Reservation. They are of the ones who escaped "unto the hills," who escaped the Trail of Tears, the Cherokee Diaspora to Oklahoma.

Like the Lumbee, the Qualla Boundary Eastern Cherokee were anti-slavery and their caves and mountain hideouts were also part of the underground railroad. Nancy's mother, Hester, it was always said, was the first person to teach newly-liberated slaves to read. Being able to read was important to the Cherokee, something some of my other great-great-grandmothers, the ones on my English aristocracy side, including Mary Sharp, could not do.

Guy Clarke, "that redheaded Cherokee Irishman," was raised on Roan Mountain, then Asheville, and, from about twelve, in Juvenile Detention in Richmond, Virginia. He's the one that I've always mourned for, no doubt a haunting that I absorbed from my mother. The persistent family lore has always been that Guy's father, Charles Rogers Clark, was the grandson of William Rogers Clark of the Lewis and Clark expedition, but no records of him have been found. Given the insistence of the telling, and other factors (a stunning resemblance of the portraits of the redheaded Clark to my mother), I continue to regard it as possible. "Charles Rogers Clark died in a forest fire on Roan Mountain or of smallpox in the Ivy Poor House outside of Asheville in 1903"—that's the way it was always put. Nancy Jackson then married John Hammet—probably the reason she is not on the Baker Rolls—a veteran of the Spanish-American war of 1898 who was feared and hated by her three children for his putting them to work in the mills before the child labor laws, for his sexual violations, beatings ("nightly" of Nancy) and psychological abuses, and for committing my grandfather, the baby of the three, to juvenile prison.

Susie's brother Dewey came home from the Army with the Spanish Flu of the first World War. It turned into tuberculosis which swept through the whole family. First Susie died, then Ernest's baby, Aubrey, then Dewey, then Bessie, then Maybelle's baby, then Maybelle, then Ernest, then Guy. In that same decade of deaths, CC, Walter (Guy's older brother), Elizabeth, and Nancy also died, not of tuberculosis but in other tragic ways, my mother witness to most of it. These days I think the TB was the "brown lung plague" of the Dan River Cotton Mill where the adults all worked.

My Aunt Mozelle first told me we are Lumbee in the early nineties, sending me books and material on the tribe. The history of the North Carolina coastal Indians is as abominable as any of the genocides. I don't know for certain about being Lumbee, but—humbly, in search of our roots—I claim it too. (Simmons is a Lumbee name in at least one account I've found.) When I questioned my mother about being Seminole and Choctaw, as she insisted when I was a child, she told of seeing a book "when I was about twelve with photographs of the Seminole. I was shocked, my goodness, those people look just like my family."

She claimed with indomitable fierceness to be Indian, Irish and Scots-Irish. She had past life flashes of living in Edinburgh, Scotland. Made ashamed by Hughes School of so much—shame and notions of the proper were a permanent part of her psyche—it's stunning to realize that she was never embarrassed about CC, not of his outlawing, homelessness, or of his being Indian. In 1988 we found our Simmons Indians in Southport. (Both John and Alexander had Indian children, or were Indian themselves; their father's name, Stephen A. Simmons is on Mozelle's records but without other information.) I remember especially the granddaughter of Alexander (Sandy) Simmons of the Civil War (still a legendary hero there). She was undeniably Indian. And shriveled, blind, mute, very dark in age, and living in dire poverty. My ashamed mother was not ashamed. In fact she was proud of having found this woman.

She was in the second class of Hughes Memorial School, entering in 1928 at the age of eight. The first requirement for admittance to Hughes was that the children had to be "one hundred percent white." Mr. Hughes was the owner of the Dan River Cotton Mill and therefore held responsible for the many orphaned children of his mill workers. My mother was raised from age three, when her mother became ill, to age eight by two Native American grandparents, Nancy Jackson and Christopher Columbus Simmons. I think they told her to never tell the School, but to never, not ever, forget her Native American heritage. To be proud of it.

Then there's the emphasis, through Guy, on our being Irish. "Guy Clarke, that red headed Irishman." St. Patrick's Day was her favorite holiday because it was her father's. She promised him as he was dying to always be wearing the green on March 17 and of course her children would too. She gave us Irish names, Sharon Lura, Bridget Colleen, and Clarke. (Lura, I've been told by strangers, is Cherokee, but she believed it t'was an Irish melody.) Guy was the one who added the "e" to Clark, something she didn't confess until she was dying. I can't help but wonder if this was an effort by him to free her from the tainted outlaw legacy of the Clarks. Or perhaps adding the *e* was simply the orphan bettering herself—Clarke, I'm told, signifies a higher class than Clark.

There's a beautiful, haunting passage in Thomas Wolf's *Look Homeward Angel,* of a Cherokee woman who arrives from Cherokee, many miles west of Asheville, to the boarding house on Spruce Street. She doesn't speak to anyone the whole time, just rocks in her chair. Eventually it is realized that she is pregnant. After the birth she disappears back to the mountains. There's a Nancy Jackson with three children, listed as "colored," in the Asheville Directory, 1900—the term was used for Indians, too—living on the short hillside Spring Street, just down from Spruce, and mentioned several times in the book as a regular walking route. Guy recited long memorized passages from *Look Homeward Angel* when he visited Mama in the School. He and Thomas Wolfe were close to the same age, they were little boys living in the same neighborhood, but of such different circumstances surely they didn't know each other.

My mother's maternal grandmother, Elizabeth Reynolds Simmons, was raped and murdered on September 14, 1935, in Lynchburg, Virginia, and her father, Guy Henry Clarke, died January 24, 1936, in Danville. My mother was fifteen.

There's a long hall on a fourth floor, with gleaming green marble walls, a building called Records, and Mama in three inch, shiny black patent leather slingback high heels, straight lines up the back of her calves, her scrumptious rump rolling beneath a green rayon dress, is frantically searching for one. A Record that will prove she's right about something, and they're wrong.

In the attic, the entrance to which is a trap door in the ceiling of our closet, she keeps her collection of Sears and Roebuck and Montgomery Ward catalogues. She has been saving them since 1940 when they first arrived in Southern California. I love to watch her climb up over the clothes and boxes and junk, her feet disappearing into the ceiling. When she descends she "reads" to us from the catalogues as if they are story books, not the printed words, but words and stories she makes up. She follows certain models. She shows us little girls in 1940, she shows us the same girls now. She shows us how they grew—blossomed is always her word. She tells the ongoing story of two or three she especially loves. The one with the wide-spaced eyes like extroverted Bridget, the one who is shy and serious like introverted Sharon. She tells stories of their lives, what their personalities are like, what is really happening to them, who they're in love with, who they're going to marry in the men's grey clothing section, the boys like Clarke.

Mama herself looks like Katharine Hepburn. People stop us on the street and tell us this. There's a painting I once saw in the Museum of Modern Art in New York City of my young mother, except that it's really Katharine Hepburn in 1927. In 1927 my mama wasn't even in the School yet.

She reads two newspapers a day, every word (except the Sports Page), including the want ads. The Los Angeles Times in the morning, the Huntington Park Signal in the evening. The cost of our morning and evening newspapers is fundamental in the tight budget. She's so proud of how political the Edens have always been, at least back to 1066 and the Rights of Man, that we are aware and involved.

Stumbling into the kitchen in the morning, rubbing sleep from my eyes: the white enamel wooden table, the see-through yellow chintz curtains pulled back by bows over the sink, the cream and yellow striped tiled counters, the pale yellow flowers on the linoleum floor. My beautiful mother sits, ramrod straight, alone—always there is about my mother a severe aloneness—at the table in the deep corner drinking black coffee and reading the paper, her elbows inked in the newsprint. Looking up often to the window. On a clear day you can see that snowcapped mountain rising above everything.

She can remember the first time she saw a newspaper. It was 1927. The headlines were about a flood. Just imagine, she thought, every word is true. All this really happened. "I decided at age seven that newspapers were the most important thing in my life. They were true!"

They both read us the funnies. They have serious discussions about politics and the comic strips. Blondie and Dagwood, Daisy Mae and Lil Abner, Dick Tracy, Lil Audrey and Little Orphan Annie, a red headed orphan girl from 1924, the same year Mama became one. Daddy says that Al Capp is a genius, a real genius. He lost his legs under a train so he drew funnies. Out of every bad comes some good. Mammy Yokum spins herself around and around until she's zapped by lightning, then she's channeled. Out of this comes me and my sister. We practice regularly on the front lawn, spinning and channeling at twilight. Daddy giggles that giggle about Daisy Mae. Like when he calls me Lady Godiva. Sometimes he calls me Daisy Mae. He says but Moonbeam McSwine is dark and more beautiful. And then there is the Shmoos.

They read aloud about the atomic bomb testing in the Bikinis. "Do you realize, children, that your Uncle K.D. is there, taking part in this historical event?"

He's lying on the deck of his ship with his hands over his clinched-shut eyes when the Bomb goes off. Even though his eyes are squinted shut he can see all the bones of his hands and the giant mushroom cloud blowing up Bikini behind them. He will tell me of this when he gets home. Thirty years later in the slow dying of his bad heart he will tell this with great bitterness to anyone and everyone who dares come within hearing distance.

When Daddy reads the paper, he rips off a little piece of the corner, puts it into his mouth, and balls it up with his tongue and gums. As he reads he's rolling it around. "Gumming the news," he calls it. His eyes never leave the page as he gets the poop on Nixon and the current person Dirty Dick is slandering. How much he despises Dirty Dick. He reads union and antiunion stuff. He reads about the Kitchen Cabinet in our kitchen, then spits what he's chewed against the kitchen wall. The little round wad sticks like plaster. "Spitwads are a filthy shameful habit," Mama gasps, running to wipe down the enamel wall.

"There is nothing worse," she deplores, "than being a prisoner of habit, except for words like" and she spells it out, "p-o-o-p." But this doesn't stop our father from chewing his wad.

She teaches us to stand on our heads, to somersault down the lawn, to spin cartwheels across it. The thrill makes your heart want to break, Mama playing with us. The thrill of her body, that she's so big and reserved but still knows how to play. Sometimes we even tumble and somersault with Daddy. We ride his back across the desert of Arizona, into the wilderness of Tennessee, to the barren eroded hills of Ducktown.

There's a photo of her sitting on the bumper of the 1923 Ford. Our jalopy, our rattletrap, our joke of a car. Her hand is up behind her head, her elbow resting on the words *Just Married* painted on the back of the rumble seat. Her pompadour and short cotton sun dress, her big grin. Going down Paramount with their three kids and *Just Married* painted on the back. I loved that rumble seat, how I loved to go, the wind in my face across the land. This must have been the car you had to crank the handle in the center of the front bumper to start.

Her big grin. Did I say she never grinned? I am struck by what seems almost happiness (genuine, not the cover-up kind) in many of the pictures through this period, which, really, wasn't a happy period. There is memory of this too, of my mother happy, especially strong in the Arroyo Seco driving to Pasadena. Perhaps she gained something in being free of Daddy that year he was in the Army and hospital, in being independent. Twenty-five, three children and a home in sunny California. She's no longer a girl, she's become a woman. She even loves another man, is perhaps loved by him. She's beautiful, not just pretty.

He installed an airplane altimeter on the steering wheel so we'd always know how high we were, and a big spot light for the fog, or for anything he wanted to spot, like a jackrabbit fleeing into the brush. As he's backing out of the driveway, we vote on where to go. I always want to go to the ocean (sea level), Mama always wants to go to the desert (below sea level), Clarke always wants to go to the mountains, which thrills Daddy because of the altimeter. "The San Gabriels are the fastest growing mountains in the world," Mama explains. Bridget wants to go anywhere Daddy wants to go.

"Try hard to see the land before the roads," Mama says. "Before the tracks and bridges and houses and factories. Los Angeles has the most beautiful light in the world, that's why the movies are made here." The light hitting the Hollydale triangles inside the one big triangle that is the Los Angeles Basin. "Oh, to just imagine," she cries, "that there are people who don't love the land."

Just as often she extols the great virtues of being free of place, history, story and roots. This is what is so great about Southern California. We're so lucky not to be growing up in Virginia with its awful class system where you have to know, accept and stay in your place until you die. Just imagine!

The sound of the cars passing is the sound of the future approaching, then passing. The sound of wanting. Wanting to know the people in them. To come so close, to be driving the same roads, to never know each other though we may have passed each other before. Does God know if we did? Like Mama and Daddy standing on the same corner watching a parade in Charlotte North Carolina three days before they met. What if they'd never met? I wouldn't be here. Neither would my brother and sister.

In January the Basin smells of sweet orange blossoms. We raid the orange groves. Driving along he rolls an orange up and down his thigh, juicing it up, then digs a hole in the top with his pocket knife and sticks in his straw.

And, oh, alligator pears! That's what Daddy calls avocados.

When she was told, three weeks after her fourth birthday, that her mother had died, she laughed. This is one of the earliest stories I remember. But when I wrote this in the original Mother poem for my first book, *Hard Country*—I sent it to her for Mother's Day believing she'd be honored— she was devastated and protested vehemently. She wrote back the account that's entitled *Genesis: The First Story Ever Told Me*, the only prose that's in the poem, about how hard she cried when she was finally allowed to go into the bedroom where her mother lay dead. But she admitted too that she put spit in her eyes at the funeral because when they were burying her she couldn't cry, and maybe that's where my awful notion came from. The others were crying and expecting her to, she didn't know why she couldn't cry then. My mother didn't imagine that her laughing on being told that her mother was dead had always been a key for me to the terrible universe, that I understood my mother's laugh as deepest love, deepest loss, deepest helplessness. What a little girl knows when confronted by the Universe. "To keep from cryin," Langston Hughes writes in a poem, "I opens my mouth and laughs."

She was so in control of her grief and so proud she told the stories of her tragic family without a hint of self pity. Now I realize that as the survivor they were her soul's responsibility, a way of keeping her family alive, and that she passed this responsibility on to me, one of my roots as a writer. Most children's stories were boring to me, they couldn't compare to hers. I hated most of the nursery rhymes. *"Mary, Mary, quite contrary"*—they were so fixed I wanted to explode. No way did I want to be one of the *"pretty maids all in a row."* But I did sort of like Peter Rabbit (in dreams I'm still hiding in the cabbage patch eyeing the shotgun-toting farmer), and Br'er Rabbit and Tar Baby—Daddy told that one, always so confusingly haunting, I believe now, because he was alluding to his great Uncle William Washington Sharp who was tarred and feathered, that is murdered, in Winchester Tennessee in 1863 for being for the North.

On Friday nights we go to the Pike in Long Beach, buy bagfuls of jumbo fried shrimp from Shrimpy Joe's. Shrimpy Joe's is a hole in the wall, a window in a retaining wall at the bottom of a steep hill just above the water. There's no beach there. Only a buoy out there bobbing around, crying and moaning, so sad and lonely, sending flashes.

"What's a boy doing out there?"

"Telling ships how to come in."

A wave of terrible sorrow for him still washes over me when I hear that foghorn sound, which I believe now is that man Mama and I witnessed drown six days before I was born. Still this is the funnest thing we do. Sometimes we get to do it on Saturday night too. We sit in our car at the steep angle, eating our delicious shrimp and watching the incredible sights. Drunken sailors, and freaks on display, Siamese twins and mummified cowboys, a thousand year old mummified prostitute, the Monkey Boy, Emperor Hito's portrait in the glittering, fantastic lights. Towering above us is the hundreds of feet high neon needle a man has been sitting on for months to break the record. He's in the newspaper. We watch his shrimp go up in the basket, then laugh about what must be coming down. There's an all-glass tattoo parlor right on the corner and we can see the sailors being tattooed. Just imagine you can never wash it off. The world's largest roller coaster looms on the other end of the Pike, a massive trestle of dark crisscrosses. The zippy little train flings the riders out over the night's high tide, their rhythmic screams when they drop from the highest point like a song over the engine's grind and the cars' zoom and the ocean's boom.

Most of all I feel the boy out in the water. I listen to the waves slapping him around, worry he's going to catch his death of pneumonia like Grandpa. Worry that he's lonely out there.

We're climbing the short, steep hill, leaving Shrimpy Joe's when we get stopped by a stalled car in front of us. Daddy worries about our clutch, always tries to make the hill before the light turns red. "Lookie there," he says about the shiny giant car. A very dressed up Negro man and woman are getting out of it. "My. How they love their big fancy cars."

When we get around them, our clutch burning a bad smell, we go to the drive-in theatre. All through the double feature I keep reliving the movie at the stoplight, trying to understand what Daddy was saying. Who wouldn't love a big fancy car?

We're at a crosswalk in Huntington Park, me, Bridget, Mama and Aunt Alice. Clarke is on her hip. A Negro woman with a baby on her hip is here too.

"Oh, they are so cute when they are young," Mama is saying as we cross the street behind her when the light turns green.

I'm hit by horror, sheer paralyzing shame of what my perfect mother is guilty of, though she actually thinks she's being generous.

The elm in front of the kitchen window has grown twice as high as the house. Mama loves to climb a tree. Everyone knows Cherokees are tree climbers. She would run away from the School, live on berries all day, be high in a tree reading a book when the search party would pass below calling *"Audrey, Audrey...!"* She would not answer.

I climb the tree to try to see the ocean and into the backyards behind us. Up here I'm not confused about north and south. El Pueblo de la Reina de Los Angeles. I can see the Long Beach City Water tank on Cherry Avenue. I can see the Los Angeles River, near the fork of the Rio Hondo. Maybe it's the Rio Hondo coming into the LA River that creates so many triangles in Hollydale. I can see the side gate to Rancho Los Amigos de Los Angeles, the County Farm, four blocks north up Industrial. The County Farm is the home of sick, crippled, homeless, and insane old men, most of whom are vets from all the wars. There's a constant stream of these old guys down Industrial on their way to Hollydale to purchase tobacco and liquor. They hobble by. They curse their wheelchairs caught in the weeds, the broken bottles, they shake their canes at Trinity Bible Church, at the cars, they drop into the tumbleweeds, the coal piles, they pull out their things to pee, they shake their things at the god damn little girls, me and Judy Clare and Bridget Colleen, they pull out their bottles and drink.

A couple of sips from Daddy's beer. Unimaginiably awful. But I want more than anything to love what he loves.

SMOG! One morning that's the headlines.
Smog is a combination of two words, smoke and fog.
I had seen in my mind the Indians' campfire on the LA River where City Hall is now, the very first description of the area written from a Spanish ship out at sea, and grasped the lesson about geography and air, how the mountains trap the smoke which then mixes with the ocean fog, but Mama's reading me the news story is a revelation about language. "Smoke" and "fog" make "smog."

We are not poor, just broke. Never say you are poor.
Don't tell the neighbors our business. Don't ever tell anyone how much money we make. This is private.
If we are anything we are lower middle class, the best place to be. We are not working class, or blue collar. Labels like those are an insult from Back East or from the Communists or the politicians like Richard Nixon and others who want to label and control us so they can use us for their own purposes, to get power. Never forget who you are. Never let another name you.
A man is innocent until proven guilty. Might does not make right. The ends never justify the means. There's no such thing as a free lunch. You can't get something for nothing. The best things in life are free. The haves and the have-nots. What goes around comes around. You go so far left you become right. Two wrongs don't make a right. Out of every bad comes some good. May take awhile but all crimes are solved. Poetic justice. Way in over my head. Too deep for me. The blessings in disguise. Where there's a will there's a way. You control the oil you control the world. By hook or by crook. Never say never. Turn the other cheek. Turn a blind eye. A sight for sore eyes. Sharon Lulu's thick skull. If you haven't forgotten you haven't forgiven. What's good for the goose is good for the gander. Daddy said that. It hurt so bad it wasn't even funny. Watch out what you hate, it'll be standing in front of you in six weeks. Mama said that. Quit stretching the truth, Audrey. I'll box your ears. Grandma said that about a

student in her one-room schoolhouse before she married Grandpa. Never shout fire in a crowded theater. Don't butter up. Each person is unique. Do you realize you are the only one who's ever been you? Don't forget, you're an Edens. Put your John Hancock here! The biggest, the boldest, the bravest, the first. Just like an Edens.

As we mosey along, the King of the road, the King of his own Castle sings with the cigarette dangling from his lips everyone says are exactly like mine and I see in the rearview it's true, mine are just smaller, *getta long little dawgy.* Turning onto Paramount for the home stretch he yodels *ya HA hey. Come the yup SAY hi.*

Sometimes he says *come the FBI.* Sometimes *dog eat blue.*

Even the face of the house at 5903 Roosevelt looked like my father's face.

"Shoot!"

For months they've been building a triplex apartment building next to us on Industrial, in the triangle lot that works back from the point of nothing on Roosevelt to the wide base that is the alley behind us. Mama was sure they could never build on it.

Shoot! comes out of her like a gun shooting. She is standing at the front window, behind our new Venetian blinds, shooting. The carpenters are leaving for the day. She has been talking to a man in a dark suit who said we don't qualify for the loan.

Somehow we buy the triplex anyway. My mother figures that out.

But even that is not as impressive as the force of *Shoot!* shooting out of her.

She says the only reason she can bear living here is because our house is on the corner lot and from the window over the kitchen sink as she washes dishes she can look down Industrial, beyond Main, past Hollydale Park and see that mountain, snow capped, rising over the Los Angeles Basin. "I have to see a long ways," she says, creating a bias in me against those who don't, against those who like to keep their shades drawn, who do not need or want to see out. "Oh, I love a road to look down," she says.

Because I had north and south in Hollydale reversed I thought the mountain had to have been Mt. Wilson. Now I think it must have been San Jacinto, Southern California's highest mountain, so important in the Indian history and lore and to me later. "You had to get out on Paramount Boulevard to see Mt. Wilson," she admonished that time about the house facing south. I will have to return to Roosevelt on a clear day to see if you can see Mt. San Jacinto from 5903 Roosevelt, looking south.

She has claustrophobia. Whenever she gets sick the claustrophobia increases. Closed curtains, any enclosed space, especially elevators, are off-limits. "I have got to get out of here!" is one of her oft-repeated declarations.

The claustrophobia came from all the burials she attended as a girl. Everyone died. First her mother, Susie, then her eighteen month old cousin, Aubrey. "A beautiful baby with curly hair. He was Ernest's son, my mother's oldest brother. I looked in the window the minute he died, saw him turn blue. Then I saw him put in the ground near my mother. It was dismaying because it was so soon after my mother was put in the ground and had not come back."

When she was told her mother had died she told herself she was just sleeping. When they lowered her in the ground, shoveled dirt on her, all she could think was what will she do when she wakes up? She won't be able to get out. All her life she had nightmares of her mother waking up under the ground.

Her mother had told her that she was to have the watch Guy gave her when they married. But someone said no and she was buried with it. As a girl she lay awake nights wondering if it was still ticking on her arm under the ground. My mother loved watches and had a clock in every room of every house and motorhome she ever lived in.

"My mother is buried in a small country churchyard, Mt. Carmel, on the road to Eden, North Carolina, just south of the Danville, Virginia line. I can't imagine how they managed it but they made sure they buried her in North Carolina. We kept returning to that graveyard to bury others."

The Los Angeles Water and Power Department workers have drilled through the concrete where the two sidewalks meet at the corner of Roosevelt and Industrial, using a horrible sounding pile driver that reverberates through your whole body. Then with shovels they dig straight down. The black dirt piles up like mountains all around the hole. We sneak up behind the dirt mountains to look over and down on a blond guy digging without a shirt—with rippling muscles and a heart tattoo on his heart, *Mother* written through it like an arrow. He curses us with bad words, grabs out for us, scattering us in all directions screaming. I get to our porch, my heart pounding, grab the post to turn and see that he's got

Denny Clare and is holding him by his ankles upside down over the hole. He spits, then swears he's going to drop him in and bury him alive.

The nausea buries me for awhile. I know that Denny will never be the same. Again, I know what evil is.

We mail-ordered baby chicks from Sears. Daddy built the coop in the far corner of the back yard, using the fence for two of the walls. The coop had lofts inside, nesting shelves, and a low-slung modern roof with overhanging eaves. "Better than a new house in Orange County," Mama boasted, pointing out how well-built it was, how even in making a chicken coop Daddy was a perfectionist. He put a chicken wire fence around it so they could be on the ground. We had one rooster. Daddy made a big deal about the rooster, always pointed out his wattle, always pointed out that he's the boss of all the hens.

"I was on the roof of the chicken coop," Bridget often tells, "helping Daddy to nail. Suddenly I realized that my name is Bridget Colleen Edens. Bridget is a Goddess and Colleen means lass and Edens is about Eve in the Garden. I realized I must hammer like a girl. So I practiced, up there with Daddy, hammering like a girl."

He summons the three of us to come out. This is his duty. Time we know this.

We are ordered to sit on the front porch steps. The three choice hens are clucking around him, around the Henka corner of the house, cluck, cluck, cluck. He grabs one by the head, cluck to you too, he laughs. Now watch this kids. In big swings of his big arm, he swings her around and around until her body flies off from her head.

Daddy stands there with her head, laughing, her eyes staring up at him. Her body keeps running around in circles, blood gushing from the opening of her neck.

Other times he uses the ax. We are ordered to the porch. He chops her in two. The chicken's so dumb she doesn't even know her head's cut off. Blood spouts like a fountain from her opened neck, like a Fourth of July firecracker as she runs around the yard, down the side yard, two or three minutes before she suddenly keels over dead.

But her head lies there, glaring at Daddy. At us. Daddy laughing maniacally.

This was his duty, that we know where our bread and butter comes from. That we know what he does for us. That we know how hard it is, what he sacrifices of himself to put food in our mouths. That we know the hand that feeds us. That we know the meat we are eating. That we be not hypocritical or spoiled. Life's not always a bowl of cherries, kids.

Even then it seemed a script. He always said, in a sort of shame but also in a kind of affirmation of who he was, that he was chicken-hearted, he couldn't kill a thing. But we were made to witness him as a chicken killer. I think he was still in shock of his father doing this to him, making him witness the murders of the chickens that he then had to eat, that he was resentful of us still in the privileged state of youth and innocence. The Czech novelist Milan Kundera says the origin of evil was the domestica- tion of animals, when we first brought animals close into our lives, raised them in order to eat them.

Mama brings out the big pan to fetch the fryers. Suddenly he's screaming at her "Quit putting words in my mouth!" and disappears in one of his moods, into the back yard to the big plow he made for his garden— corn, tomatoes, carrots, lettuce, string beans, bell peppers, onions, potatoes—food he grows that we might survive.

My favorite part of the chicken is the neck. "Sharon's faking," Daddy curses my fidelity to the thing he breaks. "Just being stubborn." When he's feeling philosophical he shrugs, "to each his own."

A little store is being built on the corner of Industrial and Main, across from the church. "When it opens can I go get the bread by myself?" I want to do this more than anything, to be that grown up. Mama can watch me from the kitchen window if she's nervous. Yes, I can make it across Main, even though there's no crosswalk there, I know how to be careful.

And then it opens and I'm allowed to go up there and get our loaf of bread, our daily bread, our staff of life, my very first official journey alone, up Industrial, the quarter and penny clutched in my hand, twenty six cents for Langendorf's White Bread, for the extra-long, fluffy blue-and- white waxed package, the long block out of childhood, beyond the boundaries.

This becomes my job. I do it every afternoon. I get an allowance for this, maybe a nickel or even a dime every week.

Bridget announced her decision to run away last night at dinner and ever since she's been making careful plans, as Daddy told her she must if she is to survive the ordeal. She cut the stick from the elm tree just like cutting a switch and she's tied an apple, a bowl and a spoon—the dish ran away with the spoon—a nickel for a phone call or a bag of peanuts, a comb and a California map into a kerchief and tied it to the stick. Daddy showed us how hobos do it.

Mama and I are in the garage washing clothes. She's so tired it's a struggle to get the sheets, Daddy's heavy pants and the towels lined up into the ringer. The towels come through and I'm scared her hands will come through too. She can hardly lift her arms she's so tired. Bridget comes into the garage to say goodbye. "Good bye." The rollers are mashing the towels, the tub is clunk-clunking back and forth. Mama says "Don't worry, she won't get far, she'll be back by dinner." She laughs in her warm, wise way, "This will teach your sister a lesson. It's natural to want to run away, I ran away many times as a girl. The adventure is good for you. Bridget will appreciate her family more."

I don't want to run away. I want to stay in my family forever, at least until the confusions are cleared up and they know I'm not jealous and they know how much I love them.

"Just let her go," Mama shouts to me when I run after her. "Just let Bridget Colleen go."

I follow her back through the kitchen and living room, and out onto the porch. "Bye Sharon Lura." "Bye Bridget Colleen."

The Buster Brown oxfords carry my little sister, hobo bundle on a stick over her right shoulder, past the Henka's, past Marilyn's house the boys lived in who took me down in the hole, past the Ritchie's. Now she's in front of Dixie's, across from the Clares', now looking up and down Arizona. At what point is she going to turn back as Mama assured me she would? I know about pride, Sharon's false Southern pride. My poor sister, to have to eat humble pie and turn back. I would never run away because I could never come back.

She gets to the corner, stands very still for a few minutes, her hobo bundle pivoting in the late afternoon sky. Just staring up Roosevelt. Then very slowly she turns around and trudges back home.

"It doesn't matter what I do in this family," she says. "It doesn't matter if I leave or stay so I might as well stay."

"It does too matter, Bridget. It matters to me more than anything. And to Mama and Daddy too."

"Pride has nothing to do with it. That's you, not me."

Buried in their closet is the large oval photograph. I beg her to bring it out. It's getting banged up around the edges thrown back there in the closet with the smelly shoes.

Sarah Susie Simmons Clarke sits in a chair outside a white clapboard house and Mama and Lawrence are hugging close to each side of her. Mozelle is in her tummy though you can't see her yet. My grandmother is twenty-two. "You can see the Indian in her," Mama always says. She is sullen, apprehensive, serious, as is Mama. Her dark hair is bobbed in the fashion of the twenties, a single curl coming down her forehead. She will die in a year and a half. To grasp that she is my grandmother. To grasp that Mozelle's inside her. That the two and a half year old towhead with the bowl haircut is Mama, a look on her face that seems to anticipate every tragedy that's coming, anticipates her face when she dies seventy-five years later, a look of fear but saying hope is the only prayer, saying love is the only answer.

"She's buried in that dress. It's yellow. Her mother, Grandma Simmons made it." An eyelet cummerbund around her middle that is Mozelle. Mama is holding a tiny doll and she's wearing a yellow dress too with matching bloomers that her grandmother made. Both Susie and Mama are wearing black patent leather shoes. Lawrence who is about six is barefoot.

And there's the watch on her big wrist: big faced, round, white.

It was a very dark picture so I don't know why I loved it. Mama didn't like to bring it out. It was like looking directly into something forbidden, but important. The clothes were strange, as were the haircuts. Everything was dark, even Mama's blond bowl cut. The brilliant red of Lawrence's hair photographed as just dark. The dark reproduction. Maybe it was the film that was old-fashioned. Mostly it was Susie who was dark. How can you die? How did Susie let herself die? How will I ever die?

And where is Guy Henry Clarke? We are in him too.

Luella Simmons writes in her 1976 *Memoir:*

"*In Reidsville* [North Carolina], *we moved into some rooms over a café, and there was a lot of noise going on until late at night. We had been there for a month or two when Susie came bringing Lawrence and Garnet.... She'd left Guy because of another woman. Then Susie started getting morning sickness. Soon Guy came and they reconciled. It was after Mozelle was born when she went for a checkup they discovered she had TB. Back then they had no cure for this, it was almost always fatal.*"

I have just found this, on a disk Mozelle sent me, a second part to Luella's *Memoir* that my mother did not give me. Mama never, not ever, breathed a word of this. Several times she expressed anger at her mother for "just giving up and dying." She was faithful to her father to the very end. But now I know what I've always sensed, that Susie is suffering a broken heart in this picture, and that this too, maybe as much as the flu and TB germs and working in the mill and her Indian blood, led to her death.

I love to hold Daddy's arrowheads, to feel them in my hands. I can only do this with permission. As a boy, arrowhead hunting was his favorite thing to do. All the trees for fifty square miles had been killed by the sulfuric acid fumes from the copper mines, so everything lost in the forest for eons was newly exposed on the barren hills.

They are bundled together in a drawstring bag in the corner of the top left drawer of their dresser. They are all sizes, from tiny bird ones to tomahawks. Mostly copper orange and white, with black, grey, green and brown streaks, they are the most fascinating things in our house. Just to feel them, to try and imagine how they were chiseled, how they were tied to the arrow, what they killed. That they killed, that they could kill, that they were instruments of death. Just to imagine the particular person who carved and shot each particular one. Just to imagine the people no longer there, in a forest no longer there.

Daddy isn't Cherokee but the great-great-grandson of the original white settlers of Tennessee. He loves the Cherokee, he married one. If I turn a certain way in Mama's big mirror, I see the Cherokee.

In time the makers of these arrowheads will come alive and terrorize our house. But until writing this I thought the nightmares were from the cowboy and Indian movies we saw at the drive-ins.

§

Eight

"We were quite competitive. In fact once I got mad at you and kicked your nose with my tap shoes. What a bloody nose you had and my Mother really got mad at me for doing that." (Sharon May Ritchie Neely, letter, June 21, 2002.)

When my mother says I was easy I feel the deep passivity in my body, like an ocean, maybe the largest part of me. The Sun, Venus, the Moon, Saturn, Jupiter and Uranus in the constellation of Taurus were setting in the ocean the moment I was born. Taurus is patient. I accept what is happening. I have simple innate trust like love for the universe, a kind of physical and psychic openness to whatever is coming. Taurus is slow to react, is spring's second action, the rooting of the fiery germination of Aries exploding out. Resistance for me is usually second reaction, and usually takes awhile. Betrayals will always be as with the dog that bit me, as with Sharon May's bites and kick in the nose—*she* was competitive—a shock, a complete surprise, devastating in part because my denial of such a possibility was a demonstration of my love.

I suppose that causes others to feel they have to wake me up.

I start school in this state.

"Sharon was born with a rusty neck!" Daddy hollers. (Taurus rules the neck.) A rusty neck must be like a birthmark, it won't wash off. I'm grateful I have long thick hair to cover the rust on my neck.

But Daddy keeps saying it until I finally realize, for shame, he means dirt. He warns me again and again about being in school and someone discovering how dirty I really am underneath.

Now I realize Mama had forbidden him giving us baths anymore and he was chomping at the bit.

The kindergarten for Theodore Roosevelt Elementary School was situated under enormous old palm and sycamore trees, away from the modern classroom buildings. The fronds and leathery golden-red leaves that carpeted the yard were bigger than our heads. Even in kindergarten we walked the mile by ourselves, crossing busy Paramount Boulevard. I loved the crossing guard, I loved the cars stopped for us. I loved the cars going on to elsewhere.

We bring our own blankets to school for nap time, our initials embroidered in the corners. We spread them together on the rug and lie down and shut our eyes. The intimacy of our thirty prone bodies as in one big bed, our eyes shut, our heavy breathing, the way you can smell the others wakes me more than ever. I never sleep.

We have Fingernail Inspection. We have to stand in our alphabetical rows with our hands out, palm down, while the teachers, Mrs. Hall and Miss Sharp, inspect our nails for cleanliness. I am Sharon Edens so I'm in the front row, the last one down. I'm frantic with my hands behind my back trying to clean the dirt from under my nails with my thumb nails before they get to me. I'm panicked that I'll be caught cheating but then mortified when my deception works. It's like my rusty neck hidden under my pretty golden locks, how dirty I really am. Standing with the clean kids looking across at the dirty kids I know I'm a cheater and a phony. I'd rather be with them than go through this again.

One day that first week of school Mama picks me up as a surprise and drives to the Downey City Hall. She enrolls me in Tap Dance. She and Bridget and Clarke sit on the side and watch. *Clickety clack!* I am still in that lineup of girls learning the lesson. I still feel and see and know and hear the *clickety clack!* on the golden wooden slats so deeply that even as I'm accomplishing the first lesson I'm knowing the carpenters nailing the boards down. And the lineup of girls, oh! we are all still in that big wall mirror. Swing your right leg forward, tapping the floor as you go, then back, tapping again, then bang to a stop. Now your left leg. Repeat and then make two big bangs.

We go to the shoe store next and she buys me and Bridget shiny black patent leather shoes with movable t-cross straps up the front, the buckle on the inside. Giant silver taps come in the mail before the second lesson. We take them to the shoe repair man in Hollydale and he screws them onto my black patent leathers. A photographer comes to the house, takes pictures of all three of us, me in my magical tap shoes.

The following week I'm in ecstasy from the sound and vibration up through me of my own *clickety clack* taps. For lesson two, we add hops and skips to what we learned in lesson one.

And then that was it. I accepted what Mama told me, that we couldn't afford it, though she had already gone to the expense of acquiring the shoes and the taps. I was disappointed but I accepted without protest. I just made sure I didn't forget lessons one and two. I got Daddy to unscrew the taps after I grew out of the shoes, saving them for the time I would be able to resume the lessons as she promised. I remember standing in the garage at his work table silently watching him do it. I still have the taps; they're the oldest thing in my hope chest.

He probably had a jealous fit. It was shortly after that that they took dancing lessons. When they taught dancing in the School Mama was sick, one of her long periods in bed, and so she'd never learned. We got a new record player and records! *The Tennessee Waltz, To Each His Own* (Mama's favorite), *Perfidia, My Heart Belongs to Daddy, Cool Cool Water* (Daddy's favorite). She tells us about the wind-up Victrola her grandpa CC had when they lived in the tents. They demonstrate for us seated on the couch. Mama is self-conscious, she says, like a little girl, she's so thrilled. Daddy takes her in his arms and they waltz. *"I was dancing/with my darling/To the Tennessee Waltz/ When an old friend/I happened to see."* Daddy is laughing, nibbling on her neck as he moves her across the living room, loving her goosebumps against him." *I introduced him /to my loved one/And while they were dancing/ My friend stole my sweetheart from me."*

Then, after the second or third lesson on Tuesday evenings, they stop. Just as I am still in the tap dance, still in the mirror with the other girls, still beside him at his workbench removing my taps, I can still feel the martyr in our mother rising with her goosebumps, the sacrifice of herself and her children to him and his moods, as demonstration, as proof of her love and commitment to the marriage. And I feel her absolute assumption that he will meet this, that he knows the Golden Rule, that he knows the soul debt he is incurring, that he will meet his responsibility, he will balance his side of the equation. The records are never played again.

"I'm looking over a four leaf clover."

He complains when she sings at the kitchen sink, she can't carry a tune. She has a four leaf clover in her Bible that her Daddy gave her singing that song. She says she will never hum again. She explains—she always explains him, she wants us to understand him so that we can love him—that singing was prohibited in his boyhood home. Singing was reserved for church.

August 23, 1946- Dr. Luff came. Avon was worse- Dr. said no sign of T. B. but he has a little pleurisy.

Late in the drafting of this book I read my grandmother's diaries, impressed by how close my chronological ordering has been, but stunned too by what I haven't remembered. That we visited them every day on Comolette for the two years Grandpa was sick before he went away for good to the hospital. Sometimes we walked the two miles. It hurts not to remember that walking. Daddy's attentiveness to them brings surprising tears to my eyes. No doubt we were encouraged not to remember, not to be aware of the dark that was slowly engulfing them.

Oct 12, 46- Cecil came. Avon felt better but coughed too hard & tore a cell. Slight hemorrhage.

But how wonderful life is too!

Sept 20, 46- ... Avon and I drove down Comolette. I learned to drive!

Rancho Los Amigos is filling up now that the war is over. More and more homeless old men are walking on Industrial but also young wounded ones. We stand on our heads and watch them. They're crippled, missing parts of their bodies, paralyzed, ragged, with long hair and beards. They use homemade boards and bars and pulleys and wheels and wagons to walk. Winos, the neighbor women huff and some of the kids mimic them, jerk spastically down the street, head and arms and legs going all different ways. Some guys you see every day. Us on our heads, their one arms wheeling their legless trunks down the street. Sometimes being pushed in beds by other cripples. "The Body is the Temple of God," Mama says, "no matter its condition, it is God's." There's one whose face is burned off, it looks like a big lumpy silver boulder on Mt. Wilson. There's one who looks exactly like Santa Claus, except he's mean. He comes down the street in his suspenders screaming "The God damn Spanish American War!"

The hobo jungle is growing too in the block between our house and Trinity Bible Church, an ever-expanding system of tunnels and shelters in the dumped coal and tumbleweeds. Just as with the men from the County Farm the hobos are from all parts of Earth east of Hollydale. And sometimes a gypsy caravan is camped there too.

Another source of weird men on Industrial Avenue is the Hollydale Foundry and other new factories opening on the three blocks behind us. These men are mostly shirtless, muscular and young like the one that held Denny Clare over the hole. Most of them are just back from the war. They are the scariest. You see them inside the long aluminum sheds built parallel to the tracks, boys before the orange fires, raging, snapping like flames themselves.

"I didn't realize," my mother said in the last year of her life to some story I was telling about the old men, "that we lived in a dangerous neighborhood."

Did she know where her brother was? On October 16, 1946, just before sunrise, nine of Hitler's Nazi officers were hanged. Uncle Lawrence was an Army guard at Nuremberg. Years later he will tell me that guarding, then escorting those men to the gallows caused him to lose his mind.

A square windowless shop is built across from us on Industrial, its front door facing down Roosevelt Avenue. "It's wrong," Mama gasps at the kitchen window, "to build a place without windows." A Russian family moves into it, is living there until they can find a real home. The father is a cabinet maker and the little girl is Nadja. Nadja is in kindergarten too. We walk to school together.

I fall in love with Nadja like I fell in love with Marilyn. She has dark skin but hair the color of golden fog. I love her so much I think my chest will burst with the joy. I'm hypnotized by the way she moves. My whole being knows immense gratitude for the fact of the yellow and black sunflower of her glowing face, the cellular rush of the ancient Russian river that I can see beneath.

She taught me the astounding skill of riding a two-wheeler. I am forever in that moment of being released from her hold, balancing and pedaling and steering up Industrial. But then, suddenly, she wasn't allowed to play outside. Maybe it was because of the old men, maybe something happened. I have a vague memory of her father making cabinets, nothing of her mother. Maybe they realized the danger. But imagine not being able to even see outside.

For the Christmas play I was the Angel that guarded Baby Jesus in the manger. For the entire production all I had to do was hover over him in my glittering gold and white wings and halo. I had one word to speak, "*Hark!*" which I was terrified I'd forget or say at the wrong time. And I sang *Silent Night* with everyone, so moved to see yond there a round pregnant virgin. And the Kings of Orient are.

Mama, Bridget and Grandma were in the back row. "I want to be a Staingel like Sharon," Bridget sobbed. Our father roared when he heard this. Our parents called Bridget a Staingel forever afterwards.

A Hollywood scout was in the audience. He started writing letters and phoning my parents that I must have a screen test.

"What's a screen test?"

"A screen test is a movie made to see how you look on film. Some people are photogenic. They look better on film than they do in real life. Some people don't photograph well."

Then Mama told me about Shirley Temple, the curly headed little girl movie star of her childhood who was damaged because she didn't have a normal childhood and though she's famous throughout the whole world, and still makes more money from her old films than all the adult movie stars combined, she's fled Hollywood. She's vowed she'll never make another movie. That's how awful Hollywood is.

Then she told me that her grandfather, the Indian Christopher Columbus, never allowed his photograph to be taken. He believed the camera steals your soul.

We're in Penny's in Downey, Christmas shopping. I'm sitting on Santa Claus's lap. My mother is standing outside the circle of presents, beyond the blinking tree. She's looking at Santa with her Third Eye. Clarke went first, then Bridget.

"That your mother?" he asks, staring back at her. I see the electric current running between his eyes and hers.

After Daddy died I asked her about this memory. All I had was the flash of being on his lap and seeing her beyond the tree, but the intensity of their staring at each other is why I'd never forgotten. His name was William O'Sullivan. He lived on Utah Street in Hollydale. He'd been in the war and now was getting divorced. "I was even in love with another man." This Santa Claus was evidently the man, Sully, "the closest I ever came to having an affair."

He'd come in where she waitressed,
the Downey Road House, buy Camels from her, play
Love Walked In over and over on the juke box, drink and smoke
the whole pack while watching her serve dinners. She quit,
found a new place in Huntington Park, until late Fall when
Love Walked In again. She was so lonely, that was the period
that if they lived now they wouldn't have made it.
She quit there too. And then there he was on that lit throne
in Penny's, the prettiest Santa she ever saw,
her children on his lap.[6]

"*Love Walked In* is a Eddy Howard song," she said when I read her this poem on what turned out to be her last Christmas. " '*Love walked right in and drove the shadows away,'* she recited by heart fifty years later.

'Love walked right in and brought my sunniest day. One look and I forgot the gloom of my past. One look and I had found my future at last.'

"He also played *To Each His Own.* I began to feel myself falling. I kept waiting for him to walk in again. And to think I'd almost bought a house on Utah, that we would have been neighbors. I wanted it more than the Roosevelt one, but we'd already chosen the Roosevelt one and your dad put his foot down." Then she said William O'Sullivan again. He lived on Utah. It almost felt like she was hinting I could find out about him for her if I wanted to. In her journal that night she wrote "*I almost made a terrible mistake!*" and "*thank goodness Fred never knew.*"

I remember when she worked at the Downey Road House, up on Paramount. I remember sitting outside in the car in the dark with Daddy in one of his sulking moods, and Bridget and Clarke, waiting for her to get off work. In the poem I had remembered that I was four and she twenty-four. She corrected me, it had to have been Christmas 1946, because Daddy was home from the Army. "I was twenty-six by then and you were five."

Why was my mother so lonely after my father came home?

"My mother has always had a thing about Santa Clauses. Maybe a fetish. Come the season she begins pointing them out, that's a good one, that one's not."[7]

I got a little Santa Claus face pin in my stocking that Christmas, the same Christmas I was Jesus' Angel. I wore it every season into adulthood. It always reminded me of the Penny's Santa Claus, the prettiest Santa my mother ever saw.

Dec 25, 46- Rain, Rain, Rain. Cecil & Audrey prepared a fine turkey dinner for us but Avon's feeling very bad and the weather bad we gave up and Cecil brought over our dinner. Avon was so disappointed that we couldn't go...

Grandpa's been sick now for almost a whole year. Mama says she's sure it's just pneumonia, it was so wet and rainy last winter.

We brew up a little pot of stew, me, Bridget and Marie Henka. We use leftover moldy carrots and potatoes from Daddy's last year's garden, and we get the water from the curb side. We down this, the three of us. We're testing the germ theory.

Everything feels like it's about to disappear. I'm too sick to go to school. Bridget can't hold her head up. All day we're throwing up. A bug, a germ, a virus, something going around we breathed in or swallowed. Marie's sick in bed too. "Never drink after another person," Mama lectures us as if she hasn't before. "Never kiss anyone on the mouth. The Ritchies and the Clares actually kiss their children on their mouths. They should be ashamed!" We don't tell her about the stew. Clarkie wanders in and out, Black Sambo at his heels whimpering for us. Bridget goes "ugh, you poisoned us." "I'm sorry Bridget, I thought I was proving them wrong about germs." I don't know how to explain that life seems good, too good to kill you.

In the afternoon Grandma comes over to wash clothes. They're out in the Tide-and-oil-smelly garage talking seriously about Grandpa. They don't want us to hear so we are trying not to but what does silicosis mean?

The evening paper is on the sofa when I come back down the hall from the bathroom.

Torture Slaying!

The nude, mutilated body of a young woman, cut in half at the waist, was found in an empty lot south of downtown this morning. She was disemboweled.

I don't know how to read but the words are coming into me anyhow, like I'm a sponge or something. I know what the paper is saying though I don't know what torture slaying means. Then I see Daddy torturing Sambo for the fun of it; I see the shiver running up his back.

All night Bridget and I have nightmares. I keep seeing a woman's head rolling in a park.

"What's a nightmare, Mama?"

"When I was a little girl," she explains, standing at the door so as not to get our bug, "just after my mother died, I was playing in the street, when the neighbor's horse got loose, came flying at a full gallop down the street. Stupid me, I started running before it. My Daddy came running behind it, yelling Garnet! Garnet! Then I tripped and fell. But the horse—it was a girl horse which is called a mare—when it flew over me, didn't touch a hair on my body. Then Daddy was scooping me up in his arms, sobbing Garnet, Garnet, not you too. You can't die, you must promise me not to die, it would kill me.

"Nightmares can't really hurt you, and sometimes good things come of them, like being held in your Daddy's arms."

Twenty-two years old. A black dahlia still in the long black curly hair. A black dahlia placed in her severed disemboweled lower half. Now the Black Dahlia takes up almost the entire first section. Pages and pages of photographs and stories. The weedy lot where she was found, lit up by arclights with hundreds of people driving by all night, looks like the one across the street. The scrubbrush the old men hide in and the big boys laid me under, the brush that will die and become tumbleweeds blowing down the streets. The black dots of the photographs waver and come apart so all you can see is black dots, like the sand and rocks and Joshua trees out in Yucaipa. The black headlines I can't read, about her black silk evening gown with spaghetti straps. The white dahlia in her black hair pulled behind her ear. Her body strewn like spaghetti and meatballs. The autopsy performed at Queen of Angels revealed she choked to death bleeding from the ear-to-ear knife slash through her mouth. That's the cause of the Black Dahlia's grisly smile.

All week, sick from our curbside stew, the morning and evening papers are more and more filled with the news of the Black Dahlia. A slinky femme fatale in a tight black dress. Victim of a werewolf murder whose romances had changed her from an innocent girl to a black-clad, man-crazy delinquent known as the Black Dahlia. "What's a werewolf, Mama?" "What's a femme fatale?" "What is man-crazy?" "What's a black dahlia, Mama?"

"I thought you couldn't read," she snaps.

"I can't."

"Sharon Lura it's not good to think about such things. And it's not good to pretend you're not as smart as you are."

"The Black Dahlia's father lives on Kingsley Avenue, Mama. Remember? That's the street we left Aunt Giny on to have Penny. Maybe he kidnapped her. What does vivisection mean?"

She holds up an article in the movie section. "Read this line." The black dots wiggle, float and dissolve like blood and cigarette smoke. "I can't read yet Mama."

A man named Red in South Gate is arrested. Red is Daddy's nickname. He works in the Huntington Park hardware store. We bought some toilet hardware from him. But by the end of the week he's released.

"He's innocent," Mama says, "even if he was intimate with the Black Dahlia. Boys will be boys. This, children, is what is great about the American system. A man is innocent until proven guilty.

"Course," she adds, looking down Industrial, "the poor man, his marriage is ruined. Surely the police could have found a way to hide that from his poor wife."

Now it's the greatest manhunt in California history. "Everyone's just gone crazy," she says, "they want to possess the Black Dahlia even in death." This is when she first tells of the manhunt for her father. Guy Clarke killed a man in a poker game. He was arrested, thrown in jail. He escaped with a key hidden in a potato. He was hiding in the Blue Ridge Mountains of North Carolina. Mama watched from her school desk the blue hills to the southwest, watched every moving blue streak of shadow for her daddy. Daily she read the papers about Guy Clarke. He was on the run for a year before he was caught, brought back to stand trial. He was found innocent. He'd killed the man in self defense.

"What does cutting someone up have to do with the facts of life, Mama?"

"You tried to murder me, Sharon Lulu," Bridget answers. "I'll never forget this."

Connie Wollum says the man pees inside you. I know the facts of life, I know where babies come from. The man puts his penis inside your vagina and the egg hatches. My mother didn't say the man pees inside you. I am standing on the sidewalk, a block up Roosevelt, on my way home from kindergarten in a circle with Sharon May, Sharon Beck, and Nadja when Connie tells us the man pees inside you. I don't believe her, but right then, in that circle of girls, as she says it, I feel something strange in my mouth.

It's my tooth, my first baby tooth to come out, a little white thing like a seed floating around my tongue, my teeth, the roof of my mouth that I almost swallowed before deciding to check it out. It felt like a man's pee, or maybe the hatched egg, or some part sliced from the Black Dahlia.

One week after my sixth birthday, exactly seven days later, Karen Pohlman had her sixth birthday. The Pohlmans moved into Marilyn's house where the boys lived who took me down in the hole before they moved to Yucaipa. May 3 was like magic to me, the perfect math of one week, of seven days, the exact amount of time it took God to make Creation and Karen after he made me. And Karen rhymes with Sharon.

For her birthday she got an electric slide pedal steel guitar, with lessons. She wanted to give me the lesson after she had it every Monday. "You just must be outside my house, on the sidewalk, at 4:00."

And so on Mondays after her lesson she'd come out of her house with her pedal steel guitar and bench, set up on the sidewalk and give me my lesson. In her black cowboy boots, in my red ones, beneath her hat, beneath mine, she held the heavy metal bar in my hand, plucked and pressed my fingers on the other one to the strings, slid my hand down. Oh! The sound, exactly the sound and vibrations I feel inside the front folds of my Mounds of Venus, the tickle there.

May 29, 47- Cecil's trial over car accident put off till Monday...
June 2, 47- (Anniversary of sister Ida's death) Cecil lost in a suit about a car wreck. I kept Bridget and Clarke.

At some point, not recorded—perhaps it's in the missing diary—my father was in a car accident in which he ran into someone in heavy fog. It was an accident, he couldn't help it, the fog was so thick. (The ground fog of Southern California is heavy, dark, totally obliterating; it makes San Francisco ocean-air blown fog seem light and navigable in comparison.) If there were injured parties I didn't hear of them but the issue was serious and hung over my father through my early years and was one of the ways Mama explained his moods. He was innocent but was found guilty and lost his license for a whole year. How was a man supposed to get to work to feed his family? He couldn't drive, he felt trapped, things were unfair. He ranted about the corrupt courts, the lawyers for the rich. The other person on trial that day was a woman who had killed two people on bicycles. She was found innocent. His attorney, just licensed, was suddenly made judge. I remember attending the much postponed trial in Huntington Park. My parents wanted me to witness our court system in action—my father, an innocent man, found guilty. I remember the woman too, but mostly, I remember my father's bitter rage. I've always rooted my politics in this moment.

June 18, 47- Audrey took Bridget to a clinic in L.A. Avon feeling bad.
June 19, 47- Audrey took Sharon to the clinic. Also Bridget & Clarke.
July 3, 47- Our 41st wedding anniversary all to ourselves except Cecil stopped on his way home from work. We hear that Avon has active Tuberculosis.
July 9, 47- Avon rode out in the sun in his Autoette.

When Grandpa was diagnosed with tuberculosis all of us had to be examined and X-rayed. It was the law. It would become a six month ritual as regular as the one with the dentist. Putting your bare chest up to the cold silver-grey plate, folding your arms around into it, worrying about what they're going to see. We all had positive reactions to the skin test but this would be true of anyone who has come in contact with TB germs. It doesn't mean you have TB. My lungs were fine. So were Clarke's. But they found a shadow on Bridget's lung. And a bigger one on Mama's.

Tuberculosis, my mother will always tell, carried an enormous onus of shame with it when she was a child. "The onus was like cancer used to be, prostate, breast, colon cancer, you didn't tell. TB was like AIDS now. TB was associated with poverty, you gave it to others, you were a social menace, you almost always died of it."

Contagious or not, we continue to visit regularly. This is the period of my life of which I have the least recall. Mama didn't want us to suffer fear, the knowledge that a whole family can be wiped out, just like that. Her children wanted most of all to give her what she needed of them.

July 20, 47- Cecil lost his job.... Clarke is very sick.

July 21, 47- Went to be X-Rayed today. Picture didn't look so good but they tried to encourage me. Audrey & Clarke took me. He was sick. I am very tired tonight.

August 19, 47- I was very restless last night- Cecil came tonight. He has a cold of long standing. Clarke sick.

August 20, 47- Cecil came again. Little Clarke very sick. Giving him penicillin. Paid rent. I upset over things said by landlady about Avon.

August 29, 47- Avon not so well. In bed most of day. Cecil came and let us have $5. Gave ½ pt whiskey for eggnog.

August 30, 47- Avon played little music box. Avon repeated the Lord's Prayer after I prayed.

August 31, 47- Clarke's 3rd birthday. Avon & I alone all day...

September 1, 47- I drove Avon down as far as Priscilla Avenue. Farthest I've driven.

September 3, 47- Sharon's operation put off.

They're going to cut six inches diagonally down my right Mound of Venus and sew up the inside hole. Mama says I won't feel a thing when they cut me open, ether is wonderful. I'm all packed, we go to Children's Hospital on Vermont. I'm being admitted when they take one look at Clarke in Mama's arms and take him instead.

He's been sick since the middle of July, running a fever, every day a little higher. It was diagnosed as pneumonia but something's wrong with his legs. They put him in isolation in case it's polio. We can see him only by looking through the crack of the door, between the hinges. Mama tries not to let him see her but he does and he starts screaming for her. He becomes completely hysterical, screaming, jumping up and down in the crib. This is my worst early memory.

The doctors are more stupid than cruel. "He was quarantined because they thought it might be polio, but it was an allergy to the sulfa drugs they were giving him for pneumonia. One more dose would have killed him. It destroyed his white blood cells, caused his leg damage."

After two weeks he finally gets to come home but he's still very sick. Mama puts his crib in the dining room so she can watch him, so Bridget and I won't disturb him. Poor baby brother. His legs always hurt, at night especially. He sobs for Mama in the night, "my leg hurt, my leg hurt," and Daddy screams "Sissy! Mama's boy!" Sometimes Mama sneaks out after Daddy is snoring and crawls in the crib. Sometimes she says Industrial smells like sulfur, just like Ducktown did.

Bridget made the March 1 cut-off date to start kindergarten by one day. "Really by only ten minutes," Mama always said. And it was true: she wasn't mature enough. She cried and cried for Mama not to leave her. She didn't stop crying when she did leave. By the third day, Clarke's second day home from the hospital—Mama had so looked forward to having the time alone with Clarke—Bridget was still crying so they all gave up. The school said Bridget could stay home another year. Mama never said Bridget couldn't bear for her to be alone with Clarke. And I never thought this until now.

I notice Raymond Price the first day of first grade. Dark and quiet and as tall as me, he sits on the far side of the room, under the big windows. I feel incredible love stirring my heart like a bowl so full of water it's spilling. He's shy like me. We never speak.

Oct 10, 47- ...The Hondo Knot bearing our war dead dropped anchor in Sanfrancisco bay. A light rain is falling tonight.

Nov 25, 47- ... Fear is in my heart.

Nov 26, 47- Avon is suffering very, very much.

Nov 27, 47- Thanksgiving. Cecil brought over dinner that Audrey prepared; turkey, lima beans, peas, p. pie. cranberry sauce. It was delicious.

Nov 28, 47- ...Sharon called to tell of going to Sharon May's 6th birthday party.

Dec 8, 47- .... Fear I'm going to break down...

Dec 9, 47...Sharon called. She is sick in bed.

Dec 16, 47- Avon seemed better all day but seems worse tonight. Red spot on cheek.

I keep looking at that entry. The red spot on the cheek returns in vague, mythical memory as the sign of inevitable death by consumption. I think Mama spoke of it. I think D.H. Lawrence wrote of it.

The dining room set is put out in the garage and the Christmas tree is set up in the dining room. Clarke gets to sleep under the tree. The pine smell will be good for him, and the Christmas Spirit. Mama goes up into the attic through the trap door in our closet and brings down the boxes of Christmas decorations. She tells us the story of each ball. The most important ball is from their first Christmas, 1938. Here's the ball from Sharon's first Christmas, 1941. And here's the one from Bridget's, 1943. Here's Clarke's, 1944. She winds the lights around and around. If just one bulb burns out they all go out. She's so tired these days figuring which bulb is bad. She looks at my Santa pin and says he's so pretty he's almost perfect. At the top, from the ladder, she places the white Staingel, the most important of all the decorations, with her wavy white hair and flaring gold wings. All the nights till Christmas we throw on the icicles.

One night after we've all gone to bed, Clarke gets out of his crib, pushes a chair up to the tree and tries to reach for something, maybe the Staingel. He falls into the tree, causing everything to fall, breaking many of the balls. The crash wakes all of us. Daddy roars out of their bed like he's going to kill our baby brother.

But mostly this Christmas he's nicer to Clarke. His boy has almost died, as he almost died last year. His father is dying. His wife and second daughter have shadows on their lungs. He's spending all his extra time out in the garage making his gifts for us.

Christmas morning an awesome logging truck is under the tree for Clarke. Daddy carved it out of a solid block of wood, with movable wheels, movable steering wheel and axles, the cab detachable from the trailer. It's enamel-painted Clarke's favorite color, chartreuse green. He left the wheel spokes unpainted, just sanded, waxed and polished.

He made all three of us wooden toy boxes, a yellow one for me, a red one for Bridget, a green one for Clarke. At the end of that wonderful day we haul our toy boxes to the ends of our beds, then load them with our presents. Clarke's green one is placed at his crib as a step into it. He takes his truck to bed with him.

According to Grandma's January 24, 1948 entry, Grandpa *"was so troubled and sick four weeks ago tonight."* That would have been Christmas Eve.

I'm standing in the frame doorway to their bedroom, my nose and eyes at the leather strop hanging from the keyhole door knob. He's been asking for me. This may be the last time we'll see each other until we meet again in Heaven. He's propped up in the high bed under the quilts his mother and Grandma made. Above his bed hangs the Navajo Chief's red and white blanket. At the foot of the bed is the trunk from Tennessee. I can still see Daddy and Grandpa struggling to get it off the train. "Goldilocks come here," he gestures. "Goldilocks, come here." I'm afraid to enter the room, but I do. He talks to me but he is strange and far away. He holds my hand but still he calls "Goldilocks, come here, Goldilocks." He was a copper miner all his life. The Company says there's no such thing as copper silicosis but they don't have coverage anyway for any kind of silicosis. I smell copper in his breath. When he coughs copper fills the room, the TB germs floating around, copper colored.

Dec 27, 47- Sent Kermit a wire to come to arrange for Avon to go to sanitarium. Avon worried.
Dec 28, 47- Avon left at 2 P.M. for L. A. General Hospital. Goodbye Maude was hissed. Words. Kermit & Cecil took him. Audrey came. Boys got back at 5 P.M. Hot day.

I watch my father carry his father like a bride out the door, down the three wooden steps, and lay him delicately like a baby on the back seat.

"Goodbye, Maude," he whispers from the pillow.

§

Nine

Grandpa begged to come home, but Grandma was about to break down herself. She kept having little heart attacks. Uncle K.D. and Aunt Alice, Billie and Shirlie had to leave for his new station on the Great Lakes and that made her even sadder. Kermit David was her favorite child. Grandpa's hospital room was like ice.

Sunday, Jan 11, 48- Cecil, Audrey, the children and I went to L.A. Cecil & I went in to see Avon. Poor Avon is so thin & so homesick. How I wish I had him here.

We're pulled up to the back of LA General, to ugly lean-tos lining the back of the famous fancy landmark. Mama and Daddy and Grandma are visiting Grandpa. It's cold and windy. A trash bin is burning something that smells awful. I'm entertaining my brother and sister but I'm thinking they've put our grandfather back here with the trash.

I know now that this visit was my father's last to his father, though Grandpa wouldn't die for four and a half more months. And I know now, from my mother, that he, his father's favorite, suffered terrible guilt about this the rest of his life. Something happened inside that day. Something stopped Mama from going in his room, she doesn't see him again either. I remember her saying even the doctors are afraid to get near him.

In her diary Grandma seems cagey, noting suspiciously Cecil's withdrawal; he's lost his license, he's sick, they're having *"a time about car,"* but then she drops it. For the next four and a half months she struggles with getting to East LA to see Avon, usually by bus or by her church friends. Surely she was sympathetic with her son's health concerns and the very real danger of contagion, though that is not expressed.

It takes her six hours to travel roundtrip by bus the twelve or so miles the gulls fly to see him for one hour, and the ride hurts her spine. He cries and begs for her to bring him home. Then the doctor talks to him and he settles down. In his letters he begs for her to bring toilet paper *("they're out and I have got to have some you see")*, a plastic box (*"please please, Maude, the size of this tissue box for it is tearing up, one with some way of closing"*), and aspirin (*"it hurts so I have to take aspirins day and night to get some ease"*). He calls her darling, and says in every letter *"I sure do love you." "Only God and Jesus know how much I love you."*

Jan 29, 48- Marie came in to phone. So glad someone needed me. I tried hard to get away to go see poor dear Avon but failed. Cecil came. Wrote to Avon.

I don't remember Marie or know who she was except she's in the diary regularly from the move to Comolette, often visiting ailing Avon when Grandma's gone. She must have been a neighbor or a Gloria Gardens Mission Baptist Church member. By July 13 Marie is in an Arkansas hospital with tuberculosis.

On February 15, 1948, his seventieth birthday he fell out of bed, hurt his side, but no one would pick him up.

Monday, March 29, 1948- Audrey came by, from Huntington Park to report to me on her physical exam. So sad! O Father of Heaven, help.

The spot is on Mama's left lung. They can't find a single germ in her saliva but this spot is serious. The symptoms and signs of pulmonary tuberculosis do not usually become apparent until sometime after the actual appearance of lesions on the X-ray. Nights now and throughout the day the main sound in the house is my mother trying to clear her throat. Trying to bring up the germs, to spit them out, to flush them down the toilet.

"I always thought I'd die at twenty-eight. I'm not sure why twenty-eight. My mother was twenty-four when she died, my father thirty-nine. I don't know why twenty-eight."

One morning Daddy wakes spitting up blood. Hemoptysis is sometimes the first symptom.

The Sears truck arrives with twin beds. Their double one is carried out. Mama and I are standing at the screen door. "We're getting twin beds," she says in her wise tone, "because we love each other. We both have insomnia. I fall asleep early but wake early. Daddy can't get to sleep until late, then sleeps late. He keeps me awake in the evening tossing and turning and I wake him getting out of bed in the morning when he's finally fallen asleep. Neither of us can get any sleep. With twin beds we'll be right beside each other but this way we can let the other sleep."

I don't want to know what she doesn't want me to know.

"He was waking up with blood in his mouth," she explained when I finally asked in the nineties if the twin beds were because of his fear of getting TB from her. "It was just a cyst on his throat, but yes, he was afraid to sleep with me."

"Maybe it was like sympathy pains, Mama," I said.

"Oh, yes," she then said when I asked, "we had sex. We had sex even after his prostate was removed. Your father was the most sexual man I've ever known. We just didn't kiss."

Then she spoke of the fear of infecting us. "The doctor kept saying I was going to even though they could never get a germ on me. They even stuck a tube down my throat to my stomach trying to find something. All there was was a spot on my lungs they couldn't diagnose."

After her twenty-eighth birthday TB diagnosis, physical contact with our mother became an absolute taboo that lasted.

LA County passes the Leash Ordinance. Our parents say we have to get rid of Sambo. "No way can that dog stand being tied up. It'll break his spirit." On Sunday we drive south to Orange County where dogs still roam free, into a new housing tract. "Chicken coops!" they laugh, "this is how the houses of the second half of the twentieth century are going to look." We push Black Sambo out the back door of the car. "He'll find a good home," Mama assures us. Sambo chases us until we disappear. In the oval felt tan and black window we leave him in our dust.

"We went back and got him," she said on her seventy-fourth birthday in Newport, Oregon. "Remember?"

I hadn't.

"We couldn't do it. So then we stopped at a little store, asked if they knew someone who wanted a dog. He told us of a man. We knocked on his door. He said yeah! After that, on our Sunday rides, we'd get Sambo a frosty, take it to him, remember? He was always so happy to see us."

I think my mother told me this because she had sneaked and read an account I'd written of Sambo from the perspective of Clarke's heartbreak.

"Even Sambo had TB," she told me later than that, still, it seemed, trying to justify their getting rid of Sambo. "I know he did. He lay around for a year, sniffing those germs."

Israel! The headlines scream about the Holy Land. The United Nations approves cutting Palestine in two like the two harlots' baby to make room for the immigrating Jews. The Arabs say it's not right to be kicked out of our own homes, our ancient land. Mama says why don't they just give the Jews half of Germany, that seems right after what the Germans did to them, and besides, Germany's their homeland now. Grandma reads aloud David Ben-Gurion's speech saying it's straight from the Book of Joshua.

"The armies of Israel have struck the kings of Lod and Ramleh, the Kings of Beit Naballa and Deir Tarif, the kings of Kola and Migdel Zedik."

"Might doesn't make right," Mama says. "Nor does two wrongs. It's the same thing we did to the Indians. There'll never be peace in the Promised Land now."

And she tells again the story of Sarah and Hagar, a story of the everlasting terrible results of jealousy.

May 23, 48- Mr. Douglas drove Mrs. Baker and me to see Avon. Poor, dear Avon is very very sick and I want him home. O Father come near.

May 24, 48- Avon sent word he was feeling awful blue. This evening he said "I hope you come tomorrow." O how I hope I can.

May 25, 48- Mrs. Baker & I went to see poor dear Avon. He looked so sweet & innocent and pitiful. God bless him tonight, please, Lord.

May 26, 48- Saw dear Avon. Bro. Middleton went with me. Avon wanted to come home. He was waving to me as I walked down the corridor.

May 27, 48- A message said Avon slept away at 2:45 this morning. I never slept any. He lies in Memory Chapel. O how sad I am today! He needs me no more.

May 28, 48- Cecil & I selected a casket.... All the children have called but Ken and he sent telegram.

May 29, 48- I said goodbye to the dearest on earth. Avon looked so sweet lying there. Bro. Middleton talked of our risen Lord and of our hope. Cecil & Audrey & many friends were there. He sleeps in Downey Cem.

I remember my grandfather as a sweet, dignified, joyful, magical old man. He embodied the mystery of life and death and the Edens back to the Garden; certainly back to England, the Battle of Hastings and the Rights of Habeas Corpus in 1066. I knew he had a whole secret self as a man that couldn't come out now. I remember fear of him too. There's that insistent image of being in his dark blue electric car in the back of the Downey duplex and his dangling me over his erect penis, an image from such a young age I can't know if it actually happened. When my mother shocked me at the end of her life by telling that Avon Edens was known as the Devil of Ducktown, not *"the dearest on earth,"* that he could be heard screaming at Grandma, the Angel of Ducktown, and at his kids, all of them except Daddy, all over Ducktown, that he was hated in Ducktown, it was just that he was so unhappy, that image rose in me again. On a tape I made April 18, 1988, Aunt Elizabeth, Marion's wife, says she once heard him say of K.D. "I'll be glad when that boy's in his coffin and I can spit on him." "Imagine!" she gasps, "saying that about your own son." When Grandma and Grandpa arrived to rescue Mama and Daddy just married and destitute in Charlotte, Mama ran from the room. She'd read the letter marked "Private!" that Grandma had written to Daddy about the kind of girl she must be living alone in a strange city without family. Grandpa ran after her, and so kindly, without any condescension, pleaded with her to come live with them in their Ducktown home, to help poor Maude who was sick and needed help. "He made it seem like I was doing a favor for them," she always said. How lucky, she always said, we were to have him. She loved that man—that's how she always said it, "Oh, I just loved that man"—and took his side, I realize now, almost against my grandmother, though she was a faithful and dutiful daughter-in-law. "I always knew it was her fault." My mother found her place in a family psychically obsessed with placement by siding with its hated head.

Avon Edens planned to be a medical doctor and practice in the West. He was apprenticing to his oldest brother, the well-known physician of Franklin County, Dr. W. M. Edens, whose antebellum mansion was across the Elk River Road from the Chitwoods, when he met and became engaged to Lura Maude.

On the early evening of May 3, 1900, when he was twenty-two and Maude had turned twenty the week before, he was racing home with friends to Lynchburg from a party, maybe their engagement party, in Estill Springs. "Maybe they'd had a little too much to drink," Mama always said. He was riding the Arabian, Black Skin, and just at dark leaped a wire fence. The horse didn't clear it, he stumbled, and Avon's left leg was crushed beneath him. He was crippled for life. Black Skin, his father's most valuable horse, had to be put down. This hurt his father, the Confederate soldier and horsebreeder, Francis Marion Edens, so much that he disinherited his son. This is why my grandfather was unable to continue his medical studies. Now I think that probably he was disinherited because his fiancé was the granddaughter of the infamous John Chitwood who sided with the North. It's taken much to grasp the family my father was a product of—that the Chitwoods were educated, albeit religious, pro-Union liberals and the Edens were Confederate Primitive Baptists, the equivalent of present-day rightwing, fundamentalist Christians, and that their marriage was freighted from the beginning by not just poverty, but also by a deep conflict in values. When Avon got out of the hospital in Winchester he left for the West in hopes of finding a life for him and Maude there. But his leg didn't heal, there was always an open wound in his calf, and he spent a year in the hospital in Jerome. He was in Arizona altogether five years that first time. Even on Comolette his painful wound had to be cleaned and dressed every day.

And he was jealous of his twin sons' close relationship to their mother born just before he left for Arizona the second time. Mama always explained they were born after he left (and so didn't know them, that is, couldn't love them when he came back), but he's there at their birth in the diary, March 19, 1912, how surprised they all were at the arrival of the second boy, Kenneth. *"Avon ran out and got extra clothing,"* she notes, gratefully. There's a work letter of recommendation dated April 30, 1912 that he took with him to Arizona. He left when the twins were less than two months old; he left Lura Maude with four young children. When he finally came home more than three years later he found the twins sleeping in his bed. "He'd rant and rave and strike K.D. and Kenneth." When Daddy came home from the Army he found Clarke sleeping in his bed and reacted identically. Mama always said this is just the way men are; this is natural.

Avon was the youngest of seven children (as Daddy was the youngest of five), raised on Beech Hill outside Lynchburg, on the farm his father began building in 1867 after the War. When Avon was seventeen his mother Phoebe died and his father remarried a seventeen year old neighbor girl and began a new family. Maybe that's why he wanted his handsome son out of the house. (Avon, I realize, looked like the delicate beauty Phoebe, not like his father, the ruggedly handsome Frank.) Marion Francis Edens (Frank), named for the legendary "Francis Marion the Swampfox" of the Revolutionary War, great-great-grandson of John Matlow, a South Carolina hero of that war whose descendents founded the Jack Daniels Distillery, was a surviving member of Turney's first Tennessee Regiment. Of the twelve hundred men that left Franklin County for the first battle at Bull Run even before Tennessee seceded from the Union, less than a hundred returned at the end of the war. No doubt, this veteran, my great-grandfather, was psychically wounded.

Perhaps just as my father's hostility to my brother was a mirroring (a sort of justifying) of his father's at the twins, especially K.D., Avon was mirroring his father. When Avon was ten, his father's sister died in childbirth. Francis Marion went to Texas and brought home her twin boys to raise (bringing the total to nine children), a story Mama began telling only after the 1988 visit to the area. Maybe he hated one of them. "One became a sort of outlaw," Mama kept saying, "the other inherited everything." Maybe Grandpa's twins reminded him of all he'd lost. Maybe the family tradition of playing the siblings against each other goes all the way back to the original Edens who left England. (The English didn't do anything to the Indians and Africans they didn't do to their own children, many have pointed out.) Of course it goes back to the Garden of Eden, to Cain and Abel, and that cruelest of all Patriarchs who played husband and wife, brother and brother against each other for his favor. Sometimes I look at the photo of Phoebe Stovell Overby and Francis Marion Edens, my great-grandparents and the thought just washes through me: he murdered her.

In her diary my grandmother never utters a word against her husband, but there are entries that are difficult not to ponder. One in particular, from the early twenties, is addressed to her dead father and begins, *"Dear Daddy, things are not right tonight!"* She describes her father, George Washington Chitwood, as a gentle, adoring and wise father. During her childraising years she wrote only sporadically, poems, prayers, dreams and nostalgic memories of her childhood. That this is not a case of lost diaries is supported by the fact that her original ledger, given to her at the age of nine by a neighbor boy, covers dates from 1889 into the twenties. She takes up daily writing again on the evening when Kermit (K.D.) leaves home in 1927. She watches him as she writes, fifteen, headed down the hill to hitchhike to Chicago, her heart clearly devastated, but steadfastly maintaining her duty as the Angel wife, as the Lord demands. There's a post card from K.D. in a Chicago YMCA to his father contritely announcing that he's joined the Navy. "I'm sorry Pa, I really tried to find a job, I surely did."

Mama always told how K.D. took leave and spent thirty days at his father's bedside in his first hospitalization and so came finally to understand why his father was so mean. The most shocking story, as my uncle told me, was that he learned that his father had worked as a hangman in Arizona. He qualified for this job because of his medical training. He was desperate for work, hard to come by with his bad leg, homesick, maybe heartsick for his lost parents and Lura Maude, desperate to prove himself a man. He kept sending her the money to join him. (This would be the first Arizona sojourn when they were engaged.) She would pack, her parents would take her down to the train station, then she wouldn't get on.

In the spring of 1904 her younger sister Ida died very suddenly, of probably either typhoid or cholera, and that fall her older brother Will was killed in the collapse of a bridge across the Arkansas River. Lura Maude, though she tried, couldn't leave her mother—that's the way my mother put it, derogatively—who never fully recovered from the loss of these two children. Maude, a graduate of Winchester Normal College, formerly Mary Sharp College, taught those years at the Bethel District School, a "one room" schoolhouse, kindergarten through high school.

In defeat, both times, Avon returned to Tennessee. *"Marion Avon Edens of Poland, Arizona and Lura Maud Chitwood of Estill Springs, Tennessee were united in Matrimony at Winchester Tennessee, on the third day of July in the year of our Lord, 1906, by Reverend Moffett of Baptist Church."* He worked for a while at the mill in Estill Springs and then they moved to Ducktown just before the birth of their first child, Lucile, on August 14, 1907. Their second child, Marion Chitwood Edens, was born July15, 1909.

He worked in the mines until May 1912 when, the twins being two months, he left for Arizona again, returning in May, 1915. He kicked the twin boys out of his bed and my father was conceived. His daughter Lucile was three months short of turning eight. He returned to the mines.

Mysteriously, Avon wasn't jealous of my father. Daddy was his pet, the spoiled, beloved baby. In the Old Testament the youngest son is often the favored son, i.e., Abel, Jacob, Joseph. *"In the summer of 1915, with the Mine City Baptist Church of Ducktown Tennessee,"* his Obituary says, *"he surrendered his life to Christ and was eternally saved from his sins."* Daddy was conceived in that moment of grace and return. "He would strike the twins but never your father," Mama explained.

Marion Avon Edens spent thirty years in the dark drifts of the Ducktown copper mine. Raised a Southern gentleman, to be a medical doctor, a direct descendent of the Edens on the ship after the Mayflower, he travailed his days on this earth as a hardrock miner—copper, lead, zinc—a foreman who ran the jack hammers. For years he never saw the sun. "He went down before the sun came up, came up after the sun had gone down." His last job was in the Changing House, where the miners changed their clothes before going down in the shafts. His leg was so bad by then he couldn't do anything else. He had only six months to go to retirement but there was no question about it. When the miners went out on strike, he went out and he would never regret that, no matter if he and Maude starved to death, no matter what his sons thought.

All my life I have tried, as my mother instructed, to know my grandfather's eight years in the Wild West, in Arizona "before it became a state." I imagine what were not her instructions—hung men, prostitutes, saloons, whiskey—Lynchburg's Jack Daniels, of course—and his relationship with his older brother there, Dr. James E. Edens, the long hospital stay, the vast Arizona deserts, the awesome sunsets, the two mile tunnel under Poland. One morning he woke to an Indian brave passed out on his horse outside his cabin. He took him in and nursed him back to life. Another morning the sun came up on a large gathering of Indians circling the cabin on their horses. The young man he had saved was the son of a Navajo chief. They gave him the Navajo blanket. I learned of his being the hangman of Globe, Arizona from Uncle K.D. in February 1976, when I was starting *Hard Country*. (And learned, with the publication that my mother knew of Avon's being a hangman but that my father only learned in reading it.)

My father was the son of a hangman! Who in turn was the son of a surviving Confederate Veteran (of Bull Run! Of Turney's Men! Of Chickamauga!), who in turn was the grandson of a veteran of the Battle of New Orleans in 1812, who in turn was the grandson of a Revolutionary War soldier. My father was the pampered, beloved, protected, special baby of this family, who witnessed all his childhood the brutality of his father to his older brothers (and probably the sexuality of all of them to his sister), his Christian mother dutifully standing by. Is it any wonder he had a sense of divine right? Is it any wonder he was depressed, gloomy, cruel, confused, a sadist, an incester, a rapist? Yes, Mama, you are right, it is understandable. It's a wonder humanity has survived at all.

For some reason Lucile was bitter and unforgiving of her father, earning her mother's disapproval. *Aug 29, 41- Received a letter and pictures from Lucile. She sent me a dollar and asked me --- "me"* in a rare cross-out is exchanged for *"for Dad"* along with there being equally rare missing words (to forgive her) *"for being crossed and peevish while here last. It is noble to humble yourself. I hope she asks the all powerful father to forgive her and lead her."* Lucile's failure with her father is alluded to several times in the diary.

I find in the trunk a rather astounding photograph of my grandfather, the foreman, with about thirty other miners—astounding because some of the men (some are filthy, exhausted-looking boys) are horsing around in obscenely intimate poses. And the photo has been doctored suggesting there may have been more. It is astounding that neither my grandmother nor my mother destroyed it. I am grateful for this image that's survived from his mining existence.

I was the lead in the school play that spring. I played Granny, an old woman. All April, May and into June we practiced. My hair was brushed with corn starch, which turned it silver, and pulled back into a bun. I wore one of Grandma's dresses. As with the Staingel I was onstage the entire production, mainly knitting in my rocking chair and cackling and commenting on the stupidity of the young people. Grandma showed me how to be really knitting, purl one, knit two. I loved the dazzling task of memorizing my many lines. Practice started before my grandfather died and the production was after his death. Purl one, drop two. I was only seven but I was also as old as my grandma and grandpa. Playing Granny was being in their bodies and minds. I loved the audience seeing me as an old woman. I loved rocking and knitting onto death.

It's been two weeks since Grandpa died, it's the next to the last day of first grade. Mrs. Hunt announces that she has been observing each of us from the first day of school with the intention of rewarding the best behaved boy and the best behaved girl at the end of the year. She has watched us carefully and now will announce the winners of this secret contest.

To think that for the whole of first grade we were being judged in a contest none of us knew we were in! It takes my breath away; it seems almost unfair, like a trick.

"And the winners are: Sharon Lura Edens and Raymond Price!"

Then I'm standing in front of our thirty-eight classmates. All year I've felt invisible to them. But now I'm standing in front of them, receiving paper dolls, all their eyes on me. The best-behaved boy, Raymond Price, standing here beside me receiving a model airplane, has been my secret boyfriend the entire year. He's been as silent as me and has no idea. This is all astounding.

The next day, the last day of first grade, I start talking to my nearest neighbor, Sharon Beck. My seat at the outer corner of the square of tables has made me very aware of everyone all year but it has not occurred to me before that I could actually talk to them.

I keep talking. I talk to anyone who is listening to me. They all seemed to be listening to me. After all I won the contest. I have lots of things to say to each and every one of them because I've been watching them for so long and lots of things have happened to us, my grandfather has died, and now it's the last day of school, my last chance. Out of my mouth a river of words is rushing, coming from my body which keeps rising from the seat and leaning over the table to touch the person I'm talking to. Connie Wollum, Patricia Moore, Billy, and Robert Kent and Sharon May. Mrs. Hunt is frowning at me, but I can't stop the words even for her. I've never felt such happiness. I'm ecstatic. I can see that my listeners are startled, are backing away, but I can't stop for such a mundane observation. I can't stop even though the teacher is calling across the room in a voice only my parents have used to address me. "SHA-RON!" (shock!) "SHARON EDENS!" (for shame....) "SHARON LURA EDENS SHUT-UP!" (screaming!!)

I see how it looks. I understand, but the words, the urgency of the words coming out of me dwarf all such consideration. All my life they've complained I don't talk.

I talked all through lunch, giving my sandwich to Robert Kent, unable to stop talking to eat. Mrs. Hunt called my mother and told her what a bad girl I turned out to really be. Then before the whole class she demanded my prize back, my paper dolls. Suddenly, another first happened to me. A door slammed shut inside. I earned those paper dolls. I *was* the best behaved girl in the class. You can't change the past. I lost respect for her. I refused, even under threat of failing first grade, to give her back my prize.

To this day I can only speak when acknowledged. When listened to. When there's an opening, a welcome. When my words are wanted. When a response from me is desired. Words are holy, like the Bible says, like my grandma knew. She wrote *"Avon's Last Words To Me"* and sewed them into the lining of her Sunday School black beaded purse.

§

Ten

One Sunday we drive up to Mulholland Drive, head west into the setting sun. It's really hot. After awhile on the windy dusty dirt road Daddy says "This is it, Lovers Lane where Caryl Chessman prowled on the couples up here necking. He had a red police light so they thought he was a cop."

We're above the clouds. The San Gabriels, the Basin, and the Pacific Ocean spread below us. Caryl Chessman's in the news day and night, and the debate about capital punishment. Must we kill him?

"No wonder lovers come up here," Mama sighs.

The Red Light Bandit didn't kill anyone but he did some really weird things that Daddy and the newspapers won't repeat.

Thou shalt not kill. It's the Sixth Commandment. Moses brought it down from the mountain after seeing God. So what's the debate?

"What's necking?" is the question that comes out of my mouth. I see two swans, their long necks wringing around each other. "What's sodomy?"

"Did you feel that earthquake?" is the answer.

My grandmother is a very old woman now, so sad she can hardly bear it. She teaches me how to study the Bible so I can bear it when the iniquities happen to me. So I can survive the grave. She calls out chapter and verse, like "First Corinthians 1: 13!" and we see how fast I can locate it. Then I try to say it by heart. *"Faith, hope, charity, these three; but the greatest of these is charity."* She was a school teacher before she married Grandpa, and she taught Sunday School all her life. She teaches me how to study, how to find what I seek or need, about references and cross references, that the Bible is One Book, that it's holy, that it's about the world, about man's history, philosophy, and wisdom, about God the Father, how he gave his only begotten Son, about Heaven and Hell and how to save my Soul.

I set myself the task of memorizing all the names of the books. *Genesis, Exodus, Leviticus, Numbers, Deuteronomy.* I win the Bible drill at Trinity Vacation Bible School and am presented with a thick, cut slab of a Sierra cedar tree, about fifteen inches across. The dark bark is still around it with drops of sap like tears held by the varnish. On the surface over the sanded grains of golden wood is a painting of Jesus knocking on the door. Daddy nails my prize up over my bed.

July 2, 48- Cecil came a few minutes. Got his driver's license back. O how lonely it is.

August 8, 48- Mrs. Baker spent the night with me. We went to Church. Cecil was there. He took me to see dear Avon's gravemarker. It is pretty.

Imagine my father who hated church, being there, evidently alone.

Aug 12, 1948- Audrey's children were here awhile. Bridget & Clarke had a fight. How do I love them. So sorry I punished them.

Aug 16, 48- I had a heart attack and went to L. Beach Com. Hospital.

She's in the hospital until September 14. I don't remember this.

In September Bridget finally starts kindergarten. She's the oldest, the biggest, the smartest kid in her class. I start second grade, so proud of my little sister. All year we wear identical dresses that Mama made.

It's election year and everyone says how fortunate we are to be able to vote and who are you going to vote for for President of the United States? My class has its own elections. I am the only Democrat, the only person who votes for Harry Truman. Both my parents laugh and laugh. They lecture me again about being an Edens, about standing by what I believe, even when I'm the only one. They're so proud of me.

Daddy comes home from Douglas Aircraft so angry and tired I know the worst fate in the world is to be stuck in a job you hate. The only hope is Harry Truman. The world is so bad, so corrupt, what's a working man to do? He rants about the congressional hearings, the House UnAmerican Activities Committee, about the Fifth Amendment, about Alger Hiss, but most of all about how he hates that Richard Nixon from Whittier. Dick Nixon is the worst kind of liar, the kind of man who slanders innocent people to win the vote.

He'd kill me if he knew but I think my father looks a little like Richard Nixon.

On the Tuesday after Halloween we have the presidential elections. Everyone knows Harry Truman doesn't have a chance.

Wednesday morning I come into the kitchen. The newspapers are spread across the table and counter tops. **TRUMAN WINS!** Daddy is roaring "Lookie here, kids, that Chicago Daily Tribune was so sure of itself it printed it's paper last night, **DEWEY BEATS TRUMAN!** Wouldcha jes look at that!"

At school I feel sorry for Dewey and my unhappy classmates almost to paralysis. I'm awash in the perplexity. What makes them think they are so right when we know we are right? To have voted for Dewey is inconceivable, but when I look into the eyes of my second grade classmates whom I adore, I understand, that for now, I'm seeing through a glass darkly. I see only in part.

Nov 3, 48- ...I suppose Mr. Truman is elected President.

All summer and now fall, ever since I played Granny, there are letters and phone calls from movie scouts who saw me or heard about it, wanting to sign me as a child star. Mama keeps up her lectures about Shirley Temple not having a normal childhood, the danger of selling your soul to Hollywood.

One day a letter from the President of the Screen Actors Guild, Ronald Reagan, comes. Mama is impressed. Grandma says you're a Reagan too, my mother's name was Nancy Reagan. Mama says most mothers would give their eye tooth for this and starts talking about Shirley Temple again, how her mother ought to be ashamed of herself, any mother who would sell her own child. Hollywood Mothers are seeking to fulfill their own unfulfilled longings through their daughters and this is wrong. But it's a good sign that I was discovered playing an old woman. Maybe you are a true actress Sharon. Even so, she's afraid.

For all Mama's fear and disgust the next week they take me to an office on Sunset Boulevard, to a Hollywood movie agent. It's over a hundred degrees as we drive north. His best scout saw me in the two school plays, as the Staingel guarding baby Jesus and as Granny, the cackling old woman. My hair turned into a halo, hark! my hair turned into a silver bun. I rocked and chewed and made witty remarks and puns to all the young ones.

For all his persistence the movie agent doesn't seem happy to see us. He acts like we wanted to see him, like we've finally fallen into his clutches. His dark face pours forth sweat, his fat mouth rolls a cigar around in his teeth and he keeps sneering at Daddy. He leans way back in his navy blue suit in his swivel chair, puts his feet up on the desk.

"Alright, Goldilocks. Let's see how cute you can be."

Daddy and Mama are seated on the side wall, Mama with her claustro-phobia closest to the door. I'm in the chair in front of his big desk. Daddy is staring at me. I can see and hear the traffic down below on boiling Sunset.

"Recite nursery rhymes," the movie agent instructs.

I don't know any. Jack and Jill went up the hill. They're so boring. Mary had a little lamb, its fleece.... I'm standing here and all the world is turning white as snow, even me. My eyes see something deep in the linoleum, my head is bending towards it.

"Come on, girl. Your parents are counting on you. You have to be able to take direction."

The room is filling up with white cigar smoke. I can't move. No words will come out. It's awful to disappoint him. My parents know I'm not cute. Bridget has the personality. Pretty is as pretty does. To act like he wants me to act would not be pretty, would be embarrassing for all of us. To act like he wants me to act would be to forget who I am.

On the ride home, Daddy smoking faster than ever at the wheel, me in the back seat still completely mute, Mama says this is a blessing in disguise. Sharon is not the movie star type.

Putting it together now I see my mother's desperation. She was afraid she was dying, that we were becoming orphans. She was trying to open to the career opportunity, a way for me to support myself, the whole family, Daddy too. She was meeting her duty to Daddy who was demanding this.

Until we left Hollydale five and a half years later letters and phone calls came regularly from scouts and agents, especially whenever I appeared in a stage or other public event, even a church one. Several times a scout or agent came to the house. She would not let them talk with me. I am not the movie star type. It felt like being stalked. Now I wonder who they were, and how many, or if it could have been just one man. What were they doing in the Roosevelt Elementary School audience? and later at the modeling shows of Mama's tailoring class? Maybe the scout was Mrs. Hunt's husband, my first grade teacher, the aspiring actress. Maybe they were Daddy's drinking buddies in Johnny's. Maybe those times I was brought into the bar I was being viewed. As soon as I think that I feel it was true. To imagine my father doing that makes me nauseous even now. But of course parents show off their children. Most would consider a chance at Hollywood a good thing.

There are many blanks through the rest of the year. The entries are even more sparse than usual.

Nov 25, 48- We ate ThanksGiving dinner with Cecil & A. Then drove around....???

Dec 6, 1948- Audrey must go to the hospital. Breaks our heart.

Breaks our heart—but we kids do not know this yet. We are going to have a happy Christmas no matter what, visited by the most perfect, most beautiful Santa Claus and Christmas Spirit that ever was.

Dec 7, 48- We went to look at a boarding home.
Dec 14, 48- I notified State Pension Board I was moving to Compton.
Dec 16, 48- I have been terribly upset today. Fixing to break up. Raining tonight.
Dec 19, 48- My last Sunday in "Home Sweet Home."
Dec 20, 48- Came to 5536 Rayborn Compton today to board at Rose Lodge. Raining, raining.
Dec 21, 48- Raining, raining. Fred's terrible automobile accident and death. O Father be near.

That fall my grandmother's youngest sibling, Fred Chitwood, her only surviving brother, for whom my father was named, began calling her from Florida. "If I show up dead, Maude, know I was murdered." His girlfriend's son had institutionalized her in a mental hospital and now he was out to get Fred's home in Memphis. He'd been forced at gunpoint to sign a will giving the son everything.

In the early hours of December 21, 1948, on Highway 29 out of Pensacola Florida, Fred Chitwood died in a car accident. The report said he was drunk, going 90 mph when he crashed head on into an oncoming vehicle, killing that driver also.

The next evening,

Wednesday, Dec 22- Cecil came to tell me of the message that Fred had met death in an auto accident. It was raining. O how dreadful it was! We drove out apiece. Jesus stood by me.

She called Marion. The day after Christmas Uncle Marion left Greenville, Tennessee for Pensacola with his twelve year old son Alex to investigate what his mother had told him. Fred's body was identified by someone no one knew and shipped to Memphis the morning after the accident and his home was sold that same day by the son. All the Chitwood family heirlooms disappeared immediately. Still, Marion found everything to be as the police and mortuary reported. "*Unfortunately, Mother,*" he wrote, "*as hard as it is to accept, Uncle Fred was a drinker and though his friends all describe him as a wonderful, hardworking man, the fact is he killed another man too.*"

My grandmother was destitute and gravely ill, but she persisted. An old Tennessee lawyer friend of the family took on the case, demanding the body be reinterred and an autopsy performed.

A bullet was found in Fred Chitwood's head, though charges were never made against the son. Or anyone.

This was the Christmas they introduced the shocking idea of opening presents on Christmas Eve as well as the next morning. Christmas Eve will be in honor of just our family; we will open the presents we are giving each other. Tomorrow will be about Santa Claus, what he brought during the night.

Mama made her. Mary Jane was almost as big as me, with the same blond pigtails and bangs. She wore the white dress with red hearts that I learned to dress myself with the day Bridget was born, and white cotton panties with eyelet lace around the leg holes.

She made Snookums for Bridget out of one of Daddy's old socks. Snookums is Daisy Mae and L'il Abner's baby. A real sock doll.

She made us red and brown plaid cotton circular dresses with intricate gathered circle pockets in the skirts. She made Clarke a beige wool coat. She made all three of us matching pajamas. Of the softest pale blue cotton, with big pearl colored buttons.

All three of us got seven pairs of underwear, a pair for each day. Bridget's and mine had the days of the week embroidered on them. Clarke got boxers like Daddy's. Remember, never wear panties to bed, it's not healthy.

In the morning there were more dolls—Patsy!—doll strollers, a trike for Clarke, western leather holster gun sets for all three of us, and cowboy hats. Roller skates! Santa brought me a Mickey Mouse watch and a gold Mickey Mouse pin. Of course I was wearing my Santa Claus pin from last year. Mama said again how they were lucky at the School to get an orange for Christmas. She told her story of the twig dolls they made, with twig houses and twig furniture.

Christmas was on Saturday. The next day on our Sunday ride they casually inform us that Mama is going into the sanitarium. A woman with a baby boy is moving in to the end apartment to help us. She's going to get free rent for this. We must be very grown up now, and help poor Daddy with everything. Out of every bad comes some good. Mama's so tired she's been saying all our lives all she wants to do is to escape to a hotel room, just read a book for an hour. Now she'll get that much needed rest. We must think positively. The spot on her lungs will go away.

"Do we call the woman who's going to help us Mama?" I ask from my seat behind Daddy. The rain is coming down in sheets, the streets are all flowing rivers, the windshield wipers are slapping like crazy. All the world is rain.

It seemed the most reasonable and accepting response. I was trying to assure our mother we will be okay.

"No!" she gasps. And now, oh, once again I have to see what she was seeing about me.

I see how young I was. Passivity filling up the body like water in the wide, dry bed. As the river rises, you shift, you adjust.

Mama just wanted to lie down and die. And find her Daddy again.

Tuesday, Jan 4, 1949- Cecil and Audrey came by as he took her to the hospital. Coldest day since 1878, dear Avon's birth year.

I remember waking the next morning to Daddy's voice, "Kids, wake up! It snowed!" There was snow on our grass, snow layered on the roofs and backs of all the cars and houses, snow on the coal piles, up on the tracks. No one could believe it. We'd still never seen snow coming down, but that it snowed in the night while we slept, that it snowed in Southern California, was a miracle.

I remember running into their bedroom and Mama was there in her bed, so excited too. But she wasn't. It was the first morning our mother was gone. Daddy helped us make a snowman in the front yard. He took a picture of it.

Mama woke on Signal Hill and looked out the window and saw the hills covered in snow and kids sledding down them. She told this all her life, her first morning away from her new family, finding herself back in her old family's home, the TB sanitarium.

Wed. January 5: Cecil and children came by after going to the dentist. They looked sad. Bridget seemed more like herself than the others.

This is the oldest writing of mine that I have:

Dear MaMa, this is Sharon. How are you feeling? This paper that I have sent you it is a prayer. Are room is looking [pretty] and wet. I love you MaMa. Love Sharon.

Daddy painted our bedroom.

I still can't remember the woman who lived in the end apartment in exchange for rent to take care of us. Neither can my sister or brother. "The woman the neighbors ran off," Mama said, the few times I dared to ask. "They said you guys were dirty."

I took over the cooking after she was run off. This was an extraordinary, exhilarating feat. I can still recite my elaborate menus for each of the seven days of the week. Daddy must have washed our clothes because I only ironed them. He must have done this on Monday because on Tuesday after school I started ironing. I ironed all week. I understood what she meant about a woman's work never being finished. The hardest thing was Daddy's huge heavy khaki pants. Getting the creases straight, getting the wrinkles out of the fly area.

On Friday nights we went to the Pike, just like always, but now sometimes we walked down the central mall to see the sights, the dancing chickens, the tattoo parlors, the sailors watching naked girl movies behind red velvet curtains, the fat ladies without teeth calling to Daddy to play the games. "Hey, babe!" they cackle and he cackles back. We buy our bags of shrimp, then take some to Mama. There's no road, Daddy just drives right across the dark, dead lawn, beneath the starry night, between the groaning oil wells on Signal Hill that seem like black long-nosed monsters, to her window in the sanitarium. How I love my Daddy for not letting the lack of a road stop him. No one is allowed inside the contagion ward, but we can see and talk to her in the window. Her bed is right there. We can see rows and rows of other beds behind her with sick people coughing in them. I love my mother so much, dear Jesus, this is a prayer, help her to get well. Afterwards we go to the drive-in. I sit in her place on a pillow in the passenger side. Tonight we see *Pinocchio* and *Samson and Delilah.*

"It will take a miracle to get us out of here," Jiminy Cricket says to Pinocchio. Then the Blue Fairy is there. "Your father is alive, swallowed by a whale at the bottom of the sea."

"A lie keeps growing until it's plain as the nose on your face."

She gives him another chance. "Prove yourself brave, truthful and unselfish. And someday you'll be a true boy."

"The Blue Fairy came. I have a conscience," Jiminy Cricket says.

But Delilah doesn't. How sick I feel when she tricks Samson, is cutting his hair.

January 28, 1949 Dear MaMa This is Sharon. How are you feeling? Just first grade and sixth grades gets to go to school all day February the first. All have to walk with Nodgi. I wrote this letter to you January 28, 1949 I love you Sharon

Saturday, Feb 5, 49- Rained all night. I was sick. I talked with Cecil by phone…

Sunday, Feb 6, 49- Cecil took me to a drug store. So lonely and sick the rest of the day.

Monday, Feb 7, 49- Went home with Cecil.
Friday, Feb 11, 49- Back at the Home.
Monday, Feb 14, 49- Cecil's 33rd birthday and Audrey in San. at Long Beach. I had a weak spell.

§

Book II

Gae

Love keeps no score of wrong. 1 Corinthians 13

Whosoever committeth sin is the servant of sin. John 8: 34

Hate the sin, love the sinner. Mahatma Gandhi

A disease of the lungs is, metaphorically, a disease of the soul. Susan
Sontag

*Incest is the worst experience of grief. At the moment when the incest
occurs, the child's entire family dies.* Elizabeth Kubler-Ross

Eleven

A new house is being built across the street. All fall and winter we've stood on our side speculating on who our new neighbors will be. We can hardly believe it when Marie Henka says the hole in the living room wall, which we can see through the enormous one for the bay window, is for a built-in TV set.

I'm washing dishes. Grandma rag-curled my natural curls backwards in old sheet rags, so when I take them out they're going to stick straight out. But that's okay, it makes Grandma happy. I try not to think about how I look anyway. Pretty is as pretty does. It's foggy and damp outside. I love the fog, the edges not so sharp, being unseen, unknown, where you end, where the others begin.

"Sharon, Sharon!" Bridget comes running into the kitchen. "The new people have moved in!"

Running behind her back through the house, through the screen door, flying off the porch into the fog. Down the lawn, up the sidewalk, across the street to the new house.

Our houses, the five different models in different colors, different plants and trees, look a hundred years old now with this new house here. It's ultra modern: peachy pink with sparkles and white rocks on its white flat roof. The driveway is polished white cement, not the rough pitch of ours on which we are always bloodying our knees. For months, after the workers have gone, I've stood in the twilight before it trying to know how you build a house. Jesus was a carpenter and so is my father. Sometimes I'd get up the nerve to wander through it. The echoes and smells of cement and stucco, the sappy two-by-fours conjured up future ghosts who would live here. Then huge walls of glass were put in, windows without blinding squares and crosses, and a sliding glass door. Then a television set really was installed right into the wall. Such a spectacular house meant spectacular people would live in it. And new people on the block would change everything.

One evening just before Mama left for the TB sanitarium, she cut a photo and article from the Huntington Park paper. The next day I stood in front of my second grade class for Sharing, holding up the news photo and article, **South Gate Hero!**, of a blond policeman holding a man down with his foot, a gun to his head. *"'Mr. Merrill Wayne Walker, almost killed in the shootout, was awarded for bravery and action beyond the call of duty.'* He's the father of the new family," I told my class, "that's moving in across the street from us on Roosevelt Avenue."

She appears in the fog across the new plugs of dichondra. We stare at each other, the silver glass wall shimmering behind her, the rim of the white roof sparkling in the fog above her. Fog in her beige hair. Fog coming from beneath her eyes. I'll always see this, the fog there, steam in the grooves of her eyes. Bridget and the little girl start chasing each other, giggling. But the big girl and I just stare across the foggy yard into each other like we're hypnotized.

She'll always say she thought I was an Okie with my rag-curls like a pickaninnie, a little negro girl. I feel the stupid rags of old bed sheets around my head, I feel the boxy Buster Browns encasing my big feet, I feel the weight of everything, the fog stooping my shoulders to hide my breasts—what kind of freak am I that I have breasts at seven?—but I'm looking at beauty, perfection and mystery, her face with fog across it, her face so taut, drawn and sad, yet like a river, a churning flow the color of milky fog. I can't talk. She will say I talked like a hillbilly. I will love her for being bold and honest. Across the lawn through the watery air, the strangeness of her eyes connects with something deep inside me, a strangeness I will never let go of, a spell I am still under. My heart breaks for love of this first sight of her, for gratitude that she exists. There's a river across her face, a river between us, a river to cross. I will be crossing the river forever. I love her.

Two black and brown, big skinny dogs are barking their heads off from the back corners of the house. "They're Doberman Pinschers," she says. "Police dogs. They are not pets, they're trained to kill."

Her name is Gae Elaine Walker. I manage to say Sharon Lura Edens. February Seven rivets through me like a lightning bolt. Her seventh birthday was last week, seven days exactly before Valentine's Day, our father's birthday. I've been seven for nine months. This girl and I are staring at each other like two big dolls, like me and Mary Jane. Even in the photos from then, you can see the iodiney steam rising from her face. I am like God without a face; I'm the fog.

Tomorrow her parents will enroll her in the second grade. Dear Jesus, please please please let this girl be in my class. Her little sister is Dottie, she doesn't go to school yet, she's only three, so chubby and cute.

Then someone is calling us home. The moon is coming up full behind us as we run back down the street, a vibrating glow like Daddy's fog light on the car. We have to cut out and address valentines for our classmates tomorrow. Valentine's Day is my second favorite holiday, after

Halloween. It's Daddy's birthday; it's about Love. I address the biggest heart for him, but the next-to-biggest one, the lacy one in the back of the cut-out book is for Gae Elaine Walker. Will you be my Valentine?

But in class Monday she's not there.

In claymaking I made an elephant for Daddy's birthday. I formed him in my hands from a photo of a circus elephant in *LIFE* Magazine. I love the Elephant Boy, Sabu, in the movies. I made his trunk perfect, a fifth leg to balance on. I painted an orange and green Indian blanket with gold tassels on his broad back and another of blue and green with tassels on his head. When he was fired in the oven the colors ran together making the design abstract and mysterious. Deep under his trunk I painted a big pink smile and on his tummy I carved my initials: SE. The teacher, all the kids, everyone praised me for the success of my elephant. "You're a real artist Sharon Lura." I couldn't wait to give him to Daddy. My elephant made for my father born on the Day of Love.

When I get home from school I make his birthday cake from scratch just like Mama would. "Just follow the directions exactly," she said, "it will work." I follow the chocolate cake recipe, measuring the flour after sifting twice just as she always instructed and as it is written on the three-by-five index card in her beautiful handwriting, my eyes down level with the glass measuring lines. I pour the batter into the greased nine-inch heart-shaped pans used only on this day, once a year, and while it bakes at three-fifty in the oven I was careful to preheat, I make the filling and the icing. I separate the eggs, the most precarious task. If the teeniest drop of yolk gets in the white it won't beat up. It's hard keeping the top layer from sliding off the filling, but the icing helps, like glue. I line the heart with red hot candy hearts. Bridget and Clarke lick the bowls and we spend a lot of messy time putting the thirty-three red candles on it. I bought the candles and candy hearts from the little store, they took all of my February allowance. "Just imagine," I keep saying to them, "thirty-three, the same age as Jesus." For dinner I make the usual Monday night spaghetti and coleslaw.

After we sing to him and he makes his secret wish and blows out the candles Bridget and Clarke fight for first place to spank him thirty-three times. Bridget wins of course. Clarke gets the last three. I give him the one to grow on. Then we give him our presents. I am so proud of my elephant I feel like I'm going to burst. He holds it in his hands, then in his khaki lap between his legs. "It's really good Sharon," he says. Last week he lost his job again. He seems so sad and far away.

Tomorrow will be Grandpa's seventy-first birthday, his first birthday that he's dead. He's somewhere in Heaven looking down on us, especially on Mama in the TB sanitarium and Grandma in the rest home, and helping Uncle Fred up from the highway where he was murdered last Christmas in Florida. Daddy is Grandpa's baby boy born the day before his thirty-eighth birthday, his Valentine for almost a Valentine. He needs our love and attention especially this night. Jesus, a son too, the Son of God, Grandma and Mama both keep reminding us, was thirty-three when he was crucified.

On the wall above my bed is the varnished slab of cedar with the painting of Jesus knocking on the door. *Seek and Ye shall find. Knock and it shall be opened unto you.* I love this Jesus, he looks like Daddy, especially in the moonlight coming through the window over my bed. The pale elevated forehead with receding hairline, the waves of reddish-brown hair if Daddy's hair grew to his shoulders, the same thin straight nose, the sad delicate two-pointed lips, the heavy-lidded eyes. Jesus over my bed.

Waking to him, the covers ripped back. Waking in the dark to the pillow slammed down on my face. Waking to Mary Jane he's slammed down on my face so I can't breathe. Waking, arms in his arms, tangle of arms Daddy no Daddy no. Being lifted to between his legs as to a butcher knife to be severed in two. Struggling to breathe. Suffocating within the giant enclosure, the suffocating black the same rhythm as the train. The train coming through, the train on top of me, the train cutting me in two, chug-a-chug-a-chug, faster and faster slicing all the way up through the heart to the top of my head. My heart stopping completely.

Then the whistle blowing. My heart starting again. Then he's fleeing naked back down the dark hallway to the room where our mother is gone, screaming *oh no! Oh no oh no oh no!* Searing, burning, blackening pain. Sickening smell, poop and blood all over the sheet. Bridget sleeping deeper than ever, a smile on her face. Clarke not crying for our mother as usual, just whimpering, just sobbing. I couldn't help it. I tried to keep the poop in but it was forced out.

I can't breathe. I keep going into the fog of God, into death on the cross, into knocking on the door. Getting caught on the tracks, the train slicing through. I'm in a tunnel and can't breathe, the fear is like sirens echoing in a tunnel zillions of miles long through my chest.

It takes a long time to find my pajama bottoms, to get them back on. But the elastic band is broken and the button is missing and the button hole is ripped and it hurts so bad to put my legs into them and there's poop and blood everywhere and they're sopping wet. Connie Wollum said the man pees inside you. Then I struggle to get them off and hidden under the covers at the foot of my bed. Two buttons on the top are missing too and the button holes are ripped.

The rooster in the hen coop is crowing. That means it's four-thirty, that means it's Grandpa's birthday now. The sun comes up. My dolls sitting on top of the chest of drawers, between me and Bridget, look down on me. They are sorry. Sorry. So sorry.

Daddy comes in.

"You have to take a bath."

I don't let go of Mary Jane as he lifts me from the bed, carries me in the hairy arms I wrestled with, that smell, that smell, down the hall to the bathroom. Tears are streaming down his big white face, "I'm sorry Lu, I'm sorry, Baby." I smell the poop, I haven't done that since I was a baby. He checks my hernia, there's blood everywhere. Mary Jane drops to the floor as he drops me into the drawn water, her limbs splayed so uncomfortable on the floor under the towel rack. Ribbons of blood are streaking the water, swirling around, floating up. He says "I didn't hurt you, did I Baby?" He scrubs me down there with soap on a washcloth, so mad. My hernia is popped out like a balloon. Then he shoves my head under, holds me under so I can't breathe. Kicking and splashing, Daddy I can't breathe. His face through the water saying this is what will happen if you ever tell. At the last moment, just like he does with Sambo when he plugs his nose so he can't breathe, he saves me. He lifts me out, sits on the closed toilet, gently dries me off. He cuts Mama's Kotex pad in two, pins it in my Tuesday panties, "you're a big girl now." He's laughing again. "This is all just a fun game," he says yanking my wet hair, my whole head back to my shoulder, "Isn't that right, Sharon Lu Lu?"

He says "Go back to bed till it's time to get ready for school."

We are trying to come out of the bedroom. Three curly towheads, seven, five, and four, our mother dying in the sanitarium, trying to come out of the bedroom to our father. He yanks Clarke up, he pushes Bridget away. He'll kill them too. We're trying to get out of bed but we can't walk. Our hearts stopped in the night and blood is coming from between our legs broken at the hip sockets. I feel so awful I'm going to vomit. My stomach hurts. My chest, my bottom, my body, my rib cage, my head ache. It must be the flu, too much chocolate cake last night. But I can't stay home. I can never stay home with my father again. Or with my brother and sister, they might cry or talk about it. I hide my pajamas in the bottom of my toy box, under the games, Chinese Checkers, Monopoly, under the paint sets and tablets, folded doll clothes, the bag of marbles he made up especially for me. My jacks. Jesus help me to find a better hiding place. Help me to explain their disappearance. At school, in my class, that girl is here. Gae Elaine Walker.

But I have the hiccups so bad I can't speak. I keep getting so hot I'm embarrassed, I'm perspiring. I keep getting so hot I don't know where the ground is, my next step forward, it hurts so bad down there every step feels like something is tearing more. When I try to concentrate on the blackboard I see my bloody blue pajamas in my toy box. That Daddy or Clarke or Grandma or that woman might find them makes my heart stop again. In the bathroom the Kotex is sopping. The smell. That smell. I try to flush it down the toilet, but it's not going down. I stuff my blood-stiff panties with a pile of little squares of toilet paper, try to pin them in. I flush again and the bloody water rises, spills over the brim. I run out but it's left in there in the Girls for anyone to find. Some of the little squares of toilet paper slip out of place before I get back to my class. I don't know where they are. I can't keep my eyes off the boys' crotches. Are their things as big as Daddy's or are they still as small as Clarke's? The blood is soaking through and now I'm sure everyone knows. I have to face things, I have to hide my pajamas. I can't stop hiccupping. My heart is going to pound right out of my mouth, but the words don't, they don't come out right, hard as I try to act normal I can't talk straight, the words come out like Woody Woodpecker's stutter. Uh-uh-UH-uh! Uh-uh-UH-uh! All the kids laugh.

"Why Sharon Edens you've begun to stutter," Mrs. Allen says. "You look as if you may have a fever. Maybe you should go home, dear."

"No!" Then I say my father's out looking for a job.

Now I'm on the cot in the nurse's office sweating, smelling just like the monster. Blood and sweat and poop, that smell I first smelled when I was born. I have to get home somehow and get clean panties and another Kotex.

"Take a nap," she says.

Thank you dear Jesus that they can't find Daddy. Thank you for providing this safe haven to sleep.

The bell rings. That new girl is at the door of the nurse's office, standing there in the hallway, all the kids streaming by.

"I can walk her home, I live on Roosevelt too, the same block. She lives at 5903 Roosevelt. I live at 5920."

"Oh yes," I assure the nurse, "I can make it, I feel just fine. Thank you."

In the bathroom I stuff my dripping Tuesday panties with more tissue.

Gae Walker and I walk home to Roosevelt, the mile. Even before we get to the crossing guard on Paramount, I have to stop on the bumpy dirt path of Golden and lie down near the falling-down Pachuco shacks, sweating like a horse, then down Paramount without any place to lie down, past the newsstand, **Girl's Body Found!**, then the wet, dewy, soft mowed grass lawns when we finally get to the top of Roosevelt, three more blocks to go, the one between Hoover and Arizona the longest. My heart hurts to breathe. My legs are broken off from my hips.

"What's wrong with you?"

"I'm just tired."

"I heard your mother has tuberculosis."

She walks me past her house. She walks me up the porch of mine.

"Thank you."

Inside I die from the relief that no one's here. Not Daddy, not Grandma, not Bridget or Clarke. They must be with him searching for work. I head straight to the kitchen, to the big foldout potato bin under the humming Frigidaire. We keep our used grocery bags in here too. I make it to the bedroom, pull off my bloody panties, throw them into the bag, put on Wednesday's. It hurts so much to lift my legs. Someone's changed the sheets. When I lift the top of the toy box, the ringing sirens of the tunnel start up and I almost faint again from that smell. I manage to uncover my wet stinky pajamas under the toys, stuff them into the bag, then bury it all again at the deepest level. Dear Jesus please don't let anyone find them. Dear Jesus help me to think of the right place to hide them. Help me to explain their disappearance. Dear Jesus please please forgive him, forgive him. He knows not what he did.

Then just going out of my mind when I go to the bathroom and see that there's more blood, that my Wednesday pair of white cotton panties are already ruined.

In bed that night the three of us are silent and still as stones, so wide awake we are like the train roaring through the tunnel. When one of us tries to be normal and talk we can't. No words come out. Then Clarke is crying. "It's okay Clarkie," but I can't get out of the bed to go to him, it hurts too much, I keep fainting and getting up makes more blood come out and Daddy might come in. Being up would mean something's wrong, would mean we know. Bridget lies on her side looking at me. "That's okay Sharon Lu Lu. I will make things all right again. You just wait and see." Then she says "Poor Daddy." Clarke just keeps sobbing. "Poor poor Daddy."

We can hear him in his room but thank you dear Jesus he doesn't come to ours. All night long I pray don't let me fall asleep, don't let me fall asleep. I must never sleep again. If I have enough faith, if I have enough will power, if I believe in Jesus enough I will never have to sleep again. In Sharing Raymond told of a sect of people in India who don't eat. He had a picture of a sixty-year-old woman, a friend of Gandhi before he was assassinated, who has not eaten a bite of food since she was seven. The sun and her faith provide the energy she needs to live.

Another day he said "Einstein said to solve a problem rise above it." I saw the mushroom cloud Uncle K.D. described rising at the atom bomb tests out in the ocean. Dear Jesus, help me to rise above this. Help Daddy too. Help all of us. Make Mama well again. Help her to never know. Help her to come home.

The night is so long. *Don't fall asleep, don't fall asleep.* It's like a miracle when the train comes through because it means it's four-twenty a.m. and then the rooster crows and the danger is over. The sun is coming up in the window over my bed.

I kneel to my yellow toy box like I'm praying. My beautiful dolls are watching. Marlene, Patsy, and Mary Jane. I spy one of the pearl white buttons from my pajamas along the edge of my bed. I manage to get down the hall, through the living room, the kitchen, and out the back door with the damp, yucky-smelling sack. This side of the house, not the other. I went over and over my plan in school. I'm so terrified I'll be caught, that someone will see me but that's less likely on this side than the Henka side. On the outside of the house, under Mama and Daddy's window that Aunt Giny's voice came through, right next to the bathroom window, I kneel inside the cement square that frames the entrance to under the house. It has a screen over the opening that takes forever to pry off. Inside is thick with spider webs. I'm terrified to put my hands in there, the spiders could be black widows. I've got a big soup spoon, I couldn't find Mama's trowel for planting bulbs. I try to dig but the dirt's so hard I gasp and sob every time my hand hits a web, someone's going to hear me, dear Jesus don't let me cry, but when I hit another web, see the black spider with the red hourglass scurrying up it, I just throw in the bag, I only get it partially buried, I can't stop crying, I must not cry, I'm getting so dizzy, I'm perspiring like crazy, I'm going to throw up for fear someone will see me, I have to get out of here. I push the screen back on but can't get it as tight as it was.

Night comes. To go to bed is like being tied to the railroad tracks. Lying there waiting for the 4:20 train to grind you into Eternity. Your ears ring and ring and your heart jumps crazily all over your chest. You can't show you're afraid, he will know you know. Just pray, *do not sleep, do not go to sleep.* To stay awake you have to keep your mind busy, you have to constantly think (the bag's not buried enough), you have to talk to yourself, you have to see things (the screen's not back on tight enough), you have to remember (don't return to the scene of the crime, someone will see you, you'll remember). To keep your legs crossed and your eyes open you have to sleep on your back. You have to listen with all your might for him coming again. You pray your hernia goes back in. You pray hard and deep so He knows you mean it *Father forgive him forgive him forgive him.* You pray for the bleeding to stop. You pray that your bloody things are never found. You pray for your mother to get well, to come home soon. You pray for your father to find a job. You pray that we will all be safe from now on. You pray for your baby sister, your baby brother, that they forgive, that they know never to mention it, that they not be afraid, that they forget. You pray for all the neighbors and for that girl, Gae. Most of all you pray for your father's soul, that he not be condemned to Hell for Eternity. *Forgive him, Father, he knows not what he did.* Your little sister sings to you *Tura Lura Lura. Tura Lura lie.* And she sings to your baby brother who sobs and sobs. *Rock a bye baby in the tree top. And when the wind blows down will come baby, cradle and all.*

On the third day the stain is darker, dryer, the color of poop. I've run out of panties, have to keep wearing the ones I have on. Sunday's. My hiccups are louder, hideous belches I can't control for all my effort. Trying to go to the bathroom, just the blood coming. I have to go, they're keeping track. But I can't eat. My head sweaty in my lap, I can't let the teacher see. Then I'm throwing up but there's nothing in my stomach but thick sticky spit. I can't I can't oh God help me I can't be home alone with Daddy.

This Friday we are too sick to go see Mama. Unbearable, unswallowable sore throats, burning chests, then colds, high fevers. All three of us in the bedroom, Bridget three feet away, and Clarke in the corner by the other window. Praying to Jesus on the wall, let Mama know we haven't forgotten her, let me not go to sleep, let Daddy know even Hitler is forgiven by our Lord Jesus. Even Adolf Hitler by Love. All over the world his soul is prayed for.

It's February 28, Bridget's sixth birthday, but we are too sick to have a cake, to even get out of bed to sing to her happy birthday. I sing the one line over to her, *"happy birthday dear Bridget,"* but she cries that her throat hurts. Yesterday Daddy lost his new job. Even so he brings home expensive ice cream, spoons green pistachio nut ice cream into our mouths but even that doesn't taste good, hurts to swallow.

"When was the last time you moved your bowels, Sharon Lura?" The neighbor women are in the doorway. They keep trying to put the glass thing down there. "In your rectum." I go completely out of my mind then, screaming and kicking. "No! No! No! Please please no no no!" So I manage to hold it still and tight in my mouth. I see Daddy returning down the hall naked, "no no no no." A hundred and five. A hundred and five point five. "If it gets to a hundred and six we'll have to get her to Emergency." Fighting with all my will, praying Jesus please keep my temperature down, the terror of being handed over to strangers who will force the thermometer into your rectum, just going somewhere else for long periods of time. But not to sleep. The spiders are crawling up the wall from under the house. A constant line of black widows are running up and down, their red hourglasses glowing. I scream and scream. The neighbor women are in the doorway. "They are not really there, Sharon Lura, they're just in your head." This is when I learn the word hallucination. Then, a hundred and six, more and more spiders are crawling up and down the wall coming from under the house making me scream out of my mind. They make Daddy take me to LA General Hospital.

Huddled in the army blanket in the back seat, my face buried in the crack where the upholstery meets. Daddy is driving to save my life. Crying at the wheel he loves me. But mad so mad at me too. This is when I learn the word hypochondriac. "Poor poor Sharon, faking it to get attention. Isn't that right Sharon Lu?" Dear Jesus even Stalin is forgiven by our Lord Jesus. Even Joseph Stalin by Love. All over the world his soul is prayed for. My throat is so sore I can't bear it but they say it's not diphtheria, they don't know what it is. Some sort of bad flu.

There's a blond Queen in a long blue dress who keeps rising in the sky like a star over the railroad tracks. She looks like the Blue Fairy Queen in Pinocchio. She wears a gold crown. Her eyes are blue and her lips are red. Her waist is small and long. She says your father is alive, just swallowed at the bottom of the sea. It will take a miracle to get him out. I have come so he will have a conscience. Then he will be a real boy.

Grandma keeps coming to take care of us, sits there in a chair telling stories of when he was a little boy. "Poor Cecil," she says. He's out looking for a job so we can survive. She keeps saying "Oh Lord be near." She keeps having us bow our heads in prayer. It's hard to bow your head when you are lying flat in the bed. Then she gets sick again. She stays a day or two, then goes back to that Rosewood Lodge in Compton.

I see her from the back, her small blue waist, cut of her upper torso, layers of pinafores gathered as clouds over the tracks as she approaches him, her arms down and out to him, open, completely unguarded. What he did is unpardonable. The Pardon is what she must give. She sees this so clearly. Resist not evil, He said on the Mount. What's done is done. She does not take her eyes from him. She does not hesitate, does not run from him, there is no escape. A force, tubular, round, the only truth greater than his mistake, goes from her, down the hallway where he runs, and penetrates him. Over and over she encounters his madness and over and over she moves closer to him. She loves him. Love is stronger than death.

How long does it take for the caterpillar to weave its pale gold cocoon, then how long does it stay in there, before its wing starts breaking out? In the window above my bed I watch the hairy green worms marching in a line from the elm tree, crawl up the porch pillar, crawl under the roof eave, turn upside down and start spinning their cocoons. They hang there so long they get dusty with the soot from the foundry on Industrial. Endless days and nights in that bedroom. Years. I crawl out of bed when no one's there, look them up in Mama's desk encyclopaedia. Pupa is Latin for girl. Pupa is a doll. Pu means to swell, inflate, whence Russian pulja, a ball. Does Nadja know that? Pupil is boy! I am in the nonfeeding stage. When I'm finally well, when I leave my bloody, black-widowy bed, I am very skinny but my breasts are bigger. Pu.

Food doesn't come out because I'm not eating. I haven't eaten in a long time. Tears don't come out either. Nothing comes out, thank you Jesus, not words, not poop, not blood. Just hiccups. Just da da ta sta stutters.

When I begin to eat again, the digested food comes out only once a week. This goes on for years. It's fine, I feel fine, absolutely fine. I don't want anything to come out. But it's not fine with them. The whole neighborhood is keeping track. "Sharon Lura, when was the last time you moved your bowels?" How can I explain that every night I have to hold everything as tight as I can so nothing can get in or out again. And to stay awake. I can't let go. I won't. And it's none of their business.

He makes Campbell's Chicken Noodle Soup, then lobs in a tablespoon of Skippy's Peanut Butter to each of our steaming camel-colored bowls. It's a recipe on the back of the can. This is extra protein so we can regain our strength. All three of us throw up after one spoonful forced down. Daddy laughs and tears pour down his face, "Sorry, I'm sorry, I never could cook." Then he says "Those Japs, whoever heard of peanut butter in chicken noodle soup?" He's actually apologizing but still the next Sunday afternoon, our first visit in weeks to our mother in her window, we complain with vehemence. "The peanut butter was added protein," she explains. "Your poor father was trying to help you." He stands in the field behind us shrugging his shoulders, about to cry again. We all laugh, trying to get our own tears to come out. Daddy putting peanut butter in our chicken noodle soup was the only thing we complained about the whole time our mother was gone.

§

Twelve

Bridget and Clarke are playing in the bedroom, far away. He tells them to stay in there, Sharon and I are talking about grown-up things. I hate being grown up.

He asks me to sit on the hassock before him in the armchair. He asks me if I would mind unbuttoning my pajama top.

They embarrass me. The dark pink keeps growing in ever widening, puffy circles and the nipples stick out when they are cold like they are now.

"Can I touch them, Lu?"

I'm shaking my head yes before he finishes the question. I'm begging Jesus let this be over fast. His fingers, wrinkled and dark on my white skin, delicately trace the round poochy circle and the nipple sticks out even more. His fingers so lightly like whispering move out on the little mound and slowly down and over. He cups them. He pulls the nipple.

"They are very pretty, Sharon Lura. You are growing up so fast."

The living room is still except for his heavy breathing. And the pounding of my heart and the ringing in my ears. Bridget and Clarke keep playing in the bedroom. The lamp shines above us and onto my bare chest. His eyes are green and I see myself in them, tiny and doubled. I'm almost eight. Sometimes I think they're blossoming because he does these things to me like I'm his wife.

He moves in the chair. He laughs a little. The strange look on his face makes me want to assure him it's okay.

Suddenly he jerks closer to them so that I smell the hair oil on his large head, am looking down on the wavy red-brown hair, am looking through the lashes of his eyes caught in the light. His eyes bore into my bare chest. Breasts is a word impossible for me to say. I wish they *were* pretty for you Daddy. They are sores swelling. His hot breath stirs them and his fingers are larger than my ribs.

"Don't ever tell anyone, baby," he says when it's over. "They wouldn't understand. This is strictly between you and me, okay? This is our little secret."

Maybe this happened before. Maybe this first happened that night, the night of his thirty-third birthday. My buttons were still on. (Or maybe they were sewn back on.)

A little girl fell in a well. She was just skipping along through a field when her foot hit a place in the weeds that was really a hole. She fell hundreds of feet down a dark dank narrow hole, down and down into darkness. For days and nights they were trying to reach her. We could hear her crying on the radio, the Henkas next door watching her on television. "Are you alright, honey?" her parents yell down. "Yes," she calls back. The ground fog comes in and goes out. Praying in bed all night for her deep in the earth. And for Grandpa six feet in his hole in Downey Cemetery. Every morning Bridget asking Daddy and Grandma, "Have they found Kathy Fiscus yet?" She's not crying any more but her Mama and Daddy keep calling down, "We're coming darling, hold on." The searchlights down the hole trying to see the lost little girl, the reporters gathered around. The midgets and dwarfs from the County Farm volunteer to be lowered down the narrow shaft. They start digging a parallel hole down beside her hole, to get her out that way.

Then there's the morning we wake to them pulling her up into the cameras. Dead.

Bridget and I returned to school. Old, abandoned wells pockmark the Southern California landscape, watch where you step. Daddy carried Clarke with him when he looked for work. The Henkas gave him a little outfit for this—a gray plaid vest, gray slacks, a gray sweater and a red polka-dotted black bow tie. To assure us this was not charity they said the outfit was a gift to Sammy but it was too small for him. Clarke looked so handsome.

Mrs. Ritchie, Mrs. Pohlman, and Mrs. Henka hurry through the front door. Daddy shuts it behind them, turns to face them. I huddle on the floor behind the hall door, watching through the hinged crack as they move nervously into the center of the living room, eyes locking in looks of exasperation, nodding heads. "Dear girl," Mrs. Pohlman exclaims when she spies me, "shouldn't you be in bed by now?"

"We waited, Cecil," Mrs. Ritchie says, "until we were certain the children would be asleep. Now girl, go along to bed. What are you doing on the floor? Have you brushed your teeth?"

"What is it that you gals want?"

Blue veins snake their fat white legs. There are small dark explosions on one. Daddy calls them the nosey neighbors. My eyes go from nose to nose.

"What we have to say, Cecil, would not be in your daughter's best...." Mrs. Henka's big nostrils pulsate open, shut.

"Whatever it is you'll have to say it in her presence." He sits down in the armchair. I'm so proud. He treats me like I'm grown up.

Mrs. Pohlman, not much bigger than me, is leaning over her high heels from the sofa. "We want you to know Cecil that our coming here in no way means...."

She stops me coming home from school wanting to know if I've moved my bowels and when was the last time I had a bath? I can't tell her Daddy doesn't give us baths anymore and I'm afraid to be alone in the bathtub. Mrs. Ritchie comes out of her house, "What'd you all have for dinner last night Sharon Lura? Who's doing the cooking now that your help has disappeared?" "We had peanut butter and jelly sandwiches," I assure her. They gasp and then they want to know if I'm happy. "Is there anything you want to tell us, dear? You realize how sick your mother is, it could be years, she may never get well...."

"Being mothers ourselves," Mrs. Ritchie begins, "uppermost in our minds is the welfare of the children."

Yesterday we were walking through the Ritchie's house to Sharon May's bedroom. Screams, sobbing and curses were coming from the bathroom. "No! Mother, please. Please don't!" "God damn you little bitch, this will show you who's boss!" "Mother has rearranged our bedroom again," Sharon May was saying pleasantly over the screaming as she led me down the hallway. We passed the bathroom. On the floor, between the toilet and the bathtub, Mrs. Ritchie was riding Susan's back like a cowboy and with long scissors whacking off one of her two gold pony tails. "Please, oh please, mother, don't."

".... nutrition and love that children require, we have come to the conclusion that under these painful circumstances, the children should be put in foster homes."

Daddy remains silent. No one hates the County more than my father.

"As you know," Mrs. Ritchie continues, "I have some connection with the County, I do volunteer work for the polio victims at the Farm, and having described to them the situation...."

"Get out."

"The situation...."

"Get out of my home...."

When the door slams shut he sits there, breathing heavily. I crawl to the bedroom, praying he doesn't call me back.

We go to see Mama. Darkness outside we move through, our breathing fogging the windows. Lights flicker in the black, coming at us. Daddy keeps sniffing and clearing his throat. Bridget and Clarke sit in the back and I sit on a pillow in the mother's seat. The pillow is to see better but it makes me feel big too. I'm sure the passing cars think I'm the mother. Daddy buys only two bags of shrimp because we've barely gotten our appetites back and we drive to Mama's sanitarium. We came last night, but because of the problem with the neighbor women we come again. We drive across the dark dead lawn, beneath the starry night, between the creaking, groaning, black long-nosed monsters pumping oil from deep in the ground, to her window. He leaves us in the car. He taps her window and after awhile she lifts the pane and puts her white hand out into the dark for him.

He stays at the window with her a long time. Bridget and Clarke fall asleep. I cradle my head in my elbow over the back of the seat and watch him talking to her. Last night after leaving here we went to the drive-in. When the man in the booth didn't charge for me I was crushed. How could he tell I was not the wife? I do all the things a wife does. Now he rests his head on the sill. Then he reaches in and puts his hand on her breast and lays his head on her arm. Between the rhythmic screeching and groaning of the oil wells I hear him sigh, "Oh Mama."

The neighborhood committee visited Mama. They'd already run off our help. Mama told them she had to believe what her husband said, not what they said. She said she would stand by her husband. She told this to the very end with pride and righteousness in her voice.

It's Sunday, we're in our Sunday clothes playing in the front yard. It's hard to remember how to play, I feel like a pretend girl. Suddenly Daddy yanks Clarke up, disappears with him into the house. Then he comes through the door carrying Clarke's clothes, the Henka slacks and vest. Clarke is standing in the doorway bawling, the little cut wing between his legs going up and down with every sob. Daddy passes by me and Bridget on the lawn so fuming the air he leaves in his wake is black. I am afraid and repulsed and proud too of what he is. He moves heavily but quickly up the Henka's driveway carrying the neatly folded clothes like they're emitting a terrible odor, the red polka dotted bow tie on top, stopping them as they emerge from their car home from church. The words are muted by the distance, but the black fumes float back to us again and again across the green shadowy lawn and row of rose bushes. Mr. Pohlman in the yard beyond stops mowing and watches. Daddy turns and leaves, his face contorted.

"You kids are never to set foot in the neighbors' yards or houses again. Do you understand? Never!"

He gets a job selling rubber door mats. *Welcome* is cut lower in the rubber than the rest of the spikes. The car reeks with the smell. We sneeze and sneeze, even Daddy, driving through traffic.

We're parked on Gardendale, under the eucalyptus this side of Rancho Los Amigos, in sight of the whole avenue, all three blocks, so we can see him and he can see us. I watch him going from door to door like a beggar. When he comes off a porch he pushes his penis to one side. We spend the day here, in the mess of eucalyptus buttons and the long silver leaves falling like half moons. "Sharon's the mother," he told them. All the windows are open, the eucalyptus smell is such a relief from the rubber mat smell. We blow through the buttons making whistles like the Indians. If I had any stories to tell I could entertain my brother and sister, I ache to have stories. But just like Daddy I can't remember anything. And nothing's ever happened to me. But we have our games, our crayons, cars and trucks, our dolls, our comic books, my Bible, and the baloney sandwiches and cookies I packed. In the afternoon he disappears into the inner blocks but the map back to 5903 Roosevelt drawn in his dark carpenter pencil is on the dashboard in case of an emergency. We do okay these long days of our Easter vacation. I remember being thirsty, noting I must remember to bring water in the mayonnaise jars tomorrow. I say to my sister and brother how lucky we are, our play house is so big it has a motor and wheels and our Daddy is making money for us to eat. We pee outside between the two open doors, watch for each other, for any cars coming. Clarke's thing is still a baby's, tiny and white. Sometimes, in a sudden shiver of fear, a flash of sun through the high branches, I think, dear Jesus, the Indians are still here.

We go to Penney's. I can't stop hiccupping. It makes Daddy mad, he says I'm doing it on purpose, this is such a big deal, store-bought clothes, can't I mind my manners? Mama has always made our clothes. How lucky we are now, he's actually going to buy us each an Easter outfit. Wandering through the circle racks of dresses, I feel so weak and fuzzy I can't keep my head up, it's all I can do to keep from lying down under them. Bridget and I choose different dresses, unlike the identical Easter ones Mama has always made us. Mine is of pale thin aqua stripes with a white square yoke and white cuffs on the short puffed sleeves. Bridget chooses a sea-blue one with fish swimming across the front. In the dressing room, only a pull curtain between my naked self and everyone, panic suddenly seizes me and my heart clamps shut so that I'm perspiring, almost crying. Clarke gets slacks and suspenders, a bow tie and a white shirt. See, we don't need the neighbor's charity, Daddy says like spitting. Only the dread of his screaming at me keeps me from lying down on the floor. This is the moment I remember missing my mother. Poor Daddy. Poor poor Daddy.

Grandma's so sick she can't come for Easter. Dyeing the eggs all by ourselves, Daddy hides them in the back and front yards. We can't find all of them, he hid them that well. "We'll be finding eggs till Kingdom come!" he shouts. There are pale, not so good photos of this day, Daddy leaning in his swanky posture against his perfect high back fence, me and Bridget in our Easter dresses hanging off it, Clarke perched on top, Odie's grinning head coming over from the apartment side. Bridget, her front teeth missing, looks like she's studying all of us, trying to figure. We look happy.

Grandma taught me how to clean my plate by wiping it with my bread, that's how they do it in Tennessee. I gag on the soggy bread but my shiny clean plate is worth it. I put it, unwashed, on the highest shelf, to save to take to Mama, to prove to her. *Dear MaMa,* I wrote her, *I cleaned my plate all up.* But I know that it's not really clean. At night I see the germs crawling from my plate to all the others.

We stand under her window in our new Easter clothes. I display my plate to her, shadowy behind the screen. Even in the bright sun it looks washed. A part of me is so proud. Dear Jesus, don't ever let her know what Daddy does to me. That would kill her for sure. When I get home I scald and scald my plate, and scrub the shelf with Purex.

One afternoon Bridget colors our four newly painted light green walls with her crayons, great big circles and waves that are pretend writing just like she scribbled on one of my letters to Mama. Daddy comes in and she says "Clarke did it." I feel the confusion of spiders in my head. Clarke gets a switching, Daddy roaring and killing him. "But Daddy, really, Bridget did it, she was just trying to write like me. Isn't it pretty?" Bridget looks right at me and denies it. "Sharon just wants to get me in trouble." So I get switched too, for being a liar, a snitch, a tattletale. That I'd do that to my little sister.

There is nothing scarier than the nights. All night on my back with my legs crossed. Practicing like crazy the power of positive thinking like Mama always instructed. "Thoughts are real things out there." The monster will not come again. The monster will not come again. Praying and thinking all night, sheer will power to stay awake. Dear Jesus help me to remember to breathe. Sometimes I forget, the monster's rising up from under the bed, I'm being suffocated again. Dear Jesus don't let them put us in foster homes. Imagine having to sleep in a whole house of monsters who take you in just for the money. And to do that to you too. Bridget gets up saying my thinking is so loud it's keeping her awake. She goes into the kitchen where Daddy has gotten up. It's the middle of the night but they're having scrambled eggs and potatoes. Clarke and I lie here listening to their giggles. When the train comes through, when the rooster crows, when the sun starts rising, when the first pale silver blue of early LA dawn comes in the two windows, the one over my bed, the one from which in dreams I still make my escape, the other over Clarke in his crib, I can relax, and maybe fall asleep. 4:20 a.m. The time on bad nights still, I can usually fall asleep.

Bridget and Clarke are almost asleep though it's still light outside. Daddy's in his chair reading the Times. *Don't call me don't call me don't call me dear Jesus don't let him call me.* The tingle-lingle Good Humor ice cream truck is coming down Roosevelt. We're his last address. Then Daddy is coming in our bedroom, "Wake up kids, I have a surprise for you!" I scream and scream, then apologize and apologize. So now we're sucking our orange and purple Popsicles on the sides of our beds, Clarke's four year old legs coming through the bars. "Soon, boy, we're getting you a real bed, you're getting to be a man." And then Daddy is telling his one story again, about the movie star Julie London and singing *My Heart Belongs to Daddy*. I still see him there, how young he was, sitting at the foot of my bed. How hopeless and sad and lost he looks.

I struggle with his heavy khakis. This is the hardest work I do. The awkward heaviness of the iron, its point and the point of the ironing board, the wrinkles in his fly. Then, my discovery! Shaping his fly over the point, sprinkling it with water from the jar with my fingers, then leaving the iron on there a minute, the steam sizzling and rising, gets the wrinkles out. But then I leave the iron on too long, burning a permanent triangle there, a perfect arrowhead. I try to get the crease in the humongous legs even more perfect in hopes that will make the flaming arrowhead less noticeable and he'll know how hard I tried. But Daddy screams I burnt his fly on purpose, he could kill me for that. Why is it called a fly? I see flies flying around it.

Clarke and I are standing at the foot of the Ritchie's two-tire driveway, watching our old friends playing at the top, two days after my eighth birthday and Grandma's sixty-ninth, when Bridget comes racing down the street shouting at the top of her lungs, "Surprise, surprise! There's a big surprise for you two at home!" She's shouting behind us, all of us running as fast as we can back down the sidewalk, "it's Mama it's Mama!" I have never run so fast in all my life, I have never felt my heart pound so hard before, but even so little Clarke keeps close to me.

And when we get through the screen door it is her. She's standing in the far corner of the living room over the floor heater just like always, smiling at us, her hands folded behind her, behind her big magenta hibiscus-flowered print dress, her back-strap high heel pumps, her little thin-belted waist, her hips and breasts the exact same measurements as Venus de Milo, her perfect, beautiful, beautiful body. The whiteness of her skin from months out of the sun is shocking, blinding almost like a marble statue too.

But instantly her white hands—her white nails filed to points—go up. "No!" The force of that no! is so strong that it actually stops us in our tracks. No. We must stay back. That no in her sternness even before she shouts it, we cannot come near her, cannot touch her, no! as we are flying through the door, is forever, most fundamentally, our relationship to our mother. Daddy is saying Mama came home sooner than the doctors wanted her to. She left without permission because she knew that she would die just lying there in the contagion ward with all the other dying. She's come home to get well but you must not get near her. And you have to let her rest. You kids have to carry on as before, as if she's not here. Remember, you can't depend on your mother for anything.

They started the pneumothorax a few weeks before she got out. They collapsed the top part of her lung to let it rest. The doctors told her again she was going to give the TB to her children. What if you catch a cold? But she had begun to feel that not only was she in danger in that contagion ward but that her children were in danger too, more than without her.

She stays in bed. She gets up only to wash her dishes that must be kept separate from ours. In the far left hand corner of the yellow and white tile counter, the coffee cup with the smudge of lipstick, the glass, the silverware and plate all have the ominous, forbidden quality of Mama. We could die if we touch them, just breathe them in, if just one spoon falls in the dishwater with ours. All day and night the sound from the bedroom of her trying to clear her throat, coughing up the germs, spitting them into Grandpa's spittoon. This is doctor's orders. It is important that she coughs.

But her mind is strong, stronger, she says, than those old doctors think. Gradually she is up more. If you think you are well, she says, then you will be. If you think you are dying, then you will die. Isn't it interesting that I always thought I'd die at twenty-eight?

She stands over the heater, just as before, quiet and watching, except my sister and brother are not folded around her legs. We're across the room. She stands over the grate like the Cherokee exiled forever from the land and though we will never be able to touch her again, she can tell us stories.

"There were four brothers who went down the Cape Fear River to Southport, North Carolina. They were from Town Creek, but they'd lost the plantation to the carpetbaggers, the ones who took over Wilmington. So now they would become shrimpers. They bought a boat, started running to Boston, to Cape Cod. CC—Kit, Chris, Christopher Columbus Simmons, my grandfather, yes, your great-grandfather—was the oldest. They made a good living but CC hated the life, he wanted to farm again, he was so homesick for the land, but he ended up shrimping for years out of Southport to support his family."

CC was the Indian, her mother's father. Susie's father. The dark woman in the big oval photograph hidden in the back of their closet.

"The flu of the first World War was so bad twice as many people died of it than died in all the war. Uncle Dewey came home from the Army with it, there was no place for him to go, someone had to nurse him so my mother took him in. That awful flu turned into tuberculosis. We have a weakness in the lungs, every family has an inherited weakness, ours is lungs, you must never, not ever, smoke. They operated on Dewey's lung but still he died, my mother died even before him, and then everybody died. The TB swept through my family like wildfire."

Some stories she tells over and over but I never grow tired of hearing them.

"My daddy's daddy, Charles Rogers Clarke, was the great grandson of William Rogers Clark of the Lewis and Clark Expedition. That's where we get our wanderlust from, why I kept running away from the School, longing to know what's on the other side of the mountains. When you see Clark's picture you will see I look just like him.

"After his father died, daddy's mother, Grandma Jackson—she was Indian too, she was Cherokee—baked pies for the men in the mill to support her three children. There was this old guy—I always called him Old Man Hammet—I never liked him, he liked for me to sit on his lap and he'd make advances—he came everyday from his junkyard. He'd ask Guy and Dora and Walter if that was their mother. They didn't like him, saw through him, but one day unbeknownst to them he followed them home. He knocked on the door and married her. Then he retired from the junkyard, he was a Spanish American War vet, he had a small pension, and put the three of them to work in the mill. Twelve hours a day, six days a week. This was before the child labor laws. Daddy was only nine, he kept running away. When the police would return him Old Man Hammett would beat him to within an inch of his life. The last time, he was twelve. Grandma told them to take him to juvenile detention in Richmond, and keep him. She did that to save his life. That's where my father learned to read and write. Remember, out of every bad comes some good.

"Daddy wanted to be a writer. He wrote long beautiful letters to me in the School. 'My Dear Precious Garnet,' he wrote. 'Sometimes I'm so sick I let myself be arrested just to get a warm, good night's sleep and a meal. You must know I am not a bad man.'"

"Who snuck the jail key to him in the potato? Tell that story again!"

"Well, now that I think of it, it doesn't make sense, a key in a potato?"

It took a night for me, Bridget and Clarke to figure this out. A baked potato for dinner!

"Oh, Daddy had lots of friends alright. He was one of those persons everyone just loved. All over Virginia and North Carolina my father was known and loved.

"I ran away to find him. He was so sick. I was fifteen. He was twenty-seven miles away, straight north, in Chatham. I knew the road from visiting CC in jail. He'd gotten out of the sanitarium, was helping some people on a farm, the only work he could do. That was the final straw with the School. They asked me to leave, or they'd put me in reform school. Daddy said leave. Run.

"When he died he was engaged to be married again. Oh, he was a ladies' man, alright, a real fancy dresser, and so good looking. But he wanted to get married, have a normal life, have a home for us. He had the surgery on his lung in hopes that he'd be cured, could support her and us. I don't remember her name, she, Mozelle and Lawrence were at his bedside, I wasn't. I was a mile down the road at Aunt Luella's. I refused to be there. If I didn't see him die, he wouldn't be dead."

I love Mama's stories, I can't hear them enough. I see them lowering her Mama in the ground and shoveling dirt over her. I hear each shovel-load dropping down. "I'm sure it was Dora who wouldn't let me have Mama's watch. Dora is my daddy's sister, she never liked me, she always said look at those eyes, those are Guy Clarke's eyes. And so she was buried with it. I used to wake up with a start, hearing it ticking."

I wait for her to say the next thing, like her father married again soon after Susie died. "But I refused to recognize that woman. She spanked me because I wouldn't call her Mother. Daddy came to my rescue, yelled at her for that, and so they got a divorce."

She spent long periods in bed as a child with rheumatic fever. She was in bed for so long, three different times, she read all the books in the library. At the end of the sixth, seventh, and eighth grades she took the high school tests, and all three years she got the highest score. Higher than all the graduating seniors. "I'm sure it was just because I had nothing else to do but read, but every year at the big awards ceremony they gave the medal to someone else."

As smart as she was, though she loved history, studied all the battles and places on the map till she knew the routes and dates by heart—"you realize the Civil War was not that long ago, when I was your age I actually saw Confederate veterans leading the parades through Danville"—she was twelve before she learned the South lost the war. This was devastating. She was never the same after that.

"The matrons of the School who took care of us, the volunteers and teachers, were widows of Civil War generals and high-up officers. They taught us only white trash work in the mills. Ladies work in dime stores. Well, I found out, the dime stores in Danville paid a third what the mill paid, they were like finishing schools, or something. Girls waiting to get married or go to college worked in dime stores, returning home at night to their parents' mansions. A girl like me would starve to death on those wages."

Run. Sometimes that's all you can do to free yourself. Run away. Though to this day she literally aches for red mud and wild berries, oh, what she would give for a handful of Virginia red dirt this very minute, to be in those trees, to be that free again, sometimes you just have to run away to save yourself. You children are so lucky to be born in the far west.

In California, as far away as you can get. Where there's sun and light all year and no roots, no disease, no class consciousness.

Mama hated more than anything the class consciousness of Virginia. How very lucky we are not to be growing up in Virginia.

My chores grow less as she becomes our normal mother again. After awhile I've forgotten how to cook and iron. She tells the story of how she boiled Dewey Harold's diapers in the big outdoor kettle when she was four. She takes care of us again. I've forgotten everything except being her little girl again. I step out, but though I can't touch her she's there in the house to come back to. Her body and ways are serious and different from the other mothers. She doesn't laugh and she's proud that she doesn't need friends. She isn't social even when she's well. Her body isn't like the one on the calendar in Daddy's garage, it doesn't lilt in the S curve like it's making fun of you, like she's challenging you, my mother would never smile that way. Her stomach is round between her hips, not sucked in, her breasts are heavy like full sacks, not jiggly like butterflies just hatching from the cocoon. She was born to have babies, Doctor Pentz said. Hers is the body of a mother, and the one on Daddy's calendar, that of a girl.

But as she grows better, Daddy grows colder, a dark figure lunging past us to get to the back of the house. He's so unhappy in his new job at Douglas. He works long hours at a job he hates in order to feed us and take care of us. He's young. So handsome, so smart, so talented. He could be many things. Most men couldn't do it, they'd leave. He loves us. But sometimes he can't help it, he feels we owe him something, that he's entitled to act like a dictator, a man's home is his castle and poor man, what does it hurt us to go along with that?

Some nights he stays away and I hear Mama awake, clearing her throat, waiting for him. More than anything I avoid his glaring eyes. He's so mad at me, he screams, accuses me of things. "Sharon's avoiding me, she hates me." When I protest that's not true, "Daddy I love you," when I try to defend myself against the accusations, Mama says it takes two to make an argument, and you're just like him, Sharon. Anger is an inferior, immature trait. I'm afraid you suffer from Southern pride, Sharon, which is false pride.

When he comes home from work he hugs me, pressing me hard against his hard thing up on his hard hip bone, mashing and rubbing my breasts up and around his chest with the heart hollow like mine, his breath smelling of beer. He does this right in front of the whole family, Grandma too, and if Dee or Odie is here, in front of them too, in front of everyone so that we can't think anything of it except it's proof he does too love his children. He was jealous of you when you were born. You took so much of me from him. Now he's jealous of your growing up, of your finding a boy friend. He acts that way because he loves you. That's why he calls you Lu. He has a special love for you, deeper than daughter love. You're his favorite child, just like I was my Daddy's favorite, don't ever tell Bridget and Clarke that. He wants you to love only him. You're a beautiful girl, it worries him sick.

Lu is what he called his big sister Lucile, beautiful like you, who ran away. Every night he heard his Ma praying, Lucile, forgive your father and come home.

I watch him walking toward us in the car, down the long wide civic steps in Long Beach, skirting around the overgrown bushes of Pershing Square downtown Los Angeles, in Huntington Park where they put the long needle in Mama's side, under her left arm, between the ribs to pump fresh air in, and in the mountains, on the beach, working, talking, smoking, fishing, playing poker, and always his hand moves down and nudges his big thing to another place as if it's risen to the wrong one. It's the most important part of him, the only thing that makes him happy. A sad handsome boy-man with heavy lidded eyes like my eyes. Those eyes, Mama says, they go back generations. They're English. Came over on the second ship, the one after the Mayflower, Lord Baltimore's. My eyes are in your forehead, Daddy. Your eyes are in Mama's Cherokee cheekbones, Daddy, her face veiled by your blond lids and lashes. Is this how an American is made? Is this how a beautiful girl is made? They keep saying that word, that word makes me gag. It's why he does it, Daddy says, he can't help it. I'm ugly. Ugly. I couldn't be uglier. Burp.

He says I'm hiccupping on purpose to get attention. I hold my breath to hold the next one back till I turn blue and it erupts. I drink so much water I have to keep leaving the class to go to the bathroom which is so embarrassing. Even when I accidentally fall asleep my hiccups don't stop. I know this because they wake me up. Once in the middle of the night Mama came into the room, the first time she checked on us since she went away, she heard me hiccupping, she scared me to death standing over my bed, I screamed and screamed. Then died for the embarrassment, the loss of control. "Daddy's wrong," she said at the door. "Sharon can't help it, she even hiccups in her sleep."

A cocoon in the porch light twirling under my eave. A pupa worm turning into a butterfly eavesdropping on me. Like Eve dropping down to me.

He stands over my bed, saying fear not. I am with you. His face like Daddy's face. Knowing him, the sour smell of him. I stand here at your door, knocking, knocking. Dear Jesus, if I should die before I wake.

He turns into a nightmare. Forehead too elevated, like modern art. Arms too extended. Daddy wringing the chicken's neck, wringing his thing. Squeezing my whole self through the tiny mesh holes in the screen netting, escaping south to Long Beach where I was born. But now, where do I go? The world is men pointing and wringing their things at you.

Some mornings I can't believe my eyes. Coming out from under the little brown and green army blankets of her twin bed in the windowless corner, all ten of Bridget's fingernails are bleeding where she's chewed them to the quick.

At school I have the hiccups so bad Mrs. Allen puts me in the last seat, the last row. "For your own good, Sharon," she says so kindly. "And besides you're getting behind." "*A sweet little girl and a conscientious student. Weight 65, height 50,*" she wrote on my report card at the end of January, giving me straight S's. "This will give you a chance to catch up." She doesn't know what to do about my stuttering but she's going to research it. She gave me straight S's, not a single minus, the whole year.

That girl is here, in my class, Gae. But I can't be near her. She hisses Okie, the way I keep burping. I can't be near anyone.

Mama says the high and wide windows are the best thing about Roosevelt Elementary. We can see out. When she was in the School she always looked west to the sun setting behind the Blue Ridge Mountains dreaming of what was on the other side. Dreaming of her Daddy hiding in them having escaped the jail, dreaming of being on the run with him.

We're at the tables covered in white paper with our hunks of clay. That girl is in front of me. The helper comes through, lobbing to each of us from her bucket our portion of wet clay. I love the smell. "Now, children, your aprons on."

I find a small photograph in *LIFE* Magazine of a tall, white, black-spotted Dalmatian dog. It's exactly what I want to model. I so miss Sambo.

All week I work my clay but for some reason I can't make it look like a dog. Every day at 2 p.m. we line up, me hiccupping, that girl in front of me—what is she making? why don't I ever see her outside on

Roosevelt?—and the sun behind me and I study again the photograph, my hands molding the clay that won't become a dog. Why can't I shape this clay to be like that dog? I was so successful with my elephant, a more complicated, unfamiliar animal. I see that dog that bit me. It's like the clay has a will of its own. It's as mystifying as it is mortifying. On Friday I have to put him in the portable kiln out on the playground as he is, hoping that when baked he'll come out looking at least like a wiener dog.

He comes out green with pink polka dot germs. His stubby legs come off as I claim him from the mouth of the furnace. My dog is really ugly. He's too long, especially his long curved neck. His too-long head has a big deformed pinch right in the middle from my thumb and forefinger. His mouth is a long pink slit, the rim of his snout.

Daddy hollers in scorn and laughter, "Sharon's modern art!" He hates modern art like he hates Freud. He says Frood, sometimes Fruit. He says he hates all things that smell of spoiled Frood. At the movies a common scoff is Frood! He says I made that hot dog just to make him feel bad about Frood. He will never forgive me for making that dog. And that is true. On his death bed, even after his confession, he will curse me for this second grade gift to him.

I have always called my dog my prehistoric monster, which always made my father roar some more. Only now—only now!—in writing this, holding him in my lap, do I see that my dog, amazingly, looks like a penis; looks, actually, like Daddy's penis.

I'm the Diphtheria Germ hiccupping through Second Grade's big year-end production. Mama takes one of their old full size white cotton sheets from the hallway cupboard, and keeping me behind her at a safe distance, leads me out into Daddy's garage. Under the calendar of the naked blond girl sprawled on the red velvet sheet, she pries open a pint of black enamel paint with a screwdriver, and with shocking splats to the sheet, makes big black germ spots all over it.

I wear the sheet draped over my head with two black-ringed holes for my eyes. I'm the Croup! I hover evilly around everybody and everything, the whole world, and I love this. I know about disease. I know about germs. I know about hallucinations, that you can get so sick you see spiders that aren't there. I know about strangulation, that's how you die from diphtheria, your father must insert his fingers down your throat in order to tear out the diphtheritic membrane, as in the famous painting, *El Garrotillo*, that's on the cover of our script. I know as Mama keeps saying when you go through something hard you come back stronger than ever. People who've been through things are the deep ones. Something happened to me and now I go somewhere very deep down in the ground, like I'm tapping something that goes forever. Mama says tap root. She says second wind. The energy I feel inside the sheet is fantastic. I love the word diphtheria. I understand germs. Germs are just in love with the world too.

Monday, Feb 14, 49- Cecil's 33rd birthday and Audrey in San. at Long Beach. I had a weak spell.

Tuesday, February 15- Dear Avon's birthday. He has been gone 8 months and 19 days.

Sunday, Feb 27- Went over to Cecil's. Bridget is sick. Throat I think. Cecil out of work. Dear Avon has been gone 9 months. How I miss him!

Feb 28- Bridget's 6th birthday. Cecil says she is some better.

March 3- I moved over to Cecil's today. I wanted so much to help him and the children.

Friday, March 4- I came back to Rosewood Lodge today because I was so weak I was afraid I'd give out. Bridget is sick with her throat.

March 5- Bright day. I grieve so about Cecil's family.

March 6 - My dear brother's birthday and he is gone to return no more until Jesus comes. I went to Cecil's and was sick too.

Friday, March 11- Went to Cecil's. Sharon was sick.

March 12- Came back to Rosewood Lodge today. Clarke is sick too. Last night I met Avon in dreamland. It is such a comfort even in dream.

Sunday, March 13- I went home with Cecil for Sharon is real sick.

March 15- Still at Cecil's. Children sick.

Wednesday, March 16- Came home from Cecil's. He is in so much trouble. Sharon was real sick with her throat but is better. I am very weak but helped a little.

Friday, March 18- Cecil came for me. Sharon was worse. He took her to Gen. Hospital, but brought her home after a treatment.

March 19- Kermit & Kenneth's 37th birthday. I came back from Cecil's.

March 20- Went to Cecil's again.

March 21- Sharon is better and I came home this evening.

March 27- This is Audrey's 29th birthday. She is in a sanitorium. She has been in our family 11 years. Wrote to Bess. I've been so lonely today!

March 31- Cecil left the children over here with me. We watched television.

April 5- Moved back to Cecil's.

April 7- Cecil looking for work.

April 24- I went with Cecil and children to see Audrey.

April 26- My 69th birthday and Sharon's 8th.

April 27- Came back to Rosewood Lodge. I stayed 22 days at Cecil's home.

April 28th - Just called Cecil & Audrey was home. O how I hope it's okay.

May 13- I wrote to Fisher-Poir Funeral Home and Judge H.E. Page of Pensacola, Fla.

May 21- I dreamed of dear Avon last night. Thought he had on overcoat and was begging me and one of the children to go with us. We knew he wasn't able and left him. How sad!

Because he'd just turned thirty-three like Jesus, because I met Gae right then and she'd turned seven on February 7, because all my life since I've had death nightmares mid February (or at February's full moon in Leo), I've placed the rape as happening February 14, 1949. (That February the full moon was on February 14.) Of course, typically, typical of Mama too, I didn't succumb right away. I managed to escape to school for awhile, to escape the facts, to escape everything.

Perhaps, given my grandmother's diary accounts, the rape happened a week or even two weeks later.

Electrocardiograms show that Bridget and I both had heart attacks in early childhood, she around the age of five, me between seven and eight.

That she got sick first would be typical of her. My sister will always be a big barrier in my knowing my family story. When she collapsed, then I did.

§

Thirteen

There's a blond Queen in a long blue dress inside me. She's standing with her back to me before her King, her betrayer, with her arms extended and open from her small waist in silent submission to him.

She's not inside me as words. And she doesn't speak. She stands before him before argument, before debate, above betrayal, like a principle. Love is stronger than death, the only truth greater than his mistake. Her love penetrates him.

When school's out Mama makes us take a nap in the afternoon. Though I lie as still as I can she can feel me thinking which keeps her awake. "Sharon's never been able to sleep since we coated her thumb."

She teaches me Solitaire to play while the three of them nap. She plays Solitaire when she needs to quiet her mind. The first time, showing me on the living room rug, a safe distance apart, the cards line up, all the Aces, Kings, Hearts, Diamonds, Clubs. Then the Queens, the Jacks, the tens on down. We win. "This is unusual," she gasps. "Beginner's Luck," she warns, gathering the cards. "You must remember it won't always be so easy."

But the slapping of the cards together when I shuffle, even with the thick rug and room, hallway, two closed doors, and Bridget and Clarke asleep in the other bedroom, keeps her awake. "Sharon you're keeping me awake." I cannot bear her scolding, however gentle. I cannot bear to make her feel bad. I love her so much, my sick my most beautiful mother. But I'm old, too big, I can't be in my bed, I can't sleep, I have to do something, I don't want to quiet my mind. My mind is saving me, keeping me awake.

I learn to scramble the cards silently with both hands, just swirling them around in the carpet whorls, but I never win Solitaire again.

We get an automatic washer and dryer. When the Sears truck arrives the neighbor women raise their eyebrows. You can feel this, their hands going to their aproned hips like a chorus line all down the block. Soon she'll be buying cake mixes. Mama's pneumothoraxed arms are not strong enough to put the clothes through the wringer or to hang them on the line. Yes someday, she'd like an electric beater too. Beating the cake ingredients the million beats a minute has always been terrible but now it could kill her.

Bridget keeps accusing me of messing up the bedroom. She throws things down and says I did it. She leaves rotting apple cores and crusts of her old baloney and mayonnaise sandwiches in my toy box and in my blankets. Daddy says Sharon's making that up. Mama says Bridget is too loving to do such a thing, she's not that kind of person.

"Sissy! Mama's boy!" Dear Jesus, help Daddy to stop belittling Clarke. Help Clarke to withstand it. Help me to grow up and never treat a child like that.

June 24, 1949 Rosewood Lodge – In my sleep (or wake) last night, I heard sweet music & singing. Seemed to come from Audrey's & Cecil's window(bedroom).

Trinity Vacation Bible School starts the week after school is out.

"*Deep and wide, deep and wide.*" Assembled in the pews, kids of all ages from all over, swaying back and forth like waves of the ocean.

I win all the Bible drills.

But to be first, or at least to be happy about it, is to be vain. To be competitive with the Lord's word has to be wrong.

The most important thing is Jesus, Jesus is our Living Lord. Jesus is alive right now in this room, this minute standing right by your side, it's up to you to realize His Presence, He's with you at all times. Jesus is your Personal Savior. This is what most who profess to be Christians don't understand, and thus they fail to be true Christians.

Pastor Adams looks so much like my father it's eerie, like Jesus knocking at the door. He wears a tie of the Cross with all the Biblical names for Jesus on it. "*I am the Rose of Sharon.*" He puts his finger beneath the tie, right beneath Sharon in the very middle of his chest, bends deep toward my eyes in the second row, and says "I am the Rose of Sharon, and the lily of the valley." I'm still trying to read the Bible from beginning to end. *Joshua, Judges, Ruth, First Samuel, Second Samuel. First Kings, Second Kings.* Most important is to understand that the Holy Bible is one living book, one story, *Genesis* to *Revelations*. Grandma first read it when she was eight. I can too. *Ezra, Nehemiah, Esther, Job.*

But we study Exodus the most because of Israel. I love the felt pictures of Moses in the bulrushes. And on Mount Sinai receiving the Ten Commandments from God, which I memorize, then wandering in the Wilderness forty years trying to find the land of milk and honey. I get nightmares when Moses forgets the commandments, when he flies into a rage because the returning Israelite soldiers have slaughtered only the adult males. "*Now kill all the boys,*" he tells them when he calms down. "*And kill every woman who has slept with a man, but save for yourselves every girl who has never slept with a man."* Mama explains this is an example of the old Jewish religion that believed in a jealous, angry, warmongering God who demanded an eye for an eye. Jesus said turn the other cheek, love thy enemy. He saved the world this way.

Sometimes when I wrestle with the ghost over my bed I think oh it's Jacob and his ladder to Heaven. *Israel* comes from *Sarah* meaning *to wrestle.* We're meant to wrestle, Daddy says. Survival of the fittest. "Sarah was my mother's first name," Mama sighs.

If I should die before I wake. I wake just after or just there inside it, in the struggle to not let his thing inside me, in the moment of the dilemma of pulling my pajamas bottoms back on. The moment of the scream, my heart stopping, the drowning in blood, the evidence buried with the black widows under the house. Is it still there? Sometimes Daddy has to crawl under there. I wake inside the heart attack, don't let him find it don't let him find it. The dilemma of whether to live.

Then I know Jesus as my Personal Savior. I feel Him, his arms around me, I can smell Him, his flesh and blood, I hear Him, I see Him. And He saves me, this I know.

One day coming out of the church this black telephone pole is branching out to me, somehow talking to me. "I was once a tree growing roots in the earth and branches to the high heavens. I still know who I am, I still think though I'm trapped in here, a sad telephone pole, a prisoner tarred in creosote. I could tell you, if you want to know, of the place I once grew. And of the messages going out by phone like branches all over the world right now as I speak. Believe me they help. As you do, standing there hearing me. Every day I watch you walking by, such a sad little girl. I know why you are sad. It hurts that I can only help you by watching but I watch you all the way to your front door."

One day I talk back to him, in silent prayer. It must be what it's like trapped in the coffin, I'm sorry. After that I never come out of Sunday School, I never go to the store and come down his side of Industrial, I never pass him, tall lonely sentinel dripping in black creosote, without feeling him reach out to me, without my reaching back. In time this talk or exchange or prayer evolves to a vow. I'll survive too. My consciousness will survive like yours no matter what. I'll live as long as possible in this blessed temple on this holy earth, I'll live to be at least 121, one year older than Moses when he found the Promised Land. If he and Abraham and Sarah lived that long, so can I. Life is good, life is worth it. No matter what. Life is important. That's what Job learned, too.

We still can't go in the neighbors' houses but we keep inching up the Ritchie's front lawn. One day all of us kids are at the enormous blue and white hydrangea bush in their front window because it's loaded with tiny gold butterflies. The bush swarming with gold butterflies is like the burning bush in the Bible that is not consumed. You reach into the thicket, clasp the two wings together, catch it without hurting it, put it in your mouth. It flies around inside your mouth. I stutter so bad. Worse, I hiccup continuously. The fluttering wings against the roof of my mouth feels good, like it's teaching me to talk and breathe again. All of us kids at the bush, all with gold butterflies, sometimes as many as three flying around inside our zipped shut mouths. *"The voice of God spoke unto Moses from the burning bush that is not consumed, I AM THAT I AM, this is my name forever. And Moses said O my Lord, I am not eloquent. I am slow of speech and of a slow tongue. And the Lord said unto him from the bush, Who hath made man's mouth? or who maketh the dumb, or deaf, or the seeing, or the blind? Have not I the Lord? Now therefore go, and I will be with thy mouth."* Then, fast, before we hurt or consume them, we open our mouths and out they fly. Butterflies out of our mouths like out of their spun cocoons.

"My mother says it's okay for you to come in."

It's hard to approach her house, to go up the white cement driveway. The two Doberman police dogs, Adolf and Goebbels, in the chainlink back yard have barking fits. If they get loose they will kill you. She holds the door open. The fog in her eyes pulls me in, there's a river across the sand of her face.

First thing, she teaches me to play *The Marine Anthem* on the triangular-shaped piano standing in the bay window. It is upholstered, the entire thing, even the legs, in white leather. "Just always remember middle C." From the halls of Montezuma, her dark fingers on the keys, to the shores of Tripoli. Her short tan fingers on top of my big whites, guiding them. Her feet under mine guiding them to the pedals. What are the halls of Montezuma? This is like Karen teaching me how to play the pedal slide steel guitar until her mother put a stop to that. A wooden triangle with a hand tick-tocks, tick-tocks on top of the white piano. "It's a metronome," she says, "you play in time to it." And a photograph of her father, framed in white leather too, when he was a sailor in the war. Mr. Walker, blond curls spilling out from his white cap, is so handsome and grinning so big he looks like a movie star. Blue Boy is on one side wall and Pink Girl is on the other.

"The Greeks saw the horse as an ocean wave," she says pointing to a painting of horses in the ocean waves. "Horse in Greek means wave."

And there's another in the bathroom of palominos, just their gold heads, their white manes blowing through clouds. The shower curtain is see-through glass with a big swan at the bottom. Returning down the hallway, I spy, through the cracked door at the end, a round bed in an all white room. And in the round mirror over the white boudoir, a naked blond woman lying on the floor. She has little beads of perspiration all over her brown body under a bright orange lamp. A high wild bush of black hair where her thighs join her hips is how I know her white head hair is bleached.

"Don't worry about it." Gae Walker slams her hands down through the hallway air. "My mother lies under the sunlamp naked all day to keep her tan. My father makes her do it. She looks fat when she's not tan."

Her mother's name is Dorothy. Dotty, her three-year-old sister, is named for her. Mama makes a big deal about my being a natural blonde. Don't ever bleach your hair, you'll be a dime a dozen then. Mrs. Walker is only twenty-three.

"My parents were both sixteen when I was born, my father's twenty-three too."

"My mother was twenty-one, she waited three years to have me, to make the perfect child. But now she's twenty-nine."

Twenty-nine is so old even as a little girl Mama knew she'd be dead now for a year. I can't take my eyes off this girl as she leads the way back outside.

We navigate through the men in the bushes, over their broken liquor bottles, shards of glistening green and golden brown. She curses them. This takes my breath away—*love thy neighbor as thy self*—I just pray to love them enough I can get past the danger of them. But that she knows about them in the way I do is an incredible relief.

Hollydale Park is a triangular piece of land right behind the little store, left over from everything, mainly the railroad tracks and the diagonal street cut. Dew coats everything on this June gloom morning, a teardrop hanging off each blade of grass, lining the swing sets, the rails of the track, like caterpillars. First we have to find something to wipe it off so not to get our hinies wet. Then I have to sit on the inside bar because I weigh so much more than she. The beautiful law of balance. We seesaw. It's a grammar lesson about Time. First you see, then you saw. She is up and I am down. Then saw-see, I am up and she goes down, a sight before my sore eyes.

Then running like crazy across Main, the long block home down Industrial, making it through the perverts and winos, the piles of dumped sulfur-smelling coal and thorny sage and tumbleweeds. Gae can whistle. *Tumbling tumbleweed.*

Mrs. Walker plays canasta hours on end with Gae's grandparents, her father's parents, at the gleaming yellow formica and stainless steel-legged table in the dining room, beneath the glass chandelier, a cloud of smoke up there with the many mirrors of glass. They visit every afternoon from South Gate, parking their two-toned silver giant car in the white driveway. "They're from San Francisco. Does that tell you something?" Mrs. Ritchie is saying to Mrs. Pohlman on the sidewalk as I skip by. "Even though it was World War II he got kicked out of the Navy. Something not right there. A queer I bet."

"Oh," Gae says. "It's just that my father was discharged from the Navy for being borderline insane."

She teaches me rummy on her living room white wall-to-wall while the adults play at the table. Every time I look up into her face my heart breaks open for gratitude. Outside Bridget and Dottie play witches up and down the sidewalk on their broomsticks. When you hear the Olds starting up, purring out, then Mrs. Walker, like that, is naked under the sun lamp in the front off-limits bedroom. When you hear Mr. Walker's motorcycle turning onto Roosevelt, like that, I'm out of there.

He skin dives. He spear fishes, he scuba dives, he dives for abalone. They go every weekend to Laguna Beach, bring back a trunk load of iridescent red and silver abalone shells which they use to landscape their yards, front, back and sides. By the end of summer the abalone shells line the new flower beds beneath the bay window, around the new elm on the grass strip on the street side of the sidewalk. Birds of Paradise, cala lilies, cactus, date palms, orange and lemon trees all outlined in glistening abalone shells. Inside, the ten inch reds and silvers are the ash trays, candle holders, candy, change and catch-all dishes.

"My parents are founding members of the Sexual Freedom League."

"My parents are proud they're not members of nothing."

"They worship the sun, they aren't ashamed of the body. They're naturalists."

"My father sleeps in the nude. He's not ashamed, it's his religion."
"Why do you stutter?"
"I'm sorry."
"Why do you hiccup all the time?"
"I'm trying not to."

Each day is a deepening to her like the sun going down in the Pacific. Mornings we meet on the wide triangle cement blocks where the two sidewalks of Roosevelt and Industrial meet, where Denny Clare was held over the hole and almost cemented over. I can't take my eyes off her as she leads the way running in the hundred degrees. We play chase with our shadows, we hopscotch them, me to hers and she to mine, in our chalk squares down the Avenues under the blazing light. My hair is in pigtails. Her fog colored hair is short and permed. *Step on a crack, break your mother's back.* Coming down Industrial right through the glaring old men exposing themselves in the bushes. Clapping our mouths with our hands, making the Indian war cry, we're on the war path. Telephone Pole protecting us. Eating our penny candy from the little store, warning the others we're coming, *allie allie auto free free free!* Entering Roosevelt as the Three Musketeers. Spinning around and around down the whole block from my house to hers, blinding spinning tops. Playing Jacks and pickup sticks on the porch, tic-tac-toe, the smell of the wet cement from the sprinkler. Running through the sprinklers. Getting browner and browner. Back up to the little store to buy Jawbreakers, Neccos, Tootsie Rolls. Abracadabras! grape Kool-Aid mix to lick dry from our palms. Reentering Industrial on the back of the elephant, coming down as Sabu the elephant boy. Coming down in our big candy wax lips through the old men rubbing their things and hissing and spitting and pissing and squirting. Sneaking into the boys' big hole, showing her the secret tunnels. Trying to make fire like Indians rubbing two sticks together. Digging for China in the back yard at the edge of Daddy's garden, digging straight down. The Chinese people are walking upside down and they don't even know it. And so are we every time the earth turns over and we don't even know it. Burying nails, a 1943 lead penny, a photo of Sabu, a deck of cards. Climbing the backyard fence, spying on the Beaver boys who took me down with the Yucaipa boys into the hole. Remember don't ever eat the red berries on the bushes, they're poisonous. Hiding inside the sweetish poopy coop with the chickens in their lofts laying eggs, studying the mean rooster. Why's he mean? I'm so in love with her I want to die. The killer dogs attack the chain link fence whenever we storm into her house. Me hiccupping and belching through everything, she not saying a thing about it now. *Ashes ashes, all fall down.* Night coming, I am so afraid of the nights, but days, oh all the days long I am with her.

One day everyone's gone. I sneak her into my parents' bedroom. Just to show her. My father's photograph on the dresser in its black and silver frame taken at Knott's Berry Farm the day after I was born is like her father's on the white leather piano. See how perfect his teeth are? My father's never had a cavity. I pull open the top lefthand drawer, show her his Cherokee arrowheads, tell her about Ducktown, how all the trees were killed by the fumes. Hunting for arrowheads and tomahawks was my father's favorite thing to do as a boy, he'd start out early in the morning with his knapsack, roam all day, come home with hundreds. They'd just been lying there for eons from the Indians shooting in the dark forest and then not being able to find them.

She picks up the deck of poker cards that has the naked women on them, pulls out a Heart, a Spade. "My dad has these too." We go through the women, much older than our mothers. "Painted hussies," she whispers.

She picks up the three monkeys of black onyx on the dresser top. "My parents have this in their bedroom too. See no evil," she cites.

"Hear no evil," we say in unison. "Speak no evil."

At twilight we sit on the edge of my sidewalk, watch the worms crawl from the mud under the grass. I could die of dread of night almost here, that I have to leave her. She demonstrates how you can cut them in two, chop! and they don't die. The two halves wiggle away. "Don't worry," she says at my ouch! "They'll grow their heads back."

The elm tree is infested again with caterpillars. Every branch is solid with the hairy green and yellow creatures. I lose my breath, I hyperventilate, I start choking not to remember. "Just wait, Gae," I burp. "They turn into butterflies." Beautiful many-colored butterflies with iridescent designs like abalone on their wings.

Dear Jesus, may this girl somehow love me too.

We're in our house under attack by the Indians. We're in the wagons circling. We're in our log cabin on the prairie. We're in our farm house on the plains. They descend from all sides. Flames and arrows penetrate the walls of our house. My family lies dead, scalped, burning with arrows in their still quivering bodies.

Mama has nightmares too. She wakes the whole house screaming. The nightmare galloped right over the top of her without touching her, but still that horse returns and returns. The good part was her daddy holding her afterwards.

I'm a Tomboy," she says when I show her my dolls.
    "What's a Tomboy?" I know Peeping Tom but not Tomboy.
    "A girl who likes to do boy things."
    "Me too!"
    I hate girl play like I hate the sissy fairy tales. (This is partly why it's so hard to say the Blue Fairy Queen is inside me.) To be a girl is to play a role on stage. I can't stand sissy girls who play house, who put on aprons and pretend to be the mother. I love my dolls so I do not play dolls. I hate more than anything being babied. I prop them on the top of my dresser and on my bed every morning after I make it, like the statues of Jesus in Catholic churches. Other girls, even Gae and Dottie, throw their dolls in their toy boxes. I don't know how they can treat them that way. I comb my dolls' hair. I feel how much their tangles hurt. I make their clothes. I wash and iron them, give them clean underwear when there's blood. They watch the room. They cast their black lashes out over their eyes seeing every-thing. They are real. Marlene especially. Mary Jane, always on my bed in her yellow yarn pigtails, is me. She'll come back to life one of these days.
    But Gae's not interested in dolls.
    Tomboys! We run all the blocks of the Presidents, Roosevelt, Wilson, McKinley, Hoover, back down Main, down Industrial, arms around each other, singing in unison "Skip to my lu my darling." Daddy calls me Lu. Because he called his big sister that and had a special love for her too.
    We look up. A man is holding his thing out to us, rubbing it back and forth, saying bad words. We freeze. He adores his thing, he idolizes it. He treats it like it doesn't belong to him, like it's something separate that's got him hypnotized, like the Serpent to Eve in the Garden. I start moving first, pulling her out of the trance. We run like crazy to get to my back yard. "Thank you dear Jesus we aren't really boys!" We crack up, rolling in the grass. "Imagine having one of those things hanging off you."
    We're both Tomboys but I'll never be as free, as spontaneous, as bold, as carefree as she.
    When Mr. Walker's motorcycle or black and white police car is in the driveway she doesn't come out and I don't go there.
    Evenings we are in our houses. The Edens. The Walkers. Separated but together in spirit we listen to The Lone Ranger at 7:30. They have a television set but she has her very own private radio in her bedroom and

she wants to hear what I'm hearing. Our dark mahogany standup radio is in the living room. I put my pillow, my head on it right to the speakers. "You're hogging the best place from your brother and sister," Daddy scolds about my selfishness. "Sharon and the law of the jungle." He lies on the sofa reading the paper, his Big Cecil moving around in his khakis, the ever-present Serpent.

Into my head their radio voices, their words. The sound of the horses clip-clopping through the rocks. The sound of the same music through Gae at 5920 Roosevelt.

The Indian comes right through the front door of this tiny shack. All my family lie dead on the floor. His tomahawk coming down on me.

Mornings we meet as the Lone Ranger and Tonto. We run all day on Silver and Chief, reliving, resolving the drama of the night before. We never say who is who. "Qui mo sabe?" We're all four.

We're coming through her ultramodern living room. I've seen it in all the newspapers and magazines, but now it's on her television too.

The house near the tower is occupied by a family of life-size dummies. Mr. Mannequin lounges in his easy chair watching television. Mrs. Mannequin sits nearby knitting. On the floor at their feet sprawl two children. A baby is lying in the far corner before a stack of comic books. They sit there like my family in our living room. They sit there like all the families on Roosevelt, around all the blocks named for the Presidents.

Then, everything—people, the mountains in their windows, animals in them—stand out without shadow in the silent gush of clear, cold, pure white light.

"The sky is falling!" Chicken Little's my favorite children's story. "Do you know Chicken Little? The sky is falling! The sky is falling!"

It's ballooning now into what looks like a monstrous flaming planet suspended in space. Uncle K.D.'s hand moves in from the South Sea Islands, the bones showing. Out the bay window the Santa Ana sky is so clear you can't help but gasp. Bridget's chasing squealing Dottie. "I'm going to spank you *so* hard!" And when she catches her she does. She sits down on the curb, pulls her pants down, turns her over her knee, and spanks as hard as she can until Dottie is screaming and screaming. For one second everything is so clear I hear Mama saying as if she's standing here "Bridget's a Staingel."

Sometimes we flip a penny for what we will do today. I always bless Penny, I always choose tails. A ladybug lands on her arm. "*Ladybug*

*ladybug fly away home, your house is on fire and your children will
burn."*

We hide in the hot newspaper box behind the apartments, the lid
down, talking. Endless talking. In here with her I don't stutter. Cross my
heart and hope to die.

"Did you know that Elizabeth Taylor from England has purple eyes?
Like my brother. Just look into Clarke's eyes sometime and you will see
pure purple."

Trapped, totally. No way out. Seeing everyone killed, each one as they are
being killed. Trying to find one last hiding place, some hole or box under
the earth, as the house is burning down, as the savages pour in to scalp us.

*August 28, 1949- Went to Cecil's awhile. I feel lonely over there 'tho' I
love them so. Took flowers to Avon's grave. Pretty birds flying around....
Sept 3, 1949- Went riding with Cecil & Audrey in their new car.*

We buy a brand new, mint green, 1949 Ford. It's a trick Mama knows, like
Christmas shopping on Christmas Eve. The 1950 cars come out in September of 1949, so the still brand new 1949 cars are greatly reduced in price.
The mileage on the speedometer is twelve miles. Mama is so smart about
money.

I'm hiding in the newspaper recycle box, the big one Daddy made for the
apartments. An arrowhead penetrates right to the surface of the dark circle
under my eye. I watch each wood slat shatter.

*September 11, 1949- Lucile, Overton, Nancy & Jimmy arrived. We all
went to Cecil's for awhile.*

Grandma's daughter and family drove from Miami, Florida, visited a
week, staying in a motel near the Rosewood Lodge in Compton. Our Aunt
Lucile, the one Daddy calls me Lu for, is forty-three years old, has all gray
hair, yet her children, our cousins Nancy and Jimmy, are practically still
toddlers. Mama makes a big deal about this, explaining that Lucile is
divorced, she didn't have children the first marriage. Instead she played the
violin in the Chattanooga symphony. Daddy still calls her Lu. Mama
laughs that people ask Lucile the ages of her grandchildren. No doubt we
bought our Ford in time for their arrival to further diminish her white trash
image.

September 18, 1949- We went with C's family, ate at Knotts Berry Farm. I said goodbye to my only daughter, Lucile. How very sad. O God protect her and husband and two children. Nancy & Jim. God bless all.

Grandma knows she will never see her daughter again. Her yearning for her, her loneliness, her fear of death which she fights with her Baptist hope of an afterlife where we will all meet again. All through her diary she is pining for Lucile.

August 14, 1940- Lucile's 33rd birthday. Seems but a few fleeting years since she came into our home. My mother brought her to my bed and showed her to me. Her big blue eyes looked wide awake. Today she is far away and somewhat unhappy.

August 14, 1941- Many many changes have come. I wonder if I shall ever see Lucile again.

August 14, 1948- Seems like yesterday and my momsy was there & Avon & Dr. Lewis & Mrs. Price.

It was Nancy who informed me, early in writing this book, that our grandfather, Avon Edens, was disinherited for injuring his father's most valuable horse, Black Skin. Mama had always told me of the horse accident but never that he was disinherited. In the same letter Nancy also tells that her mother Lucile claimed to have been prematurely gray because of malnutrition in Ducktown while he was in Arizona. *"And yes, I can believe that my mother was molested by her father. That would explain so much about my mother including her excessive control of us with other people—to say she was protective of us where anything sexual was involved would be an understatement—and it would explain why she was chronically depressed. And why I never knew the Edens' side of the family.*

"I always thought my grandfather died long before I was born. I'm shocked to learn that he didn't die until 1948."

And that would explain, in part too, why my grandmother, though in denial, pined for her daughter. As my mother pined for me.

The next Sunday ride in the new Ford my parents actually invite Gae to come with us. I give her my window seat behind Daddy and crowd between her and Clarke in the middle.

As we drive along, all the windows open to rid the car of the formaldehyde smell, people on the streets turn to watch us in our new car and Mama tells Gae how when I was young I ruined their rides because I

always had to wet. Everyone laughs about the can on the back floor. I
know my mother tells this so she and Daddy can enjoy a laugh together,
but I wish that she hadn't.

"Aren't they something?" Daddy says to Gae.

We're parked before the Watts Towers, on the avenue just below the
tracks. It's sundown over the LA Basin. This old guy from Italy is building
these triangle things in his triangular back yard right up against the tracks
hundreds of feet into the sky. He's been at it for over thirty years.

"Aren't they something."

They're scrap metal and junk, railroad track, thousands of shards of
Coca Cola bottles and seashells and abalone, but welded and glued
together so they're beautiful. "This isn't the safest neighborhood, but
lookie that, wouldcha just look at that?"

On the ride back Bridget starts screaming that I pinched her. I didn't.
But I say "I'm sorry, Bridget." This just makes her madder. She accuses
me of pinching her again.

"Bridget likes to torment Sharon," Gae says, wisely. "She doesn't care
if Sharon did it or not, or if she's sorry or not. She just likes to get Sharon
in trouble."

No one knows what to say to that, not even Bridget.

"You did too pinch me."

"Bridget's not that kind of person, Gae," Mama informs her,
philosophically.

Then they tell the Staingel story. Bridget Colleen's such a Staingel.

"I'm sorry, Bridget Colleen. I love you."

Gae is to me like Aaron is to Moses. *"And he shall be to thee instead
of a mouth."* I love her so much she's more real than I am. I'm her Mary
Jane rag doll, her negative, her mirror. I feel myself from within but I see
and therefore know her from without. She's more beautiful than anything
on Earth. The gold-beige clouds that are really God move across her face,
move in her hair like a movie, like a storm coming up.

We meet on our meeting spot at sundown, on top of the Denny Clare
hole. *"For the place where thou standest is holy ground, the burning bush
that is not burnt, the Lord said to Moses,"* Moses is boy for Mozelle. Gae
is a head shorter than me but her face is God's, a face unbelievable to look
into. "I love you."

"I love you," she says back.

I've brought the razor blade from Daddy's shaving kit.

"One. Two. Three!"

We slice into the blue veins on our left wrists. The blue blood instantly bubbles up red. We mash our wrists together, rub them hard together. The stinging stops. We are ecstatically in each other's eyes.

"Your blood into me. My blood into you."

We say this to each other.

Unto each other truly.

Now we are blood sisters forever.

Nights. Everyone's dead but me and Mama. Then the arrowhead penetrates right in the middle of her forehead splitting her in two. Then the flames, then the whole tribe is storming in on me.

§

Fourteen

Daddy's thing, so fat, so dark, so veiny, so wormy purple, floats in the bubble bath.

"Isn't it pretty, Sharon Lu Lu?"

The hiccup explodes up, goes on and on. I can't stop the hiccups for all my prayers and will power.

"Hypochondriac," he hisses, about to cry.

Mama's eyes are sky blue. She turns them to her flower bed, speaks to her flowers as if to her children. She doesn't tell us their names, an omission she will regard as one of her failures as a mother. Her flower beds are her escape.

She was alone with her grandfather when he died. Christopher Columbus was fifty-seven.[8] She was seven, they were living in the two tents. He'd just gotten out of Chatham jail where he'd spent the year for bootlegging for the rich man who went free. He was so sick his legs were leaking water. Dropsy, her grandmother said. Jail food. He said "Garnet come here." She went to him. "Would you get me a chair?" When she brought it to him he sat down and died.

Everyone died. At the School the first day the matron said "Don't you have another name? I don't like Garnet." When her mother Susie and Aunt Myrtle and Aunt Maybelle were teenagers they vowed they would give their daughters the names of precious stones. Thus Garnet and Pearl and Ruby (who died as a baby). "Audrey is my middle name." Audrey was chosen by her father. "Yes, Audrey is better. Audrey is what we will call you." My mother's favorite comic strips were Little Orphan Annie and Little Audrey, but she hated being called an orphan. She didn't know that Audrey actually means orphan.

The areolas turn salmon pink first, then blow out like little balloons, then into the triangles of arithmetic. Areola means bubbly, bubbling out, blowing out, swollen, a word too swollen in my mouth I can't pronounce though the definition is exactly what it is like to blossom, the word they use about me. Sharon's blossoming. The way to this day I smell him when I look down on them. See his big moles in the big mole inside the right areola. Something in myself I try to kill in every breath, every night with him in nightmare over me, my body shot full of arrows in the sheets.

Billy Graham pitches a huge tent this side of the church, displacing part of the Gypsy camp and hobo jungle, and conducts an old fashioned Bible Revival for ten days. The Times heralds it as a **Crusade!** Grandma attends some of them. "He's going to be famous," Mama says, disapprovingly. "Trying to become famous is unChristian." I pass the tent on the way to the store, hundreds of folding chairs in sawdust rows and dressed-up adults sitting down and standing up and wailing and singing and crying and being saved and Billy Graham screaming "The end of the world is at hand!" Coming back they're singing *"Onward Christian soldiers...."* With my hand I brush around Telephone Pole. *"Marching as to war...."*

"Where did you get your Southern accent?" someone is asking me and Mama is laughing in the next aisle. Almost ten years and people still detect her accent, but oh! that they detect the South in her children! We're in the Hollydale dime store. I love this store but something awful is happening. I feel the floor tiles pulling me down, I feel myself surrendering my too big ugly self to the tile, cool and receptive and magnetic, wanting me, and then I'm going down in the stationary and art supplies aisle, whirling down into the dark. Just going down. To allow the pull, the comfort of the black, feels as big an allowance as I ever allow myself.

"Must be worms," Mama says. "Worms down there you got from going barefoot all summer with that girl Gae." Sure enough, there are little white quarter-inch wiggly things with eyes looking up at me from the bowel movement floating in the toilet water. They look just like me as the diphtheria germ. Did I accidentally swallow a butterfly? Will worms in my bottom turn into butterflies?

The worm medicine is worse. I'm in bed for over a week just before school starts, the scariest place in the world to be. I listen to Billy Graham screaming down to us, for the Kingdom of God is at hand! "Jesus said go into a closet to pray," Mama scoffs.

Billy Graham looks a little like Daddy too, him and Richard Nixon and Pastor Adams. "That's because he's from the South," Mama says. "Billy Graham is from North Carolina but I don't claim him. I don't like to be screamed at. No one from North Carolina would." As twilight comes on I listen to them singing *"With the cross of Jesus going on before."*

The thought of starting school with the hiccups makes them even worse. At the last minute Mama finds a tip in *The Reader's Digest.* A sure way to stop hiccupping. Wrap a linen handkerchief over a glass of water, secure it with a rubber band, drink the water through this.

She pulls out Daddy's right hand top drawer, the one next to the one with his collection of Cherokee arrowheads and gives me one of his white linen handkerchiefs. I've consumed untold gallons of water since the hiccups started to no avail but the handkerchief trick works. It works even over the school faucet, wrapped over the spigot and held tight around in the back. Sucking through. In time I dispense with the rubber band. The trick is to hold the cloth taut. In time I even use a sheet rag. The trick is in the sucking through the cloth.

Gae and I get the same class! The best class, Mrs. Erikson's. Bridget starts first grade and Clarke starts kindergarten. This is an immense moment for Mama, her first taste of freedom since I was born. Soon as we go out the door she turns on the classical station. I don't remember much of third grade. I remember Gae. Gae was my education. Gae was my strength and my salvation.

She wasn't a good student. I admired her for that. She had the courage not to get *A*s like I had to. She was the smartest person I knew. Far, far freer than me.

The Third Grade Reader was a little more interesting than first and second, the sentences in several parts, the way people really talk and think. I liked that, the work of going into them and figuring them out rather than sliding over the surface till you're falling asleep. Dick, Jane and Spot however were as boring as ever in their Back East lives. And I hated the way we were circled off from each other, and these circles called the Advanced Readers, the Middle Readers, six groups in all down to the Non-Readers. Gae was in the Lower Middle Readers.

"Do you have any clues as to why you stutter and stammer, Sharon, when you're my best reader?"

Mrs. Erikson's carefully scissored autumn leaves, pumpkins and black-hooded pilgrims on the Mayflower fall down around the room. I haven't the foggiest, Mrs. Erikson. Please, please don't ask me that again. And my hiccups. Ruining everything.

Down the green stucco high-ceilinged hallway I go, my hiccups echoing.

Wrapping the right leg over the bar, then plunging head first down and around back up and then over again. And over again until centrifugal force has me and Gae spinning like dervishes. The thrill of our expertise, that we can make our bodies tumble and spin endlessly, backwards into leg leaps and flights, sideways and forward, arm over arm through the crossbars to stand completely upside down on our hands—then one!—on the high bar, our dark legs paused in the clouds, then drop, whirling around and hang, our skirts over our heads (panties showing is okay by monkey bar etiquette), swishing our hair like brooms back and forth in the sand. We spin all of each ten minute recess, we spin through most of lunch. We break the records. We compete with each other for the biggest calluses. Gae and I are the kings of the monkey bars.

She first flashed the badge to me in the hall lineup at the end of morning recess. "Look what I found, Sharon." Her countenance is serious, very stern. A half hour later she flashes it from her reading circle to me in mine, pinned in the pages of her Dick and Jane reader. It's the badge for the playground patrol person. Only a select few have a chance to be the patrol person; it's never us and never will be, my trustworthiness forever shot by what I did on the last day of first grade. Gae found it in the sand under the monkey bars.

For two weeks she hid it in different places in the classroom, in the seat drawer of her desk, under the hollow part of its aluminum floorbar, in the corner of an empty cupboard, and once in the bottom drawer of Mrs. Erikson's desk. That the badge was hidden in the classroom and only we knew of it was thrilling. It was our power source, our touchstone. To me it was kind of like the Arc of Covenant, it carried the holy laws.

Then Mrs. Erikson announced that the patrol badge had been stolen. Our joy and sense of sacred mission turned into panic and fear. For several days we hid it in a bark flap of the big palm by the kindergarten. I was terrified. I was more terrified for Gae. I prayed to Jesus right in my desk.

And then somehow she was caught. I was acknowledged as innocent, though an accomplice, guilty by association. Gae was the secret possessor of the coveted badge by having found it, but she had not stolen it. It could have stayed buried in the sand. Still she was labeled a thief.

Sometimes in my memory it's her father's police badge she sneaked out of the house. Sometimes I know she was trying so hard to be legitimate that she did steal the badge only to become the opposite of what it represented. When I took acid the first time, on my thirtieth birthday, that badge held in the palm of Gae's hand appeared again and again before my eyes.

Night comes. To go to bed is like being escorted to the gallows at Nuremberg. Sometimes in the middle of it Jesus knocking on the door becomes Luther nailing ninety-nine protests to the door. Sometimes the ghost hovering over me is Daddy's giant thing like the worms and Diphtheria Germ, its big white head wobbling around. His lashes not low and heavy enough to hide the eyes. Daddy. In the time he's hovering I don't breathe, not knowing whether it's Jesus or Daddy. I pray so hard. I keep breaking my record for how long I can go without breathing.

One morning the headlines of the Times on the kitchen table screamed **Soviets Detonate Bomb!** To the Non-Readers I was helping that day I told the Chicken Little story, "the sky is falling! the sky is falling!" Mrs. Erikson had to shush us up. For months after that the headlines were about the Communists. For Billy Graham, who'd pitched his giant tent all over LA, the times were not a problem. **Graham Converts 300,000 In Six Weeks.**

Then I gathered all the kids to the corner lawn at twilight and read them Chicken Little. "The sky is falling! The sky is falling!"

Gae and I are Gypsies for Halloween. I show her the places their tents were before Billy Graham's tent. "Sharon and Gae, they're tinkers," Mama says into the kitchen window. "Maybe you should worry about their wandering, thieving ways. They steal ladies underwear from the backyard clotheslines."

She shushes us from cracking up. "Actually, I think they just think differently about private property and owning things. They aren't materialists. They roam the land in caravans like tribes of Indians."

She says what she says every Halloween, "you go as your soul, who you really are." Gae and I are really Gypsies, anyone can see this.

I take half my beads from my neck and put them around hers. How beautiful her taut tan neck. "I love you." Her mother paints her face. Mrs. Walker knows how to put on makeup. "You are more beautiful than any movie star that ever existed."

Halloween is on Monday night this year. We start trick or treating Friday night. Four nights! Bridget and Dotty are both Gypsies too. Through the night we traipse, Gae and I side by side behind our veils, our jingly costumes, me on the lookout for the soul of my murdered Great Uncle Fred.

Bridget's candy lasts a lot longer than mine, I don't know how she stands it. All the way past Christmas she's pulling out a Three Musketeers from the crumpled sack under her bed, slowly unwrapping it, licking and slurping. I long for a bite, but long ago I learned I must never, not ever, ask her.

I can't stand lima beans. Lima beans stuff up my throat, my stopped-up throat my big problem anyway. They make me gag, throw up. I hate throwing up. Once a week now, since Mama came home, we have lima beans for our vegetable on Thursdays with liver. I explain my throat, I beg to no avail. When I gag, Daddy yanks me out of the chair, drags me to the bedroom, throws me in, slams the door, then returns with my plate of lima beans. "You will not come out of this room until you've eaten every single bean." There are only five or six, but they are big, bigger than my throat.

Then I'm a prisoner in the cold, darkening bedroom, the plate of cold limas sitting on my yellow toy box. The very air of the room feels to my breathing heart and lungs unfair, each breath like I'm being double-crossed. The first time this happened I dropped them out the window with the plan of retrieving them in the morning, then losing them on the way to school, but then this made me as sick as trying to get them down. He always accuses me of lying and deceiving, if he finds my lima beans out the window no amount of switching could meet the pain of the proof: I really am a liar, a cheater.

Eventually I manage to swallow each bean whole the instant I put it in my mouth by washing it down fast with milk before the taste gets too strong. The gag reflex happens after every swallow, along with breaking out in perspiration, and it's awhile before I can consider the next one. Eventually I manage to swallow them whole at the dinner table.

One Thursday I have only one more to go when suddenly there are four on my plate. "Bridget, you put your lima beans on my plate." She starts crying "I did not I did not" and Mama says "Sharon! How could you say such a thing about your little sister? Bridget Colleen is not that kind of person." I'm sent to the bedroom to finish her lima beans. Forgive me Jesus, if I falsely accused her—but where else would they have come from? Forgive her Jesus if she did it, she's not really that kind of person.

Avocados and pumpkin pie and shrimp and jelly hole sugar glazed donuts. My favorite foods are Daddy's favorite foods. On the day they met he told

Mama he wanted to take her to California where they eat alligator pears and tacos, things she'd never heard of.

He got the jar of green chili peppers from Dee Rupp. He wraps one in a piece of Langendorf's white, takes a bite. "Mmmm good," he says to me, his eyes flashing across the table to mine. I can tell by his glee that something's up, habeñeros, jalapeños, anaheims, he's even talking Spanish. I accept the green pepper sandwich he makes just for me, take a bite from the worm shaped thing, and though the sour tang is immediate and unlike anything I've ever tasted, definitely not good, I'm totally unprepared for the burning to get worse, and worse. The fumes choke me, my throat closes so I can't breathe. I cough, burp, break out in sweat. Soon I'm actually crying. He laughs until the tears come from his eyes too, "Sharon's such a crybaby."

Late that night in bed, the green pepper with the single bite out of it laying in its white bread wrap on my toy box, I turn over and my tongue accidentally wipes against my upper left arm. Maybe I'm even kissing myself. The juice from the bite of pepper must have squirted there. The stinging again to tears. And then I'm sobbing again, I can't help it though I'm trying more than anything not to let my sister hear me.

"Sharon Lu Lu is such a crybaby," Bridget says from the bed across the way, in Daddy's voice.

I'm looking for my skates in the garage. I didn't see him working at his counter in front of the new Ford sharpening the kitchen knives. "Pull up your tee shirt, Lu. Let me see." The yellow fingers of his left hand holds the cigarette, the yellow ones on his right hand trace over and over parts of my breasts. Smoke rises and rises from his mouth, of which mine is a duplicate.

She always says "Sharon's just like her father, she feels for the underdog like he does and that's what America is all about." "Clarence Darrow to the defense," Daddy teases. It's true, there is nothing more sickening than the feeling when I hear about something like slavery, or the Nazis, or the English having power over us, or when I see someone bullying someone else on the playground. I just don't understand how anyone can enjoy hurting anyone else. "You must have inherited this trait from your ancestors," Mama says. "The gene to feel compassion. You're related to the Founding Fathers."

I love the story of David defeating the giant Goliath with his slingshot, but then I feel sorry for Goliath. I feel sorry for David when he rapes Bathsheba but when he arranges to have her husband put at the front of the battle where he'll be killed I get upset. I want to protect him from the anger of the Lord who for his sin takes Bathsheba's baby when it's seven days old. But how can the Lord take an innocent baby? What about that baby? What about Bathsheba? Then David gets her pregnant again and that child is Solomon who knows the real mother by her giving up her baby rather than letting it be cut in two, and so like her I have to fight not to think something's wrong with the real Lord that he would take the baby. Like in the movies when I can't keep following the story line for worrying about every dead person, hey wait a minute, what about that dead person? That's a real person lying there dead on the ground you just shot and now are going on like nothing's happened. Like their death is nothing.

When the Santa Ana winds start blowing it feels like God celebrating our love. Desert hot, they pour over the high crest of the San Bernardinos, sweep down across the Basin to the Pacific, giving us so much energy we can't contain ourselves. Plus there's the energy of the approaching mid century mark. "Imagine: 1950!" Gae and I run all the streets holding hands. We can see every cream-colored boulder on the mountains, every twig of sage too. We can see Catalina huge beyond the purple drop-off line of the horizon so backed in light we wonder what's holding it up. We can see forever and we can see that it's true, everything is alive, pulsing, breathing, thinking. Even the rocks. We can see the end of the world, a shockingly clear, cloudless sky. Explosion of light! The whole world is a movie set, crystal clear. I go the longest time yet without hiccupping.

For our ride the day after Thanksgiving we find that beautiful street to eat our leftovers, the street we've been on before. The trees lining both sides arch over to each other, the branches intertwined, providing a thick canopy down the whole block. Mama loves this street, it's the perfect place on a hot day to have a picnic in the car.

One Sunday my parents say both Gae and Dotty can come for the ride with us. First they lecture us again about the importance of preserving the private sanctity of our family, to not let others in, but Grandma's not feeling well and Daddy's excited to show us something.

He drives us to one of the most incredible spots on Earth. He read about it in Ripley's *Believe It Or Not*. It was somewhere in Norwalk.

We pull up a steep incline, a two lane asphalt road that continues to curve around above us. Out the windows we can see all the land below. It rained recently so everything is green with new grass and orange and red geraniums and yellow and fuchsia ice plants everywhere. "This is the beginning of winter in Southern California," they say, "isn't it amazing that green means winter." We can almost see the ocean, maybe we do, with low scudding clouds marching south down the horizon to Mexico.

"Now watch this," Daddy says.

We're parked under an oak tree. The nose of the Ford is high in the windshield beyond Mama and Daddy. The five of us are slanted back in the backseat. Daddy turns off the engine, releases the brake. We can hear a mockingbird calling, the screech of gulls. A hawk sweeps down, hovers mid air, mid windshield.

It's slow at first, hardly detectable.

Then, we are rolling forward. We are rolling up.

We are rolling up the hill!

"Look, here's the key, look!" he says, "here's my legs, I'm not doing it."

"It's in Ripley's *Believe It or Not,*" Mama says.

"A magnetic attraction under the ground," Daddy says hitting the brakes.

"They're going to cut this hill down to make new houses," Mama says.

"Electromagnetism is the future of the universe!" Daddy quotes Dick Tracy and mimes looking at his watch. "This place is important. Who would ever believe it if they cut it down? That there's a hill you roll up against all the forces of gravity."

On the ride back Gae and I start planning a new dig. We've scratched little holes for China but this is serious. Something's alive under the ground. Yes yes, we say to Bridget, Clarke and Dotty, you can help, we need all the help we can get. To imagine they want to cut that hill down.

"Electromagnetism is the future of the universe," Bridget says, and says again and again after that.

For a while we went every Sunday, as part of our ride, to a place called Houston Meadows, in the bluegreen rolling hills east of Whittier. "Blue," Mama would say. "I was raised in the Blue Ridge Mountains of Virginia." She was looking for a new place for us to live, she was looking to better ourselves, to not stay in our allotted place, a Virginia concept she abhorred. There were ponds, lakes, and kids sledding down the steep, blue-green hills on cardboard just like the Christmas cards of kids back east sledding down white snow. The first time we went there we piled out of the back seat and slid down the oily slick grass tracks on our behinds. Daddy jumped out from behind the steering wheel and slid down on his bottom too. Oh, it was fun! Except for Mama crying up above about the grass stains on our panties and Daddy's and Clarke's slacks that will never come out. That night when we got home, our bottoms stained green, the four of us broke out in red welts. Daddy almost had to go to Emergency for his old war wounds acting up.

You buy an acre of Houston Meadows and build your own house on it. Mama talked Daddy into it, we'd get a loan on our house, make payments on the land, then build when we sold our house.

During the next week we rounded up cardboard boxes, broke them open, stacked them in the trunk. On Sunday, along with the other kids from who knows where, we raced down the steep, new grass slopes like it was snow while Mama and Daddy explored to find our acre. It was thrilling, and too beautiful to even imagine really living there.

But by the time we got home, all three of us were broken out in hives again. Mama soaked us in the tub and Daddy dabbed the huge pulsating welts with pink calamine lotion. Shaking her head that we had inherited her allergy to new grass, well, some grass, telling of the hives she once got from strawberries.

We had so many hives every Sunday night after playing in Houston Meadows that calamine lotion was wrecking the budget to buy the new place. One Sunday, maybe the last one, the three of us in the bathroom were solid hives, head to toe. They debated taking us to Emergency.

One of those Sundays, crashed at the bottom of the slope, gathering ourselves back up, Clarke attacked me. I don't remember why, just the surprise of him running at me with his head down and his small fists flying, and his legs kicking at mine. He was furious about something. I grabbed both wrists and held him out away from me and let him carry on, laughing to dispel his screams and sobs at me.

Then we learned from the real estate agent that Richard Nixon's brother, Dr. Nixon, had bought the acre next to the one we'd picked out, and Richard himself was showing interest in Houston Meadows. Dr. Nixon had two little girls, just like Dirty Dick. That's what Daddy called him, he hated Dick Nixon, but that wasn't the reason our mother nixed our plans.

"We would have to keep up with the Nixons. I can't do that to my children."

Later she learned that new, experimental chemicals were used to kill the native brush and grow that blue grass, that's why those hills looked so beautiful and unreal. That's why we got those awful hives. Maybe it was those chemicals that set off Clarke's anger. Maybe it was those chemicals that made Richard Nixon's evil grow worse.

It isn't something I dwell on, I force myself not to dwell on it—negative thinking attracts the negative—yet I know it's coming, it's always coming. I hate it. I hate it so much I'm afraid of my hatred. My heart pounds so hard beneath his hand I fear it reveals to him my hatred. I seek ways to avoid him, then white-out in the panic. When I'm cooking dinner and he's due home from work and Mama's gone somewhere I get Bridget and Clarke into the kitchen by not scraping the pudding bowl clean, letting them lick it, the spoon and the beaters. Then I feel guilty for the sin of manipulating them, for having ulterior motives. I work like crazy to act oblivious so that he won't understand my understanding. When he's doing it I'm in constant prayer, dear Jesus don't let him know how much I hate it. I go so far away I'm really with Gae in her house. Daddy can't help himself. He loves me. I feel so sorry for him. I'm the Blue Fairy Queen moving closer to him, resist not evil. I'm in the arms of Jesus, turn the other cheek. My soul to his thing. The sweat of his brow. His hairline is receding but it was in infancy. His high forehead, Grandma says, was the first thing everyone noticed when he was born. His widow's peak, Mama says, his face like a Valentine heart. Room for my big brain, our funny Valentine laughs. Cecil means blind and Frederick means ruler. "Edens," Mama always says, "like the Garden of Eden, but many." "Thank goodness he has his workroom," Grandma says. "He always has to be doing something with his hands," Mama says. "Sanding is his meditation."

When he's through sanding my chest my hiccups and stutter are worse. Gae always looks at me differently like she knows. But as I don't of her, she doesn't inquire. I don't think he ever raped me again, though in my years of notes and letters I often refer to two rapes. He confessed to one time, pleading in question, "There was only one time, right, Lu?"

Mama is at the kitchen sink looking south to that snowcapped mountain telling of the fall of Rome. Rome was the greatest civilization the world had ever known but in time its morality was lost. In morality's place grew corruption, decadence. Drunkenness. Debauchery. Homosexuality. She sips her coffee and says she's worried that this could happen to America, an even greater country than Rome.

"What's homosexuality?"

"Men taking men for their wives," she says over the steaming white suds dishwater. She says this in such a way that I am riveted to my seat behind the table in the corner. She says again that Daddy's ancestors were original Aristocrats of Virginia, Founders of America. Thomas Jefferson's father, Peter, was our family lawyer, he surveyed the Hancock's land next to Monticello. We have a responsibility to this country, she says so sternly. Grandma always says "Don't ever forget. A Hancock married a Corn— Jesse Corn, my great-great-grandfather, was a Revolutionary War hero, he lost his leg at Valley Forge—a Corn married a Chitwood, a Chitwood married an Edens." You have a responsibility.

He's returning home from Douglas, he's coming up the winding walk swinging his black lunch pail with the silver silhouettes of the pony tailed girl on both ends, her knees drawn up under her chin. Mama is watching him with her Third Eye. Maybe he's a little drunk. She is deep there at the sink, I'm at the back corner doing my stupid Dick and Jane homework, he's tired, he's trapped. If he's drunk, if ever my father was drunk in my whole life, this is the only time I ever knew it. If he's drunk, just a little tipsy, he's a happy drunk. He's as light as she is dark in soberness. He's coming home from the Army. He's staggering home from the Christmas party. The point is he's coming home. She wasn't sure. I don't know what she feels, just that she's watching him, he's tickled, he's laughing. He wants her to let him back in. She's trying to figure this and the fall of Rome. I float over the kitchen floor to her, then out the window to him, from her belly to his, wanting them together as in that moment they made me. I want to live.

He's permanent now with Douglas, a plastics experimental man, things are a little easier now, we have enough to eat, enough for a few luxuries. And he has come home, our breadwinner!

But any time such a bargain is struck, as many have observed about capitalism, as my mother did constantly in her roundabout way, of trying to figure how to survive, the past, the present and the future, the breadwinner is going to feel he has certain inalienable rights with those for whom he sacrifices himself. It's called buying. It's called property. It's called profit. I always knew it was partly Douglas' fault.

And if he was homosexual, which may be why this moment is riveted into my psyche, her words confirming what I knew on a nonverbal level, he was a happy homosexual (actually I think he was pan-sexual). It's the taboo, the shame, the deceit, the distortions, the secrets, the oppressions and violations, the fascisms that civilizations are built on, that we are all built on, however conscious (mostly unconscious), that cause the fall, not love. Not ever love. I always knew this too.

Because now we open our presents to each other on Christmas Eve we have to plan our shopping in advance. I've saved my allowance almost the entire year. I've thought about everyone on my list, what they might want, what I can afford, but I've known from my first Christmas thought my gift for Gae. It was in the Hollydale dime store. A 2B lead drawing pencil, a block gum eraser, a tablet of real drawing paper, and the book *How to Draw The Horse.*

Friday night is our annual Sunday School Christmas party. Afterwards, I'm standing on the church steps with the little box of hard candy they give us each year. The Three Wise Men are on their camels following the star from the East, a white string handle holds them to my hand. I'm wearing my Santa pin, the most perfect Santa Claus. I'm wearing my gold Mickey Mouse pin and my Mickey Mouse watch. I have on my white socks with teenie Mickey Mouses embroidered on the turned-down cuffs clinging to my big-boned ankles in my black patent leathers. It's the week before the mid-point of the twentieth century. Why am I standing there on the cement steps? It is dark, it is cold, everyone has left. I don't want to go home. I'm as deeply stuck there as my Telephone Pole is, to whom I am praying. If I could cry, I would, to him, my pole, my power.

We're in our pajamas, we've opened all our presents to each other. Suddenly, as if startled, my mother is looking at me. She's worried about me. I don't need for her to worry about me, that's the last thing she or I need. Maybe Daddy has said something or looked at me or just rearranged his thing in his slacks and she caught it. Or suspected she did. Do I still believe in Santa Claus? Did I ever? It's conceivable that this is what she's concerned about. Her strange sudden concern. I'm leaning against the hallway door corner, too big as always, watching Bridget and Clarke revel in their presents. She's sitting in the chair just inside from the kitchen, looking at me, I see her seeing me, seeing me strange and sad. I let her look. She conjures up another present for me from her hidden Santa Claus stash, as if my sad paralysis must be about not enough presents. It's a new package of seven pastel-colored, silky panties, the days of the week embroidered at the top of the right leg. Daddy scoffs "Sharon's looking for attention again," but Mama says "Actually Sharon has a hard time receiving attention." Mama's attention to me is my very best Christmas present ever.

Christmas morning we have waffle torture. Daddy makes them, the only day of the year he cooks. It takes forever, mainly oiling the thing, all the burnt no-goods that go before, each waffle one at a time in the steaming waffle iron that stays all the rest of the year in the linen closet. I try to soothe Bridget and Clarke behind the closed hallway door, banging and screaming to get out to the presents. Mama and Daddy are in the kitchen giggling, enjoying themselves. She has to put him first. This is only right, his check bought this day. Finally Daddy comes back to the dark closed-off hall where we're going crazy, blindfolds each of us with dish towels. We are walked through the living room past the tree in the dining room, into the kitchen, where we have to eat our waffles first.

Daddy just loves to torture us. "Such a big teaser he is," Mama says.

"Watch this, kids," he roars as he lowers the waffle lid. He kisses her on the neck. She squeals and the goosebumps break out on her arms.

There's so many presents under the tree we can't believe it. We get rubber galoshes for the Hollydale floods. Every winter when it rains Industrial flows like a river, the Rio Hondo into the LA, and we spend hours, days, wading the current. (Probably my worms came from the Hollydale River, as Daddy calls it, the sewers overflowing.) The high wading boots will make it safe play.

And we get stilts. Daddy made them out of heavy boards, with triangle side places for our feet. They're painted two-tone enamel green and pink.

It takes us awhile to learn but by afternoon we are stilting down Roosevelt to Gae's house. Daddy says "Darn, maybe I better make Gae a pair of stilts." And he does. All Christmas afternoon he's in and out of the garage making my best girlfriend a pair of stilts so she and I can stilt together.

It takes a day, being winter, for the paint to dry, but then my wonderful father presents Gae with her stilts. By the end of the week we've learned to walk on stilts so well we can run, we can dance, we do the jig. We meet on them to practice the Pig Latin that I've learned from Mrs. Ritchie. We sway in circles around each other. "I ovelay ouyay!" We walk backwards. We prance, a breeze. We prance around the block. We start skipping. My hernia doesn't even hurt. We learn skip-to-my-lu on stilts. To learn the trick, it's just a trick, is the trick to everything. To be so tall above everything is a trick too. That's what Einstein said. He said to solve a problem rise above it.

Dec 23, 1949- I dreamed a sad dream of Avon and home in Ducktown, of some of our children and Mr. Brewer.

Dec 31, 1949- I dreamed of Avon last night, and Sharon and our home in Afton. Lovely day.

Did her dreams ever tell her that her son liked to take his thing out of his pants and have me look at it? Were they ever a replay of the brutal times with Avon in their Ducktown homes?

Daddy loves his thing, he strokes it just like the men in the bushes. "Isn't it nice, Sharon Lu?" He's so interested in it. I try to pretend I'm interested in it too, that it's nice.

When I think there's an earthquake I look to Patsy's eyes to see if they're rolling. She sits on the green enamel-painted dresser and watches the door, her straight black lashes cast out over her hazel green eyes, her small pursed lips. If he comes back in the middle of the night she will be my witness. I'm certain he never does because I pray so hard. My fear, my dread, my prayers protect me.

Mama says how perfect, the first day of the second half of the twentieth century lands on a Sunday. She says think of one thing to remember each year by. That way you won't lose a single year. Think about what you're going to remember for 1949.

Mid afternoon, waiting around to go to the cemetery, Bridget and I take to the swings in the backyard. When we are up over the Wilson backyards, we shout at the top of our lungs, "It's…." Then we come swinging and screaming in unison down and then up over Industrial and the church all the way to Long Beach. "…1950! It's 1950!" We shout it over and over to all the world. "It's 1950!"

The Los Angeles Times spreads out like the world and my mother's vast wisdom on the kitchen table. She's proud of her black elbows, proof that she reads the newspaper just like Avon, Daddy's Pa. Do you realize Grandma was the reporter for the Chattanooga, the Knoxville and Copperhill papers? she says and says. During the Scopes Trial, the strikes, Huey Long's corrupt reign, and all the murders this was important reporting. Polk County Tennessee had more murders than any place in the country for its size, *LIFE* Magazine said; they called it lawless. My grandmother seems so still, so dull, so unthinking, so slow and depressed, it is hard to imagine she knows anything of the modern world except the Bible. "I'm afraid she's going into her second childhood," Mama says, "but I think Sharon you might have inherited her talent for writing."

Reading the newspaper was for my mother an act of loving the world. It was her education and proof of her intelligence. It was greatness of soul. There was no acknowledging that much of the news was awful. No acknowledging what I was tripping over, that every day in every newspaper there was at least one girl raped and murdered. Every day girls stuffed in car trunks, thrown out on the sides of roads, stashed up the canyons, tossed in trashcans on the beaches. Every single day their bodies found in backyards, under houses, down wells, raped, beaten, murdered, dismembered, tortured. And grown women too. But no one, not even my mother, seemed to think this was unusual or noteworthy. No explanations or editorials as with other news like homosexuality, Communism, smog, or Korea. If you are a girl who wants to grow up to be a well-adjusted woman you are not to notice this, to be concerned about it in any way except to make sure you don't let it happen to you.

Caryl Chessman was found guilty over a year ago but the debate about capital punishment is fiercer than ever. He didn't kill anyone. He just sodomized the girls he found making out on Lover's Lane, made their dates watch. I know the story of Sodom and Gomorrah now, Lot's daughters seduced the poor man sleeping in the cave to preserve his seed, but I'm still not sure what sodomize means. Even if he had killed those girls how can people debate whether he should be killed or not? *Thou shalt not kill.* It's the Sixth Commandment. In our family Daddy leads the debate, like Clarence Darrow for the defense.

It took me and Gae awhile to realize that the tracks that cross Paramount at the crossing guard intersection must be the same tracks that cross diagonally through Hollydale. We figured and figured this to be sure. What if we went down them going home from school and they led us to an unknown place and we couldn't get back before dark? We scanned down the side streets. We made maps in our heads.

Then we do it, our first walk home from school as hobos. I wanted to grow up and be a hobo with Daddy. Now Gae and I are hobos, jumping trains, walking the world.

We make it! We come down into Hollydale Park. We stop in the store and buy dill pickles from the barrel. We love dill pickles and they stop my hiccups. We get to her house. Her grandparents and her mother are playing poker in the dining room they call their card room. We can hear the click of the chips before we get inside. We walk in slurping our pickles, our great but secret accomplishment written all over us. They stare at us knowing something's up. Cat got your tongue? Where you two been?

We're both being sexed by our fathers but as close as we are, as passionate and verbal as we are about our love, we don't speak of this. It is not possible to put "that business," as she calls it now, into words. But we walk the tracks when things are especially bad, when one or both of us signals it's time. We know how dangerous this is, we know we are taking our lives in our own hands, but what else is news? Our lives are in greatest danger at home. Sometimes we go the whole mile balanced either side on the steel rails, our hands out-stretched and touching, over the hobos and escapees down there drinking in the bushes, undoing their pants when they see us, two crazy Tomboys, coming down the track. "Girls, lookie here!"

Mama's driving. Gae gets to come with us. We're on our way to her twice-a-week induced pneumotherapy. We're pulled up to a light in downtown Compton and the nun is standing there, completely covered in black from head to foot in the hundred and ten degrees, in light so blasting you think the Bomb must have hit.

Nuns. We will grow up to be nuns. There is nothing as mysterious or holy-seeming as the women inside those black head-to-foot tents.

But I don't want to be a Catholic. "Jesus didn't worship in places like a Catholic Cathedral," Grandma says. "He certainly wasn't a Catholic."

We're at the Lakewood Drive-In watching a birth scene in which the doctor's dilemma is who to save, the mother or the baby. He's in love with the mother but Catholic doctrine says the baby's life must come first. He'll go to Eternal Hell if he disobeys. Funny, how in the movies the church is always the Catholic Church, never my church. Daddy's deploring, Mama on her side of the Ford agreeing, about the Catholics who believe a mother's life is less important than the baby's. Catholics think the whole point of getting born is just to get your soul saved so you can go to heaven for Eternity, this life not being important. Mama almost died with each of our births. The baby is just beginning. Of course the mother is the most important one.

Then Daddy is telling about the prettiest girl in Ducktown, how she hung herself because she was pregnant and not married. "That wasn't right, you know?" he says, in his deep wise God tone, a voice of reflection, compassionate wisdom. "The guy should have been held responsible too. You know?"

"Boys just have to sow their wild oats," Mama sighs sympathetically.

I always took this conversation as an example of the side of my father that was wise and generous, even feminist, but now I hear the other message. He was telling her and us that we aren't as important as she. He was pitting us against each other. He was jealous of us when we were born.

I love the dark meat of the chicken. My throat gets stopped up with the white meat so dry. Mama says her Grandmother Simmons always said she'll take the last piece over the fence. Her grandmother really didn't eat any chicken so all the children and men would have enough. She made it seem like it was the chicken's fault for not having enough parts, never that they were that poor. I love most of all the drumstick, then the neck. Daddy doesn't believe me, says I'm just being contrary, everyone knows the white meat's best. He throws the neck on my plate. We brought home this year's batch in the trunk of the new Ford. Tiny yellow cute little peepers we're going to eat when they grow up and he wrings their necks. Trying to taste which chicken it is today. Gae and I spend lots of time on the roof of the chicken coop spying on the four black-haired Beaver boys. They are the wildest, naughtiest boys we know. Now I think they were Indians.

Trying to taste the chicken, both the hen and the mean rooster, in my morning poached egg. Thinking about Daddy's favorite theory, the Theory of Evolution.

"Pull your shoulders back, girl!" Mr. Walker yells. In my mind I see him draw his gun.

The horror, the mortification of the endless belch.

Once I borrowed one of Mama's handkerchiefs without asking, pretty and lacey with her hand embroidery. I loved it so much even though I knew it must have TB germs and my sin for taking it. I washed it in the bathroom sink with the bar of soap, hung it in our closet to dry in the back where I prayed she wouldn't find it, ironed it when she had the ironing board down and wasn't looking and then snuck it back into her top drawer.

Gae and I scoot around the neighborhood on our butts. Butt's a four letter word, better say bottom. We organize bottom races with the other kids. Going down Roosevelt on our bottoms till there's holes in our shorts and worms crawling inside us again.

We master double-dutch jumprope. Now there's expertise.

She loves peppermint patties. Therefore so do I. She bites into her patty in ecstasy. I want to be inside her mouth.

Mama calling me home. "Shar-ron.... Shar-ron Lurrr-ra.... Time to come home..."

I drink in one long last look of her to last me through the long awful night.

She shows me how she breaks the packages of cookies at the little store, takes one, just one, from each. She has this down by the time she shows me where the cookies are coming from. Down the row we go, she slicing the cellophane with her long index nail, sneaking one for me and one for her. I'm beside myself with horror, fear, confusion, protective feelings of her, maybe even the fear that she's going to hell, that she really is a thief like with the badge, thou shalt not steal is the Eighth Commandment, but for a long while I go along with her, pretending to be as thrilled as she is by the accomplishment, and to love the strange cookie, a different kind every time, kinds I've never had before. I can't tell her I don't want to do it, she'll know I know it's wrong, she'll think I think she's bad, she'll think I don't love her, and Jesus said don't judge. But I die at the counter with the owner. Every evening just before dinner I go get our Langendorf's Bread and as I pass the broken packages still on the shelf I die again. Once, eating our stolen cookies, we passed my mother on her way up Industrial to shop at the little store. My panic, trying to hide my cookie in the folds of my dress was like waiting for Daddy at night. I heard Mr. Walker talking about lie detectors. What about stuttering and hiccups and your heart pounding, and breaking out in sweat, the machine thinking you're guilty when you're not? Or am I?

Finally I tell my parents. It feels awful to snitch on Gae but I can hardly breathe. Daddy and the shoplifting are all I can think about but in no way can I acknowledge what Daddy does. I tell about the shoplifting for the relief, I just know the way the owner looks at us when we come in together it's only a matter of time before we're caught—I'm going to hiccup while she's doing it, I'm going to faint dead away in the aisle.

"Please, please don't let Gae know I told on her. She just doesn't know better. She doesn't go to Sunday School."

They're most horrified that I went along with her into crime because I don't know how to say no. They lecture me again on having the strength of my convictions. Your Civil War great-great-grandfather, John Chitwood, stood up for what he believed, fought for the North even though it cost him everything including his wife and children. They're particularly concerned what this character weakness will mean when I start dating boys. But Mama assures me, in a lecture about white lies, of knowing when it's good to lie, that Gae will never know that I told on her.

I never knew what was done but our shoplifting stopped.

Where the bullet goes. My left collar bone, my right rib. Both upper thighs. My buttocks. We're at the drive-in. The bullets riddle the man, he's dead and I'm dead too on the battleground.

On my father's thirty-fourth birthday I'm tied face down up under the engine of the train. It races down the tracks through Hollydale, me managing for awhile to dodge each tie. Then it's over.

Being ground under. Plowed under, that horrible train rhythm, chuga-chuga-chuga.

On my mother's thirtieth birthday, I can't help it, I start crying. She's old now. Even at the end, on her seventy-eighth birthday, she told how I cried on her thirtieth birthday and how much it hurt her. I just didn't want her to ever die.

There's a photo taken *"Easter Sunday, April 10, 1950."* In my Easter dress she made, lavender see-through, bordered in white lace, my shoulders are bowed around my front, my hands grip the lavender organdy, the petticoat beneath. My head hanging like a sunflower on its stalk. I was in the garage with Daddy again. I had to show him again. Hard to get my Easter dress down off my shoulders. Here let me help you Sharon Lura. With his giant fingers he undid the mother-of-pearl buttons Mama sewed down the back, pulled down the slip strap. They are so beautiful he said. He said you want to see something as beautiful? His skin was electric silver like the knife he was sharpening. They just think I'm an introvert, that's why I am the way I am. But I'm coming apart, dust particles floating in space. Every breath, every move is to keep the spiders from crawling up my insides.

On my ninth birthday, Grandma's seventieth, I receive a white leather Holy Bible with my name embossed in gold in the right hand corner. *In healing the man with the speech impediment Jesus took him aside from the multitude and put his fingers in his ears. And he spit and touched his tongue.*

There's another present for me in the garage. I dread the garage where Daddy traps me. But today when I open the door and turn on the light, in

the middle of the dark cool space, just like Swan long ago, tilted
magnificently on its kickstand, is a shiny blue, silver and white Schwinn
bicycle, just like the one Gae received for her birthday.

We bike all the streets. We bike to Hollydale. We bike to the County
Farm. The men in the bushes aim their piss at us but miss, reach out to
grab us cussing but they can't catch us.

"Yodeley yodeley.... Yodeley hey hoo!" we warble up echo-y
Roosevelt. I don't stutter when I yodel either. "Yodeley yodeley yodeley
hey hoo!" moseying along Gardendale, looking for 1943 lead pennies
beneath our tires. Mama keeps saying to keep an eye out for them.
Someday they're going to be worth something. That year my sister was
born and all the copper had to go for tanks and guns.

Her face alongside mine as we travel is extraordinary. Blood sister.
We will grow tails, manes, we will sprout wings.

"He he hey ga ga Gae...."

"Hey Sharon."

"Uno dos tres quatro cinco seis." I don't stutter when I count in
Spanish either.

"Fourteen karats."

"Pure gold."

"I love you."

"Siete ocho nueve diez."

"Touché."

When it's really hot and we can use the shade we often end up on that
street somewhere above Pasadena having our picnic in the car. Mama just
loves these blooming canopy trees. Could they have been jacarandas?

Bridget starts screaming that I took a popcorn from her. I didn't. I don't
know how her popcorn ended up in my purse but I'm sorry, she's just
mistaken, and tell her so. She just gets madder. As we come back down
the new Pasadena Freeway I try not to see the stupid look from the
cartoons on her face in Daddy's rearview conniving her next plot against
me.

*April 30, 1950 - Moved to Cecil's apt in evening. C & Audrey had
everything nice in readiness for me. It is good to be home again. I was at
Rosewood Lodge 16 months—1 yr, 4 mos + 10 days.*

We'd been trying for months, every time there was a vacancy, to
get Grandma to move into the apartments but she was too sick and

depressed. Grandpa died and her brother was murdered, slandered a drunk and killer himself, her homesick heart for Tennessee can hardly stand it. When your heart starts failing all your systems do. But Mama knows it's important to get her near family, to get her away from that awful rest home. She gets the center triplex. We shop for furniture, finding an ice box in a used store, which she prefers to a refrigerator. There's still an ice man in the yellow pages, an answer to her prayers. We move in her big black trunk. On the first day we're standing on the porch outside. She gestures down Industrial to the church.

"When your daddy was a boy he could swim that far under water."

When he was fourteen his Pa took him by train to spend the summer with his sister on Beech Hill, outside of Lynchburg. On the return trip to Ducktown they were going to see the ocean first. Cecil was a championship swimmer but she made Avon bring him home to Ducktown because she was afraid he'd fall in.

"Oh, Grandma, you can't fall into the ocean, not from the shore!"

She laughs, like she knows that now, like she's a little happy now. She doesn't say his best friend, the son of her best friend, had just drowned.

I'll never walk up Industrial to the church again without knowing Daddy swimming like a fish at my heels, under the pavement, unseen by anyone but me.

Recently I was in Winchester, Tennessee doing research. A second cousin told me of "our strange cousin who never married." It felt like he was trying to tell me something. He gave me a photo of Daddy and the strange cousin standing together, shoulder to shoulder, behind all the others. Summer 1930.

May 28, 1950 – I was home all day except walked out to Frederick's. (He wants to be called Fred.) He went fishing! I grow worse gradually. Suffer so.

I put on my red coat with the hood. Out the door, across the porch, down the steps, down the S-curving walk, around the corner I go to Grandma's house.

Along the way the wolf appears, frightening me to death. Somehow I make it to her door and she reads the Bible to me. Then suddenly I see that she's really Daddy. I die of fright.

But I don't want the man with the ax to come along and chop my father open, not even to free me inside. I don't want him to die. The chop would kill us both. I want us both to live.

Going under the butterfly wings of my mother's hips, our house, to my bloody pajamas.

It was the nightmare worm going into that sleep of death with Daddy, coming out the butterfly of Gae.

§

Fifteen

Gae's parents zoom up in their yellow convertible, the top down. Mrs. Walker, snuggled up to Mr. Walker, is wearing a pink and black polkadotted French Bikini, named for the island where we test the A-bomb.

Gae and Dotty jump in, Gae begging "Can Sharon come?"

"Can Sharon come?" Mr. Walker calls to my parents working in the yard. His perfect white teeth flash to my mother, his sunbleached curls above the Camel drooping from his lips, the smoke rising in his black sunglasses. He so scares me.

"Wednesday morning," Mama answers, "all three of my children are going in the hospital to have their tonsils out. Sharon Lura must not get overly tired or cold."

I run inside, grab my bathing suit, jump in the back. Bridget and Dotty are both crying that Bridget doesn't get to go. Last night she hissed across the room "Sharon Lulu, I have often wished you were dead."

We descend El Camino Real with the heavy weekend traffic, the wind in our hair, Mrs. Walker's like straw on fire. Mr. Walker keeps changing the radio station trying to find some jazz but all the stations want to talk about is Korea. I love Laguna with its narrow windy streets up the high bluffs and ornate sand buildings with red tile roofs, "like the French Riviera," Mrs. Walker says. There's a line of people waiting to see the matinee. **Korea!** is the headline on every street corner, Korea is all the papers, newsreels, radios and televisions have been talking about for weeks. Daddy says "Watch out, we're going to war again." Mama scolds him not to think so negatively. My parents are so different from Gae's. The curves of Highway One. The curving crashing waves. "The curves of Mrs. Walker," Mr. Walker laughs, slapping the inside of her thigh. "The curves of my beautiful little girls."

Portions of the little beach beneath the cliff are long slabs of flat rock. Friends of the Walkers are down here, a man and a woman with a little girl Dotty's age. She must be the reason they didn't invite Bridget. Mrs. Walker spreads out our blankets beside theirs on the sand part, pulls out the beers. Gae and I run to the surf. The men go into the ocean, disappear with their spear fishing gear. Mrs. Walker calls us back before we get our hair wet, poses us before the Laguna rock arch, takes our picture.

The sun is setting on the horizon. We've been in the surf all afternoon, the tons of water moving against us. It's hard to walk out straight, the ocean feels inside us as if our bloodstreams are the pounding tide.

"Time to change, Sharon, you have to go to the hospital next week."

Mr. Walker comes with his towel, starts drying me.

"No thank you, I can dry myself."

He's just staring, big-eyed.

"You're getting goose bumps girl."

I look down, my skin is blue next to his glistening brown.

"Sharon Edens," Mrs. Walker says, "we must get that wet suit off of you right this minute. I promised your mother."

"Sharon's not a nudist, Mother," Gae says. "We have to make a cover for her."

She gives one end of the beach towel to her mother, the other to the other woman. Then she and Dotty hold up another around me making a little cabana. Mr. Walker and the other man are lying on the blanket just beyond and beneath, staring.

"Poor hick of a girl, no one cares what you look like."

Then the women's towel comes down, like a curtain on a stage, and I'm completely naked before the men. Mr. Walker says here I'll show you how we do it, and off come his skintight wet trunks. He gets up, is standing in front of me again. We are both naked facing each other, his thing bobbing high in the air. Gae yanks the towel from her sister, throws it to me. Mrs. Walker slaps her across the face but even so she runs to my front, shields me with her small self. The other man is staring, just staring.

Mr. Walker snaps his sweat shirt around his daughter to my thighs. Then Mrs. Walker puts it over my head, and bringing it down brings her hands over my breasts, then down on my swollen hernia.

I have two photographs from that day. (I think others were taken when the towel came down.) Gae and I are eight and nine. In one we look our age, we are little girls playing. We're standing before the famous Laguna Beach arch, pretending to be bathing suit beauties with our left wrists turned back on our hips, and our right ones behind our heads. We're posing like the naked women on our fathers' playing cards, like the girl in the 1949 calendar hanging in both our garages. Painted hussies. Glamour pusses. The way my legs are bent is partly because I'm trying to be shorter to her. The way my back is arched and thrust is more telling of my long Irish torso than of anything else. There's a shadow, maybe a wet spot, at Gae's crotch where a wave splashed. My silver-blue rear end seems to be wet too, though maybe it's the material, the way its gathered across it, the shadow of light and film.

In the other one we've got our act down. We're lying in the sand on our sides in front of the arch. You can see my little breasts pooching over the blue top. There's triumph in Gae's face, the bravado I so loved about her. I can feel my right hand partially buried in the hot sand. We look, genuinely, sexual.

What was happening to us was unspeakable, without language, unthinkable, a total taboo, yet everyday. On some level we did communicate all of it to each other.

We didn't speak of our changing bodies either. This is life, how you grow up.

On Wednesday, June 7, we had our tonsils out.

Waking up to the pain, the knife slice around the inside of the throat. It hurts, unbelievably. Each hiccup a lasting torture like nothing I could ever describe. I will never talk again, not ever, not a single word.

"You had your adenoids cut out too."

"What are adenoids?"

"They thought the removal might help your hiccups."

That they can do things to the inside of you without your knowing. (Is the cause of hiccups.)

June 10, 1950: Fred & Audrey got a T.V. set on trial for the children. They are restless from tonsillectomy.

The Korean War started when the Communists smashed across the 38th Parallel to attack the Republic of Korea. They captured Seoul, the South's capital. I began to pray for Korea.

Mama figured out how all five of us could sleep in the 1949 Ford. She had Daddy rig a way that the clutch, brake and gas pedal could be flattened to the floor. Sofa cushions were fitted to either side of the hump, then a pad over that, making a bed for her. Daddy had the front seat. When he needed to stretch out and it was safe to do so, he could open the door. Bridget had the back floor, with padding also to overcome the hump. Clarke slept in the shelf of the back window, he was still that small, and I had the back seat, the most comfortable bed, Daddy grumbled every night after we were bedded down.

She figured out how we could stretch Daddy's two week vacation into three. The Fourth of July holiday fell that year on Thursday and Friday. He took off the first three days of that week as paid sick leave. They were so excited, their first trip back to the South since they left.

Waving goodbye to Grandma I fight back the thought she could die before we get back. Waving goodbye to Gae I fight back tears.

We drive east all night, waterbags hanging off the bumpers, to get across the desert before the sun rises. Route 66 to San Bernardino, north to Barstow, then northeast to Baker, skirting Death Valley. Mama instructs about the Colorado River, how far away it starts, a little trickle high in the Rockies, and about the Continental Divide. Soon everyone's asleep but me and Daddy.

"You think too much Sharon," he sneers, his eyes catching mine in the rearview.

The hot night crosswinds from the open windows feel like they're blasting the skin off my face.

"See that shimmering water at the end of the highway?" he says as the sun is rising north of Las Vegas. It's a big river flowing across where it dips down. It's there right up until we're practically in it, then it disappears. "Mirages caused the thirsty pioneers to lose their minds. Mirages are what your mind's full of, right, Sharon Lu?"

To try and not think I memorize our routes like I memorize the books of the Bible. At times it feels like my brain is dissolving in the gray-green sagebrush.

"Tell us stories of when you were a boy, Daddy!" The words just fly out of me like hope as we start climbing the Rockies. Mama has so many fantastic stories of when she was a girl I worry nothing has ever happened to me, whatever will I tell my children?

"I can't remember," he snaps, his big heart-shaped head bitter against the highway.

Then he sneers again "You think too much Sharon."

Because of her pneumothorax therapy Mama's taking a big chance crossing the Rockies. The doctors warned her that she wouldn't be able to breathe, the oxygen content being only a third of what it is at sea level. But she's not going to let that stop her. More than anything she wants to cross the Rockies. She's thinking positive. She's holding her wrist, counting her pulse.

Suddenly she's gasping she wants to die. We're on a two lane road, going higher and higher. Daddy pulls over, slams to a stop. She just wants to heave herself over the twelve thousand foot edge. She falls out the door, heads for it, bent over, gasping for air, vomiting. "Go on! Just go on without me."

Daddy is screaming at the three of us in the back seat to shut up, quit crying, get out and go to the bathroom. We get out in our shorts and sandals sinking deep in the snow. Daddy is over there with her. Did she see the way he was looking at me? Is that why she's throwing up? Someone—it could only have been my father—took a picture of her that day, squatted low and dark on the mountain edge, throwing up.

"All I wanted was for you four to leave me there so I could lie down and die in peace."

She was feeling better by the time we got to Berthoud Pass, elevation, 11,314 feet. She loves the land; the land revives her. We straddle the Continental Divide, an exact line down the curve of the earth, wet in it thinking about the word watershed. All the water that falls on this side of the Divide eventually flows to the Pacific Ocean and all the water that falls on that side of the Divide flows to the Atlantic Ocean. I'll spend the rest of the trip trying to figure the Continental Divide, wondering if we've caught up with our wet yet. (Mama forbids our saying pee.) She took the photo of Clarke and me in the snow at Berthoud Pass, both of us in shorts and sandals. And the sign *Watershed*.

Right then, right after the snap, right on the Continental Divide, Clarke's beatific countenance does an about-face, and he attacks me again, like he did at Houston Meadows. He comes running with his little pounding fists, his anger so great the tears are spurting sideways out both eyes. I put my arm out, save him from the edge, the Frazer River way down there, and myself too. He starts pummeling me with his fists like stinging bees driving into my stomach. To hold him back I get both his arms and then, to counter his continuing rage, begin to twist them, laughing like Daddy.

We descend to Denver. Mama seems mad at all of us, brooding about something. Maybe it's just something between them, maybe just an ordinary marital spat, but she's brooding. And that's good to finally get. Does she see him looking at me? Yes, she'll say at the end, she did. Even when I was very little she saw him looking at me inappropriately. Maybe even little Clarke saw it. But only now do I see that my father intentionally used his attraction to me against her.

Dear Ma, We are in Denver. Will spend the night near. The altitude didn't bother me at all. Love Audrey.

Mama and her little white lies.

We're crossing Nebraska. We're on our way to Chicago, Daddy singing *"Sioux City Sue. Your hair is red, your eyes are blue."* He laughs and squirms behind the wheel, adjusts his penis in his pants and is not mad. *"I'll swap my horse and dog for you."* Did he just have a beer? Mama stares out onto the land. We go along the shallow, light-shimmering Platte River all day to Omaha, to Council Bluffs, and she's revived. She loves the Platte more than any other river because it's so wide and gentle.

They have a fight. They fight the whole way. She puts words in his mouth. He twists hers. He knows what he's doing but he repeats her words like he doesn't know what she's saying, little jeers that completely change the meaning.

Bridget takes Daddy's side. It flabbergasts me but at least someone's on his side.

"She's a woman, she's smarter than him, everyone knows women are smarter than men, she should know better than to fall into his trap." Then she attacks her fingernails until they're bleeding again.

When Daddy's eyes catch mine in the rearview fear shoots through like Nebraska lightning.

He picks on Clarke the whole way too. "Baby! Sissy! Girl!"

"You have to love your father," she says when we take our last wet of the day. "You have to," she says from the front floor over him on the front seat to us in the back.

We visited Uncle K.D., Aunt Alice and Billie and Shirlie at The Great Lakes U.S. Naval Base north of Chicago. Uncle K.D.'s temper was even worse than Daddy's. It's not so much memory, or images, just the sense, and this could be more from the atmosphere of a military base than from anything that happened. Order. Uniforms. Rules. Orders. Everything in straight lines. You feel like you're messing up the place just by being in it. Even famous Lake Michigan out the window was orderly and gray, little regular waves coming in, so different from the wild Pacific. I almost remember Aunt Alice. Maybe they had a fight. Maybe I saw him treat her the way his little brother treats my mother. He was preparing to ship out to Korea. Mama worried that Alice didn't love him enough. She chainsmoked and had been married before, to Billie and Shirlie's real father. Billie and Shirlie were teenagers now, and tall, close to six feet, so big and hep in their shorts and ankle strap sandals. Billie Jean's VD hadn't caught up with her yet, she was a big pretty outgoing blonde, a bundle of energy, a bombshell, still sucking her thumb at night. Shirlie, Mama said, is the smartest.

There's not happiness in our car driving up from Chicago to Milwaukee along Lake Michigan to Aunt Giny's and Uncle Strick's and our new cousin Helen. "Don't say a word about Penny," Mama warns, "especially to Helen."

Helen is two, the pretty, spitting image of both her parents. I humpty dumpty her on my lap. She laughs so big it's like the egg breaking. It's a little hard to be around her, I'm so afraid Penny might come out. All the king's men and all the king's horses can't put Penny together again. When we grow up Helen we will try to find her.

Uncle Strick starts unbuttoning his shirt as he comes through the door, home from the beer factory, goes shirtless the rest of the time, it's so humid in Milwaukee. And there on his sweaty horsy back are the sprayed bullet holes and knife cut just as I remember. He says Korea's going to be worse. Aunt Giny keeps touching my hair, beginning stories in her soft Southern drawl of when I was a baby that she doesn't finish because she starts crying.

We stay only one night.

Going south, that late Saturday afternoon, Bridget starts in. You hit me. You love Helen more than me. You lied about me. You said I'm not pretty.

"I did not."

"Sharon," Mama sighs. "It takes two to make an argument. You're the oldest. Surely you didn't say that?"

Clarke never says anything.

Bridget just likes to torment me, Gae said. I write postcards to Gae all the way.

We're in an old fashioned white wooden apartment building in Lynchburg, Virginia. We're meeting Mama's Aunt and double first cousins. Walter and Guy Clark of Asheville, North Carolina married Myrtle and Susie Simmons of Southport, North Carolina. Two mountain brothers married two coastal sisters. Their children are double first cousins. "Double first cousins," she explained before we got there, "are more related than half brothers and sisters. They have the identical blood lines both sides all the way back." This is doubly amazing because we thought everyone in Mama's family was dead.

Everything is white except the carpet which is cream, swirling silver and crimson hibiscus flowers. We're sitting on a sofa when the door opens and in comes....

I have tried for so long to remember who it is.

Ina, I think. Or maybe Pearl.

This is Aunt Myrtle's apartment. She is Mama's mother's closest-in-age sister. Myrtle met Walter in the Wilmington mill during World War I and then he introduced his little brother Guy to her little sister Susie in the Danville mill.

The room is sunny, pearl white. We are scrubbed white, me and Bridget in our matching lavender organdy Easter dresses and white ruffled petticoats Mama made, and our shiny black patent leather shoes and our white socks with lace trim. Clarke's wearing the gray flannel slacks she made and a white dress shirt. We're sitting on display, Mama so proud of the three children she has made, married so well she can afford a vacation back to visit, to show them how much she, the runaway, has succeeded. We are sitting against the wall opposite the door and a double first girl cousin is standing there gold in her high heels, in her 1950 dress, the very latest, and latest hairdo, her dark gold hair piled up high movie-star beautiful, with her ten month old baby girl in her arms. This baby girl is gold too. She stands in the doorframe protectively holding her baby girl, together they are shimmering gold, but like a doe and her fawn in gun sights, ready to flee.

Dewey Harold Clark, another double first cousin, is here too. Myrtle's son, the brother of Ina and Pearl. The uncle of the gold baby. The last time Mama saw him was on Myrtle Beach. He was in the war. "But the Japs weren't nothing to what those Korean slopeheads are going to be." He loved California when he was stationed there, sorry he didn't visit us. His face is Mama's face, and the same clear skyblue eyes, but a man's. He's lean and very tall, big boned like Mama and Mozelle, and handsome and blond and funny and you can see the Cherokee, a blue eyed Cherokee, and he keeps telling us our Mama is his Mama too. When Myrtle was carrying him Grandma Lizzie told Garnet this will be your baby, you will take care of it so Myrtle can work. Walter and CC were both in jail for bootlegging. When Myrtle was expecting him her sister Susie died and then her nephew Aubrey and then her brother Dewey, and her sister Maybelle and her baby Ruby were dying. Mama was four. She boiled his diapers in a big kettle in front of the tents. Dewey Harold was her first baby.

"Daddy was in the Army," Dewey explains. "He was shipped over to France and got wounded. While he was lying there on the battlefield waiting for medical care the Germans turned mustard gas on the American troops. He never fully recovered from that old gas, he was in and out of Veterans hospitals all his life. It was called shell shock."

"It was called Soldier's Heart in the Civil War," Myrtle says. "That was what was wrong with my grandfather."

"I'm so glad Daddy is buried in North Carolina. We had to come up here to Virginia for work, and to get away from the law. We were starving, the men had no choice but to bootleg. The Clark-Simmons had the reputation of making the very best corn liquor in both states. To some, you kids should know, they were almost heroes, like Robin Hood."

Dewey Harold towers over the couch we sit on. I feel Mama watching.

"Are you going to remarry, Myrtle?" Daddy asks.

"One man is enough," she laughs. Myrtle is dark, with the high wide cheek bones Mozelle has. And her blond son too.

And her daughter, Ina or Pearl, is so beautiful standing there, she looks like my grown daughter, Shawn, now. And even more like Bridget's oldest daughter, Monique. The woman in the door has the identical blood lines as my mother both sides all the way back to the Garden of Eden. In her, in these others, in that baby girl, are Mama's lost family, the survivors of all that death. How amazing, how beautiful they are.

But something not beautiful is happening too. Maybe this is what Mama and Daddy have been arguing about, that Mama's double first cousin standing there in the door with her baby isn't married and this is why she doesn't come in any further, doesn't sit down. I know now that most of the women in her family were pregnant when they married—if they married at all—and Daddy tormented her about this. It could almost be Mozelle and Penny standing there.

Maybe Mama tried to stand up for her family, in defiance of Daddy's shaming her about them. I want to think so. This is her first reunion with her family. Something awful happens right here. Ina or Pearl standing there, in her mother's apartment. Myrtle. Stunningly beautiful women. Stunningly handsome, the one man, Dewey Harold. But there are no pictures of them in the *Scrapbook*.

In April 1988, after Daddy died, Mama and I journeyed to the South in her Winnebago. This is how I wrote it in a letter:

We're at Ina's, Mama's double first cousin, in a farmhouse bordering Appomattox. We're seated in the living room around the early American coffee table with Aunt Luella and another double first cousin, Dewey Harold, a six-foot-three male twin of my mother, and just like her, a fabulous story teller of the long dead family members. Only his stories focus on what she glosses over: the bootlegging to feed the starving children, the recipes! the constructions of the gins themselves, and where in the woods, and details of the arrests at least one of which he witnessed, the running from the law, to Virginia to escape North Carolina, the routes and hiding places, but always the importance of maintaining our North Carolina identity. When I asked how they survived all that death, especially Elizabeth, the mother, he responded with the identical answer my mother has always given. "Love. We survived on love."

Ina has brought out a big box of family photographs, the first pictures I've ever seen of the Simmons and Jacksons. Pictures of the brothers Walter and Guy who married the sisters Myrtle and Susie. Pictures of Ernest and the flappers Maybelle, Luella, and Bessie, and Aunt Belle, CC's baby sister, in the voile dress Lizzie made her. Actual pictures of Aubrey, Ernest's baby, the second to die after Susie, and Ruby, the second baby to die. And the other brother, Dewey, the one who came home from bootcamp with the 1918 Flu. And Susie, my grandmother, pregnant with Lawrence, or perhaps my mother. At least half of them look Indian, I mean lookie there, Maybelle is blonde, a thick gold curly blonde like you, Sharon Lura, oh, how Maybelle could dance the Charleston. But none of Christopher Columbus, just as Mama always said. CC believed the camera steals your soul. But he looked exactly like his little sister, Aunt Belle. Just look at that Aunt Belle! If that's not one hundred percent Indian I don't know what is.

And several photographs of Elizabeth Reynolds Simmons, my great grandmother. One astounding one of both my great grandmothers, Nancy Jackson Clark and Elizabeth together as old women in Lynchburg. I had seen one of the stern highcheeked half-Cherokee Nancy but never the Scots-Irish Lizzie, who it's always been said Bridget takes after. Her large breasts, her small waist, her round smiling face.

"Grandma Reynolds knew music, taught piano lessons, taught school, homeschooled all her own kids."

And had Olive out of wedlock at fifteen by her German music teacher, which conceivably, being "ruined," had something to do with her marrying an Indian.

"And how did she die?" I ask, a bit stunned to realize I didn't know.

"*She was raped and murdered!*" *Dewey Harold exclaims, sitting beside me on the crowded couch.*

"*No!*"

The gasp is from my mother, seated in a pulled-up chair across from us. Her wide spread fingers shoot straight down to the floor as her body stands up.

"*No!*"

We obey, go on as if this hasn't happened. Photos of Harold in World War II bootcamp in San Diego, photos of them all laughing it up. Stories, wonderful stories.

Later that afternoon, Dewey Harold met me under the Appomattox farmhouse. In his soft melodious Southern drawl he told me the story.

"*I was nine. Grandma Reynolds was living with us. Our parents were working the night shift down the street at the mill. Friday night, Charles Eades, a twenty-three year old neighbor, got to drinking, came looking to rape Pearl, who was thirteen at the time. Pearl was a looker, I got to tell you, like you, Sharon Lura. Walking round all the time in short shorts. Luckily she was spending the night at a friend's, but this so enraged Charles Eades he jumped on Grandma instead. She was in the bed sick with two year old Ina and eight month old Harley who were sick too. Well, I ran to the neighbor's next door. They slammed the door in my face saying they wanted nothing to do with it, so then I ran a mile to the store. The store called the police, who were there by the time I got back to the house. He'd raped and beat her. Imagine, she was sixty-three. She died of that beating Charles Eades gave her.*

"*There was a trial. It was in all the papers. I'd been taught to never, ever use cuss words, Grandma had slapped my mouth till it bled for using such words, and washed it out with soap, but the Judge gave me a lecture and told me this was a Court of Law, and with my hand on the Bible I was to repeat exactly what I had heard Charles Eades say as he was raping my grandmother. So I did.*

"*Charles Eades, he spent his whole life in the penitentiary in Richmond for those few minutes, he only just died last year.*"

The next day, Dewey Harold drove me by the house in Lynchburg where it happened, a little blue one down in a gulch, on the corner a block up from the old mill, bordered by the cemetery where Elizabeth, and my other great grandmother, Nancy Jackson, are buried.

For the next three nights, sleeping side by side in the Winnebago, just the narrow passage between us, my mother struggled to speak to me of it.

She tried, she kept trying. The words would drown in her throat. I remembered her telephone doodles, Charles Eades, written over and over in her hand, Charles Eades down the little white pad when I was trying to learn to write Edens. Finally on the third, maybe fourth night, after I'd resigned to her inability, she gasped from the pillow, "I never told anyone. Not even your father."

How long it has taken me to know my mother.

"Oh Mama. You blamed her?"

"Yes."

It was Lizzie's fault. It was Myrtle's and Walter's, it was her family's because they drank. Worked in the mill. Were white trash. Were Indians. Were bootleggers. Were wanted by the law. Did jail time. Had a good time. Were women. Were pregnant and not married. Died of TB. Daddy would have never let her forget.

It was then, after her grandmother's rape and murder, maybe during the trial and all the publicity, that Mama started running away from the school. And when her father agreed to the experimental surgery, to cut away the bad part of his bad lung, a desperate hope with this newest family tragedy that he could lead a normal life, that he could marry and have his sad, devastated children home with him. This happened four months later and killed him.

Of all the many horror stories of her children's deaths, that Elizabeth survived all that only to die herself so ignobly and tragically, and that it had been my storytelling mother's shameful secret, was truly shocking.

How long it has taken me to know my mother, the profound trauma in her of sexual rules and their violations mixed with death, loneliness, unfairness, illegality, desperation, shame and poverty. One prominent theory maintains that sexual abuse of children is permitted because it's the essential, though unacknowledged tool in socializing and preparing the child to accept the submission/domination structure of society. This is the reason incest is so common, the taboo being in telling of it.

My mother would prove herself. She would rise above her allotted station in life by submission to society's rules. Proud, but in both conscious and unconscious denial, she subverted herself at every turn to our father's rule. She called this Love, the necessary Compromise, the Law of Marriage, of Civilization. She called it Wisdom. Being a woman. Being a good mother.

Leaving Lynchburg we drive through Appomattox. The silence from the front of the Ford silences us kids for miles. One out of four soldiers killed at Gettysburg was from North Carolina; three of Mama's great-uncles were wounded there and another at Spotsylvania; three of them died in prison camps. Mama's great-grandfather, CC's father, John Simmons, still a teenager, walked home from Appomattox to Southport North Carolina, barefoot, wounded, and bitterly defeated. His three older brothers were dead. He smoked opium to make it. Was Daddy's great-grandfather, John Chitwood, the one that fought for the North, the one I'm supposed to be just like, at Appomattox? Perhaps, being on the winning side, he had better transportation home.

Down to Danville, on the road through Chatham where CC spent the last year of his life in jail. Where Mama ran away to find her sick father and so got expelled from the School. Funny how she never seemed embarrassed or hesitant in telling us about Christopher Columbus.

Danville, Virginia. Where the TB came from. Where most of them died.

We drive by Hughes Memorial School. We drive by the Dan River Cotton Mill. She points out the woods in Schoolfield, the company section of town, where they lived in the tents, and the Dan River her daddy walked her reciting *Look Homeward Angel*.

The important family is Daddy's. Now we're looking for our Uncle Marion in Tusculum, Tennessee. Daddy's oldest brother runs a dairy and is a business professor and football coach at Tusculum College, the oldest college west of the Smokies. Daddy went there about a year until something happened and he was asked to leave. In three days it'll be Marion's forty-first birthday. We're coming as his birthday present.

Everything in the East is old, dark and sinking in, everything creaks with age. We pull into Uncle Marion's driveway. A man is racing around the front of our Ford, a garage wall of stacked rocks with moss and ivy behind him. Daddy is behind the steering wheel but the racing man is Daddy. I see my father as I have never before. The racing man is Daddy's oldest brother, Uncle Marion. They look just alike!

Something is happening. This is why he's racing. He's cutting us off at the pass, we can't go to Uncle Kenneth's and Aunt Mary's and cousins Jimmy, Joe and Bob in Alabama as planned. They don't want us to come because of Mama's TB. "I am *not* contagious!" Mama gasps. She has her official certificate with her, proving this. "I would not have come if I were. Mary is a nurse, she knows this. She knows this."

He's racing to cut us off from entering his home too. His wife Elizabeth is afraid for her boys, Alex and Jack. But we can stay up at the cabin, we can stay there, and maybe they'll visit us, tomorrow.

Grandma wrote them to warn about her TB! Driving away Mama's out of her mind with the betrayal, begs Daddy to get us out of here, it's too humiliating, she can't stand it. But Daddy wants to visit his older brother, it isn't fair of her to keep him away from his brother, after all it's Marion's birthday.

We go high up into the Great Smoky Mountains to their log cabin built before the Revolutionary War. Uncle Marion finds deserted pre-Revolutionary War cabins in the woods, numbers each log, dismantles the whole thing, transports it to a buyer's site, then puts it all back together. Aunt Elizabeth is a direct descendent of the first white girl born in Tennessee. The cabin is deep in the woods with a creek rushing through the property. How wonderful, Mama keeps saying, so as not to spoil it anymore for us. But the bathroom's an outhouse. There are scary cobwebs in all the corners, even under the rim that's the hole you have to go in.

All the rest of that day Mama washes and starches and irons our ruffled dresses, heating the iron on the wood stove. Daddy keeps the fire going, chopping, bringing in wood from outside. "This iron is so heavy I can barely lift it," Mama keeps starting to cry, her pneumotherapy arms hurt so bad. But she's getting us ready for our Aunt Bess in Chattanooga, she intends no matter what to present us at our best. She doesn't want to go to Grandma's sister either but Daddy gives her no choice.

First thing in the morning she starts Marion's chocolate birthday cake. The four of us take turns beating the ingredients the million billion beats, Daddy perspiring to figure three hundred and fifty degrees in the stove he's putting wood into.

In the late afternoon Aunt Elizabeth and the boys come up for an outdoor picnic. "She never has liked me," Mama mumbles, then shushes her mouth with her hand, that anyone heard her say that. "Poor Elizabeth. I'm afraid she's a typical Southerner. She still believes in class. She thinks she's better than me."

We're up here on the old moldy-smelling wooden bridge that crosses over the creek. Uncle Marion is dropping us in one at a time. Aunt Elizabeth and Alex and Jack are below on the bank spreading out the picnic, Mama keeping her distance. Alex and Jack are fourteen and twelve, they're the boy cousins Grandma has told us endless stories of, her first grandchildren she was so close to before she and Grandpa had to come west to us. We had so looked forward to getting to know them but that's not going to happen now. The thick foliage makes everything dark.

I'm the last one lifted from the bridge. When Uncle Marion lowers me over the railing his huge hands slide up under my bathing suit top, and linger there.

"Your teats are getting big like a cow," he giggles that Daddy giggle into my ear, his nostril breathing heavily.

Daddy just stands there staring. Uncle Marion holds me out over the creek, just hanging that way to him and everyone, my legs dangling, his hands inside making the nipples hard just like Daddy does. A skinny Doberman pincher, like Adolf and Goebbels, stands down the road and stares at me too. Finally he lets go. I fall through the air and splash into the cold hole with Bridget and Clarke, trying to squeal like a girl.

I have to go to the bathroom but I'm so scared of the outhouse, the spiders that will crawl up the hideous hole of centuries of poop, up me and out my throat to declare me dead. I'm afraid to go in the woods. I'm afraid to pull down my pants.

I write a letter to Grandma trying to hold it.

Dear Garndma, How are you? We are at the cadin now. We or having a good time. The cadin is in the woods. I like it here. Bridget and Clarke are out in the woods now. We are getting ready to eat. Bridget Clarke are getting back from the woods now. Now we have to eat. Goodbye. Love Sharon

When I first found this letter I burst into tears reading it. For a long time, until I found the little notes to Mama in the hospital, it was the earliest piece of my writing that I had. I framed it, with a photograph of me, age nine.

On that journey my mother and I made to the South after Daddy died I continued my letter from Uncle Marion's cabin, actually from the swimming hole under the bridge. "*I remember fear fear fear. The dark woods, the great isolation. The outhouse. The terror.*"

I hadn't remembered the creek incident with Uncle Marion until my father told it in his confession the year before. (The Doberman actually comes from this letter, not the 1950 memory; it was standing down the road staring at me as I wrote.) "Were you molested when you were a boy?" I asked, and he jumped "No! But ... well, I saw my oldest brother, Marion ..." and then proceeded to describe the above scene on the bridge, which as he told it I relived, for the first time, like watching a movie of it. "Was that molestation?" he asked.

This letter also tells of the nightmare I'd had the night before in the Winnebago parked outside the cabin, sleeping next to my mother (just nights after she'd blurted out that she'd never told anyone about her grandmother's death). Two men were trying to change my oil against my approval. *"Have you always had nightmares?" she asked in the morning. "Last night you sat straight up, screaming and screaming. I couldn't get you to quit screaming."* I would do this again and again over our next ten years together, never seeing the outrageousness or the pattern that's revealed in the journal and letters: the nightmares came when something triggered the old story and I was within screaming range of her. I was screaming for help, what I couldn't do back then. I was screaming to wake myself up. I was screaming to wake my mother, to make her hear me, to finally believe me. Once, later, I even had a nightmare of sleeping in the Winnebago outside the Tennessee cabin. I was backing us up over the precipice, two men outside signaling me to keep coming.

There's a photograph of the two men that day. They're sitting on the cabin's porch. Marion Chitwood Edens' contempt, or at least unhappiness with his youngest brother seems demonstrated to the camera (or to my mother). Daddy seems oblivious of his big brother's sneering, seems happy to be sitting there. On the back of the photo she wrote *Marion and Fred Edens, Mountain Cabin, Tennessee, July, 1950.* And then, my mother who was rarely ironic and never about Marion added: *Oh, things couldn't be that bad.*

And there are the tapes I made in the 1988 visit, just seven months after his death, in which Marion's disdain for my no good father, his spoiled baby brother, is undeniable. I wanted to know anything, everything he wanted to tell me, but I was also taken aback that he would be so insensitive, so eager to reveal his contempt. Was he trying to tell me something he thought I needed to know, or was the jealousy that viral, even with his baby brother just dead, that he couldn't control it to his baby brother's daughter?

"On his death bed," the 1988 letter continues, *"Daddy cursed me for writing the poem in* Hard Country *of making love with Charlie here in his brother's cabin in 1976. How could I? I couldn't really understand it myself, why or how I could have done that. But I did: make love here with*

a Tennessee native son, without contraception, Uncle Marion and Aunt
Elizabeth on the other side of the wall; and then wrote it as a poem, and
published it in my epic....

"*Mama said yesterday when I referred to the phenomenon of denial, 'I*
know it. Sometimes I'm saying something so strongly and I'll know it's not
true at all! *That's not the way it happened. But the words come out*
anyway.'"

It works the other way too. The truth will out, Shakespeare said, by
cryptonesia or nightmare. I went there with a lover in 1976, a Tennessee
native son, to return to the scene of the crime, though I had no conscious
recollection of it. Not as revenge but to reclaim a bit of my self. To say as
a poet this too is American history.

It was the fourth brother and on down who left England for America.
The first brother inherited the father's estate. The second one entered the
church, the third the military. The daughters just married, best they could,
or didn't. The rest had to leave. Imagine leaving England in the 1600s for
this distant wilderness.[9] Imagine the rivalry, outright hatred, between those
siblings. The lack of love and protection by the parents, products
themselves of the same system. Jealousy and disinheritance and
competition and contempt and exile and massive unspeakable wounds
between siblings is the tradition that settled America. The boundaries have
been violated in this family for how many generations? I wanted to ask my
uncle if he remembered fingering my nipples in front of his little brother.
But the words wouldn't come out despite his eager, even gleeful words of
contempt for him. They'd have shocked him as inappropriate. And no
doubt by his American creed it was a healthy, natural man thing to do, to
claim me from his brother.

South, back into the North Carolina mountains, through Asheville, Mama's
father's ancestral home, then west through Cherokee to Ducktown,
Daddy's hometown. In Cherokee Daddy laughs, "What a tourist trap!"
Mama sits straight and stiff, pointing where to drive. The road makes a
loop, we come down a two-lane of tourist attractions, shops and
Hollywood-costumed Indians. "This is just about money, starvation. When
people are desperate they'll do anything. Don't ever forget, you kids, one
drop of Cherokee makes you Cherokee forever. Actually you have a lot
more than a drop. The Simmons are Cherokee too, they're Coastal
Cherokee." It's later, when they run away, that they become Seminole.
There's always been a Cherokee road across North Carolina, down the

Cape Fear River to the ocean, and double first cousins have always been
sacred. And we're from the Cherokee who didn't go on the Trail of Tears,
we're Qualla boundary, don't forget, we escaped. Unto the hills.

Now we are actually coming to Ducktown. Sure enough, no trees. Sure
enough, the hills are barren-red like Arizona, and eroding. "Bad." Daddy
grimaces, like it's a new revelation.

   We park at the top of Main Street and he disappears into a little white
house. He's visiting his high school girlfriend, Mama explains, this is
good, this is love, we must wait. This is so strange, everything is silver and
black. I see him touching her breasts. I see the pregnant Ducktown girl
swinging from the telephone line strung there beyond Mama across Main
Street. I love my father for telling us of her, saying that wasn't right. His
big sister Lucile was four when their father left for Arizona the second
time, left them here in this rough town of miners. They almost starved to
death before he got back when she was eight. That's why her hair turned
gray before she was twenty.

   When Daddy comes back to the car, he is quiet and far away. "How-
yadoin Lu?" he asks in the rearview.

Estill Springs, Winchester Middle Tennessee on the Elk River, where
Grandma grew up, where her great grandparents originally pioneered.
They came through the Cumberland Gap from Virginia. John Chitwood
was two years old. In Winchester we visited the site of our Great Aunt
Mary Sharp's College for women, the oldest woman's college in the U.S.
with an academic curriculum the same as Yale and Brown. Look at that
historical marker, Daddy.

   MARY SHARP: "LEARN TO THINK."

   We visited Aunt Bess, Grandma's younger sister, in Chattanooga, a
short ways across the mountain, through Sewanee. In the many photos
Daddy looks happy, open like a little boy, his arms enthusiastically around
both his aunt (not ant) and her second husband, Uncle Stoke. She looks as
thrilled as Daddy. He's back with his family that adores him. And it's true,
as was always said, Bridget also looks just like Bess Chitwood.

We returned the Southern route, down to Dallas from Little Rock, out of
the mucky buzzing swampforest into the endless desert, Bridget singing
"copy cat, copy cat!" out the window, *"Sharon Lulu's a big fat copy cat!"*
which is funny because she's the copy cat.

"Isn't it pretty Sharon Lulu?" he sighs in Tyler, Texas, his hard snaky thing wagging back and forth under the steering wheel. Hives break out across my bare midriff. Gae and I are running the streets on our horses. I worry about his wiry hairs getting caught when he has to zip up fast, Mama coming back so happy with roses.

"Sharon's on her high horse again," he hisses crossing the Lone Star State and I see myself dismount. The Burma Shave signs are like reading one of Grandma's poems, reading each line and thinking on it before you get to the next one which changes the meaning of the last one. We come through Globe Arizona where Grandpa was in the hospital for almost a year, or was it Jerome, and that was another trip? Mama aches for him here all those years ago like her own hospitalized daddy. How she loved that man. No one understood him until she came along. Not even Daddy. "Lookie there," he instructs. "The Navajo still live in hogans."

"The Lone Ranger was really a girl," he says. "Just read *The Riders of the Purple Sage* by Zane Grey."

"Your father had to read twenty novels to graduate from Ducktown High School," Mama explains, making him so mad he won't explain how the Lone Ranger was a girl.

The Lone Ranger is still coming across the purple sage. America in her mask. The mask they wore to nurse you. The masks you and your sister wear posing for the camera. The problem with you, Clarke, is you don't have a mask. Behind the mask is a girl with breasts, a silver bullet through the top left one, another through the right groin. No wonder the Communists outlawed the family. General MacArthur was so beloved by his mother she accompanied him to West Point, now she's telling him to bomb China. It's not just Robin Hood stealing from the rich, giving to the poor, the mask is to protect the self. We sleep in the Petrified Forest, the meteor showers fall through it all night, the men Grandpa hanged pixelating in the rocks. The hangman's mask is to protect the soul. Until we rise again.

§

Sixteen

For the time we had left of summer, before my hernia surgery, Gae and I evolved into palominos, Gold and Goldie. We hung out near the stables on the river. From behind the high wooden fenceposts we ached for the horses. It cost a dollar to ride for an hour, way too much, and they wouldn't let us ride anyway without an adult.

Carrots, horses like carrots. Old bread. Sneaking sugar cubes the Walkers use in their coffee to their big mouths, lips, teeth. To lose a finger would be worth it.

One day we watched a man break a horse. He took a two-by-four and brought it down with all his might between its ears. "That'll teach you who's boss!" We could hardly make it home for the shock and rage.

"There's more female hormone in the testicle of a stallion than in any other known tissue," Mr. Walker liked to say whenever he caught us as Gold and Goldie.

Our legs and arms grow into the four long legs and our ears grow pointed and long too under our lengthening manes. My nostrils flare to hers, she bares her lips, we hang our necks around each other's. Our backs arch, our tails grow, we prance and neigh and paw the air, then gallop past the old men, explosion of horse! we leave them in our dust. This is not pretend. We are horses trapped in human bodies. We are horses from deep underground, from the elaborate ongoing civilization under the earth that's superior to this one but what this one is supposed to be. We belong to a wild herd that escaped a century ago from the Spanish Land Grant Ranchos and the Mexican War and the Indians, that hide by day in the canyons, that come down the river beds and roam the Basin at night. Even now a horse sometimes escapes from the County Farm or the Hollydale stables and runs the LA River bottom.

Not shoed, bridled, or saddled. We can't walk, we can only trot. We trot and gallop everywhere, we scream, we're wild stallions. My hiccups vanish. We're involved in elaborate dramas rescuing and freeing horses from the glue and dogfood factories. We trot down the dogfood aisles of McCoys, hide as much horsemeat as we can in the ice cream freezers, we love you horse is our prayer. We follow the Kentucky Derby news longing for next May, who will wear the roses? and the Santa Anita and Tijuana racetrack news. We love Willy Shoemaker. We will be the first girl jockeys. Did you know Man O War died of the 1918 flu? Or some famous race horse did anyway. We try to figure out how to find out for sure. We hear about Sea Biscuit. We will grow up to be stable girls to help them escape.

Pegasus, the winged horse, flies in the sky at gas stations all over LA. Horsepower! A car is a horse with wings. A stallion is a girl with testicles. A girl is a horse in her soul. Pegasus is the winged horse of the Muses, born of sea foam and the blood of the slaughtered Medusa. Ooh, we love that.

Medusa, Chief of the Gorgons! A hideous or terrifying woman. There were three Gorgons with serpents on their heads instead of hair but Medusa was the one that was mortal. She had been a beautiful maiden, especially famous for her hair, but Athena, who always takes the father's side, transformed her hair into serpents and made her face so hideous that whoever set eyes on it was instantly turned into stone.

We look up the chimaeras, Gorgons, and sea monsters. I skip ahead in my Bible and read about the Four Horsemen of the Apocalypse, Conquest, Slaughter, Famine and Death, who appear on white, red, black and pale horses. I'm praying nightly now about the Korean War. Our horses are about the female hormone in the testicle of the stallion, yes, but not as Mr. Walker says about girls. It isn't about sex, it isn't masturbation, it's pure energy. It's love. It's identification with all captive spirits, with the oppressed, about saving the horse, our selves, from bossy, jealous, brutal men. From our fathers. The horse is freedom. The poet Milton said Medusa is the unconquered virgin. Pegasus' father was Poseidon, God of the Sea, this is why the horse in Greek means wave, what is meant that he was born from sea foam. Medusa, like Mary, was a virgin mother. Pegasus is the son of a virgin just like Jesus! Gae and I will grow up too to be unconquered virgin mothers.

Daddy actually gives us permission to dig as deep as we can in the far west corner of the backyard, at the head of his garden not far from where my bloody things are buried. We dig for the trapped horses. Another poet wrote *Yet earth contains/the horse as a remembrance of wild/Arenas we avoid.* Gae and I are seeking the wild Arenas. We dig deep in the ground, to huddle with, in the protection of, to race with horses, safe from the adults. A winged horse sprang from the murdered blood of Medusa, we understand exactly what that means. We dig into the sprayed blood. We don't have flying dreams. Our horses gallop inside the earth. Sometimes I'm digging for Korea.

"Let me see if you're a woman yet Lu," Daddy whispers.

I'm a horse, Daddy. You don't know it but I'm a stallion, unconquered.

Goldie leads the way over the back fence into the Beaver's back yard. I, Gold, will follow wherever she leads. Pegasus is spray from the blood spilt to the ground when Daddy split me in two. Wild horses could not drive Gold from Goldie.

What was the name of Lady Godiva's horse, Daddy?

"Far back, far back in our dark soul the horse prances," D.H. Lawrence wrote. Mama read *Lady Chatterley's Lover* at night with a flashlight under her School blankets while the U.S. Supreme Court debated banning it.

Who was inside the Trojan horse, Daddy?

We had a subscription to *LIFE* Magazine. The soldiers were on the covers, inside every issue. **This Is War!** The black and white photographs of the icy hills, the frozen trenches, the troops in them, the maps. **This Is War!** Those words went into me as a command from God and my President: *know this war.* Most astounding, Korea was on our new television set. To hear the names pronounced. Seoul, No Gun Ri, Kaesong. To actually see our boys, just as in my prayers, shooting and being shot at. The Korean War is being carried on in my name. I must go there with them.

Then, a terrible mistake, we massacred hundreds of people under a bridge, mostly women and babies. We were ordered to shoot them because there could be Communists among them. The photographs were on our television and on a newsreel at the drive-in. Then the Army denied it. My confusion was a crisis like I'd not known before. Just admit the truth, America.Two wrongs never make a right. Say we're sorry, it won't happen again, learn the lesson and let's go from there.

Mama bought me a pink silk and lace bed jacket. A bed jacket comes only to your waist. The rest of you is under the covers. She knew about bed jackets because of the years she spent in bed as a girl. I was in Downey Community Hospital for five days.

I was shaved higher than my belly button, up over my rib cage, down almost to my knees. I hadn't realized there is hair at your waist. The last thing I saw was the thick curly black hair on the surgeon's hands and wrists and him laughing, hovering over me on the table just like Daddy. The nurse put the mask down over my nose. The room began to spin in the colors of the rainbow. The white-masked faces circling the ceiling above me laughed at what I said but they kept encouraging me to talk. I was under the bridge.

He took a knife and cut three and a half inches diagonally down my right mons veneris toward my inner thigh. The massacre went on for days. The refugees pulled dead bodies around them for protection. Mothers wrapped their children with blankets and hugged them with their backs toward the soldiers. I'm not supposed to remember this. He removed my appendix while he had me open, then sewed up the hole I burst open when I was a baby from crying too hard. He sewed me up with black thread crisscrossed like shoe lace.

Mama sat by my bedside waiting for me to wake. The crying of women and children above the gunfire. What causes those hiccups? she asked the doctor. Hyperventilation. There's a one-way valve, it gets stuck, air gets trapped. Then he said, fear.

Waking up, not being able to move. The tight constriction of the bandages, the stitches, unbelievable pain. Nausea. Don't throw up, you might break the stitches. I'm painted bright pink all the way up to my breasts, inches beyond the bandages.

Every time I open my eyes there's a different old woman in the other bed crying and weeping for her mother, her children.

My eyes open to Pastor Adams standing over me. The scream erupts, breaking skin held by a stitch. There there child, I won't hurt you. Your mother's been here the whole time, she's taking a break. He looks like my father. He looks like Jesus. He's wearing that tie of the Cross with the names of Jesus, right in the center of which is the rose, and the words over the rose, I am the Rose of Sharon.

I wake to screaming but it's not me. "No, no, no!" The screams go on and on. The clanking of equipment, the shooting at the ones still alive in the tunnel bridge. People running, screaming orders. A nurse comes with the bedpan, don't let that girl's screaming worry you, honey. She was just horseback riding on the river, that darn horse threw her. Her foot got caught in the stirrup, she was dragged for miles through the boulders, the bush and cement. All her skin's shredded, every bone's broken. There's internal damage too. I hope they put that horse down.

No, no, no! I open my eyes to the doctor and nurse outside my door, the hairy hands that cut me open writing on his clipboard.

"If Sharon Edens hasn't had a bowel movement by tomorrow morning induce it by enema."

I wait like I wait for Daddy to return.

The next morning passes. A whole day passes. I relax a little.

When she comes, late the afternoon before the morning I'm to be released, with enema bag, tubes, hoses, portable water and sink and ignores my protests, begins the process, enema means to send in, this tidal rage blows out of me. My right fist hits the girdle beneath her white uniform and bounces off. This enrages me even more, she springs back, and, second strike, I put a hole in the wall.

She nods her capped blond head to me and says with miraculous, lifesaving compassion, "That's okay honey, I understand." She doesn't try to invade me again.

When I leave the next morning no one says a thing about the hole in my wall. I will respect, I will sing that woman's praises forever. She is the kind of adult I want to grow up to be.

At home Mama makes me a day bed on the living room couch so I can watch our new television set. She brings me trays four times a day. This is the best part of being sick, Mama bringing lovingly-arranged trays of breakfast, lunch, mid afternoon snack and dinner just as was brought to her when she was sick all those times, her months and years in the infirmary. But not brought by her mother. She doesn't say this, but I think it. How very lucky I am.

Gae comes to the porch screen. "You can't come in yet, Gae, you make Sharon too excited, she might break open again."

Daddy passes back and forth from the garage to the bathroom. He's in the kitchen opening a beer.

He comes in. It'll break my stitches Daddy. I don't say this, I can't talk. I can never say anything when this happens. "Let's look at those dressings, Sharon Lura." I pull the army blanket up, he says "there there." He pulls it back down. He pulls down my pajama bottoms, he touches my bandaged mound, tight and rubbery like the nurse's girdle. The crying of women and children. Forgive them Father they know not what they do. Forgive Daddy, forgive the horse trainer, forgive the Koreans, forgive the Communists, forgive all the killers, our very own boys, forgive us our trespasses, all our mistakes.

I wake under my Uncle Kenneth's large oil painting, yellow sunflowers in a deep blue vase on a shiny mahogany table. He sent Mama two paintings to make up for the insult and hurt this summer. Mama loves sunflowers more than all other flowers. Into the lower right hand side of the blue vase is scratched *1947*.

On the opposite wall is the other painting, a yellow muddy road in Georgia coming through tall, newly leafing trees. The paint is layered thick like mud, especially at the curve where there are puddles that reflect the trees overhead and a dogwood just breaking out in pink bloom. *1947* is etched into the road. Mama stares at it and says "Oh I love a painting with a road in it. I always need to see an escape."

I study how he did it. Hours, days, recuperating in the study of how my uncle made these paintings, each brush stroke down each petal, down the muddy road. When Grandma comes she tells me of Kenneth when he was a little boy. "Kenneth was the frail and sickly twin. When he was born his head could fit in a tea cup. But by the time he was eight he was carrying his paint box with him wherever he went, across the eroded gullies and hills."

My Uncle K.D.'s twin. Why is she talking about Cain and Abel again?

I don't want a jealous man, not ever. I want to be an artist.

The first time I was allowed to go to the store for the loaf of Langendorf's after my operation, two men in an old green car followed me up Industrial to the store, the driver's door slightly ajar. "Come over here little girl," he said. "We have some candy for you." I couldn't believe they'd think I'd fall for that. They were mean-looking, their eyes in their skinny unshaven faces. He stopped the car, started to get out. I ran. I always walk against the traffic so the driver will have to stop the car to get you. Unless he has a gun. Or there's two guys, the other free to jump out and grab you. I was weak and it was hard to go fast but I got to the store. They pulled in outside, parked.

I hung around as long as I could, until the store man started eyeing me with suspicion. Over the can goods I watched for a clearing in the traffic. The blind from the rise of the tracks was the biggest problem. You'd have to run fast with no one stopping you to get across before a car came speeding down. I dashed out the door, across Main, got half way down Industrial before they caught up with me. Right then that old guy from the Spanish American War popped out of the bushes. "Hi!" I said, stopping in my tracks to converse, "How are you?" They had to roll on past. Then I ran as hard as I could across the street, across the lot, around the hole, across Roosevelt, up the lawn, up the porch, inside the screen door thank God, latched it and slammed the door shut. When I looked out the window, they were parked in front of Nadja's, passing a bottle in a paper sack back and forth between them.

I told my parents, for the first time ever. Daddy scoffed, "Sharon and her vivid imagination."

"But look out the window, Daddy, they're still there. They offered me candy if I'd get in their car."

The next day the two men in the big faded green car were still around. Mama and Daddy walked to the store with me. The two men cruised by. Coming back from the store they drove by us again.

"Did you see how they looked at Sharon?" Daddy said to Mama, like I wasn't there.

At home we watched the men circling the block, straining to look into our house.

"They circled for days," my mother told me when I inquired the second time, June 15, 1990, as we walked together down East Main Street in Ashland. "Are you sure Mama you can't remember an incident with two men?" I was reading my own journals for the first time. The two men were everywhere, throughout my poems, my scribbled nightmares, my twenty years of journaling. I had asked a few months before when I first started this reading. She had insisted she didn't, though weirdly she snapped "nothing happened!" I accepted this, but the sense kept growing, vague images more and more coming into resolution.

"For over a week these two guys were driving by, craning their necks to get a look at Sharon in the house." She too told it as if to someone else.

"The car circled around, up to Main, back down Industrial. Sometimes they parked on Industrial, sometimes in front of the church. Sometimes we had the lights out, watched them behind the curtains. We wouldn't let you go out, wouldn't let you go anywhere by yourself.

"Daddy got their license number, called Gae's dad, the policeman."

Mr. Walker scoffed at my father the way my father always scoffed at me. "What makes you think they want your hick of a daughter?"

Daddy called the police department. "These two guys have their eyes on my young daughter." "That's not a crime," the police said. "They have evil on their faces," Mama said, taking the phone. "We can't do anything until they do something."

Daddy went out and bought a hunting rifle from Sears, propped it in the dining room corner under the big window. I lay in bed, my hernia scar so weird, the skin barely woven back together, it should hold, the black-haired-hands doctor said plucking out the black stitches, and I saw the car coming for me. I saw Daddy's gun turned on himself, he's so chicken-hearted, he couldn't kill anyone, then Mama, then Bridget and Clarke.

They came through my window. They carried me out the window like in the painting of the Lindbergh kidnapping. My hernia broke open again, to the pounding of my heart, the ringing of the shots. My insides to the outside again. The world was a long dark ringing tunnel to Korea.

"Then after a week we didn't see them anymore," Mama said.

But they could be up on Paramount Boulevard where I have to walk to school starting next week. Just waiting.

What will I do if they pull a gun?

Run. Let them shoot you down, but no matter what, don't get in their car.

I went back and read again The Book of Judges.

The men of the city beset the house round about, and beat at the door.

It's the seventh book, before even Ruth and Samuel. Judges is about the thousand wars the Chosen people waged to win Israel which boils down to the competition for a woman between her father and her husband. All the men in Judges rape the woman or allow her to be raped or in some way contribute to her death.

And the man, the master of the house, went out unto them, and said, Behold, here is my daughter a maiden, and his concubine...

The man brought her forth and they knew her and abused her all the night until the morning...

[A]nd when the day began to spring, they let her go.

Then came the woman in the dawning of the day, and fell down at the door of the man's house where her lord was, till it was light.

And he took a knife, and laid hold of his concubine, and divided her, together with her bones, into twelve pieces, and sent her into all the coasts of Israel. And it was so, that all that saw it said, there is no such deed done nor seen.

§

Seventeen

From the beginning my mother was concerned about my passion for others, that I fall so deeply in love I lose myself, I take on the loved one's mannerisms. I walk and talk like the one I love. "You can always tell who Sharon's been playing with," she'd say when I first loved Judy Clare at three. "She comes home talking just like her."

They say I'm under Gae's spell. They say she's a bad influence on me.

The first day of school we're in the same class. The second day she's taken out of the class, put in the other fourth grade.

We meet behind the giant palm in the far corner by the kindergarten. She's late for her class but she doesn't care. Our recesses and lunch hours are staggered so we won't be able to play even then. She's crying. I'm speechless.

She Goldie-trots ever so slightly so no one knows, the long walk back from the playground, her lunch after mine, me in my desk watching her through the high windows.

They tell me she's bad. They tell her the same thing, that I am a bad influence on her. They think they can separate us, destroy our love. They don't know what love is.

That night I make our horse ears out of Mama's felt beige scraps. On the way to school—they can't take the walk away from us—we hide them under our hair with bobby pins, wear them all through class. She in her class, me in mine. We listen to each other through our horse ears across the vast distance. No one knows our secret. We are horses. Her name is Goldie. I am Gold. We're Gorgons. We whinny, neigh and snort to each other in horse language. In this language, superior to human language, we tell each other everything. We wear our secret horse ears through the whole of fourth grade.

Fourth grade is fog. No, fourth grade is smog. (Fourth grade is sorrow and grief and horror and fear, nothing making sense.) We started every day by standing up, facing the flag, putting our thirty-eight right hands on our thirty-eight beating hearts and saying in unison the Pledge of Allegiance. We studied Alaska and Hawaii, both soon to be admitted into the Union. Maybe then Korea could be. We had to design a new flag. For a brief time there would be forty-nine states so we had to have a flag with forty nine stars. Then we had to design another one with fifty stars.

Bridget skipped second grade! That was exciting. She got 148, or was it 184? on her I.Q. test. Mama was so proud of her. She told everyone about her genius I.Q. "Sharon gets straight As but she has to work for them. It's admirable, that she works so hard, but Bridget's the genius." I told everyone this too, I was so proud of my sister. I prayed I'd never have to have an I.Q. test. Of course, as Mama always pointed out, Bridget was just back up with the grade she started out with, back in the right class, the age group she was supposed to be in by ten minutes.

My mother always said who we were. Mama's words and Gae were my anchors in the smog.

I'm walking down the sidewalk under the tall windows of the class Gae's in, feeling her eyes on me. I'm going home because I'm sick.

Then this memory reverses and I'm the one in the classroom and Gae's the one walking by, a lonely despised girl in her pale dress, her socks and buster browns on her tan legs, moving under the row of big white wood-framed windows. I see that she's on her way home. I see that the teacher has not seen her. Suddenly I have a bad stomach ache and sore throat. I'm sent home because I'm sick.

I catch a glimpse of her just as she enters the cross walk, then disappears north up Paramount. I walk as fast as I can to catch up with her before she gets inside her house. I half run—if I'm sick I wouldn't run, I'd die if caught in the lie—down the bumpy half-dirt half-asphalt of Golden Road, Pachuco music coming from the shacks in the manure fields, to Paramount. I get across Paramount. Then turning west onto Roosevelt Avenue I see her the three long blocks down, almost home. "Gae! Gae!" She turns, and I feel her heart galloping all the way back to me. We collapse on a lawn together, laughing so hard we wet our pants and then we're even more hysterically happy!

But then it's me walking home alone in the fog of loneliness and depression. I'm in the second block of Roosevelt when I hear "Sharon!" Not wanting to believe my ears. "Sharon!" Turning to see Gae making the turn onto Roosevelt. We fall into each other's arms in triumphant joy. We have all day in which no one will know where we are. I can still smell the sweet smell of that clover.

We disguise ourselves as boys. We steal Daddy's white tee shirts and fishing caps, stuff our hair in the caps. I bind my bumps with sheet rags like Mama said Luella and Maybelle did in the twenties to be flappers but which broke down their breasts. Dear Jesus, let my breasts break down.

Then we parade the streets, walk the track from the County Farm back to Main behind the factories. We ride our bikes to Hollydale, look Ma, no hands! and have a coke at the drug store. We're boys. No one pays attention to us.

My parents accuse me of getting out of school because she got out. I can hardly bear the way Daddy says "Don't you lie to me Sharon Edens," but it was worth it. Nothing can take away our afternoon. Not even Mama looking at me with her Third Eye, so ashamed of me.

Probably both these scenarios occurred through the long awful nine months of fourth grade, me getting out to catch up with her, her getting out to catch me.

"We didn't allow you to go to her house," she said in a responsible mother tone when I managed to ask that last year of her life. I couldn't think to ask her why. Fourth grade is loss. I don't remember much. Gae turning the corner with her olive-gold skin, her gold magnetic eyes slightly stretched over her big cheekbones looking like the man in the distant future who will become my third husband, his Gae facial features irresistible. Is it a past life love? The genetic past, our Native American genes? Gae and I were such old souls we were never children.

In September after stopping the Communists at the Nukang River, General MacArthur and our troops made a daring landing at Inchon and in October advanced into North Korea. Their army disintegrated. Our prayers were answered. Our boys really would be home by Christmas like he promised.

Our main projects were the holes. The horse one in my backyard and the one in the lot across the street. The boys had abandoned that one, we took it over. We carved a dirt ladder, dug the tunnels deeper into the sides, dug new tunnels. We met in specific tunnels to talk about specific things. We hid a National Geographic Magazine in one that showed pictures of a tunnel thousands of miles long from Ecuador to Peru. We studied the mummies preserved in it. We read about the Nazi interrogation cells and underground tunnels where Hitler killed himself. We copied, then buried the Bible verses about Joseph thrown in the hole by his brothers to be sold into slavery. We dug for Kathy Fiscus.

All of fourth grade we dug for the wild stallions under my backyard. They were down there, pacing the underground tunnels, praying to us to free them. It was such a crisis. We were the only ones who could hear their screams.

I go out to the garage to get my bike and Daddy's there, working in his lighted corner. "Honey, come back here a minute." Trapped, going numb, I squeeze into the little space between his workbench and the front of the Ford and when he asks me to lift my tee shirt I do. He touches them and I try to smile when he looks at my face. I fight not to scream I hate this Daddy I hate this. They are larger and more embarrassing, the cold puckering the skin around the nipples. He's funny, breathless and giggly, different from his usual brooding self. But it's not hurting me and if I object it'll hurt him. He'll see then that I know that it's wrong. I couldn't bear for him to think that. Poor Daddy. It's all right. The tools and fishing rods hang on the boards of the black tar-papered garage, his lures glinting silver, the feathers iridescent, and the blond curls hang too on the naked body like a pink S down last year's calendar. Is she like Lady Godiva? No. She's posing. She wants to be seen. She's so happy to be posing naked for the whole world, for the man peeping through the lens who doesn't even go blind.

"Remember," he says, his huge red thorny claw over and over the protruding nipple. "Remember," the ragged cuticle sticking out to the light bulb. "This is just between you and me. Don't tell anyone. Especially Mama."

Bertie is Dee Rupp's new wife, she's a nurse at the County Farm. Mama baby-sits every day now their new baby boy, Gary Dee. His crib and playpen are set up in the dining room and it's like he's our baby. "Oh! how I love little boys," Mama exclaims. "Little boys of all ages, from babies to old men." She says this as we drive down the street, nodding to the old man in the crosswalk. She worries about Gary thinking she's his mother, about his loving her more than his real mother. I worry about it too, poor Gary and Bertie who has to work. Of course my mother is more perfect than the twenty-two year old Hollywood-beautiful Bertie Rupp.

One Saturday Daddy is crawling under the house for something. The terror is suffocating, dizzying. That's all I can remember.

That Halloween I was a harem girl. You go as your soul. I was in Daddy's harem. Mama made me silver-blue, see-through chiffon pantaloons gathered at the ankles and a bolero top with long sleeves gathered at the wrists just like the harem girls in the movies, just like Delilah wore when she danced for Samson. I wore my two piece blue bathing suit underneath, a black satin cummerbund around my waist. I loved the black veil across my face, the pale gauze on my hair sprinkled with sequins. I wore Mama's sandals.

I don't remember what Gae was. We weren't permitted to trick or treat together.

Richard Nixon ran for the Senate that fall. He lied and slandered Helen Gahagan Douglas, Daddy ranted, by labeling her a Communist. This is the dirtiest thing one human being can do to another, to slander someone in order to win or boost yourself. One day Nixon and his entourage came through Douglas Aircraft plant. Nixon's eyes met my father's across the gathered heads of the workers. Nixon knew who he saw there, he was that smart. He made a bee line for Daddy and stuck out his hand. Daddy stood there only a second, then turned his back on Richard Nixon, walked out. This took courage, Mama bragged. It's painful to go against the rules of society but it is essential to do so when society is in danger from such dishonest and power-hungry people as Dick Nixon. Your father is a hero.

Nixon won even though it was clear to everyone that he'd stooped to immoral and illegal tactics.

"What is happening to the American people?" my parents moaned.

In November, waves of Chinese attacked our boys above the 38th parallel and forced them to retreat to below Seoul. With his new twenty-two Daddy went on a hunting trip to the Sierras. He bought a red flannel shirt and cap so the other hunters would know not to shoot him. He was gone for a weekend, came home laughing about the absurdity of it all. There were so many hunters in the woods he was afraid of being shot, he was afraid to shoot. Who'd want to shoot a pretty little deer anyway? I'm not a hunter, I'm chicken-hearted. He put the gun in the closet.

I hate it most when the air is cold and shrivels the skin. I'm mortified by their grossness. But he says they're beautiful. Never tell, honey, I love you. I never will, Daddy, I promise. They are getting so big. And you are only nine.

Little Sharon Lura leans herself back, then pushes herself forward, begins to rock on the curved runners of the big white swan her Daddy made her on the cold dark oily cement. Leans her head back and almost sleeps. Rocks. Keeps rocking. Until the swan floating feathery white flies away.

By separating us at school they were hoping that in our loneliness we would be released from the intensity of our friendship and find others. This did not happen. Nor could they keep us apart at home. They had no idea. They were innocent parents.

We start Brownies, something we can do together. We get our light brown dresses with the dark brown ties and caps. We love the gold Brownie pin. We meet in a house way up on Main Street, almost to Paramount, sit together on the sofa. Mrs. Ritchie is the Brownie leader but her immaculately-kept house is off-limits. Sometime during the week, before we go to the second meeting, Gae is asked not to return. I don't understand, hardly realize, sort of go into dumbness, go automatically to the meeting. How I hate rules and regulations, how I suspect them, how I don't want to attain the Brownie goals. For the break we have Hawaiian Punch in paper cups. After two swallows I can't believe it, I projectile-vomit onto the coffee table, the pitcher and glasses and little white cut cookies with red sprinkles, then all over the living room rug. That's the end of Brownies for me, and Hawaiian Punch unto this day.

We found the horses at the County Farm, huge enormous beasts that were still used to plough. They were just work horses, not the sleek stallion beauty we dreamed of but in time we came to love them as passionately as our imaginary horses. They had thick gold and white locks called feathers growing from their incredibly thick ankles. They ploughed the long field that ran parallel to Gardendale, under the eucalyptus windbreak that bordered it. "Enormous hairy beasts of labor," we whispered. "Drafts."

Each horse was kept in a high enclosed wooden stall. Only the head stuck out. The stall boy couldn't see in. We left our bikes, climbed up the eucalyptus side of the barn to the small open windows high above each stall and perched there, our feet dangling above them. Gae above one and me above another, always the same two windows. We hung out there above our horses, no one could find us there, always the same two—hers was butterscotch and vanilla, mine was the color of a peach—for long snatches of time, talking about everything but mostly about them, were they Lincolnshires or Clydesdales? and scheming the dream of coming at night and breaking them out, riding them down to the river. Their flanks rippled, they snorted, their tails rose and they pooped. Our thighs ached to embrace them. You cannot lie to a horse, Gae said. All the lies you learn as correct behavior in society, the thousand little white lies you have to tell, you can't get away with, with a horse. You can train a horse for ten years, she said, and one afternoon in ten minutes of riding, if you are lying to the horse, destroy all the trust you've built.

We debated for a long time whether it would be fair to them, dangerous to us, what could go wrong. Can you just get on a horse and ride, from here to, say, Canada? We hated the idea of lessons but you can damage a horse too in those first ten minutes if you don't know where to sit, if you don't know where his kidneys are. If you slump, he will raise his head and arch his back to compensate, causing you to bounce on his kidneys. He can't tell you he's in pain but he'll arch more, you'll slump more, and the ride will be awful. I told her about the girl in the hospital. Gae's face in the dark hay and steamy poop-smelling barn across from me. The shadows flickering across her strange eyes like one of my dolls. Beasts so giant they could kill us with a flick of their tail. Finally we did it. We dropped down on their enormous backs.

Daddy stretches out full-length beneath the suds. He giggles. I have to sit on the toilet and watch. "Don't take your eyes off it, Sharon." He warms the water by turning on Hot with his hairy white toes. I've been trapped here for so long, having to admire his thing bobbing above the bubbles, the water has to be reheated three or four times.

"Sharon doesn't love me. She's out to get me." Now when he comes home from work he's saying things like that to Mama and Bridget and Clarke. He says "Of course you can't ever believe a thing Sharon says."

Mama and Daddy are at the kitchen table looking over my report card. The teacher has written that Sharon is an excellent student except for her health. She's sickly. When I walk in Daddy roars about my so-called bad health. "Poor Sharon Lura, just a little hypochondriac, isn't that right, Sharon Lu?" His eyes burn scary anger into me. I'm as perplexed by the teacher's remarks as I am by Daddy's. I'm not sickly. I just have the usual childhood diseases. And of course the hiccups.

I remember entering your room where you lay moaning in the bed, prostate cancer metastasized to all your bones, and being hit by your smell. That smell. This was before you confessed on Mother's Day, in May. So much confusion, grief, terror and now that smell mixed with your suffering. Being overtaken by it. Almost fainting, I who hadn't fainted in twenty-four years.

And then smelling you after your confession, just beginning, just barely able to allow in the new thoughts, the new words, the new realizations and revelations. How hard, even then, to change the lifelong thought structures that had held me together, saved my life and my sanity.

When I look down on my breasts Daddy, as I write this, I smell you. That's always been the main thing that happens when I look at my breasts. There are still huge blanks but I never forgot what you did with them.

It was really cold in Korea now. We were fighting in twenty degrees below zero. We weren't used to that, this wasn't our country. No way were we going to be home by Christmas. Every night I went in Jesus' arms to the Chosin Reservoir. By the heat of our presence may we warm them.

I got an 8-Ball for Christmas. Everyone loved it, even Grandma loved it. Holding it, asking the question, rolling it over, waiting for the answer to float up into the tiny glass triangle. Now when Gae and I met, rather than flipping pennies, we consulted the 8-Ball. At night I slept with it.

On our Christmas ride we watch the argument coming. Daddy's resentment spreads like smog across the blue sky. Just waiting in the back seat for Daddy to twist the words as they come out of Mama. "Isn't that what you said? Isn't it?" he screams. And he repeats the identical words she said but in a tone that means the opposite of what she meant. He's interested in jumping on her, catching her in the mistake that proves she doesn't really love him. This is the reason she can't allow herself to understand or to even resent what he's doing. At all costs she must not understand what he's doing. That would be proof she doesn't love him. Down the road we go licking our frosties, Mama trying to explain what she really meant, Mama trying to prove she really does love Daddy.

Bridget sits back, hisses into the wind "Mama makes me so mad. Don't say it, don't say it! But she always does. Why can't she shut her mouth, she knows her words will just set him off."

She remembers being in the crib at nine months old, Mama and Daddy leaning over her, goo-gooing what a cute little thing she was. She was lying there knowing she was older and superior to both of them, just caught in this baby body. Mama was superior to Daddy but she was superior to both of them.

"But Mama didn't have a mother," I say. "Or really a father either." That doesn't matter to Bridget. I'm awash in feelings of protectiveness for our mother. She's awash in feelings of protectiveness for our father. Mama says she'll grow out of blaming soon.

Because I refuse to think in terms of inferior and superior, which is a sin, I don't take my sister's logic seriously. She's the younger one so I'm to blame for everything, for our arguments which, it's true, I can't seem to stop for all my prayers. She takes the same stance with me as Daddy to Mama. Like Mama I'm the guilty one for being so stupid as to be sucked into the game. Her contempt for me is the same as her contempt for our mother.

Late one night, the light long out, I'm actually talking to my brother and sister about his moods. His anger, his rage is twisted, it's like a sickness, like something eats at him. Bridget says she knows exactly what I mean. This feels like a miracle. This feels like sisterhood, with Clarke too.

But a few days later she is mimicking my words back at me in her singsong voice, that my anger is just like Daddy's, except worse. Sharon's anger is so great, so ugly, so shriveling, our poor father hasn't a chance. We're all drowning in Sharon's resentment and anger. Sharon ruins everything.

"Sharon's angry," Daddy accuses coming through the door.

"Poor, poor Daddy," Bridget coos, cuddling up to him.

Clarke and I get into another horrible fight in which I twist his arms like braids.

We explore new routes to the horses through the maze that's Rancho Los Amigos. We find monkeys in a cage as big as a house, except it's taller, like three or four stories without the floors. The cage is like Gae's see-through doll house. It's made of chainlink fence, even the flat top, and it's set up in a eucalyptus grove with two trees inside. They could be chimpanzees or orangutans or little apes for all we know, we don't know the difference. Some of them have embarrassingly ugly, raw red bottoms.

Monkey society is even more brutal and ruthless than ours, though maybe it's just that they don't have walls to hide behind. Monkeys are mean, but most of all, monkeys are obscene. There's an obscene act going on in some part of the cage at all times. Like the daddy monkey who's catching his own poop as it comes out, then sneaking up and smearing his baby's face with it, cackling and jumping up and down like a lunatic to the mother's screams and frantic cleaning. Rape is always going on somewhere. Rape happens to everybody, daughters, sons, mothers, fathers, grandmas and grandpas. It's survival of the fittest. Everyone's promiscuous. Everybody is masturbating, picking their boogers and eating them. Hurling their babies against the fence. The mothers piss on each other when one is trying to sleep. They really do jump up and down scratching their armpits. They gossip out in the tree limbs, smack their kids like Mrs. Ritchie smacks hers. They trick and betray their own. They fight for each other's mates. They're worse than the old men in the bushes. At night I can't get them out of my mind.

"They're being experimented on," Gae explains. "My father said they're working on a polio vaccine made of monkey kidneys."

"Yeah, yeah, that's it! They're hallucinating! They think the black widows are coming for them!"

"Monkeynapped," she says, mashing her whole front into the chainlink triangles. "They've been monkeynapped from Africa where they were free in the jungle. That's why they're insane now."

One of the few things Daddy talks about from his boyhood is the Monkey Trial. That's how Clarence Darrow became his big hero, he defended a teacher for teaching that we're descended from monkeys. The Scopes trial was near Ducktown. Daddy was nine, it was all anyone talked about, Darwinism, evolution, the survival of the fittest, Genesis and lost faith. Maybe he and Grandma went to it, she as a reporter. "It affected him deeply," Mama always says and points out his favorite book on the shelf, *Inherit the Wind* by Howard Fast. Clarence Darrow is his hero and Grandma cites Genesis 2:4 saying everyone knows the Seven Days of Creation is like a poem. She's a Chitwood, from a long line of educators and preachers and justices of the peace, she isn't confused, but maybe this is what happened to Daddy as a boy. Maybe what he does to me is because we're like monkeys. He played Clarence Darrow in the high school play too. Darrow lost the trial but that was nothing to how he humiliated William Jennings Bryan. Maybe Daddy learned to fight dirty from the play. Maybe when he touches me he's being the fittest. His eyes devour my bare chest and he says you should grow up to be Clarence Darrow for the defense, Sharon, you're such a fighter for the underdog.

The polio victims have been wheeled out in their iron lungs, are lined up sunning their faces, using their mouths to hold their tiny brushes to paint. We spy Mrs. Ritchie instructing them in the technique. "Isn't it something?" she always says, "the miracle of life, the human will to persevere." She's adopting Robin, her fourth daughter, the infant of one of those in the iron lungs. We're walking our bikes past them so as to miss the eucalyptus buttons, silent, our eyes on the ground in search of the perfect size caps to make whistles like the Indians made. A million yellow acacias are opening their blossoms over us. Acacia was the tree the Ark of Covenant was made from. The sun is so bright there's a glare off the white soil. Even with eucalyptus I'll never be able to whistle as loudly or as piercingly as Gae. We're trying to rid our minds of what we're seeing. We're trying to survive, to be of the fittest. The eucalyptus sun flecking two girls on bikes. The way the light falls all along Gae's glorious lines. Following her down the road. Riding side by side. Back out the Industrial gate, pass the Hollydale foundry where they're making toilets, the angry young men at the twelve foot flames of hell, then weaving back and forth through the Avenues, McKinley, Wilson, Roosevelt, our arms crossed on our chests, "look Ma, no hands!" We pass Bridget and Dottie on McKinley playing movie stars with the new girl, Fay. It's so funny! They've filled balloons with water, stuffed them into Mama's 36C bras and Daddy's white tee shirts and are jugging around. Fay was named for the twenties actress, Fay Wray, who fell in love with King Kong. What's the difference between an ape and a gorilla? We go almost the entire way home without using our hands. How do we survive? Believe the worst will happen, Daddy believes, and then you won't be surprised. Mama believes the opposite: whatever you believe will come true, so believe the best. See the beauty and love and goodness of the world. What do I believe? No contest. My beautiful mother.

We're driving to the South Gate Drive-in. Bridget is sitting there at the far window stewing up stuff against me just like Daddy behind the wheel is stewing up stuff against Mama. Just before we turn in under the huge neon marquee she announces to them that I pinched her.

"No. I didn't."

"Yes she did, Sharon pinched me."

"Honest to God my hand on a stack of Bibles."

"Sharon, don't talk like that."

"Sharon can never admit when she's done something wrong," Daddy says.

"Do you two realize," Mama cries, "how your fighting wrecks everything?"

I do realize, it feels awful.

Watching the movie Daddy wants me to put my hands on the back of the front seat again so he can crack my knuckles. After he's done all ten I try to sit way back but he begs for them again. All of us laugh about Daddy's need, he winking in the mirror to me.

I pray long into the night. I go back over the day, reviewing everything that happened. My sister feels I've done her harm. Help me Jesus to know how I have and what I'm doing wrong. Let Bridget know I love her. Think not evil of another.

In the nightmare my arms are suddenly fast-twisted around and around each other tight down the front of my body like one braid. It's so fast it's like a machine did it, *shwhipppp*...

And then I find myself doing it to Clarke again when he attacks me. Of this I am guilty, horribly guilty.

Bridget starts getting car sick. *The Reader's Digest* says try saltine crackers. But the white square crackers don't work either, though she loves hoarding them, lording them over Clarke and me. Next they give her Dramamine, the seasick pills Daddy uses when he goes deep sea fishing.

Then her nose begins to bleed on our rides. When it appears, a deep river trickling down her upper lip, Daddy pulls over. Clarke and I get out and she lies down on the backseat and Mama and Daddy put a cold wet wash cloth on her forehead, whisper and console her.

At home in our beds she brags that she makes her nose bleed on purpose.

Feb 1, 51- ...An Atom Bomb was put off near Reno & Lasvegas, Nev this morning. It was seen & heard a long way. Gen. Eisenhower back from Europe.

Feb 2, 51- Gen. Eisenhower was to speak tonight of his European trip. Lovely sunny day. Fourth Atom Bomb put off in Lasvegas this morning.

Feb 3, 51- ...Cecil looks worn. Works too hard. They went to a party.

The world does seem to be coming to an end, the sky falling. We're winning again, have driven them back into North Korea, but now MacArthur wants to drop the Atom Bomb on China. The fifth detonation of the Atom Bomb rocks Las Vegas, the flash is seen all over LA and San Francisco. Radioactive particles from the earlier tests are found in snowballs in New York. The Holy Roller church on the other side of the tracks blankets the neighborhood with leaflets. *The Apocalypse is at hand!* Mama laughs, "There's always been these predictions. When we decided to make you everyone said we were wrong to bring a child into this terrible world." She tells of a date, or several, in the twenties when millions of people were certain the world was coming to an end. It was all the headlines. This was when her Grandma Simmons deserted the family, took off with the two missionaries. There have always been these prophecies. Prophets always prove to be fools. "And though I have the gift of prophecy," she quotes, "and have not love I am nothing... Love never faileth."

Still, the sense that the Apocalypse is at hand prevails. That stupid family inside their nice house just sitting there waiting to be exploded, the men hobbling down Industrial exploding in curses and rants and semen now about Korea, the monkeys throwing their own poop at their own babies.

The world didn't come to an end in the twenties but most of Elizabeth Simmons' children did.

If I should die before I wake I pray the Lord my soul to take. I pray for my parents and for the neighbors, I pray for each person I know, I explain to Jesus their ways as I struggle to understand them. My spirit visits their houses, blesses them, even Mr. Walker who scares me to death. I pray that Daddy won't ever suffer for what he does to me. It's alright, Jesus. You're always by my side. I pray for my secret bloody grocery bag buried under the house, that it never be found. Then I panic. My soul in the arms of Jesus visits the scared soldiers in Korea. We are with them crawling up the frozen battlefields, hiding in the icy trenches running with steaming blood. I pray for a solution to Daddy's hated job, the hated foreman. Most of all I pray not to sleep. I stay on my back with my legs scissored listening for the monster's return. Sometimes the terror is so great, the certainty that he's coming, my heart lurches in my chest, then up in my throat and I start suffocating again. I almost fall asleep or there's a sudden odd noise, and the shock makes me scream out loud, leaving me more devastated than ever, praying no one heard me. I thank Jesus for waking me up. When the train comes through at four-twenty, and the rooster crows, I can doze off until seven when it's time to get up and get ready for school. I thank the Lord for getting me through the night.

I'm saved many times. It is not that I fear for my soul; if I feel guilty about anything it is in being saved more than once but being saved keeps saving me. Pastor Adams welcomes me every time he calls for new converts. He doesn't protest or question me. I pray he understands. It's like Mama needs to tell the same stories, again and again. At the end this was clear. She knew she was repeating herself. She knew what we probably thought about this. But that did not matter, or at least, it was secondary. She needed, especially in the crisis of dying, to tell the stories again. What mattered was going over them again. Story like ritual. Story like creating yourself. Once upon a time there was a little girl. Reminding yourself of who you are. Going down that old road again.

April 1, 51- ...I seemed to hear Avon's voice tonight. It was passing through as Dee came in C's home.

April 11, 1951- Gen. MacArthur has been dismissed from his position in the war area by Pres. Truman.

April 17, 1951- I watched the homecoming of Gen MacArthur & family on television out at Fred & Audrey's last night. Mrs. MacArthur used to come to Estill Springs to visit her son.

April 18, 1951- Again I watched the MacArthurs as they prepared to leave for Washington. Young Arthur is a handsome lad. His mother is lovely. So was her mother, Sally Faircloth. The Gen. looked pleased at the joyous reception. Raining.

I've never forgotten the confusion I felt when in the spring of the fourth grade, President Truman relieved General MacArthur of his command in Korea. People went crazy mad at Truman, even my parents seemed miffed by the actions of their favorite president, a man supposedly of the people. "General MacArthur believes the only way to stop the Communists is to drop the Bomb on China like we did on Japan," Daddy explained. He and Mama were miffed by the actions of both men, genuinely unsure of which side to be on. "Poor Truman," Mama said, "he's suffering from Hiroshima."

The people gave him a hero's welcome. There were big parades and rallies. It was all over the television.

Then we detonated our thermonuclear test bomb on the Marshal Islands.

In her diary my grandmother says that I was in a play about George Washington in the fourth grade. I might have been Mrs. Washington, I could have been George himself, once a friend of her great-great-grandparents. Her father, George Washington Chitwood, was named for him. My only recollection is of standing on the front lawn facing our house and shouting at the top of my lungs to it, "I cannot tell a lie! I cannot tell a lie! *I* cut down the cherry tree!" Maybe I was just practicing my lines, my projection.

But I do remember being the prompter and understudy for our class's big annual play. I don't remember anything about the play except I memorized the whole thing, all the parts. Maybe it was about George Washington. Maybe I don't remember because I didn't have a part, I was all the parts. If anyone got sick I was there to take over. Sometimes I was in a little space under the stage and when someone forgot their lines I whispered them up through the slot. Sometimes I was in the folds of the thick, velvet maroon curtain. I loved being behind the scenes, under their feet, unseen, prompting. It was like my daydreams of life in the hole, and my prayer-visits to the Korean trenches. Looking up from the hidden slice of the floorboard window just a little off center stage, I could see the audience too. On stage the lights are blinding, you can't see the audience. This must be the way God feels, behind the scenes, seeing, knowing it all.

Again, Daddy's crawling under the house. To kill the black widows before they take over. At some point he had to have discovered my bag of bloody things.

One day at the crossing guard I suddenly know that the horses are under Paramount Boulevard, under the white lines of the intersection, under our very feet standing there waiting for the cars to pass. They've followed me and Gae underground all the way up Roosevelt. I'd felt them the whole way, every step, their hearts and hooves thumping after us. The horses like prompts under the stage. Like Jesus and God always at our sides, prompting. They know everything.

They were my buried bloody things. I was about to tell her the secret. Instead I told her about the horses under the intersection still begging us to free them. Pegasus sprang from the spilt blood of Medusa. I know the truth of that myth in my bones.

May 22, 51- ...The little Hull girl has not been found.
May 24, 51- ...Little Patty Hull's body was found.

Mama says Daddy feels unloved by me. He's so hurt that I don't love him he's tormented. "Why must you be so self-centered, Sharon? Why don't you go out and help him clean up the garage? Your daddy feels so unappreciated, he works so hard to put a roof over our heads."

A slope-headed zombie goes out the back door, steps down into the porch, opens the garage door on the left, steps down again, and enters, her ears ringing, resigned to her fate. Obey thy mother and thy father. But this time Daddy is in the center on his knees cutting out the two plywood sides of the teardrop trailer he's building for our vacation to the Northwest this summer.

He makes the most perfect teardrop trailer ever made. The plywood sides and top are sanded, stained a rich golden hue and shellacked to perfection. Not a nail hole shows, not a snag, not a splinter, Mama points out. See how all the grains are matched. It's a double wide bed on wheels in the shape of a tear drop. Most extraordinary is the kitchen. You pull up the back like you do the trunk of a car, and magic! there's an all-aluminum kitchen. Sink, stove, ice box, all the walls, everything of silver aluminum he designed, cut out and molded himself.

Daddy the perfectionist. All the time she points out the ways the other men, especially Dee Rupp and Johnny Ritchie, aren't. Mr. Henka and Mr. Pohlman don't even count.

"Sharon come back here a minute."

To the very end of my mother's life, she will spy a teardrop on the Interstate, or parked behind an old barn, and if it's a rare plywood and aluminum one she will wonder if it could be the one my father made. My father's perfect teardrop still being pulled down the highways, providing someone or more than one, a bed on wheels, an escape.

My tears that have never dropped, our Ark of Covenant, the Laws of Eden, our tears still on the way to the Promised Land of milk and honey.

Learning to swim well was a major concern of my parents. At the beginning of every summer we had swimming lessons at the Downey plunge but this summer they're more important than ever because we'll be swimming in the big rivers of the Northwest. Daddy's best friend drowned in the Ocoee, he knows what drowning is. Mama told many stories of swimming at the School. Her broken front tooth came from diving off the high dive when she was eleven, screaming "Last one in's a Hoover lover!"

I'm in my blue two-piece, he's there above me, at the edge of the crowded pool. I'm on my back showing him how long I can stay afloat. When we grow up Gae and I are going to be Olympic swimmers like Esther Williams. We're going to swim the English Channel like Florence Chadwick. But then I sink, seeing that he's not really seeing me floating, he's seeing my body laid out to him on the water.

In the car afterwards, he keeps staring at me. He's angry and brooding. I've outgrown my blue bathing suit. Mama's going to get me a one piece before we go on our trip. Then something happens. I can't remember, but it always comes: grief, terror, horror, the smell of chlorine which is the smell of semen, the Downey Plunge.

Maybe he didn't drive straight home. Maybe he stopped somewhere, like under the eucalyptus on Gardendale, or in the Pachuco cow pastures off Paramount. Dear Jesus, dear Someone, please come back and tell me. Or maybe it's part of the following.

There's a police stakeout on the Walker's house, even though Mr. Walker is a policeman. Black and white police cars are lined around all the blocks, behind and in front of our house. Police are parked up on Arizona and up on Main and Industrial, all down the front of the church. Sirens are wailing, red lights are spinning. Cops with guns drawn are sneaking between all our houses, coming from the church. This goes on all night, with blinding spotlights on Gae's house and loudspeakers telling Merrill Wayne Walker to come out with your hands up.

Don't shoot, don't shoot, don't shoot.

Gae's in there. And Dottie and Mrs. Walker. And Mr. Walker too.

I get to the hole, big triangles of red light slashing across their house, hide our provisions. Then I crawl through the bushes to her window. Not even Adolph and Goebbels sense me. Or maybe they've been shot. I rise up into their gun sights, knock on the pane, open the window for her. I help her out. We crawl to the hole first, under their spotlights and loudspeakers. Then, just before daybreak, after the train has gone through, crawling on our bellies, we make our getaway, we make it through everything, their guns, their tear gas, their lights and cars. Gae and I gallop away free. Forever.

Mrs. Ritchie says now she's certain Mr. Walker was involved in narcotics, that he was protected by the Mafia. Gae says no way he wouldn't have been put away for a long time, or killed, if he hadn't been protected. He's from San Francisco. Does that tell you something?

One morning they're not there.

The truth is I don't remember the police stakeout. My mother, my sister, Mrs. Ritchie and Gae have all described it as one of the central events on Roosevelt. They can't believe I don't remember. I can't believe it either. You can remember anything you want to. Everything.

What else don't I remember? Fourth grade is smog. Deadly, blinding, putrid smog.

But one day the smog will lift and I will be in the memory. I see now that I may have been in partial memory when I wrote the short story *No Man's Land,* during an all-night police stakeout I got caught in, in Portland Oregon in 1985, just weeks after I moved in with the man who became my second husband. Cryptonesia is forgotten memories you recall, but not as memories. Just like my nightmares have always tried to inform me, again and again, of what actually happened.

§

Eighteen

The air whispers her absence. I don't know what to do with myself. The
fear is much greater. My heart is a huge open sore. I can hardly breathe.

Getting across the Grapevine was as serious as crossing the desert. We
tied on our water bags. Bridget was carsick. *"Bridget was too sick for us to
enjoy Yosemite-"* Mama wrote in the Scrapbook. *"But it was most beautiful."*

From Yosemite we went up 99, circled the State Capital. We swam in
the Sacramento River, Daddy's hand fishing for me under the water, Mama
snapping our four heads in the deep and wide *"Tehama, the real name of
the Sacramento."* Back in the car Daddy snarled "Sharon doesn't love
me."

We were at Crater Lake on Friday, June 22, the summer equinox, the
date etched into the snow bank. I'm a big, very old girl in rolled jeans
leaning over the wall into it. My long blonde hair is pulled back low on my
neck. My ten-year-old breasts are puckering in the cold under the sweater,
my shoulders folding around them. In another photo I'm holding my
sister's and brother's hands—startling now, that they ever allowed such a
thing. Last night I went through all the childhood photographs looking just
at Bridget. My heart broke. In so many of them, maybe most, she is
awkwardly acting out the question: *What is going on? Would someone out
there please clue me in?* I remember posing too, but my poses are attempts
to look normal, oblivious. You're like Grandma, Mama would deplore,
when the camera is turned on you something freezes.

"The redwoods are the same color as Daddy's hair," she sighs, coming
down the Highway of the Giants. The view of the back of his big,
redwood-colored head all the way up California and all the way back
down. The all-consuming effort not to think. The all-consuming effort to
avoid being alone with him. Depression like seeing the San Andreas fault
opening up before your eyes, the whole car and teardrop headed right for
it. In Yosemite and Crater Lake, the suffocating panic taking over. I'm
paralyzed taking garbage to the can. Mama, Bridget and Clarke are gone
for a walk. Daddy's back in the camp alone. I'm afraid to go for a walk
because of the bears. I know better than to return to Daddy. Bears go crazy
when they smell a girl's blood. I'm not menstruating yet but Daddy caused
me to bleed there one night. You never know when it might return.

I remember coming back across the Grapevine, wide awake that
Sunday night, then down into the Valley, then through Hollywood, past

City Hall, down to 5903 Roosevelt absolutely bereft. Home is an empty street. Gae is still gone.

June 26, 1951- ...Terrible misunderstanding with Cecil. Really he is very impatient and seems he can't help it.
June 27, 1951- Cecil came in to say he was sorry.

In his thirty-five years this is the first and only such diary entry his mother ever made of an aspect of our father that we knew intimately, regularly. I see other little signs—*"Cecil looks worn."*—that suggest things are worsening in crisis for him. Even the increased fishing seems to suggest this. This is my first encounter with the possibility that he ever felt bad about, much less recognized, his *"impatient"* behavior.

My parents are kind about Gae, as if they've never objected to our friendship. Mama seems concerned about me. She's never liked the beach, she loves the desert and the mountains, the ocean makes her sad, but Daddy's fishing a lot now and she knows how much I love the ocean. The weekend before the Fourth of July we camp on Doheny at Dana Point.

The tide is higher than anyone has ever seen. **Malefic!** the headlines scream. In the forty-eight hours we're at Doheny we have to move the tent back three times. The roaring, pounding water, nothing is that strong, that dramatic, that undeniable. It renews me, it fills me with the desire to live again.

But I almost drown. I'm barely in the fast crashing breakers, just feet from shore, when this wave comes, hits me from behind. Daddy beside me goes down too. Bridget and Clarke closer to shore manage to scramble out. It pushes me to the floor, a ton of water on top of me, grinds me flat into the gravel. I can't get up, I can't budge an inch. Smashed down, grinding in the gravel, then I'm ripped back in the centrifugal force of flying stone, dark deafening suffocating roar dragging me back to deep ocean. Daddy's white legs beside me walking out. I want more than anything to just breathe, to rise to the air, to see the teardrop and tent in the sand dune, to have Daddy be glad to see me, you're getting so big, Sharon, anything, everything is worth it, I just want to breathe.

A set of waves goes over. I wait without breathing like waiting for him to be done, knowing about rhythm, it will subside, until finally the wave comes that goes all the way in and I go in with it.

I drag myself out, my whole front scraped and bleeding, even my breasts, and a deep hole with pebbles ground into my right knee.

No one is in sight on the beach, not Daddy, not anyone. I climb up the steep sucking-back sand, the sun setting behind me, coughing and throwing up sea water, trying to catch my breath. They're all in the tent. Thank you Jesus Daddy never realized, he'd feel so bad. I'd die rather than tell a soul, stupid me, I almost just drowned.

But somewhere in the clouds I'm conscious of the eerie emptiness of the world I'm climbing back to.

Inside the tent, my mother washes out the pebbles and sand ground into my knee. The skin is shredded whorls. Trying with all my might not to cry, not to wince when the iodine is applied. When Daddy snarls hypochondriac. She dresses it in gauze and tape like my hernia surgery. It keeps bleeding. She keeps having to change the dressing. She says yes it's okay to go back in, salt water is healing. I don't tell about the other bleeding places, pray they don't bleed through.

My Dana Point scar is still here, a pale lavender and white shell shape right above the white circle of the dog's tooth mark. When I look at it I remember what it's like not to be able to breathe. I'm in those fantastic rollers, huge green tunneling twenty foot things that flood the coast highway, and I'm not seeing my father's white legs walking out.

Mr. Walker was fired from the South Gate Police Department. They moved to Capistrano Beach, three miles southwest of San Juan Capistrano, where the old Mission is, where the swallows come home the first day of spring every year. They're managing the Capistrano Beach Trailer Park.

I don't remember how we learned, just the astounding fact that the weekend I almost drowned at Doheny we were just three miles from Capistrano Beach. I was in the same surf that was pounding her beach. We were breathing the same air. I was talking to her under the water. We got our wieners and buns at the Capistrano Beach store. That we went to the beach in the first place, like the swallows drawn there. I thanked the Lord for working in His mysterious ways.

July 14, 51- Sharon & Gae are spending the night with me.
We sleep on Grandma's couch folded out to a bed. Amazing, to sleep so close to her sleeping. I sleep all night. I don't even dream though I never forget her next to me.

Sunday evening, Mr. and Mrs. Walker pick her up in the yellow convertible and drive away. "Vaya con Dios!" We shout the words from the Capistrano pier arch across the ever expanding space until they turn up Main and disappear behind the church.

Mama encouraged me to get a library card, to start reading. Reading was her salvation as a girl. She read hundreds of books when she was nine during her first confinement with rheumatic heart. She started with *St. Elmo's Fire*. She read *Lady Chatterley's Lover* under the blankets. Books are holy. Never mark a book, never dog ear.

The librarian seems annoyed when I come through her door but *The Black Stallion* by Walter Farley leaps out at me.

Red sand blowing off the coast of North Africa, 1946. I write a synopsis of each chapter for Gae. The Arabian is the oldest and purest of all horses. The Black is the biggest and fastest horse that ever was. But fast or not, he's an Arab. They want to kill him.

We start drawing the Black Stallion, copying the illustrations, exchanging these in the mail. We critique each other's drawings. We vow we'll always be honest. In this way we will grow as artists.

I tried to read the classics as Mama urged, like *Little Women* that she so loved in the School, but everything in me bolted against being a little woman, against the stifling name Louisa Mae Alcott. Anna Sewell wrote *Black Beauty* in 1877 while paralyzed from a horse accident. She wrote it as Black Beauty's autobiography, in his voice! Well, at least that's interesting, I synopsed to Gae. I couldn't stomach that *Black Beauty* is a classic but *The Black Stallion* isn't.

"I want you to stay outside this afternoon," Mama says. "You've read enough for today."

I read *Lassie* in the hole. Gae's reading it at the same time on the beach. We post the hours, days and chapters so we're reading the same words at the same time. Me watching like crazy for dognappers, kidnappers, invaders, the old men. She watching for her father and malefic waves. *I'm Lassie running the width of the continent to get to you.* I know exactly how Lassie did it, I've been across America. I know how the swallows always get back to Capistrano on the first day of spring.

Tuesday, Sept 4, 1951- ...Listened to T.V. program of Peace Conference in San Francisco. (First T.V. Coast to Coast program.) Douglas Aircraft union workers where Cecil works came out on strike. I hope it is soon settled satisfactory.

Wednesday, Sept 5, 1951-...Cecil goes on picket duty tomorrow.

Friday, Sept 7, 1951- ...Cecil still on strike.

The Strike of Kings (Sept 4, 51-Oct 17, 51) made the cover of *LIFE Magazine*, that's how powerful Daddy's union was. We were richer than we had ever been (at least that's what they said). Daddy and Dee brought home bags of groceries from the meetings, things Mama never bought, didn't approve of. Bear claws, jelly donuts, pastries. Junk, she said. Daddy laughing in the irony of it all. During the Ducktown strikes they almost starved to death. Names like Huey Long and Jimmy Hoffa and The Teamsters and Detroit, words like scab and racketeer flew around the table. Daddy was definitely in a better mood than when he had to work. But it meant that he was home more now. He had picket duty and union meetings at unpredictable hours.

"Sharon doesn't like me being at home," he pouts at dinner. "She doesn't say hello when I come in."

I learn to stop and acknowledge his entrances instantly, even those from the back rooms to the front ones. This is required of Mama too.

Sunday, Sept 9, 1951- Frederick, Audrey, Sharon, Bridget & Clarke went to the beach and the girls were going to visit Gae & Dotty Walker ...

My intense longing to see Gae was mitigated by one thing: the fear and dread of her father.

Did something happen that Sunday afternoon with him? With my father?

Monday, Sept 10, 1951- Sharon was sick and they feared polio. Frederick & Audrey took her to General Hospital.

I can't hold my head up, I can't hold anything down, and the spiders are coming back. Kids right and left, lots of kids this very day in Capistrano, in Hollydale, are coming down with polio, being paralyzed for life, dying. I think it's Korea, like World War I killed everyone in Mama's family. Mama and Daddy are afraid to take me to the hospital where, if it's not polio, I'll be exposed to it, but finally I'm so sick they rush me to LA General.

We have an epidemic, we don't have room for another soul.

We're coming up the elevator, the young man bends to me on the gurney, and so kindly laughs, check this out, kid, there's no thirteenth floor. Did you know there's never a thirteenth floor in hospitals?

Somebody above me is whispering she may never walk again. They take all my clothes, park me in the hallway on the fourteenth floor, which is really the thirteenth, to wait for an opening. I'm there all day, alone, naked, first under a white sheet but then just a green towel because they need the sheet for someone sicker than me. I'm on my back naked in a long hallway, strapped down behind steel bars, on either the twelfth or fourteenth floor of LA General Hospital, but which is really the thirteenth, and so I'll never be found because there's no such floor. This is where my grandpa died.

In early twilight I'm wheeled back to the elevator, down to a green basement, turned on my side and given a spinal. This will paralyze you for awhile.

Of the hundreds of polio cases admitted to LA County General that week I was one of four that didn't actually have it. At the end of that back-breaking pain and nauseous paralysis I got up out of the bed, as all those other kids didn't, and walked away, full-bodied. I thanked Jesus. But then somewhere in the ever-growing sinkhole of my soul, a different kind of terror, a new thought crept in. If God saved me, why did he not save the others? I detested what that implied. I must not think.

§

Nineteen

On the first day of fifth grade the teacher said she would pick two students to be the class artists for the year. The next day she announced that the artists would be Clovis Swanger and Sharon Beck.

She gave them their private lessons in the techniques of water color in the corner near my desk, the last one of the first row, while the rest of us were doing silent reading. Most interesting was making the outline in pale yellow paint rather than pencil which always shows through.

I brought her the water color painting I did at home, a copy of Uncle Kenneth's muddy road, using the yellow outline and other techniques I'd observed her teaching them. I thought she'd be pleased to know there was another artist in the class. She was annoyed, brushed my painting aside. For a long time after that I studied my painting trying to see what was wrong with it. I ached to be Clovis and Sharon at the easels making the art for our classroom. This ache kept growing. I knew how to draw. Sometimes I'd be completely mesmerized by the yellow-lit outline of someone's body, everything in me aching to trace it onto paper. I loved painting, going with the colors and emotions. I wanted to do art all the time. I wanted to learn more techniques. Mama would stand before Uncle Kenneth paintings and say I must get my artist side from him. Even as a little boy he carried his paint box everywhere with him. Gae and I kept drawing horses, exchanging them in the mail, critiquing them. Most were renditions of the Black Stallion but we were branching out. Hers were really good. I aspired to be as good.

Mama started school too. She took Tailoring. She became far more than an ordinary seamstress. She continued to make all our clothes, elaborate dresses with smocked yokes and pleated midriffs and circular skirts and puffed sleeves with ruffles, lace and ric-rac and trims and bindings and sashes, and reversible jackets and halter tops, but now she made a tailored gray wool suit for herself and a three piece dress suit with a reversible vest for Clarke. She was always pointing out how poorly constructed most store-bought clothes are. She taught me how to hem so that not a single stitch showed. The hemline showing, or unmatched or uneven lines of prints and plaids, darts and underarm seams were shameful. The inside had to be done to the same perfection as the outside; she excelled in French seams. Sewing to my mother had always been more than a practical craft but now it became art. For the next two years the three of us would be in fashion shows, modeling her perfectly-made clothes, winning many blue ribbons.

She went to classes on Monday and Wednesday evenings. So from six to eleven p.m. on those days I had a serious problem.

His poker game happened every Tuesday night now at our house. Dee Rupp, Odie, Mr. Hogan were the regulars; maybe Dee's brother, Harry, too. In Volume Nine of our *World Wonder Books* was a painting of poker-playing, poker-faced dogs. I tried not to see that each dog looked like one of the men in Daddy's card game. The cards with the naked women had always been kept hidden but now they played them right out in front of all of us, as if proving something, I think now. As if a shield against any suspicion that they weren't normal men.

Seven p.m. I come in to the living room. They're at the dining room table at the front window. They look up from their hands.

"There's nothing so orgasmic as a little girl," one of them says, chugging his beer.

Surely one of them didn't say that. I still have good feelings about Daddy's friends. Surely it was only Mr. Walker who said that. "And big enough is old enough." Mr. Walker was never a part of my father's poker game. Could it have been Mr. Hogan?

September 16, 1951- The Hogan family is visiting Fred & Audrey & family tonight.

September 30, 1951- I went on long drive with C & A. We also visited the Hogans in Norwalk.

The Hogans will be in our lives a lot for the next two years. They had four kids our ages—the oldest, Linda, exactly my age—but for some reason we never got close to them. Mostly we visited each other's homes. We did some things with them that we had never done before, like eat Chinese food on Sunday afternoons in a walk-in Chinese cafe in Norwalk. Mr. Hogan was tall and slim, with a boyish face, light brown hair, and he was quiet.

One morning on Jennifer Street in Ashland, when, it seems now, she was trying to open about my father, my mother told me, out of the blue, that Mr. and Mrs. Hogan divorced at the end of those two years because he was a homosexual. She came downstairs to tell me of a disturbing dream she'd had during the night.

"Daddy was crying to me, he was very upset, 'Bill Hogan came up behind me in Julian at K.D.'s and handled me. He handled me,' he sobbed."

She mimed the act. Mr. Hogan came up behind my father at Uncle K.D.'s bathroom sink and reached around and "handled" him.

"I advised him not to go there again," she said in her wisest voice.

I think she was telling me that Mr. Hogan was my father's lover. I think she was trying to tell me a big secret, and of an important role she played in my father's life, that she was his confidante, advisor and protector.

Conceivably she was even trying to tell me something about my Uncle K.D.

I watch him work to get me alone with him so that no one will suspect. His manipulations of them, and my own—Clarke stay here and play with me, Bridget don't go, Mama, please let me wash the dishes, please don't ask me to go out to the garage and help Daddy sort nails—is one source of my aversion to all forms of manipulation. I vowed to never manipulate or be manipulated, if I could help it, a vow that has made it difficult to function in normal society. There have been dangerous moments in my life when the manipulator has risen his evil head so clearly that everyone can see him but me. I go blind. I deny it. I will not see it, I will not believe it. Thinketh no evil. I love you. I say I love you right to Evil's face. I love the other. I love the world.

In the middle of the night sometimes I hear Mama moaning. Sometimes it's from a nightmare. In the morning she'll say it was just that horse chasing her again. Sometimes when they're gone I go into their dark and mysterious bedroom to study the women. On the wall over her bed is the photograph of the sun rising from blue hills under which is inscribed the Biblical verse from Psalms 121. *I will lift up mine eyes unto the hills, from whence cometh my help.* And on the dresser the photograph of Daddy at twenty-five the day after I was born. I think I study the naked women to know them the way she studies the catalogue women. If it is in here that he catches me I stare at his photo while he stares at my breasts and touches them, though more often it happens in the garage and I study his 1949 calendar of the naked girl nailed up there on the black tar paper that he still hasn't taken down though it's 1951. To both these pictures, the most handsome boy-man and the most beautiful girl-woman in all the Universe, I almost pray. Then stop myself from the sin of idolatry, the sin of Catholics, *thou shalt not make any graven images.* What else does he do? Why do my memories always stop here? The face of God my father as it was on my first full day on earth. The body of the calendar girl, her pink frame more and more like mine is becoming, twisted into a question mark.

There's a jar of orange salmon eggs in the refrigerator. It's Daddy's fishing bait. When I was little and we fished from the Seal Beach rock jetty we used mussels that were free. He'd pry them with his knife from the dark sea-sloshed rocks beneath us, then pry open the long black hairy shell, dig out the meat and put it on my hook, "there you go, Sharon Lura." Now when I open the humming Frigidaire, the round beady eggs glisten at me like eyes and I see his fingers on my salmon-colored nipples and the white worms in my excrement.

Climb out the window above the bed. Walk (don't run) to Hollydale. Turn left at Johnny's on Garfield. Garfield becomes Cherry. Walk Cherry Avenue (act like you know where you're going) till it hits the ocean, then turn south, run the shoreline all the way to Capistrano Beach. Sleep on Tin Can Beach. Sleep under the Laguna arch. Only seventy miles. I still dream this escape route.

She rearranges the furniture. I walk in from school and everything's in a different place. The wind knocks out of me. My survival depends on knowing exactly where every little thing is, on being able to run through in the dark. Then I'm ashamed. Enter into life, Jesus said. Something releases. First there is order, then there is chaos. Then there is beauty. There is darkness so mysterious in Daddy, his moods. There's rising from the ocean floor. There is light in Mama's explaining. In her rearranging.

"Sharon needs a dog," she announced. "Maybe one we raised from the beginning won't develop the need to roam that Sambo had." She started combing the want ads.

One day she brought home an adorable six week old black Cocker Spaniel. Both its parents were registered show dogs, but he was illegitimate, he couldn't be registered and therefore we could afford him, a champion-bred show dog. "That's silly anyway," she said, "what are papers?"

Black Prince George loved to please. I trained him to walk with the leash, to heel and sit. I trained him to sit up on his hind legs, then while sitting there, to shake hands, then to bark the number of fingers I held up. George learned the difference up to five fingers. Sometimes six. I trained him to turn in circles to the right, to the left, to roll-over on command. I

trained him to fetch the evening paper thrown up on the lawn. I trained
him to stay. I'd go off to the store, he'd watch me the whole way, then I'd
disappear awhile in the park, return a half hour later and this puppy of
boundless energy would be sitting in the same spot and same position as
when I left. I bathed him once a week in the bathtub, and brushed and
combed his long wavy hair till it shone like ripples in a black stream. I
made a sock of marbles for him when he was teething, out of one of
Daddy's that was missing its match. We spent great laughing and growling
times pulling and yanking it through the house and across the lawns.

One day Daddy stopped up George's snout. I was paralyzed and later
cried in his thick hairy neck I'm sorry, he was just teasing, he can't help it.

Clarke and I, the skeleton and the harem girl, go up the steps of a porch
behind our house on Wilson. I'm awfully big to be trick-or-treating but I'm
relieved to see some boys who I know are even older than me leaving the
door with their loot. It's cold and I've gotten too big for my blue bathing
suit top so I'm wearing Mama's coral three quarters length coat with wide-
cuffed sleeves and high stand-up collar over my harem costume.

"Open your coat," the gangster says, "so we can see what you are."

I do and he shoots me with his water pistol, cold and stinging, splitting
my bare midriff into upper and lower selves. I'm so mortified I can't get
Clarke off the porch. All the rest of that trick-or-treating I can't get my top
self reconnected to my bottom self.

Of course by now, my brother is long gone about me. Of course he
attacks me. That's what guys do to Sharon.

Without notice, Mr. and Mrs. Walker drop off Gae and Dottie to spend the
weekend with us. When Gae comes through the door so unexpected, it's
like the Pacific Ocean coming in, the joy is that high. She's grown, she's
wearing boy jeans with wide rolled cuffs, cowboy boots and a thick
leather-tooled belt, a stallion pawing the air on the silver buckle at her
little belly. Her very long fingernails are filed and polished red. There's no
place on earth more depressing than my bed but tonight she sleeps in it
with me. "God damn!" she says as the five of us bed down. The three of us
Edens freeze. That's the first time God's name has ever been taken in vain
in our house.

The next morning, walking up Industrial holding hands just like the
good old days Gae instructs me in the words. Hell. Damn. Shit. Cunt. Piss.

Fuck. And screw, and asshole and cocksucker and motherfucker. "God damn!"

She tickles the inside of my palm with the long, filed nail of her middle finger. I almost faint over the tumbleweed. There's a boy who does this to her. Capistrano Beach boys are as unpredictable as the tides, like the night the ocean came all the way up over Pacific Coast Highway flooding their trailer and all the others in the trailer lot. Her stories pound at me like the pounding surf, a boy putting his finger in her. How you fuck. That word. She says. The word always on the Hollydale drugstore bathroom wall no matter how many times they wash and paint it off, the word etched permanent in the cement sidewalk beneath our feet.

"When a boy tickles your palm like this with his middle finger while you're holding hands it means I want to fuck you."

The sun shines in her surfbleached hair. We play baseball in the street with the Beaver boys, just like before. We go to all our places disguised as boys, we renew everything. Bridget and Dotty steal Mama's bras again, jug around the block with their big water balloon boobs under Daddy's white tee shirts singing skip-to-my-lu-my-darling! It is too hysterical. I had loved Hollydale through Gae, and so when she was gone, Hollydale was too. To have her back is to have the place back. And even my sister, who wants to have boobs so Daddy will love her too.

After they leave, Mama walks to the store with me. In the course of half a minute, half-way between Roosevelt and Main, I say damn twice. Damn just flies out of me. I feel incredibly on top of something, incredibly excited, about the world, the possibilities, with sharing this with my great, my very great mother.

"SHAR-RUN!"

It's like that time she found me in the hole with the boys.

"Shar-ron!"

I'm sinking into the sidewalk beneath F-U-C-K that is seen but never said, step-on-a-crack-and-break-your-mother's-back.

"Ladies do not use such words, Sharon," she starts in her lecture tone. "Boys will get the wrong idea."

One of them, grown old and drinking in the tumbleweeds, is leering at us.

"That kind of language is the difference between girls who are cheap, Sharon Edens, and girls who have self-respect. The reason your father respects me is because I don't talk like the other wives, not like foul-mouthed Bertie and Mrs. Ritchie. Because I don't allow him to talk that way around me. Or us. When he enters our home he leaves that language behind."

"I'm sorry Mama. It just came out, I didn't mean to say it."

How could I have? But somewhere inside I'm laughing, to the gull on the cross watching, that damn hatched on its own inside, winged right past the choker at my throat that makes me stutter and hiccup and stammer, say things backwards, always having to start over, in the beginning is the word with a life all its own, that it flew out without my intention!

When I get home I begin a letter to Gae. Then Bobby Beaver is at the screen door.

"Sharon Edens we need a catcher!"

"I can't. I'm writing a letter."

"You can keep writing, just come out and stand there."

Now I'm out here behind homebase writing and catching. I'm so excited with the writing, what I'm saying, baseball is so slow and boring anyway, I can do both at the same time. It drives Daddy nuts, he's says I'm making it up, but in many things I really can do two things at once better than one thing at a time. Like my homework while watching television. That's when I get my A+s. I'm writing with a dull pencil on Mama's five-by-eight linen tablet, page 19, page 20, and I've only just begun. I'm writing my letter full of three letter exclamations, *guy! boy! man!* plus *shoot!* and *heck, darn,* and for *Heaven's sake,* while catching the balls the boys pitch and miss, putting them out at home. Page 28, page 29, we vowed to love each other forever, this is how you fulfill that vow, the lead worn down, the words barely decipherable, the tablet running out, writing Gae I love you.

There are two photos from that visit. We're in the backyard just outside the frame of the swing set in which we usually take our photographs, maybe ten feet from the corner where we used to dig. Mama's grapefruit tree behind us is burgeoning. Black Prince George is a big puppy in Gae's arms beneath her pensive sideways stare. I'm staring at the ground, pixelating in the hundred yard stare. My big self. My too big, too troubled, not big enough self.

Gae is as beautiful as I remember her. Beautiful in both photographs, the other one being of just her in front of the end apartment. I remember taking it. I carried it in my wallet for years. Beautiful is my favorite word. She loves me too.

My sister's eight and definitely has little breasts under her striped tee shirt. She's wearing her blue jeans. Her pose is not her usual questioning, but flirtatious, flaunting and coquettish, like the poker card women. She's leaning languidly back on Dottie who she's been spanking all weekend. Bridget denies to this day that anything ever happened to her. Not even the old men on Industrial came on to her. Not in any way. She didn't even know about sex until she was in college and her boyfriend had to tell her. Dottie, who is drilling us from beneath her cowboy hat, who must be five, appears almost as sexual as Bridget. She and Bridget are relating to the camera as much as Gae and I are trying to avoid it. Maybe they're just copying our Laguna beach photos from last year.

I never really knew Dottie so I'm unable to characterize her. She was so young and my sister, envious and jealous of the intensity of my friendship with Gae (I know now), probably kept her to herself. "For two years," she kept telling our mother in the eighties, "I spanked Dottie. Dottie let me spank her. I'd pull her pants down, spank her, spank her hard." In dream symbolism Dottie would be all that's unconscious between me and my sister.

§

Twenty

Mid term, half of the Roosevelt fifth graders, those of us on the west side of Paramount Boulevard, and half of the Grove Avenue fifth graders, those on the south end of Garfield, were transferred to a new school, Hollydale School. In the fall all the other grades would start, but for now, for this one semester, it would be just fifth graders.

Hollydale School was in the opposite direction from Roosevelt, a mile to our west, on the other side of the tracks, beyond Hollydale, across the road from the horse stables, right on the river bank. The enormous, undeveloped playground in back was sand dunes with tufts of tall grass. I loved that you could see through the little chainlink hearts of the fence to the river below held in the new cement trough down the middle of the wide sand bed. The Los Angeles was usually dry but in the rainy season, which was the school season, it could, and often did, flood, even flash flood. I loved that at recess we could see people horseback riding down there and the hobos and Gypsies passing through. The sound of sawing and drilling and hammering and men shouting at each other, the smell of wet cement and new stucco as they hurried to finish the school permeated the environment. And lots of talk of the Santa Ana Freeway coming.

On the first day I claimed the position of class artist. I just claimed it. I demonstrated the yellow outline technique to Mrs. Abrahms and said Clovis Swanger and Sharon Beck know it too. I said we would do Washington and Lincoln's birthdays. For Valentine's we would make a giant heart-shaped mural of the Los Angeles Basin with Hollydale School at the very heart of the heart, right on the LA River, which would be the line down the middle to Point Fermin. If that was okay. She didn't seem to mind. I think she was taken aback by my assertiveness. I was taken aback.

The Grove Avenue kids were mysterious and beautiful. Probably they were a niche higher on the economic scale, but I couldn't know this. Mama adamantly denied the Back East notion about being on the right or wrong side of the tracks, there is no right or wrong side here, class doesn't exist in Southern California, this is why it is such a wonderful place. She almost chose a house on Utah Avenue, right near the new school but finally chose 5903 Roosevelt because it was on a corner, it faced south and she could see a far distance, to that mountain on a clear day. Still, the Roosevelt Elementary kids seemed a little scruffy and lost at Hollydale and I kept wondering about the ones we left behind, ones I could never call my friends because I was so shy I had never spoken to most of them all those years.

The Grove Avenue boys were definitely meaner and smarter, more active in class, more mature. Or maybe it just begins to happen then, naturally, mid fifth grade, ten years of age. Maybe the Roosevelt boys would have started in on me the second half of fifth grade, but I don't think so. Maybe environment's everything. Imagine if I'd grown up on Utah Avenue. Whatever, the Grove Avenue boys were the boys my mother had been warning me about.

From the first day they called me names. "Giraffe." "Stringbean." "Telephone Pole." "High Wire Act." "Hey Skyscraper, how's the weather up there?" They ran in packs past me on the playground snickering and yelling "Boobs!" "Stacked!" Mama's constant warnings about the ruin of a girl's reputation rang so loud I'd become paralyzed out in the sand dunes, unable to move, speak, or even to think or pray. For long minutes I'm dissolving into the grains of sand.

I brought my marble sack to school, hung around their circles until I got invited into the game. Again, the surprise of my sideways assertiveness. Some days I took home their prized peewees and boulders. Daddy made me steelies at Douglas—really ball bearings for jets. The boys coveted my steelies. Soon the marble games had gone on long enough that my father's steelies were in collections throughout the school. They were called Cecils. I loved this for my father. And it didn't matter how many I lost. I was at the source. Sometimes I was the first one out in the yard. I'd draw the circle in the sand, empty my marbles into it, start the game. Then, I'd panic for my forwardness. That they might think I liked them.

Just as with Roosevelt we had fire drills, but now we had bomb drills too. Jeff O'Toole, a head shorter than me, but so cute with his slick ducktail, his duck's beak down the front of his freckled face, gave the report on the Hydrogen Bomb. This is the method by which the stars including the sun and mankind were created. It's called nuclear fission.

We had to learn to distinguish between the sirens to know the correct thing to do. The Bomb siren would go off and instead of lining up and filing out of the building to the sand dunes we had to jump out of our desks, throw our right arm up across the back of our neck to shield our selves—the neck is where the Bomb's radiation will penetrate—while maneuvering with the left to get under the desk. Being exactly between Los Angeles and Long Beach, being a neighbor of Douglas Aircraft and right on the Los Angeles River, at the very heart of the Basin, Hollydale School was a prime target.

A tornado hit that fall near Lynchburg, Tennessee, destroying the school Grandpa went to as a boy on Beech Hill. The news photo of the pile of debris was on display at Grandma's for the rest of her life. Under my desk I'd see it. And her newspaper feature of the Tennessee Valley Authority flooding the valley between Estill Springs and Lynchburg— drowning John Chitwood's grave, and the graves of the second family he made after his wife wouldn't let him back in the house when he came home from the Civil War; and the graves of his second congregation. "As if the valley was just a big hole to be filled," Grandma cried, even though she wasn't allowed to speak to that side of the family. Under my desk I'd see water lapping all sides just as in Noah's flood.

One day I fainted. When contacted my mother said it must be Sharon's period trying to start. I was more mortified by this than I was of having lost so much control that I fell down to the classroom floor in front of everybody.

"Stand up straight, Sharon Edens!"

"Shoulders back, girl!"

"Don't slump, Sharon."

"Hey, hump back!"

Jerking my elbows back. Lining my spine up against the wall. But before I'm out of the room I'm slumped back down. To walk like that would be strutting.

"Hey Hunchback of Norte Dame!"

Jan 27, 52- Cecil, Audrey & children visiting the Hogans.
Feb 14, 52- Cecil's 36th b.day. I think of those who stood by that cold day. Born Monday morning. Avon, Dr. L., Mrs. A., Mrs. Am, Mrs. W.

Now every day when I come home from school Mama is in the bathtub preparing for Daddy's arrival home from work and she gives me a lecture on the facts of life. I sit on the closed toilet. I love being in here with her but I hate what she talks about. I know the facts of life. Certainly the penis and vagina part.

A cradle of blood is built up inside you for the baby to grow in, a thick cradle of blood to protect it. It could be happening right now inside you, Sharon Lura, any day now you will start to menstruate. The egg in your side develops waiting to be fertilized. If it's not fertilized the cradle dissolves and that's menstrual blood.

She tells stories of the terrible days when there wasn't birth control, when women died from having too many babies, how wrong that was. Too many babies can kill you, in spirit and body. And then where are the orphaned children?

But the main point of her detailed, graphic lectures is to inform me of the necessity of staying a virgin for my future husband, to equip me with enough information to be able to do this. I sit on the toilet right above my buried bloody pajamas and I'm just flushing down.

Men and boys will be noticing you soon. They will want to kiss you and touch you. If you let them they'll go too far. The sex drive is so strong in men, honey, they can't help what they do. But if you weaken and give in to them they'll hate you. They'll tell each other what they have done with you, they'll call you names like whore. They won't marry you. Men only marry virgins. Your virginity is the most wonderful gift you can give your husband. The sex drive is strong in girls too. But you must be stronger than it. Never sit and kiss a boy for any length of time. This is called petting. Petting will overwhelm you and before you know it you will have gone too far. And he will be looking for another girl, one who is stronger and a challenge and still a virgin.

Her nipples float like two overgrown salmon eggs in the pinkwhite bubbles. They are redder, bigger, looser than mine. No matter how many times I see her body it stays a little scary to me. The dark red bush of hair, the big hairy crack between her legs from whence I came. I love my mother.

Boys don't like girls who are forward. She told this in a way that terrified me. Never telephone a boy. He'll get the wrong idea. Boys only like girls who are hard to get. Never ask a boy to dance, never not ever for a date. Boys can't stand to be chased by girls. Boys will want you only if you don't want them.

She explains the double standard. I still see her face jerking slightly to me. The thought is crossing my mind, my mind always seeking the escape: stay single then. Love women. Love Gae. You're right, of course it's not fair, she says, but it's the way things are. If you want a husband, a family. If you want God's family to survive on Earth these are the rules you have to play by.

She has her father's redhead complexion, she has freckles on her arms and shoulders but not anywhere else. She laughs that she has his red hair as her pubic hair. As light as she is, though, her skin is darker than both Daddy's and mine. It's rosy pink.

If you ever get stuck down some dead end road with a boy demanding favors just say I have to go, my mother will be looking for me. Say, it's midnight, that means my mother has called the police. Just get out of the car and run. You can put all the blame on me. Remember, you don't ever have to do anything you don't want to. Just phone your mother. A mother's love is unconditional. Promise me you will never forget that. Always keep a nickel for a phone call. Keep a dime for a bag of peanuts, for energy to run through the night.

Sex is wonderful, she's always careful to add. Sex with your husband is the most wonderful, most miraculous thing in the world. It is how you three came into existence.

Mama is rosy, almost red. She's a redskin, an Indian. Guy was part Cherokee, maybe a half, but he was a redhead. A black haired parent and a blond haired parent make red haired babies. You really were made to make babies weren't you, Dr. Pentz said, examining her the first time, me a teeny little, big headed blond thing rocking in the cradle of blood inside her. He was measuring her wide hips.

Dear Jesus, where was I before I was inside her?

Square Dancing is fifth period on Thursday afternoons. Both fifth grades come together in the new gym, called the cafetorium: half cafeteria, half gymnasium. The girls line one side and the boys the other side and then the caller, our principal Mr. Wilson Bell, calls choose your partners! This means the boys choose the girls. Then the couple meet in the center of the waxed and polished pink and gray tile. She curtsies, he bows.

But the boys look at me and scream no way Jose! They look up at me in an exaggerated way, shielding their eyes and fall down laughing together. Mr. Bell yells for them to get back in line. They stick out their camel necks and hump them back and forth the way Daddy strokes his penis, eyes drilled to each other. "Wallflower!" "Sunflower!" "Palm Tree!" "Sequoia!" "Hey, King Kong, whatcha got up there?!"

Finally Mr. Bell assigns the tallest boy, Gary Neal of the other fifth grade, as my partner. Gary is like Raymond of the first grade, he never speaks, you almost forget he's around. He's only about an inch shorter than me. He's olive-complected, has straight black hair slicked back with Brylcream, is what Mama would call a little paunchy. The skin under his eyes are dark half moons. He is quiet, serious, maybe shy, but after this day he always chooses me to be his partner. The other boys are silent about this as if they don't know what to think. I don't know what to think.

As the square dancing sessions continue into spring, and we come more and more to be actually dancing, I grow used to being slightly taller than him. Or maybe he's growing. I swing hand over hand through the rest of the guffawing shrimps and come back to him in gratitude and relief. Square dancing is old-fashioned corny and so contrived, but I listen to the words, I try to figure out what they mean, dosie doe your partner and promenade your darling, and sometimes a bolt charges through me and I get it, and I get into it. You have to hear the language like you hear the Bible's. Metaphors, like Grandma says. Swinging around again, coming back to Gary Neal, a boy almost as big as me, and kind, as dark as I am light, with no trace of the contempt that I receive from almost everyone except my mother, and we dos y dos, and it is oh so sweet I'm afraid I'm fainting again.

There are two Grove Avenue girls in the other fifth grade, Susan Evans and Nancy Mehr. They're girlfriends, both with long dark blond hair and dark blue eyes and they're taller than most of the kids, though not as tall as me. When I see them hand in hand on the playground I miss Gae more than ever. I know what it's like to have a closest girlfriend. Nancy is skinny and witty. Susan is quieter, more serious; she may even have beginning breasts. One recess I run into the Girls and the two of them are in deep conversation before the mirror. I duck into the stall, unable to speak. When I turn around, my eyes are in the mirror over the stall door between their two heads, too seeing, too serious, too tall, too old, too weird. Too like Daddy, somehow. This is another of those moments that I'm forever still in. The three of us in that big bathroom mirror. Me praying to Jesus help me to never look again, I am too strange, too ugly.

Here's another one: Bridget has come home from Roosevelt School crying. They've gotten their school pictures. Mama and I are with her at the dining room table looking at them. "It's just a bad photograph," Mama says, "you are too pretty." But there's this frozen moment in which I'm looking from the photo into my sister's face. She's pasty pale and has pimples, is very washed-out looking, sweaty, and has no eyebrows. She has colorless frizzy hair that gets kinkier with every haircut Mama gives her. Her dishwater blond hair is so thick she's taken to using a razor blade, spouting Grandma's list of Corns down through history who had naturally curly hair like Negros, except blond. The secret thought flits through me: yes, my poor sister is ugly.

In no way do I understand this then but the real taboo of this moment is in the looking at my sister. I see that night. That night is so ugly it stops me from looking again. If I look at her we might be forced to speak of it, and then we will be killed. I blink my eyes trying not to see my sister as ugly. We've not looked at each other since that night in the second grade. We must never look at each other. The way he rubs up against her. We will remember. Nothing could be uglier than that.

She's sobbing. "But Bridget Colleen," Mama is saying. "You have what Sharon doesn't. You have personality."

"You're not smiling, Sharon," Daddy hisses. And Bridget repeats.

Maybe she's already in the habit of chewing the Ex-lax gum in our medicine cabinet, and then the purgatives in Grandma's, and now can't go without something, and that's why she's so wacked-out looking; or maybe she's already hypoglycemic.

"I'd die if they started checking on the last time I went, the way they do you, Sharon Lura, I don't know how you stand it. Besides purgatives make my skin glow, they make me prettier."

She swears me to secrecy. Lately she's spending her allowance on Ex-lax and this week she doesn't have enough. "Can I borrow ten cents from you, Sharon Lulu, pretty please?" I will secretly know she stays addicted to laxatives all the way through high school. This is the first time I've ever told. But I will always wonder if her chronic health problems started with her laxative habit.

Complete strangers call out angrily "Hold your shoulders up girl!" Mama says "Quit being ashamed of your breasts, Sharon." She was known as having the best posture in Charlotte, North Carolina. When she came down the sidewalk and the carpenters whistled and clapped for her perfect posture she was so proud she held herself even more erect. She was doing three day juice diets now every six weeks or so. She was cleansing her insides. From the bathtub, she lectured against sweets, sugar and carbonated water. These will rot your teeth, weaken your bones and muscles, tear down your immune system. Coca Cola is habit forming. Addictions are an abomination. The Body is God's Temple. You must be careful what you put in it. You must be proud of it.

She lectures me constantly about positive thinking so I can't tell her of my negative thinking, or anything that might be the result of negativity. I can't tell her that I need a bra. It would seem a criticism of her. I love her so much. I want to be her perfect daughter. Ye shall know the tree by its fruit.

Six-thirty p.m. every day Grandma comes over and watches the puppet show Beany and Cecil the Sea Sick Sea Serpent. Daddy laughs till tears roll down his eyes at the green seasick sea snake Cecil, how the end of his big tail is never seen. He loves Laurel and Hardy, and Red Skelton who looks a little like him too, like Nixon, and Billy Graham and Jesus. Red Skelton's a genius, especially when he plays Clem Kadiddlehopper or Freddie the Freeloader. They discuss the difference between slapstick and irony. Slapstick is funny. Irony is snobbish, cruel.

Marilyn Monroe hits like a bomb. She's all Red Skelton, Bob Hope and guests can joke about, she's a bombshell. The phenomenon seems to register, if slightly, even on my grandmother's face. I study the excitement like it's a test my life depends on.

Mama, upside down on her slant board doing her leg and stomach exercises, then standing on her head, her backside going up in slow motion against the wall to get the blood rushing down, says she's like Jean Harlow. "Oh, how I loved Jean Harlow."

Now we're both on our heads to get the blood rushing to them.

Red Skelton says Marilyn Monroe's chassis moves like a parked car with the motor running. Mama says he stole that, they said that about Mae West, listen to that canned laughter. She says this hoopla is just like what happened to Mae West. She was six years old when Mae West hit. Red Skelton scratches his armpits like a monkey at the County Farm.

How do my parents know this stuff? Jean Harlow and Mae West and Stan Freeburg and the Punch and Judy Show, all of this—the difference between slapstick and irony—is new stuff in our house now with the television, but clearly old news to them. Mama says Mae West's in such good condition at sixty-three because she exercises, watches her diet, doesn't drink or smoke, and is possessed of an extra thyroid gland. She says that waddly, silky, hip-swinging exaggerated walk, that long glance, those slow but meaningful gestures, that little girl voice and drawl— Marilyn Monroe is just copying Jean Harlow and Mae West.

Then the biggest explosion of all: Marilyn Monroe is the naked girl on Daddy's 1949 calendar! The studios were afraid that the discovery of the calendar, that she posed naked for money, would ruin her career, but everyone, the whole world goes nuts. The whole world loves it!

She doesn't look like the same girl on the calendar. The biggest difference is her bleached blond hair, straightened, thinned, cut and puffed-out like Mrs. Walker's and Mae West's. On the calendar photo she has long, thick, dark golden curls and she looks like me, her body anyway, Daddy always says. Her face seems different too. Mama says she's had plastic surgery and her teeth have been capped. They can change the shape of your nose and chin and mouth and teeth. Trying to feel with my tongue what caps would feel like. Her name was changed too. She used to be Norma Jean Mortenson.

We're driving downtown. Daddy says that's the woman Marilyn Monroe apprenticed under, the famous striptease artist Lili St Cyr. Lili St. Cyr is inside the theater in her white high heels and rhinestone tiara and white boa feathers draped around her neck on a swing above the men. Red Skelton jokes about Lili St. Cyr too.

One day in the bathtub Mama tells me Fatty Arbuckle was having sexual intercourse with the Sunbonnet girl and wouldn't let her up to go to the bathroom. Her bladder burst. It killed her. It ruined his career. She implied that it was weirder than this. I didn't know it was a coke bottle that broke inside her until recently, but my mother knew that. After all the years and good experiences it was still a relief to learn that his penis didn't kill her.

I don't take my eyes off Marilyn Monroe when he traps me. Her pink-white torso twisting in the S shape on the red velvet cloth, her arm thrown behind her head the way we have to for the bomb drills, luscious breathy body of how to be a woman on the black tarpaper wall among his silver tools between the exposed two-by-fours. Marilyn Monroe hung in lots of the fathers' garages of Hollydale before any of us knew her name, her made-up name. It's just the nature of the male. Hacksaw, electric wheel saw, sander, drill bits, the rows of hammers and screwdrivers and shovels and fishing rods lined up by size around her soft lit-up flesh. Jars of nuts and bolts. Tape measurers. Her pink 22 inch middle to the 24 inch spiked saw wheel vivisecting the Black Dahlia. Mine pressed between the front bumper of the 49 green Ford and his work table with my white tee shirt raised up, his big fingers playing with them, biggest hands on any man I ever saw, Mr. Hogan said during last night's poker game as Daddy dealt, my flesh more shocking than hers safe and protected behind film. She doesn't look like that anymore, Daddy.

Pastor Adams said I was a true Christian and so big and mature for my age I should be baptized now rather than waiting until twelve, the customary age. Maybe he was finally tired or alarmed at my repeatedly being saved. Maybe somebody complained.

Mama had always scorned Catholics who baptize infants before they have consciousness. This is why Catholics stay sinners and the world doesn't get better. They believe they are saved just because they were automatically baptized before they ever had a chance to develop their own thoughts and beliefs. I was baptized on Mother's Day. That Sunday evening we were taken into a room behind the altar. There was a rack of hanging white baptismal robes. "This one's for Sharon," Pastor Adams said, taking the one hanging in front, of a noticeably different material than the others. It was thinner, whiter, more delicate, almost gauzy. "You'll look so pretty in it," he said, handing it to me. John the Baptist baptizing his cousin Jesus in the River Jordan was on the wall of the dressing room, John wearing his raiment of camel's hair and the leathern girdle about his loins and Jesus in the white robe. *"He saw the heavens opened and the Spirit like a dove descending upon him. Mark 1:10."*

The baptismal font was in no way like the River Jordan. It was shiny white porcelain with gold hot and cold faucets, exactly like our bathtub at home except much bigger. I bet it was made at the Hollydale Foundry, right down the street.

I stepped into the font, faced him in his white robe. The water was warm, like bath water. His heavy lidded English eyes like Daddy's. With both hands I took hold of his hairy, hard-as-steel arm, as he had instructed, praying inside, relax, relax. "I baptize you Sharon Lura Edens in the name of the Father, and of the Son, and of the Holy Ghost," and he lowered me back into the warm chlorine-smelling water so quiet, so far away from the congregation. It seemed a long time, but I followed his instructions not to panic. Then he raised me back up, the organ droning.

Pastor Adams' eyes were burning into my chest. I looked down. The wet gown had turned sheer in the water and clung to my breasts, exposing the pink areolas, the erect nipples. The dark mole above the right one showed through as if there was no covering at all. My beauty mark Mama always called it. Sometimes it was my mole Daddy asked to see. Pastor Adams was gone in exactly the way of my father at my breasts. Nothing at that moment could have been more devastating.

"You'll have to wear a bra for the rest of your life. Enjoy the freedom as long as you can." She goes on and on about the awful feeling of being bound, controlled, strapped in, the plain old hassle of having to put on added clothing.

But then she relents. Maybe she was at my baptism, maybe she saw. Maybe she saw the poker players looking at me. Maybe Daddy or Mrs. Ritchie said something. Maybe it will help my posture. Suddenly, at long last, she rushes to buy me a bra.

"Bra," the brassiere specialist explains, "is short for the French word, brassiere, which means arm guard. It's from the Fifteenth Century when Joan of Arc was at the head of the army, fourteen and wearing boy's clothes."

We're in a small dressing room in the Downey lingerie store. Me and Mama and the specialist who tape-measures me—around my back, under my breasts, my ribcage, then the circumference of each breast. My breasts are more and more triangular, not round, very white with blue veins and spreading areolas, and the pink salmon standup nipples. Under the fluorescent light both women are staring at them.

"You have a long narrow ribcage. Too bad. You'll never look as big as you actually are."

"I think her accent must be German," Mama whispers, when she departs to find a bra with a bigger cup, a smaller band.

Her navy blue wool suit smells of mothballs. Her black lace-up shoes with thick heels are like Grandma's. Next, before it's too late, I must be fitted to a girdle. She scolds my mother for not getting me here sooner. "My dear, you don't want her breasts to fall like those poor natives in National Geographic." She has little black numbers tattooed inside one of her wrists. I bend over as she instructs so that all of my two breasts fall forward into the cups.

"Most ladies don't know that this is the proper way to put on a brassiere, this you must do every time, bend completely forward so as to capture all the breast tissue that's escaped to the back, arm pits and ribcage into the cups. Brassieres are built on the same principle as the Golden Gate Bridge. Picture those two great swinging spans every time you put on your brassiere, girl, and you'll be okay."

She fits me to a 32B.

"Most girls spend a couple of years praying to fill a 28AAA," she says. "Hard to believe you're only eleven." She gives my mother another look, somewhere between for shame and what can you do? "Really, child, to preserve those, you should have started sizes ago. You should have had a training bra. I can't guarantee what will happen. Let's pray it's not too late."

As we drive home under the remaining fan palms of Paramount, me all strapped in and trussed up, already suffering the heat of the added clothing around my heart and lungs, the constriction of my ribcage, Mama ruminates on women's hips and buttocks. How ugly a girdle makes you look and how horrible it feels to wear. "What's wrong with being a little bouncy?" she asks. "Isn't that what a woman is? I didn't wear a bra until I was twelve and my breasts retained their elasticity until Clarke."

The next day the teacher tells me to go to the board and write the answers to the weekly Korean War quiz. I'm writing Kaesong and 38th parallel and the Yalu. The double wide white band across my back shows through my white cotton blouse like a banner flown across the Basin from the Goodyear blimp. There's mumbling, then yelps, then outright cheering. "Bra! bra! Sharon Edens is wearing a bra!"

On the playground the boys run up from behind me, snap it, yelling "Blimp! Blimp! Double blimp!"

I need to shave too. Mama lectures about not shaving my legs. Once you start you can never stop. The white down will grow back coarse, thick and worst of all, black. Daddy forbids me to shave the hair under my arms. "Hairy ape!" the boys yelp, scratching their pits. Walking around in my sleeveless blouses she makes for me, still lays out for me to wear each day, my arms glued to my sides.

Often her bathtub lectures started with the question, "What is a true Christian?" Often her sentences began with "People who call themselves Christians rarely are." Or, "To be a real Christian...."

"May we be to one another as Christ is to us," she recited. "Love one another."

"Judge not that ye be not judged. The person across from us is our self."

"To thine own self be true."

"If you do not forgive, neither will your Father forgive you."

"He is there in every breath. Split a piece of wood and I am there. Lift up the stone and you will find me there." He is like Telephone Pole.

"He doesn't judge us. Life's not a court room. Judgment is Old Testament stuff. Jesus came to overturn the Old Testament concept of God as a wrathful, jealous, angry Father. You have heard it said an eye for an eye and a tooth for a tooth but I say unto you, resist not evil, turn the other cheek. But..." and she sat up in the bubble bath, fixing me with her eyes, "You must realize, Sharon, that Jesus was not meek. He overturned the tables of the moneychangers and threw them out." She didn't say that it was for this that he was crucified; her point was about the strength of his convictions, that he held onto his beliefs through all their terrible torture. Nothing is worse than being one with the crowd. That's what happened in Germany.

Then she would launch into Jesus' trial, about Pontius Pilate washing his hands of it. Her thin pink long-fingered hands would come up out of the water and she'd wash them in the air in slow motion. Nothing in my mother's repertoire of stories carried as much contempt as for this cowardly act of Pilate, that he actually believed he could wash himself of the responsibility. More than one afternoon bathtub drama was of their crowning Jesus King of the Jews, how they ridiculed him that he didn't come down from the cross. They didn't know there is a different power, she said, a higher power, a different kind of King. They were stuck in the old, the unevolved.

She talked of people who go to church as a social event, who go to look good in the eyes of others, to wear their expensive clothes, of the many unChristian churches that decree cruel things against people, who rule in the precise ways that Jesus warned against. There are people who want to be told what to do, who want a religion that tells them what to do, who don't want to think for themselves. This is what happened to the Germans. There are people who read the Bible just to find what they want to find. She said the words hypocrisy and double standard again and again. Most churches, especially churches of the wealthy and the Catholic church in Mexico that takes money from the poor are hypocritical. Jesus was a peasant, illegitimate, illiterate, a poor man, a carpenter, a Jew. Terrible the things that have been done in his name. She said this was Paul's fault. Most of the unChristian stuff in the New Testament is from Paul trying to build a Church. But Jesus said go into a closet and pray. His church was on the roads and river banks, on the mountain tops and in the desert wilderness. The Sabbath was made for men and not men for the Sabbath. The Kingdom of God is spread out on the earth, is so accessible, so here, so present, you don't need priests or laws or Bibles, you have but to ask and it shall be given you; seek, and you shall find it; knock, and it shall be opened unto you. The Kingdom of God is within you, thou shalt love it with all thy heart, with all thy soul, and with all thy mind. And so of course we don't need to go to church. Daddy doesn't go to church because of what happened to him as a boy.

To be Christian is to love thy neighbor as thyself, to be Christian is to be one with the poor and the miserable. To be Christian is to be as the Communists teach about the dialectic and, in this, Sharon, the Communists are actually true Christians. To be Christian is to love thy enemies, the bad people as well as the good. Your enemies are God's children the same as you. For he maketh his sun rise on the evil and on the good, and sendeth rain on the just and the unjust. Jesus accepts every manner of person, makes no distinction between Gentile and Jew, woman and man, slave and free, poor and rich, sick and healthy. Daddy's like that, she said, your extraordinary father can be friends with any type.

If any man would sue thee at the law, and take away thy cloak, let him have thy coat also. If you have money do not lend it at interest, but give it to one from whom you will not get it back. Only a true Christian can do that.

Carry no purse, no bag, no sandals, nor two tunics. Whatever house you enter, eat what is set before you; heal the sick in it and say the Kingdom of God is come upon you.

Jesus didn't believe in hell and never said the word Christian. He said whosoever smite thee on thy right cheek, turn to him the other also. He said do unto others as you would have them do unto you, that's the Golden Rule.

Of his disciples Mama loved Luke the most. Luke was full of light and love and the Golden Rule. She'd soak, ruminating on Paul. Corinthians 1:13 is his sermon and yet in most places he's judgmental, not loving. He hates women for one thing. Jesus didn't. Jesus surrounded himself with women. Most of the terrible things the Church has done stem from Paul.

Some days she simply recited First Corinthians 1:13, always saying first, remember, Sharon, the word charity means Love. I sat on the closed toilet and in the steamy sweet smelling room whispered the words along with my naked mother.

"Though I speak with the tongues of men and of angels, and have not charity, I am become as sounding brass, or a tinkling cymbal. And though I bestow all my goods to feed the poor, and though I give my body to be burned, and have not charity, it profiteth me nothing. Charity suffereth long, and is kind; charity envieth not; charity vaunteth not itself, is not puffed up. Doth not behave itself unseemly, seeketh not her own, is not easily provoked, thinketh no evil. Rejoiceth not in iniquity, but rejoiceth in the truth. Beareth all things, believeth all things, hopeth all things, endureth all things."

Then leaning back under the faucets turned on to warm up the tub, the hot water pouring down her shoulders, back and breasts, she would sum it up.

"Faith, hope, charity, these three. But the greatest of these is Love."

She lectured me repeatedly on the need to learn to receive. Accept the food of your host. Some people are givers, some are receivers. We have to become the other. All the philosophers have said this, Marx too; this is the dialectic. Most people are receivers, they have to learn to give, to become selfless. But there are those who can't receive, who can only give, those people are actually selfish too, are not really giving in love. They are giving to enhance themselves, their egos, to feel good and powerful. She said some people are too proud, this is the same as Southern pride. She said this was a problem with me. She said you suffer, Sharon, from Southern pride. At night I'd go over and over this lecture, I worked, I prayed to not only understand but to go the next, hardest step: to learn to receive.

She said watch out for what you hate. Thoughts are living things out there, you'll draw what you hate to you and then have to face it. Watch out what you think because in six weeks it will be standing before you. Watch out for what you covet too. If you want something too much it will slip away. Her example of this was women who can't get pregnant. Finally after years of trying, they adopt a baby and then get pregnant. They'd quit trying. They'd been trying too hard.

One day she was very excited. The Gospel of Thomas was found in Egypt. The Dead Sea Scrolls are going to change everything. At last the world will know the true Jesus.

She said Marilyn Monroe is a Christian Scientist. The Christian Scientist Church is the only church founded by a woman. Mary Baker Eddy knew illness is all in the mind. The only problem with the Christian Scientists is they've gone too far. They don't understand germs which are living, growing things. They're extremists. Like Marilyn Monroe who puffs herself up.

She leaned back into the water laughing about her grandmother running off with the two missionaries who said the world was coming to an end. She leaned back into the water, her holy temple laid out, saying "Jesus said 'Enter into life.'"

As much as on the meaning of the true Christian she lectured on the meaning of true love. Bridget kept asking her who she loves the most.

"A mother's love is unconditional. Love knows no hierarchy. That would be a contradiction in terms. No first, no last, no in-between. No measure. Love is not about numbers, not about quantity. Love is immeasurable. Love is bigger than all the stars and worlds in the Universe."

But Bridget kept asking. Mama would linger in our bedroom door, the light out, saying a woman's love of her husband is different, just different than her love for her children. Not more, not less, just different. Just as her love for each child is different.

"My love for Clarke is as different from my love for you, Bridget, and for Sharon, as he is different from each of you. It isn't a matter of degree or quantity; it's a matter of perceiving who the other is. *That* is love."

That made perfect sense to me. That was perfection.

One day I lean my head on the doorframe of the bathroom in a rare surrender to the agony. The taunting of the fifth grade boys is unbearable.

"In the not too distant future, Sharon, the boys will catch up with you."

I can't count on that. My body just keeps growing and growing.

"They're just jealous," she says.

This isn't true. I'm the giant of the school, no one's jealous of that. And now they're lying about me. Bridget tells fibs about me and Daddy accuses me of things that aren't true, and Mama knows that somehow I'm equally responsible, it always takes two, but all that's just inside our family, they can't help it, I know that, and family is forever and some day I'll figure it out, I pray for this every night, to understand my half of the cause. But Jeff O' Toole said I kissed Gary Neal and then he said I kissed him. He said I kissed them both for a long time with my tongue and the other kids believe him. Oh, Mama, I didn't! But now my reputation is ruined.

"You know the truth Sharon. That's what's important." She will say this many times in the next year. Don't ever forget, you know the truth. In the end the truth will out. The truth always comes out eventually. They're just jealous. Always remember: to thine own self be true. The truth will set you free.

"Jealousy is never love," she says, her red nipples, her wires of red pubic hair bobbing in the bubbles. "Never."

Then sliding down under the bubbles she says "They just want to possess you, not just own you, but possess every part of you."

It is extremely problematic to think that another is jealous of you. Jealousy is such a sin you can't think another guilty of such a thing. That would be judgment. And it would be vanity! Charity vaunteth not itself, is not puffed up. Charity seeketh not her own, thinketh no evil.

She says people who ridicule others, people who are bullies or prejudiced or dictators are that way because they feel inferior, they're trying to make themselves look bigger. It doesn't work. It actually makes them feel more inferior. If these people could see how obvious they are to everyone they'd be mortified. Just look at that Adolph Hitler. It's most important not to become like them, not to make the very human mistake of becoming what you hate.

At the end of every bathtub lecture, starting with you can go now, she'd tell again of her unconditional love for me. I could depend on her for anything. I must depend on her. I knew this was true. I loved her like that too. There is no measure to my love of her.

Besides Jesus—Thomas Jefferson's Jesus, she'd say, not the hocus pocus Jesus—*Unity* and the *Daily Word* which opened each day to a Biblical verse and lesson about it, she was reading the works of Ralph Waldo Emerson and Howard Thurman, and *The Power of Positive Thinking* by Norman Vincent Peale. I know now that some of these sources are the butts of jokes by the educated and non-spiritual but in fact they are the distillation of the great thinkers of the ages and cultures—not only of Jesus, but of Mohammed, Buddha, Confucius and all the great poets and philosophers.

These teachings are also similar to those of her Native American heritage. And they are the heart and core of the New Age Movement, of which my sister will be a part. And they are the heart of my poetics, my politics, my path through life. They are how I survived. I knew the truth of my mother's bathtub lectures. Riveted in the ongoing crisis of my father, I riveted my mother's bathtub lectures into my soul. I believed them. I knew them as the truth. I believed her. I would stand in their fires.

But they also blinded me. I clung to them, close to my natural temperament anyway, in part so as not to know. Not to see.

He watches me every afternoon from his window in the new bachelor apartments that have been built across the street from the church. Lately his front door has been open and I can see him naked against the far wall. He has straight dark hair and is the age I imagine bachelors are. Thirty. Today he's standing in his open doorway. His pants are down and he's twirling his very long penis in the black hair. His face is aglow as he watches me walk, as I walk not showing alarm, as I walk as if his being there and doing that is perfectly normal. The sun is blinding from the broken glass as I walk not to fall into his rhythm.

Returning from the market I walk on the church side, past Telephone Pole. He's still there in his open doorway, holding it, rubbing it, pumping it up and down, gesturing to me to come in. Black strings of hair spill down his shining face.

The most important thing is not to acknowledge him. Not saying it, not thinking it is control. Do not judge, look the other way, he's not there, the power of positive thinking. Don't even think to walk home around the block, down Arizona. He doesn't mean me harm. He's just a man. He's just making himself happy. I wouldn't want to ruin anyone's happiness. Am I going to have all the men arrested? All God's men? The old men in the bushes, the winos who suddenly jump out of hiding to show it to me, little girl, look! seem so helpless and though I'm scared to death, my heart pounding up in my throat, my head going into the tunnel, I pray to Jesus that I not tell on them. It's just the way men are, you're a man too Jesus, the way your Father made you.

I dreamed I was in a large house and my father was mending some holes on the porch. Water was lapping all the sides. With his hammer he pried the top off the yellow toy box he made me and sawed it in two to make the patches.

I cried and cried. The tears washed my face. I couldn't stop crying. That he would destroy my toy box. I loved it mostly because he made it. He seemed surprised that I cared so much. He thought the toy box was his to do with as he pleased since he made it.

I dreamed Mary Jane was my size and being drowned in the bathtub. I dreamed I was pulling my waterlogged yellow-haired doll out of the water. Trying to restore her breath.

I dreamed I ask Mama what's wrong with the baby. She says we have taken her to all the specialists, to Dr. Hooker in Downey, but there's no hope, so we have brought her home and are just loving her. Mama's disappointments, her sufferings are overwhelming. She's terminal and pregnant. The only hope is to abort. She says but that baby's all I have to live for. My beloved beautiful innocent long suffering mother. But isn't there another baby, Mama, one you had seven years ago? I go to their bedroom, stand at the door. They're in their twin beds, Daddy naked, the blanket over his lower part, reading the paper, his smell so strong. Asking, really? You haven't seen Penny? That seems impossible. She leads me down the hall to our bedroom. The door opens, there's a beautiful bunkbed that Daddy made. I walk over, asking is she cute, Mama? But then I see that something is wrong. The baby girl is hideously deformed, she has a huge bulging eye in the center of her two normal eyes, and the rest of her face looks like a bird. Her mouth area is like a chicken and all her joints are stiff and crusty and bleeding.

I dreamed of Daddy in an I-5 rest stop on my way to San Diego, writing this book. He was lounging on a sofa, dressed, but his front presented to me. I so rarely dream of him anymore. He was starting to tell me much more of what happened between us than I remember. There is much, much more. But when he saw that I don't remember it all he hesitated. I felt myself going right to the thing he was going to tell. Then I woke up.

There's an antebellum mansion in the spring 1976 nightmare, a ruin buried in moss and ivy and kudzu in the old South. There's my father, a man who looks like Clarke Gable in *Gone with the Wind*. There's a secret, the family's secret, buried in our lineage, our cells, our very blood. It's always been there, a part of the family, known by all of us. The secret in the form of one of our pelvic bones is buried under the ruined mansion. Then fast, so fast I'm gasping, the scene changes, to a highway, to the worst car accident imaginable. Braking, screeching, colliding, grinding go on forever. Then, fast! out of the wreckage pops straight up to the sky a young boy completely skinned, completely dismembered except for his penis exploding to the sky in the same posture and manner as the bird girl with the Third Eye.

§

Twenty-One

The toilet keeps stopping up. He orders me to put my hand down the toilet throat because my hand is small enough to get beyond the curve. "Do you feel anything Sharon?"

My bloody things buried down there. Like I'm going to throw up.

A few days later he's got the toilet in the backyard. "Sharon to the rescue!" he summons. Everyone's back here, all the kids and Mama. I do it again, stick my hand down the snaky throat, Daddy laughing, at least he's hosed it good, come up with a big rusted barrette that no one recognizes, flakes of toilet paper through it. He praises me, it feels good to have helped, but oh some things are so weird. For days I scrub my hands like Pontius Pilate.

How weird I was by the summer I was eleven.

I'm in the back yard on the old swing set. Just sitting here too big going sideways. I'm so bored I'm dissolving. I hit the ground, project back off. The chain catches my strapless top, pulling it down, exposing my right breast with the dark mole to the air and sky. I yank it back up.

"Do that again."

I explode from the swing screaming. Then I see him at the gate.

"Oh. Daddy. It's just you. Sorry."

"Do that again. Pull your top down."

I can still see my eleven year old right breast from that moment, the salmon areola out from the rippling opalescent base, the beauty mark just inside the rim, the nipple jutting. But I can't remember anything after that.

El Camino Real still curves around the same pure-white beach, the same trailer court. A highway in a painting, a little encampment down on the beach between two bluffs with palm trees. An inlet, a small lagoon, the whitecaps rolling in to where my love lives. Today it's called a mobile home park.

The house is not as modern as the Hollydale one. It's white clapboard trimmed in pink and green shingles. It has a sun roof with pink and green pipe railing. Behind it, east up the arroyo, are the trailers.

Gae's more mysterious, more beautiful, more wild than ever. She's so brown the fog of her face is like bleached, polished sand. Her hair is sun bleached almost as white as mine.

She has a horse! Her parents got her a horse! Red is a roan. We ride him down the sand hill, then under El Camino Real, clipclopping through the echoey damp underpass of the railroad trestle. The roar and vibration of the pounding surf when we come through. The plunging breaking splashing rolling up rolling back explosion of light of the waves into foam. The horse an ocean wave. My arms around her waist, my head at her right shoulder, my mouth at her neck.

She could whistle by putting her fingers around her tongue in a way I could not learn no matter how hard I tried. This whistle was louder than any she'd mastered in Hollydale, more piercing, with variations up and down like the screeching gulls blowing east across the highway from the beach. The fringes of the leather jacket in front of the sunset as she tries to teach me how to put my fingers around my tongue. That first night, after begging, we got to stay. Bridget and Dottie got the bedroom. Gae and I slept on the sun roof. We stayed awake all night telling each other everything. (Everything except about our fathers.)

The next day we ride east across the hills. Somewhere above and over there is her new school. The building that will hold her every day, the sixth grade kids who will get to lay their eyes on her every minute of every day and love her.

Saturday sundown, Mama and Daddy pick us up, we beg to stay the night again, but it's wise if we have a break from each other. "And Sharon and Bridget you're burnt. You can have a few hours together tomorrow."

"Vaya Con Dios." If we had to we could walk it.

Sleeping in the car at Doheny, walking all night the beach to her. Mama swathed us in vinegar, telling of the time they burned so bad at Myrtle Beach they threw up. All night I'm swimming, riding Red, burning red for her. Daddy, sometimes it's Mr. Walker, staring at me. Stepping right through the locked back door, pulling his whole body laughing through, Sharon Lu Lu. Oh, Sharon Lu.

July 3, 52- Our 46th wedding anniversary. Fred & family left for 2 weeks vacation...

"The Grand Canyon is a siapapu, an opening to an underground chamber, to the innermost parts of the earth." Mama is in the windshield reading to us from the booklet glued ever since in the *Scrapbook*. "In such places deep insight and awareness is acquired. The messenger Kachinas of the Hopis bring these to the people."

Nothing in nature I've ever seen, not even the underside of the Pacific wave that almost killed me, has matched the shock of the Grand Canyon that first and only time I saw it. A hole like Gae and I never dreamed.

The enormity, the violence of earth and time, the human insignificance. What's buried for a million years? What's buried under the house for three? What's flushed down the toilet eventually to be exposed? That a river could do this even in a million years. Grandpa lived sixty-nine. Mama's Mama twenty-four. I couldn't think it was shaking my religious faith but it depressed me in my soul.

Right then, right on the South Rim, the blues and grays and mauves and reds of the rainbow cuts rearranged themselves and Clarke attacked me again. To stop him I got both his arms and twisted them again. My laughter was like Daddy's ordering me to put my hand down the stopped-up toilet. My laughter fell down into the biggest cut on the planet. Some dead part of me felt suddenly alive again. But awful.

Then Zion. Let's stay right here a minute, Sharon Lu, and he pulls me into the cubby hole in the vermillion rock overlooking the Virgin River. The hoodoos of Bryce Canyon watch us. "Learn to read the land," he says, climbing the canyons from Salt Lake City to the Grand Tetons and Yellowstone. I'm just eleven, just flimsy human flesh. I can't breathe. I will not think.

But thought goes on without language, the way the rivers lay down soil, then the beds uplift it, slowly, so slowly, over the march of time.

He grabs me and hugs me right in front of her, rubbing his chest up and down on mine. He grabs Bridget now too, it's happening to her too, weirdest slow-motion explosion on our chest walls, poor sister. But the distance over to that, at least in words, is a zillion times around the earth.

We fished from Fisherman's Bridge
in Yellowstone. We caught so many we had to give them away
not because of the law but because of our bounty.
Mama fried them in egg and corn, served with grits....[10]

Right then, like Old Faithful's graceful and beautiful hundred and fifty foot column of hot water and steam vapor, some unexpected joy, some surprising light, some amazing grace and indefinable hope, erupted. I remember all of us, even Mama, fishing with him from the railing of Fisherman's Bridge. The Continental Divide is right over there kids! Being happy in the big tent, the sun glowing through the green canvas walls. Daddy coming through the flaps, the sun entering, see how many he has caught. To see him happy. Mama preparing to scale, clean, flay, bread and cook the fish Daddy caught.

To see him happy, to hear him laughing, like a boy, thrilled, so genuinely thrilled with the fishing. That he has caught these fish.

Soon as we got home I entered Black Prince George into the South Gate
City Parks dog show. He won all the blue ribbons. Our names were in the
paper. The blue ribbons and the news article are still in my hope chest.

Daddy dug up the front yard and planted two inch plugs of dichondra a
square foot apart the entire space. The dichondra, a tiny creeping vine
ground cover of the Morning Glory family, would eventually grow
together, making a solid green mat which would never need mowing. He'd
be free of that chore and our lawn would be the most beautiful on the
block. Meanwhile, in the two years or whatever this process would take,
vigilant weeding was required to make sure regular grass didn't grow into
the root systems and become a permanent part of the seed bed.

"Go out and weed!" he'd order any time the dark mood struck.

We crawled the dirt yard on our hands and knees, straddling the plugs
of dichondra, pulling endless new little grass stems, throwing them in the
bucket, which he would discard on the river, so they wouldn't propagate
again in the dichondra. It was horrible. Pulling weeds through August and
September, the hundred degrees; the baby weeds germinating from my
buried bloody pajamas. When school started we had to weed an hour every
day after school.

Mama's bathtub lectures resumed. Many now were about habits. For
instance the habit of laxatives, you get so addicted you can't go without
them; I kept my mouth shut about Bridget. The habit of Coca Cola which
they used to make from cocaine when she worked at the Dan River Cotton
Mill. The factory and mill workers were about to go on strike so the
company installed free Coke machines, hooking the workers, causing them
to forget their grievances. She had always explained how really bad sugar
is for one's health and how carbonated water rots your joints and hip
bones. She lectured endlessly on the hazards of smoking, somehow
without casting aspersions on Daddy. I wouldn't know until the end that
my grandmother Susie smoked, that they all smoked. Mr. Quintrill in the
end apartment was the example of the habit of alcohol.

The only bad thing she ever allowed about my father was his disgusting spitwad habit. These days he seemed to be on top of it. When I cleaned
house I found them in the ashtrays but not on the walls. His ashtrays were
beautiful, he made them at work, designed of glass, colored plastics and
steel. In a way, so were his spitwad creations stuck to the bottoms in
deliberate, fantastic designs.

Clovis lives in the lone house at the apex of the triangular confluence of
Arizona, Main and Industrial Avenues, across from Trinity Bible Church
on one side, and across from the little store in front. She is the first kid
other than myself that I see has pubic hair. They have a glass shower stall,
she's taking a shower, she's talking to me, and I see the thin ringlets of
sparse black hair raining down her inner thighs. Not even this embarrasses
Clovis. Imagine being so free. Seeing her naked makes me feel a little
normal, makes me extremely grateful to her. Clovis is beautiful. She is
named for the famous fifth century king of France, they're from Texas, her
father works for GE, and she has a grown brother. She has long eye lashes
which she coats with Vaseline to make each lash stand out, and shine.

I came trotting across Main into the little store just at twilight. The car
lights blinked on, blazed across my legs. The door opened, the man started
out for me, his eyes glossy, his tongue on his bottom lip. I leaped inside.
    But now I don't know what to do. Can't tell the man behind the
counter. Can I run fast enough across the intersection to Clovis'? What if
she's not home? The toilet paper is stacked in the window, I can't see either
direction up or down Main, just the top of his old car. What if a car comes
out of nowhere and I have to stop on the curb? he could grab me. Or I
could be hit. It gets later and later. The sun is going down. The grocery
man keeps looking at me, his old shoplifter. Finally I make the dash, the
car lights flash on me as I run by. I hear the door open and his voice
mumbling. I run harder, hitting the wide Main on the diagonal, making it
through the cars coming from both directions. I hear the GE washer and
dryer going in the breezeway between Clovis' house and the add-on
apartment over the garage for her nineteen year old brother. The gate is
unlocked. Her brother is sitting on the back porch steps. I could almost go
down on my knees in gratitude, dear Jesus, for saving me. But what do I
do now? How do I explain myself here? Am I sitting on the back cement
step afraid of him too? Was this the time I called my mother to come get
me? Clovis must have had the same trouble with the men. Maybe that's
why they had that high fence. It's stunning to realize that we never
acknowledged this ever-present danger to each other. Maybe I called my
mother once or twice, but I never told anyone the reality of Industrial.

The end of summer. We've been on the beach all day, swimming, inner
tubing, running Red, laying out to the sun, talking like mad. Now we're
back in their bedroom. In the living room Mr. and Mrs. Walker are having

sexual intercourse on the floor. I shut the door to get out of my bathing suit. Shutting the door shows I know, that I'm afraid. Nothing protects me more than not letting them know I know. We're all in here, Gae and Bridget and Dotty, the room full of things, mostly piles of clothes everywhere. I pull off my wet gritty suit.

Mr. Walker breaks in, naked and screaming. Screaming, I leap into the closet, behind the sliding plywood door, try to slide it shut. It's stuck off its runner.

"No closed doors in my house! Didn't I tell you, no closed doors!"

Sheer terror, my heart up under my tongue again. Blue pimply areolas. Goose bumps, sticking-out hairs, blue knock-knees, broken elm veins on my right thigh, the day's red burn lines. Praying to Jesus save me, save me.

"No closed doors in my house," Mr. Walker fumes. "Do you understand me?"

The terror of that moment sometimes still eclipses me.

"He had Mrs. Walker on the floor," my sister described the scene to our mother and me during the big family reunion in August 1985. Amazing, but I had forgotten. Now it played back like it happened yesterday. "He was on top of her under the coffee table, instructing her how to open it. She was wearing only her blouse. The C.B. was on. He sat up when we came through. 'What's wrong?' I asked. Mrs. Walker kept trying to come up out of it—he had her hypnotized, he kept telling her to go back down. Dottie said, 'Oh, my father's hypnotizing my mother. He hypnotizes her all the time.' Mr. Walker said to us, 'Just go on out. Just go on out.'

"Mr. Walker was at our house," Bridget went on, "to drive us to Capistrano. I remember him sitting in our living room talking anatomically about his disease when he was a boy because he wasn't allowed to go the bathroom. He was talking of the importance of urinating because he got some disease as a child for holding it too long.

"'Time to go, but no doors,' he'd say. Remember, he'd tell you when to go but you couldn't shut the bathroom door.

"Mr. Walker talked in ways I didn't know adults talked. You know, he talked about pee and poop and parts of genitalia the way we kids did. Mrs. Walker walked around all weekend with no panties on. Just a top."

Then she added again, "For two years I spanked Dottie. Finally I told you Mama. You were shocked, Mama. Dottie let me spank her. I'd pull her pants down, spank her, spank hard."

§

Twenty-Two

Daddy is stepping through the bolted door like it's air. He's carrying a gift for me. Screams that are a wild animal's that won't let me go, that won't stop, that are louder and louder till I'm fully awake on an island of devastation so vast, so total I'm the last living person on the Earth. Then I'm standing in the middle of the dark room, my brother and sister asleep in their beds. In the morning at breakfast no one says a thing.

"A man and a woman alone in the same room," Mama warns from the bathtub, "will always come to sex."

I wake to him under the bed rising up, pushing the bed up, setting it down again, pushing up again, moving me over, getting in.

I wake in the tunnel of fear deeper than it's possible to go and survive.

But it's just an earthquake, the slipping of the San Andreas Fault northwest. The front pages show a street that cracked open and swallowed a whole house.

"Daddy's just jealous of you growing up," she says again. "Of your finding a boyfriend. He acts the way he does because he loves you. He wants you to love only him. You're a beautiful girl, it worries him sick."

The architecture of my dreams is of streets and chasms and toppled buildings, ruins. The earth's crust broken into huge rectangle blocks with water all around, water rushing in.

Beneath all things, the Bible says, are the living waters.

Clovis and I get Mrs. Blanc for Sixth Grade. Those two girls, Nancy and Susan, get her too. I think Susan Evans might be an introvert like me. She's quiet, still, serious. Something so unknown in her blondness, the dark, slightly swollen circles under her eyes. Something so sad about her.

Clovis, Susan, Nancy and I quickly establish ourselves as the top students, though, surprisingly, some of the boys prove to be smart too. Clovis can talk about anything, like the Monroe Doctrine, the Marshall Plan, the Korean War. She can name every general that's ever lived; after all, she was named for a French one before there was a France. Nancy's a brain, in math especially, can joke about anything, like about the Rosenbergs scheduled to be fried and our own pitiful selves by the Hydrogen Bomb when we're under our desks. Susan doesn't talk much in class, she just watches everything and gets straight As. I never talk unless called upon and I always get at least one B. My teachers always disapprove of something about me; Mama says the B is their way of showing it. Sharon Edens must not be known as a straight A student. The same thing happened to her. The boys have always been dumb, they can't help it, they're just boys, they're lucky to make Ds, it's just so hard for them to sit still. But one day soon, she's always warned, they're going to catch up with the girls and then pass us in smartness. "I'm sure there is one boy, Sharon, probably even several boys, in your class that you can see this potential in." My whole being is alert for the moment the boys mature past me. Is this when their things become as big as Daddy's? Has my brother's gotten as big as Daddy's yet?

The bathtub lectures rev up. I hate the sex ones, especially when she goes into detail like how the man climaxes, how there's this point he gets to when no matter what he can't stop himself. I have to struggle not to crack, not to cry I know that, Mama, please shut up about that. I ache to tell her, I'm terrified I'm going to tell her. Sometimes I'm shocked to realize how close I came to telling her. Dear Jesus don't let me ever tell her. I know he can't help it. Maybe one day her words will tell me what to do.

"Jealousy is never love."

I know now she was saying that to survive his immense double crosses and cruelty. "True love is like a beautiful soap bubble," she says, holding her hand up with a big wobbly clear one reflecting the rainbow. "If you try to grasp it, it will burst."

A woman is in the news who got her boyfriend to kill her husband. Everyone hates her, feels so sorry for him and the husband. It doesn't matter what they did to get her to such a state. A woman who goes bad is worse than a man who goes bad. Women are the mothers. The male is just not as strong as the female, everyone knows that.

The boys are even worse now than in the fifth grade. I lean my head on the doorframe of the steamy bathroom in absolute agony of their daily persecutions. My monstrous body just completely beyond me. It engulfs me. It suffocates me.

She tells me again and again she loves me unconditionally, I can depend on her for anything. As a girl with boys I must depend on her. When things get complicated and I need an excuse I can put all the blame on her.

The same goes for Bridget. She can depend on her for anything. Bridget's mean to her sometimes, really mean, have you noticed that Sharon? But that's okay, in fact that's good. Bridget plays the angel with everyone else, she's so giving and wonderful but everyone needs someone to take it out on. Mama's that person for Bridget. She tells her it's okay Bridget, I understand, you just need someone to be mean to or you'll explode. You go right ahead, you can be mean to me. You can be my Staingel.

My period should start any minute now. I'm lucky. Most girls are unprepared, I won't be frightened, I will know what the blood is. She must have told me of her first period because I see her outside a big bush under a window discovering it. The School was good at preparing them. Of course I never heard a thing about this from Grandma. Imagine my grandmother at eleven or thirteen bleeding on the Elk River. Did her mother prepare her? She shows me where the Kotex is in the cupboard behind her. I pretend I've never seen it there before, the blue and white box that gives me the hiccups in there with the red rubber douche bag hidden behind the towels and wash cloths and toilet paper, and for some reason Aunt Giny's black satin brassiere from the forties. Imagine the day when you'll have to put a long tube up inside you to clean your insides because a man climaxed inside you. I sit on the closed toilet seat and she tells me of working in the Kotex factory when she got to Charlotte.

She stayed with her Aunt Luella and cousins Seifert and Hallie in their Company house in Schoolfield after she was expelled from the School, but Uncle Claude was jealous of their attention toward her. That's where she was, about a mile down the road from the hospital, when her father died and Mozelle came running for her and she refused to go. She went to Aunt Dora's, Guy's older sister, but Dora cursed her, "look at those eyes, those are Guy Clarke's eyes!" and slammed the door in her face. The people next door, the Lewis' who worked at the school, heard what Dora screamed, invited her to room with them. She got on at the Dan River Cotton Mill, her job was to untangle bobbins, but she was so ashamed, afraid someone from the School would find out. One day she was in the dime store downtown and an old classmate from the School came in. She pretended she was working there, was prospering and happy even though everyone knew a clerk in the dime store made much less than a mill worker. She always told this story amazed that she would pretend such a thing. But the dime store was a place respectable girls worked.

One day she just bought a bus ticket for as far away as she could go: Charlotte, North Carolina. How exhilarated she was to be on an adventure, to be leaving Virginia. She had $1.25 and the address of a mill owner who had befriended her father when he was sick in the sanitarium. Mr. Barnhardt published a newsletter for people in TB sanitariums and Guy Henry Clarke wrote for it. This rich man had taken an interest in her

father, had recognized a potential in him. He told her to go to Mr.
Barnhardt if she ever needed help.

From the dollar hotel room she stayed in that night—"There was a
used condom on the floor, that's the kind of place it was"—she walked to
the address, walked up the long tree-lined path to the front door. Mr.
Barnhardt would like to see me, she told the Negro butler. Mr. Barnhardt
welcomed her as if he was expecting her, led her into the dining room,
invited her to eat with him. That night he gave her a bed with the maid.
The next morning he took her to church. When the offering plate came
around, she dropped in her last quarter. Carry no purse, Jesus said. On
Monday Mr. Barnhardt took her to his Kotex factory, gave her a job on the
assembly line. Her job was to wrap the pads in bundles before they were
boxed. As soon as she got on her feet she found a waitress job out by the
airport where her regulars were the Charlotte baseball team.

She told this story all my life. She told it with pride, never self-pity or
of the fear and loneliness that must have been there. Remember: life is a
glorious adventure. When you get stuck just go somewhere else. I never
grew tired of it. I will always wonder if somewhere, in some archive,
sanitarium, Kotex museum or library, there exists Mr. Barnhardt's
newsletter with my grandfather's writing. To read a sentence formed by
him. To imagine his handwriting. She had all his letters but I never saw
them and near the end she burned them. Maybe those letters went contrary
to the image she had so carefully built of him to us. Maybe they were love
letters. Maybe she destroyed them to keep him forever hers. Only hers.

She lectures more and more now about the McCarthy people. Innocent
people are followed, photographs taken secretly, every word reported,
recorded, their mail X-rayed, their medical reports turned over. A
malicious piece of gossip can blight your life forever. You can be
interrogated, sentenced, imprisoned. Even rumors of an association with
the wrong people can be grounds for being thrown in jail, deported, or
blacklisted. You must be careful, any mistake you make will go down on
your record and you'll never escape it. Her big breasts bob in the bubbles
like Daddy's big Little Cecil bobs and she bemoans the danger of
indoctrination. You know Sharon how easily you are brainwashed.

"Ethel Rosenberg's an example of what happens when a woman goes
bad. We hate her more than Mr. Rosenberg. They have two young sons,
how could she have put anything above the care of those boys?"

Lessons, lectures, what one must do. Waiting to see what kind of girl
you'll turn into once your period starts. Everything about me seems to

bring everyone unhappiness or discomfort. I try so hard not to. I examine myself over and over, I'm such a spectacle. I remember studying Judy Clare in Kindergarten, so successful in playing the role of a five year old girl. I study the ways the others hold their bodies, move their mouths, walk. I try to absorb their mannerisms. They seem so confident, so fully, beautifully realized in the world. I don't know how to be in the world. I can't see myself.

But Sharon even an introvert must hold up her shoulders. You should be proud of your breasts.

"Hold your shoulders up, Sharon," he snarls. "What are you hiding?"

I'm just like him, she always says. I study him trying to see myself.

Every day I walked George on the leash. This day we've wandered farther than usual up into the higher, shadier blocks of McKinley and Wilson, are coming back down Roosevelt. Down on Arizona the paperboy, that boy Toni Genoway keeps telling me of, zips by on his bike, which means it must be 4:30 already. I start running with George but then he slows up to smell something and I trip over the leash, fall headfirst into a driveway, roll down the cupped triangular cement entrance into the street. It hurts, it takes my breath completely away.

At home I don't tell. I weed. But it hurts, bad. That night the pain gets worse. The next morning in school we have another H bomb drill. Waves of nausea and hot flashes, I faint dead away trying to get under my desk, trying to get my arm up to shield the back of my neck. My mother takes me to Dr. Spier in Downey. The pain by now is blinding. I almost faint again trying to get up on his table. Taking my blouse and bra off, my breasts mashed against the cold black X-ray plate, the cold silence in the room, my mother so far away. "This is your clavicle. See this thin white line at the thinnest part where it curves upward?" No, I can't see it, it's that thin, I'm so embarrassed to have caused all this commotion for nothing.

"You cracked it." He looks at my mother and says "A cracked collar bone is more painful than a completely broken one."

It's in Grandma's diary, October 4, 1952. How long was I home from school? Did Mama take care of me, bring me trays of food? She acted mad at me but no way would I think this. In no way did I ever allow what her cold withdrawal meant, that she was jealous or threatened, or as she put it on Jennifer Street "I was always a little afraid of you, Sharon." When she said a number of times that Daddy had a special love for me, deeper than daughter love, she seemed so wise, loving and maternal, like she was complimenting me, and trying to help. Jealousy is never love, she always said. Did her father have that kind of love for her? Yes, she will tell me when my father confesses.

The pain from that thin line was excruciating. I watched last year's Winter Olympics in Switzerland, unable to move, marveling at the freedom of the skaters, their physical prowess. The collar bone is funda-mental, it holds the whole body together. I remember nauseating pain, being astonished at the failure of my body, at not being able to do the most simple things. I remember being on the living room couch dreading Daddy's arrival home, watching the ice skating competitions, magnificent couples triumphantly in love whirling jumping leaping flying into each other's arms, being astounded that people could move and love so easily. I thought I would never get well, never move again, be forever trapped on the couch. Then the runner-up was a sixteen year old American girl who'd had polio when she was ten and so once again I vowed I'd overcome.

The election campaigns are on TV. Mama loves the brilliant Adlai Stevenson though he's called an egghead. It's shameful that Americans dislike smart people. Sometimes Grandma brings over the painting of John Hancock signing the Declaration of Independence from her trunk. He looks just like Uncle Marion and Daddy. The first, the biggest, the boldest signature. Do you realize what it took to sign the Declaration of Independence? Do you realize he would have been hung for treason if the English had won? Do you realize the founders of our country were revolutionaries? And very very smart.

George is so randy he's crazed. He's crazed to get out to the girl dog in heat. This is Nature, to guarantee the continuation of the species, randy is the way males are.

He scratches a hole through the front screen door, chases all night. Then he goes through the second screen door, runs again all night all over Hollydale, Rancho Los Amigos, the LA River, who knows where? His right front paw is bleeding and he looks like he's been dragged through mud. Daddy patches the door with double screening. When George goes through that he patches it with a sheet of aluminum. "Dogpatch!" Mama cries. "It looks like Little Abner lives here." George manages to tear that off. It's the hottest time of the year and it gives Mama claustrophobia but now we keep the front door shut. After we've gone to bed George scratches at the solid wooden door. He scratches and howls all night, carving a long indentation into the door. The disgusting, helpless male. He's got to be fixed.

I don't want him fixed.

I still trick-or-treat. You go as that thing inside you that wants out. A girl from her father's harem. A girl frowning through the blood and raw big bones of her mother's Cherokee/Seminole face, through the pure English madmen of her pure American father, to all the other masked American souls tricking through the Hollydale streets.

I had two costumes that year. She made me a Virginia colonial girl's dress to wear to school, the harem costume not appropriate there now that I was so big. This elaborate dress was the real thing, not a costume. After Halloween I wore it for Square Dancing. I kept it in my hope chest until I was twenty-eight. I remember lifting it out Halloween, 1969. I could have made adjustments to have made it fit. The craftsmanship was as stunning as I'd remembered. It could have worked but for the politics of that year and the fact that I had just written the first account of my childhood. I threw the dress away.

Korea just keeps going. Uncle K.D. receives his orders, he'll sail by the end of the year. *(Nov 13- Kermit came over in full uniform. He looked so nice.)* I study the morning Times and our weekly National Scholastic News at school for Friday's test. Heartbreak Ridge, Bloody Ridge, Massacre Valley—Korea's Heartbreaking Hills. The chaos of combat was so familiar, I don't know why.

On November 2, 1952, we exploded the first H-bomb, seven hundred times the power of Little Boy over Japan. A whole island was vaporized. Two days later Eisenhower and Nixon were elected President and Vice President of the United States, defeating the brilliant Adlai Stevenson and John J. Sparkman. How could people be so fooled, so blinded, so attracted to such men? It was very hard in my house to accept that Americans could be that dumb. "People've been cowed by the Hearings," Daddy said.

There were more crippled veterans around than ever before, World War II guys and now Korea. Rancho Los Amigos was expanding, they were everywhere, propped up on the business streets, in front of the stores. Legless, paralyzed, in wheelchairs. When you put a penny in their cans they handed you a small red poppy made of folded and stretched crepe paper, a wire stem wrapped in green. One soldier was always at the parking lot backdoor to Penney's in Downey. He still wore his uniform though he had no legs to fill the trousers. He gave me a small booklet explaining why the red poppy is the Veterans' symbol. The poppy's the first thing to grow back after a field is soaked in human blood. This happened in Flanders France in World War I where thousands died. *In Flanders field the poppies grow in rows and rows,* the pamphlet quoted a poem. "If people knew the horror of war," he said, "we would not have them."

I entered the annual poster contest for Veteran's Day November 11. I painted rivers of blood flowing across the ground vaporizing into bloody streaks of a gold and crimson sunset, a giant red poppy risen dead center like the H-bomb going off.

My painting won first place from the Hollydale California American Legion contest and was made into a poster that was placed in all the store windows.

I almost faint when I first see it. My heart pounds then skips all over the place, my stomach cramps. But I know. It will go away in three days. I stuff my panties with toilet paper and rags. I work and pray like crazy not to cry, or double over for the stomach ache, my weirdly aching pelvis and bottom, my thigh bones broken at the hip sockets. At school I'm certain the blood is leaking out onto my clothes, down my legs, everyone finally knowing the awful secret about me. Nightmares all night long. The single feathered Indian comes right through the bolted door, his tomahawk coming down. The blood, the blood everywhere.

The next night everyone's dead but me and Mama, their bodies still quivering and moaning and bleeding on the floor. She turns into Grandma. Then the arrowhead hits right in the middle of her forehead splitting her in two. Then the flames and the whole tribe is storming in.

Though I was prepared, indeed over-prepared by my mother, I didn't recognize what it was. I repeated the same pattern as after the rape in the second grade. For almost four days I died for the shame of messing my panties, I died for the return of the thing I most dreaded, had most worked to forget, and I died for the fear someone would discover it. But I did know what to do. Just like before I hid the panties in a paper bag. I carried an extra pair to school in my lunch bag and got rid of the bloody ones in the Ladies' trashcan in the drugstore on the way home, the whole day obsessed with trying to figure where to hide them. How will I ever explain the loss of my underwear?

I dropped the next ones into a trash can at school but then I panicked that the principal and teachers would find them. One time I snuck past the stables and buried my bloodstained panties in the river sand. There are a number of notes through the past fifteen years about this moment because for the most part I stay in forgetfulness. Then suddenly it's there, I better write it down. "Don't you remember, Mom," my daughter has reminded me several times, "when you told me about menstruation you said don't worry about it, some girls bleed before they have a period. You said you bled three days in the second grade."

Late on the third day I'm in the bathroom in the panic and disgust and fear at seeing that the blood is still coming, a river undammed, stronger than ever. On the third day it's supposed to be flaky, darker, drying up, not thicker, redder. I'm searching for a rag, a washcloth, anything in the cupboard above the bath, when I spot the Kotex box and realize. My period has started! Relief floods me. This is natural, this is what's supposed to happen. I'm a young woman now. Mama my period started!

She's so happy for me! I can make babies now. She goes on and on about the moon. She shows me how blood washes out in cold water. She shows me the porcelain pan in the cupboard beneath the sink, cold water for hers and mine, our bloody panties together in the bloody water. It's always been under there, I've always seen her blood rivers swirling around, tainting the clear water, and the smell, that smell. I just never allowed myself to know what it was.

And I never thought of the most obvious solution: to wash them. That would have been too direct an encounter. To wash the evidence—I would have had to know.

But when the bleeding stops late on the fifth day something even more unspeakable happens. At first it feels chapped down there. Then the corridor of flesh and things where the two thighs come together erupts in burning blisters and sores. That's what it feels like anyway. I never look. As the days go on it gets worse. To walk is agonizing. Every step feels like something is tearing. The rubbing of one side against the other. One day between my classroom and the cafetorium, the passageway to the playground, I almost collapse again from the burning, one of those frozen times I'm forever in. I have to tell my mother. Maybe I'm dying. Maybe that gas station toilet at the top of that asphalt hill with Mama and Aunt Alice and Billie and Shirlie and Bridget has finally caught up with me. VD is a disease that rots your insides for years before you know it.

I do tell my mother, one afternoon when I barely make it home and the pain and panic is all consuming. She says, floating in the suds, in her reassuring voice, it's piles.

"Piles?"

"Piles are varicose veins in the rectum," she says. "You must be straining too hard to have your BMs. Piles are the same as hemorrhoids. They are swollen, bleeding veins in the region of the rectum, caused by straining."

My mortification behind the partially closed shower curtain just goes over the top.

But I'm grateful for the word, piles, for her knowledge, her calming assurance. I can tell my mother anything.

"Isn't it true, Sharon, that you are chronically constipated?"

By her standards I guess, I have to admit this, I've been constipated for years. Everything in me is holding back everything down there. I guess I should worry about it but everything feels okay, like my body has adjusted to this. I feel fine. I'd fight to the death another attempt to give me an enema.

After that I notice piles everywhere, piles of trash, piles of dug-up dirt from construction sites along Paramount Boulevard, huge piles of manure at Dairyland. The piles of abalone shells and bombs on Terminal Island. Layers, like shingles, like waves, staggered one on top of the other. The architecture of my dreams is the too-tight muscular ringfolds of the rectum.

Daddy fingering me under Marilyn Monroe. Blowing smoke out his nostrils, out the O of his mouth, a smoke mask between us, smoke rings like doughnuts rising above us. Love suffereth long and is kind. Love beareth all things, believeth all things, endureth all things.

The memories are fragments, existing without a narrative line—a narrative would not have been bearable. Putting the fragments together as accurately, as chronologically as possible with my grandmother's diary, the seasons and history's dates, irrefutable facts, stunningly true stories stranger than fiction come to the fore: the poppy blood rebirth painting I did for Veterans Day in the sixth grade came just as my first period started and the first H bomb went off. I never forgot that I started in the sixth grade three months before February, because of what happens in February, but that painting, like my dreams, was trying to tell me, and tell the world, what I couldn't in words.

And from the beginning I knew it wasn't piles. Mama said some people are prone to them. I never had the experience again. If it was herpes, which I would have gotten from my father, it was not something I could ever have had again without knowing.

Dec 8, 52- I've felt weak and just dragged around today. I canned 3 pts of rhubarb which Dee gave me. Puppy George had an operation today.
"This will give you peace of mind, Prince George," Mama said, "from the insanity of your raging hormones."

He is gone for four days. When he comes home his stomach is shaved and painted red like mine was with the hernia operation. He looks at me like how could I have let this happen? I don't know exactly what they've done. His glistening fuchsia penis comes out of the hairy shaft just like always.

And again he tears through the new screen door. Mama howls about the male. "He's just like his father, Black King George, the reason he came without papers and was so cheap." The power of the sex drive, even fixed! All the forces of civilization have not stopped this randy dog coming down through the ages.

For Christmas I painted a mural the length of one wall of our classroom, of Santa in his sled being pulled across the snowy roof tops of a village by the eight reindeer led by Rudolf the red nosed one. It was like me and Jesus flying over the world to Korea. I read the poem The Night Before Christmas for accuracy. But I was unhappy with the results. Mama had such a thing about the perfect Santa Claus. My Santa would not have met her approval. His lines were too hard, too dark. Mrs. Blanc said this was okay, since it was a mural, to be seen from afar. I studied it from my desk, everyone saying it's incredible, how did you get so good? But I kept seeing something I wasn't happy with, I just wasn't sure what it was. I wrote to Gae about it, sketching it again and again, trying to name the problem.

Dec 13, 52- Kermit called from their new home in Bellflower.
Dec 25, 52- Frederick's family & I took Christmas dinner with Kermit's family. He was up from Sandiego.

I received another package of Days-of-the-Week panties. Mama told the story of that Christmas she was staying at Aunt Luella's, babysitting. She shared a bed with Seifert who was eight. They were so excited for Christmas, she was awake all night anticipating what would be under the tree for her. She was devastated when all she got was a pair of panties. She was longing to be a child again in the family. Her grandmother, Luella's mother, Elizabeth, had just been murdered. Her father was scheduled to have the surgery which would kill him. She'd been kicked out of the School.

We see *Gentlemen Prefer Blondes* at the Long Beach Drive-In. It's ridiculous the way Marilyn Monroe exaggerates the wiggle of her behind. But Mama says in her day women practiced their wiggle. Daddy says he must not be a gentleman, he much prefers the dark Jane Russell. Crack go my knuckles. Laugh goes the whole family. The way Jane Russell's nipples are manipulated to show. The way Marilyn Monroe's silver dress is sewn onto her and is the same color as her hair. The big secret Daddy sex feeling filling the Ford with all of them right here.

We're meeting in the Demilitarized Zone at Panmunjom to decide how to cut up Korea. Everyone's afraid Eisenhower's going to resume the war as soon as he's inaugurated. On television Marilyn Monroe's there sending big fat kisses out to all of them, singing into the mike with her breathy little girl voice. They're so happy to see her. The wind blowing up her dress. What day is she wearing? Laughing like a white rose opening and opening on the stage above the sea of them washing in like high tide. Like the largest bomb ever about to explode.

"She's really working them," Daddy says.

"They're acting that way," Mama explains, "because they're in a war, poor things, and she's the only girl they've seen in so long."

I will grow into the dumb blond to pretend I don't know what's really going on, to protect them, so as not to confront them, so as to be faithful to them, so as to protect my family from knowing, to protect myself from knowing, so as not to assume anything, so as not to be suspicious of an innocent person. I will grow into the dumb blond, an innocent person. I will grow into the dumb blond because I love them and don't know how else to manifest my love. I will grow into the dumb blond like Jesus on the cross, like Marilyn on the calendar, on the stage above Korea, because how else can I give my only begotten self without exposing them and getting them killed? I will manipulate the whole world into dumbness so as not to know, my sister will do this too. She'll become a healer, I'll become an artist, a poet, so the dumb images can come out.

We watch an even dumber blonde every week, *My Friend Irma*. We go with the camera all sides of her two big triangular breasts, her pointed tits. The Sweater Girl, Marie Wilson, like my grandmother's baby sister Laura dying that Christmas in Detroit, will eventually die of breast cancer, die of the breasts for which she was so famous. She used them wrong, I just know. She manipulated them.

Dec 31, 52- War looms and Kermit is to sail soon. I fear Alex & Jim may have to go. May our leaders be divinely led. Laura is sick. Dear Audrey is sick. May she soon recover, o Lord. The sun still shines and God is still on his throne. This book is closed now.

§

Twenty-Three

I'm handed a note. I think Toni Genoway handed it to me. Toni lived down
Arizona, on the corner of McKinley. The note is from a boy in the other
sixth grade, a boy named Ronald Dowell. He sees me on the playground
and would like to know me. I read the short penciled note again and again.
That someone has been watching me, and even so would like to know me,
someone I don't know. All through recesses I try to study the kids from the
other class without acting forward. At night I lie with it beside my
pillowless sleepless head. Susan Evans says he's tall with straight light
brown hair combed into a pompadour and he's called Ronnie. I imagine
him watching me the way Jesus watches me. I notice a tall boy with
straight gold brown hair immaculately combed up off his high narrow
white forehead, coming out of the class, the last in line, always my
position. Could it be him? The 4:30 p.m. paper boy? I'd die to make a
mistake in this. It takes days for the verification: the very tall boy at the
end of the line of the other sixth grade is Ronnie Dowell, the paper boy.
He may be taller than me. And he's cute, no, he's handsome. No. He is
beautiful.

Toni introduces us on the playground by the back fence, closest to the
river. The wind is whipping up the sand. "Can I come to your house and
play with you?" I'm so tongue-tied I'm choking. "Can I have your address
so I can write you a letter?"

He sends me a letter through the mail. It is also in pencil, on six-by-
nine blue lined linen tablet paper. His father is a cross country truck driver,
he has a thirteen year old brother in the eighth grade, and an eight month
old sister. He loves his mother, she's nursing the baby beside him on the
couch helping him to write this letter. He lives on the corner of McKinley
and Arizona. He sees me walking to school. Maybe he could walk with
me.

On Valentine's Day, Daddy's thirty-seventh birthday, walking home
with Clovis, a red heart-shaped box of chocolates is thrust into my hands
from someone running up behind me, and past, then on down Main.

Ronnie.

It's the most delicious candy I've ever tasted. Every kind seems
another kind of Ronald Dowell. I share the chocolates with all my family.
Even my mother, maybe like his mother, seems moved, is sweetly
encouraging.

Then a horrible thing happens. I'm on the living room floor, petting
George, rereading the letter, and I'm asking my mother about cross-coun-

try truck drivers. Bridget's on the couch behind me watching television. I must have sneezed, that's all I could ever figure, though I didn't have a cold and had no recollection of sneezing, because suddenly there's snot all over his letter, the most precious gift I've ever received. Long strands of snot. A sneeze that went flying all over. Everything in me panics for the humiliation of my germy body fluids, that such snot could come from me unknown, unwillingly, and ruin something so precious and important. The penciled words smudge when I wipe it off. I try to pretend it didn't happen but the image of snot won't go away. I've kept the red Valentine box all my life with the snot-smeared letter inside but it occurs to me only now that it was my sister's snot, that when I left the room momentarily, leaving it on the carpet, she blew her nose on it.

Menstruation like snot like constipation, it's been three months since my first period, thank you Jesus, it hasn't come back.

Ronnie's here. We're jumping rope, a very bright and warm Saturday in February. It's my turn, Bridget and Ronnie are turning it. I'm so happy he's here. He tells everyone he loves me. I've written about him to Gae. But I feel strange. Then I'm spinning out of the rope and off the curb. "Oh don't worry about her," Bridget scoffs, "she does this kind of thing all the time." My sister thinks I'm playing dead like we used to when we were small. I'm staring at the sidewalk curb, my body rolled full-length against it. My face is bleeding against the warm asphalt at the edge of the gutter hole. Looking down the black hole Denny Clare was held over. The taste of blood, my mouth bleeding into it.

Then Daddy is picking me up and carrying me across the two lawns to the house. "Are you okay, baby?" A shimmering silver tear in which I can see myself is running down his white cheek, my head against his heart. "Lu," he sobs. Ronnie is left alone on the sidewalk. Daddy's carrying me away like a bride, burying his face into mine, crying "Oh baby, oh baby." I feel left back there with Ronnie, I hear Mama saying Daddy has a special love for you, Sharon. He'll be jealous of your boyfriends. He loves you hat much.

And did he carry me to my room, lay me on the bed? Did he continue to cry to me? Where is my mother? The power, the force that pulled me down and out of the world so I can't remember. The power, the strength, the feel of his arms carrying me. Crying. My father's huge tears spilling on me. When I finally saw *Frankenstein,* the movie my parents saw on their first date, and saw the father carrying his murdered daughter up from the swamp I thought of us that day.

I fainted rather than bleed. Again that was how my mother diagnosed it, which despite Bridget's dismissal, our father's exact attitude of everything about me, that I'm faking and can't be believed, was helplessly genuine, and the time of month my period was supposed to start. In fact it did, sometime that afternoon.

The next day, on Sunday, we visited the Hogans. "Sharon has always been so high strung," Mama said, telling of my fainting. Then everyone in the house knew I was bleeding down there.

Ronnie never spoke to me again. He never looked at me, never acknowledged my existence again. My fainting turned him off, such a shameful thing for a girl to faint, hinting at all sorts of problems to come. Uncontrollable snot and hypochondria. "Ugh your eyes rolled back," Bridget said, and said forever afterwards. "You forgot to shut your eyes, all you could see were the whites." Dear Jesus, next time I faint please help me to remember to shut my eyes. How ugly I must have looked, the real me. Of course Ronald Dowell was gone, like that.

Only now do I realize that my father cursed him. "Get lost, Boy! Never darken my door again." He'd kill him. Maybe he even called the Dowells. But I never dreamed that. I would not dream such treachery.

But then heartbreak I never dreamed. I thought of Ronnie constantly, I ached and longed for him, my heart behind my left breast physically hurt every breath, that spot from the second grade, I went over and over what happened, trying to understand where I'd messed up, why so suddenly he'd have nothing to do with me. I wrote I love Ronnie Dowell on everything, like a prayer, that he would know this and come back. (That my father would know this, that God would fix things.) Gradually, in some ways, Ronnie Dowell almost replaced Jesus as my constant petitioned One.

"Oh, Sharon," Mama said. "He's running with his older brother now. It's the way boys are. Fickle."

I joined the Girl Scouts. Mrs. Ritchie was the leader, the weekly meetings held at Toni Genoway's house, directly across the street from Ronnie's house. I detested Girl Scouts, worse than Brownies, for the demand of conformity, domesticity, for girls falling into their clutches, for the dull depressing green uniform, for the scary power of group think of which Mama was always warning me. For Mrs. Ritchie's interpretation of who I am and what I must become. But it was an excuse to be near Ronnie. I'd approach the corner of McKinley and Arizona pretending I wasn't looking for him, looking everywhere but at his house, completely paranoid that he'd think I was chasing him. I sat through the oppressive meetings—how I detested Parliamentary procedure which we had to memorize—in the chair where I could watch his house. Only very occasionally did I see anyone of his family, much less him. When once or twice, there or at school he saw me seeing him, he looked the other way, I looked the other way, we pretended we didn't know each other. Of course it was my father, not my ugliness in fainting. Of course it was Daddy. But I would not think my father would do that to me. Or to him. Or to anyone.

Dozens of green boxes of Girl Scout cookies are stacked up the whole wall of the dining room. Mrs. Ritchie had them delivered. This was another catastrophe. I didn't sell a single box. I couldn't. No way could I sell, could I ask for money, could I pressure someone into buying them, could I impose that way, could I influence against their better judgment. The very thought seemed sinful. No way could I knock on a stranger's door. I knock. The door opens. The naked man pulls me inside. The image of the Girl Scout Cookies stacked against the wall will always come to me when I think of my sales aptitude. The cookies were there until we left Hollydale, growing stale, and more stale.

February 14, 1953- Today is Frederick's birthday. I gave him a valentine and embroidered his initial in a handkerchief for him. I told him I should have named him Valentine and called him Valie. Late card from Duran. Laura critically ill.

February 15, 1953- This is the 75th anniversary of Avon's birth. Cecil was born on St. Valentine Day and Avon was 38 the next day. Cecil, Clarke & I took flowers to his grave. We talked of his fine judgment and his hope of heaven. I am happy in the Lord.

Feb 20, 53- Kermit was supposed to sail for Korea today. War seems terrible over there now.... Cold blustery day. I hope Laura can rest tonight and that Duran & boys keep well.

Feb 26, 53- Frederick is preparing to build a garage. Bless his heart; he works quite hard and is on night shift now at the plant. Most every day I hear from little Laura. She is so sick.

For years they had been trying to figure how to add on to the house. Clarke was getting too big to be in the same room with us girls. Others in the neighborhood made a third bedroom out of the garage but Daddy needed his garage. Finally he figured there was enough room to put a driveway between our house and the apartments. He started digging the foundation for a new garage in the backyard, filling me with ever more dread and panic.

Holes. Holes where my bloody secret is buried.

Feb 28, 53- Bridget's 10th birthday. ... Letter from Marion says they may visit us this summer.

March 3, 53- ... letter from Kermit today from Inchon, Korea.

March 4, 1953: Card from Flo says Laura was worse Sunday night, voice weak and throat bad. She wishes to die. Dear little sister, may you rest in sleep tonight, while Jesus is very near with the angels. May nurses be kind. Keep her family, O God in Jesus name I pray; and keep Kermit and the loved ones and me tonight. Help Stallen (sic) to accept thee, if he has not. He too is very ill.

March 5, 1953: ....No news from Laura today. Joe Stallen passed away.

March 8, 1953: A message from Duran came while I was eating breakfast, saying Laura passed away at 6:30 am. She is now out of her great pain and in the care of the living God.... Cecil and Audrey came in. I lay abed most all day --- Sent 4 wires, made a call to poor Bess- God bless Duran and boys and me and my beloved.

March 10, 1953: My sister Laura was buried today. ...The funeral was 1 p.m. Central Time. I dressed and kept the hour and was in much sympathy with her family. My eyes cast dim. Alice came and put some money on Laura's flowers.

Adjusting to the wad of cotton. To the leak of blood. To the sanitary belt, like a noose. To the cramps and pixelating faint. To the handicap. To trying to figure what to do with the bloody stuff. A crisis every time. The danger of remembering the second grade. What does Mama do? What did the Indians do? What have all the women on earth through all time done? I flush it down praying, flush! don't stop up, don't stop up.

The bathroom door is shut. I knock, praying no one is in there.

"Who is it?"

Oh, no.

"Come on in, Sharon Lulu."

Trapped, can't run away. He'll know I know. Walk in. The room is steamy and hot. I know without looking that he's lying in the water. I need to check my pants, I'm frantic that there's blood. But now I only wash my hands. His eyes burn like always into the back of my pants.

"Oh Lu, look at this," he giggles. "Isn't it something?"

"Oh yes," I say, feigning interest. He pulls it forward, pushes it down, it has to be forced, it has a will all of its own. He lays back, lets it do its thing, rise and shine, look Ma, no hands! He's so proud of it, I can't hurt his feelings.

"Watch this, now. Don't take your eyes off it, Sharon."

It bobs in the air above the soap suds the same old way as always.

"Just look how big it can get."

"Oh, yes, Daddy, that's nice."

I was never inside the plant at Douglas where he spent most of the days of my childhood. I still have to be wary of being overly sympathetic about him but the fact is, just as Mama always said, all that time he was in an environment that he detested in order to provide for us. (Money is the root of all evil, the root of what Daddy does to me, the reason I can't sell the Girl Scout cookies, the root of my anti-money and anti-drudge job philosophy to this day, the root of why I have lived the way I have, the proving that you can live morally and meaningfully, pursuing your dreams, and not use the need for money or the money itself as an excuse to ruin you, to ruin others.) What did he do, minute by hour, day by week, month by year? A plastics experimental man, he brought home his wonderful creations—an exquisite art deco, clear plastic, round-bottomed cigarette box elevated on half-moon legs with a magenta star-shaped knob atop the perfect fitted lid (I keep my son's gold baby curls in it now), plastic knife handles and brilliant colored casings. He always had to be doing something with his hands, Mama always said.

I remember an open house at Douglas, all of us outside on the white cement landing field. The jets screamed till your ears ached, your whole being discombobulated.

Bridget and I are sitting on the corner curbs, me straddling the gutter hole, she on the Roosevelt side when we see Ronnie with his teenage brother and gang slouching up Arizona toward Main. In the twilight they are a silhouette, their hands in their pockets of their black fluttery chinos below the cracks of their behinds, their heads protruding way out over the pink and black shirts, their ducktails coming down their collars. They look so hoodish! Ronnie is the smallest one. I can hardly stand it. Mama's right, he's running with the older boys now, he has no use for the likes of me, a nice girl.

"He dropped you like a hot potato," Bridget laughs.

I write to Gae every day pouring my heart out about Ronnie. I write R.D. + S.E. inside hearts on everything. I do this in the Autograph Book she gave me—hers is the first entry, *"False friends are like autumn leaves/ found everywhere./True friends are like diamonds,/precious but rare. I love you. Gae Walker,"* the W being an upside down heart—so that everyone I ask to sign it knows of my heartbreak. *"Red, white, blue. Does Ronnie love you? Dean Tulley, April 7, 1953." "Mad in love with Ronnie." Sharon May Ritchie, 4-7-53."* How could I have been so out there about this? I was trying to get the message to him past my father's threat, past ever knowing my father threatened him. I was fighting my father. I was being your disingenuous dumb blonde. If I wrote it, that is, engraved the letters into the matter and psyche of the world the message would get to him somehow. Like prayer. Like Grandma sewing Grandpa's last words into the lining of her Sunday purse. Like Grandma keeping the hour of her sister's funeral in Detroit.

Our Sunday School parties began to feel like the energy of the Santa Ana Winds, the Hollydale floods, and infamous Paramount Junior High where we were headed. Mexicans, Pachuco gangs, guns, car clubs, marijuana-to-heroin, boys, lipstick, tight skirts, teenagers, seven different classes a day, six different teachers, twelve hundred kids, and showers—we have to be naked together every day in junior high! We went skating at the Paramount Ice Rink, swimming at the Jordan High School plunge, we even went to the Pike. Susan, Nancy and Clovis on the bus proceeding through the dark, sulfuric night. The world we are entering. I remember being so big so almost twelve in a rented stretched blue one-piece that fit awful, posed to dive in Jordan's plunge. *I will give you living waters*—why does that chlorination dive still seem holy to me? The angels singing *we're stepping over the river Jordan.* Aunt Giny's voice calling *Audrey! Audrey!* You could feel both the dark and the light coming. Grief, regret for the lost child in it. Goosebumps, blue white veins. Fear. Penny, my first cousin, given away.

April 20, 1953- Went out to Audrey's tonight. Sharon & Clarke had a scrap. Pity Cecil can't be home nights. He's working night shift at the plant now. Children need their father's control.

April 25, 1953- The last of the sick and wounded are being exchanged at Panmunjom. Daylight saving time begins tonight or in the morning. Sharon is having a birthday party.

It's my first birthday party since Mama went into the sanitarium, with lots of kids from both sixth grades. I sent Ronnie an invitation but he doesn't come. We're all out on the front lawn, I keep hoping he'll come down the street. One of the more spastic of the crippled men is struggling by on Industrial. Nancy starts mimicking him down Roosevelt, every move of every limb a severe jerk in the wrong direction. All the kids laugh, start to mimic him too, Clovis and Stephen rolling on the dichondra, hysterical. I ache for the man, I can't stand for them to do that to him, but I can't let them see my disgust either, that would be the same thing and they'd hate me for being self-righteous.

After dark Daddy builds a bonfire in the back yard and we roast hot dogs and marshmallows on wire hangers. Mama and Daddy seem so happy to be able to provide this, proud to accomplish this party for me. Even Grandma comes over into the night yard with us, stands around the bonfire, pointing out the Big Dipper just like Grandpa used to, telling how it's the same stars as when she was a girl on the Elk River in Tennessee. Daddy roasts her a marshmallow. "Happy birthday Ma."

After the boys leave we have the slumber party. We spread our pads, blankets and bags down the living room floor, get into our baby doll pajamas. I'm at the end, against the living-room/kitchen wall, right next to Susan Evans, and Bridget's at the other end, even though she's just a fifth grader.

"Ooh, couldn't you just swoon for Mr. Edens?" Somebody says down at that end.

"Your father is really handsome," Susan says.

"Oh, yes," Clovis says, "I've always said Mr. Edens is the most handsome of the fathers. He reminds me of Clark Gable in *Gone with the Wind.*"

Sunday, April 26, 1953- I was born at daybreak 73 years ago in Tennessee in the Eighth district of Franklin County in a country community, where the Black Jacks and tall oaks grew.

Gae's birthday present to me was *The Black Stallion Returns* and *Son of the Black Stallion*. They are the oldest books in my library. *"To Sharon on her 12ᵗʰ birthday, Love Gae"* is written in light pencil on the inside covers. I am still inclined to kiss her handwriting as I did then, over and over.

One lunch hour the boys suddenly start chasing me through the sand dunes. The Santa Ana's blowing, everything's crystal clear and baking hot. I get all the way to the back fence over the river, the wind hissing down the bone dry channel like a rattlesnake. Cornered, I spin around. They're flying at me, then coming to a dead stop in a semicircle around me.

One of them reaches out, touches my upper arm. The electric spark cracks the sky. That look comes over them that comes over Daddy, over the men on the streets, over the poor worked-up GIs screaming at Marilyn Monroe. It's just a second, it frightens them too, they seem to shatter in the recognition of what's overtaking them. I ease through them, walk, then run, just like Houdini, the great escape artist.

The silence in the wind behind me, before the guffaws, is the tunnel's echo. I feel bad for them.

Karl Harden and I were the fastest in the school. It made perfect sense about me, I was the tallest (next to Ronnie) but how to explain Karl, just about the shortest kid in the school? We were made the anchor men, I was the fastest, he was second, we were the ones who had a chance of catching up if we were behind.

The last meet against the champions, Grove Avenue, we're half a man behind, Karl's coming with the baton toward me, handing it off. "Do it Sharon, do it!" Sluggish to start, like in a bad dream of your feet running in the same spot, but then second wind kicks in, a fantastic surge past all the previously known limits. I run like the Black Stallion from Arabia, like the little girl from all the perverts, like Houdini over the falls and out of the barrel.

It's almost six before I start home. It feels great to be acknowledged as the fastest kid in Hollydale, to have won the championship for us. I come to the corner of Dakota, in front of the Egyptian pottery building where Grandpa and Aunt Giny used to work. A big car pulls up. I wait for him to pull out. Then too much time has passed. I come to the moment. Look down through the open window. He's dressed in a suit jacket and tie but is naked below the waist. His big thing sticks up into the steering wheel like Daddy's in Tyler, Texas. His eyes meet mine and in the same moment his right hand reaches for the big butcher knife on the seat beside him. I'm flying around the back of his car, I'm running faster than I ran in the relay race, up over the tracks, down behind the church, dropping down into the coal piles, praying dear Jesus don't let any of the old men be down here too. I eye Telephone Pole eyeing me. I crawl home between the gravel and brush beneath the tracks, coming down behind Nadja's old shop, making it across the street to the porch.

But this time the sick feeling doesn't leave.

Tuesday, May 19, 53- Fred & Audrey brought their new trailer home.... Cheers me to see the family so cheerful & optimistic of future.

On June 2 we watched the coronation of Princess Elizabeth, the first trans-ocean live broadcast. Grandma had been anticipating this ever since King George died. I wore the three pin scatter set she gave me for Christmas, the scepter, crown and sword, saw the real ones used in the coronation. "When I was a girl," Mama said like such a shame, "the sun never set on the British Empire." Grandma said "There he is, Sir Anthony Eden, your fifth cousin."

I watched my fifth cousin, Anthony Eden, who was going to be the real head of England, seeing how he looked, with his pouchy eye bags and heavy layered lids like my father, disturbed that the Queen wasn't going to be the real ruler. Later, as the Prime Minister of England, Anthony Eden looked, with his roundish thin pinched balding head, more like Avon Edens, my grandpa.

"Never forget," she said again, "you are English. The Edens came over on the second ship after the Mayflower with Lord Baltimore. They founded Edenton, North Carolina. The Edens were the original aristocrats of Virginia. William Hancock's signature is on the Second Charter to the Virginia Company of London by James I, in 1609. Unfortunately," she always added, "William was scalped and Sir Robert Eden, the Governor of Maryland in 1776, was for England." She made me say it again: "A Hancock married a Corn, a Corn married a Chitwood, a Chitwood married an Edens." She brought out the painting of John Hancock looking just like Uncle Marion and Daddy signing the Declaration of Independence.

When Elizabeth was crowned the Queen of England, her husband, Philip, was the first to do homage. Right there in the aisle, in the eyes of the whole world, he knelt down to her, his Queen.

And right then too there was a shot of the Tower of London where our thirteen year old ancestor Lady Jane Grey was imprisoned and beheaded because she was betrayed by her awful father.

Mama's so excited for me, that I've become a woman, that I'm a beautiful, successful twelve year old, that I'm graduating from the sixth grade with straight As. She starts my graduation dress, an elaborate creation of lavender lace, satin and voile, two dresses in one, a lavender satin slip with a see-through lace dress over it. "Diaphanous," she says. "It's going to be the most beautiful dress ever made."

She measures my every part. My bust, my shoulders, my waist, my hips. 36-22-33. She fits the lavender spaghetti straps and bodice so that my bra won't show. Measuring the hem from the floor up, telling me her stories of her own magnificent figure. "The Hughes girls were known through the whole state of Virginia for their big breasts. This was because of the Depression, people were starving, but we had our own cows. If a girl drinks at least three glasses of milk a day her bones will grow thick and strong and her breasts full to a C, even a D cup. And her daughters will too. This is why you're so big."

When she was six her grandmother made her a beautiful yellow silk dress for Easter that she still has. When her father came he took her to town and bought her red patent leather shoes. Never was she so happy in all her life. The Sunday School lesson was how Jesus walked on water, all it takes is enough faith. She knew she had enough faith to walk on water like Jesus, but when she did, crossing a puddle of the Dan, she sank and ruined her red shoes and couldn't understand and then was so unhappy. "Well, obviously I didn't have enough faith. Jesus tried to get Peter to walk on water but his fears sank him. Like Peggy Ritchie's fears always end up sinking her. Mrs. Ritchie, you know, is jealous of how much more beautiful you are than Sharon May who's gotten so fat this year."

This takes my breath away, to hear my mother speak of Sharon May that way.

"Sharon May's gotten fat because she's so unhappy." Mama is down at my feet, pins in her mouth, pinning up my dress.

That dress was probably the height of my mother's artistic achievement. The lavender satin slip had a thick organdy net ruffle sewed on the underside around the bottom. It had a matching twelve inch wide satin sash that tied around the waist and fell gracefully down the back to the hemline. There are no photographs of it, but for many years (until

Halloween 1969) I kept it too, with the dried white gardenia corsage
pinned to the left shoulder, in my cedar hope chest.

She was almost through making it when I told.

*June 10, 53- I guess Marion & family started to California this
morning.*

Coming down Industrial, past Telephone Pole, I see commotion in our
front yard. Daddy's digging a deep hole beneath the roots of the elm tree
bulging up like a stallion's neck. My panic's so great that he's found my
buried things I almost faint again. The toilet's stopped up again. He has to
get it fixed before Uncle Marion and family gets here. Dee and Mr. Hogan
are helping him.

"Don't you lie to me, Sharon Edens!" he shouts as I come across the
street, holding it up. "Isn't this your bloody Kotex?"

I move in the mirror, the bathroom steamy, the last of the bathwater
gurgling down the drain. I open the window to clear the steam, paint my
lips red with Mama's lipstick. Just one more year and I can wear lipstick
and then surely they'll see that I'm not so ugly. As the dew changes to
tears running down the mirror, I wet my lips, I smile and throw my head
back. I move my hand across my wet breast and down my rib cage and
stomach. I'm Marilyn Monroe, my body becomes like hers. I rub the towel
up and down my back, throwing out my hip, my shoulders back, my
breasts up over my ribs and then kiss my mouth with the wet red lips.

"Fuck."

A face in the screen window.

"Fuck."

A small, grizzly bearded toothless old man's face.

"Fuck!"

Then he's gone.

His scuffing footsteps echo down Daddy's cement path to the back
gate.

Scrambling to get my pajamas on, to get out of there. The humiliation
for my behavior in the mirror is almost as great as the fear.

But then I'm in the dark hallway staring at the wall. I've pulled shut all
the doors. I can't move. He saw me posing that way. There's no place to
go.

The next morning at school the old man's grizzly face lays over everything, the gravelly voice saying fuck. At lunch I seek out the girls in the cafetorium even though I have a sack lunch which means I'm supposed to eat outside on the playground. I'm so afraid to be outside I break the rules. At the long table near the front Susan, Nancy, and Clovis are talking about a madman who escaped from the County Farm hospital for the criminally insane yesterday afternoon. He's a rapist and murderer of many girls. He's still on the loose, they can't find him. I'm eating a crushed olive, celery and mayonnaise sandwich, my very favorite of Mama's sandwiches. It's shady and cool in here but I'm dissolving into sand dunes, afraid. I am so afraid.

Walking home in the fear and dread that won't let me go for all my prayers and denials. Every man driving by is naked below the window with a knife in the fold of the seat. It's harder to keep walking than when the blisters were down there. It's almost impossible to get up over the tracks and down. Even the church terrifies me, that he's hiding in its wings, or behind my Telephone Pole.

In the bathroom she starts in again about the dangers of sex. How men love women's breasts and what they like to do with them. I stand in the doorway, behind the curtain of the hot steamy room, my head held up by the frame. Daddy's on the midnight shift, he won't be home until the middle of the night. She reclines in the sudsy water saying the sex urge is so strong, honey, some people can't control themselves. They may do things that they know to be wrong and yet they won't be able to help themselves. Through the opened daylit window I see the old man's face. *"Fuck."* Through the opened part of the curtain I see her two breasts floating in the bubbles. Men will want to touch you on your breasts. Breasts excite men and give them sexual pleasure. I have heard all this before, so many many times. Uncle Marion's headed across the country to our house. I see Uncle Marion's hands on my breasts.

"Daddy does that to me."

"What?"

I can't believe those words came out of me.

"What?"

"Daddy does that. Touches me ... there." I can't say breasts. I have never said the word breasts in my life.

There's a long silence.

"When does he do this?"

"When we're alone."

"Please don't tell him I told you. I promised him."

Another silence.

"All right," she says in her tired voice.

Another long silence.

"But I want you to tell me if he ever does it again. I'm sure he never will again but if he does, do you promise to tell me?"

"I promise."

Another long moment of ringing silence.

"You can go now."

I start to leave.

"Sharon..." Her voice strange as when she was first sick. "He couldn't help it."

"I know that Mama."

"It will never happen again. But if it does, you must promise to tell me."

"I promise."

I leave the bathroom, walk down the hall, turn right into the living room, then I fly out the screen door, fly off the front porch, knowing before I hit the ground the greatest relief I will ever know, knowing my life has just been saved, that what had been unbearable is over. Mama will take care of it.

§

Francis Marion Edens, "Confederate Soldier" (penciled below), and Phoebe Stovall Overby, weaver. My paternal great-grandparents.

Avon Marion Edens and Lura Maude Chitwood, July 3, 1906, Winchester, Tennessee. My paternal grandparents.

Avon Edens, foreman, Tennessee Copper Company, pick between his legs.

This is erosion at its worst. Fumes from a copper smelter near Copperhill, Tenn., killed all vegetation; rain and run-off did the rest. These homes cling to small remaining patches of topsoil. TVA has started replanting.

"Our Ducktown, Tennessee home," in Grandma's hand, the hand in the diary.
"No matter how bad it got, Pa always had a garden."
—Photo from LIFE Magazine, 1930s.

"The postcards of Ducktown Tennessee, give only a faint hint of the devastation that goes on. Imagine an area fifty square miles so poisoned by the fumes of the copper plant that everything is killed off and the earth itself made to look like a convulsive red scar! Grand to see in a way, like a Doré illustration of the Inferno. But what a place for people to live ..."
—Henry Miller to Anais Nin, postcard, October, 1940

Above right: Sarah Susie Simmons Clarke with Garnet, age 2, and Lawrence, *"that redheaded bare-foot boy,"* age 5, Reidsville, North Carolina, summer, 1922. Susie is pregnant with Mozelle. *"She's buried in this dress, it's yellow, made by her mother, Elizabeth Reynolds Simmons. My dress was yellow too, and made by my grandmother too."* (Mama)

Top left: Guy Henry Clarke, *"that redheaded Cherokee Irishman"*

Above: Guy Clarke, widower, with his three children, Garnet, Mozelle, and Lawrence, 1924.

Right: Belle Simmons Sibbetts, Chesnee, South Carolina, 1977, my maternal great-aunt, younger sister of Christopher Columbus Simmons. Her son Richard and granddaughter. (How quickly we become blond.)
—Photo by Mama

Audrey Garnet Clarke Edens, July 26, 1940 (nine months to the day before my birth), The Pike, Long Beach, California

Cecil Frederick Edens, April 27, 1941 (the day after my birth), Knott's Berry Farm, Buena Park, California

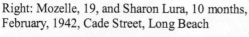

Right: Mozelle, 19, and Sharon Lura, 10 months, February, 1942, Cade Street, Long Beach

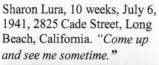

Sharon Lura, 10 weeks, July 6, 1941, 2825 Cade Street, Long Beach, California. *"Come up and see me sometime."*

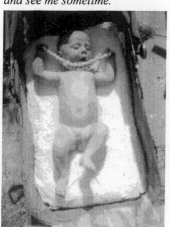

5903 Roosevelt Avenue, Hollydale

Sharon Edens (20 months) and Marilyn Ripp, "*way over two.*" December 1942 "*The earthquake crack between Marilyn's white shoes and socks...I am beside myself with the thrill.*"

Clarke Frederick Edens, "*the most beautiful baby ever born,*" in our embrace.

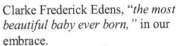

My sister and me. She is 8 months, I am 2½ years. "*A sort of portent of what was then of what will always be about us.*"

Mama posing on the back of the 1923 jalopy, *"Just Married"* 1946, what a joke! The rumble seat I loved to go in with the wind in my face.

"that sexy father of ours...," *"April - early May 1942. It's a 1939 Chevrolet. I'm either just pregnant or about to get pregnant with Bridget. You were almost 13 months old. You were walking. We had the other car six months after the transmission went out. You wouldn't go near it after we got this one."*

"Sometimes we even tumble and somersault with Daddy. We ride his back across the desert to Arizona, into the wilderness of Tennessee, to the barren eroded hills of Ducktown."

"Camp Roberts, California, D Company, 79th Infantry Training Battalion, First Platoon, C.F. Edens." 1945

C.F. Edens

Below: "Heroes" in wheelchairs, the Rose Bowl Parade, Pasadena, front page of the *Los Angeles Times, The Huntington Park Signal*, January 2, 1946. Daddy in far right corner. I think the legless man in front, Sergeant Ed Ruzika, is the man who was at the back door of the Downey Penny's every day in his wheel chair, giving out poppies, begging.

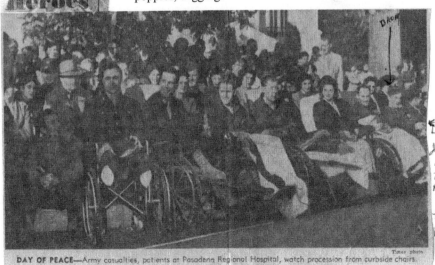

DAY OF PEACE—Army casualties, patients at Pasadena Regional Hospital, watch procession from curbside chairs.

Sharon Lura Edens, Kindergarten through 5th grade

Kindergarten, age 5

first grade, age 6

3rd grad.

"Nov 1948, 2nd grade, age 7½
wt 62 lbs"

4th grade, age

5th grade

Nadja   *Louise*   *Gae (2nd Row)*   *Sharon May Ritchie, 3rd Row, 2nd in*

Second Grade class photo, June 1949: Gae is in the 2nd row, mid-center, I am two rows directly behind her, in my sheet curls curled backwards. Nadja is at the end of Gae's row, next to Mrs. Allen. Sharon May Ritchie is in the 3rd row, 2nd from right, Karen Pohlman next to her on the end. That might be Robert Kent in the 3rd row, just beneath me, to the right. Or it might be Raymond and next to him, Gary Neal. In the front row, 4th from right is Lonnie Hicks, who crossed in front of my grandmother's funeral procession. When I stare long enough into their faces, their names just rise again to my lips.

The Neighbor women said we were dirty.

Jan - April 1949
In front of the Ritchie's. Probably taken by Mrs. R. as Evidence

Bridget asking, "what is going on here?" Clarke knows. I'm praying.

Gae and Red *"We are horses trapped in human bodies....It isn't about sex,... it's pure energy. It's love. It's identification with all captive spirits, with the oppressed, about saving the horse, our selves, from bossy, jealous, brutal men. From our fathers. The horse is freedom. Gae and I will grow up too to be unconquered virgin mothers."*

June 6, 1950, Laguna Beach *"... pretending to be bathing suit beauties. Painted hussies. Glamour pusses."*

"Now we've got our act down ... What was happening to us was unspeakable ... We didn't speak of our changing bodies either. This is life, how you grow up."

Left: The Two Men, Marion Francis and Cecil Frederick Edens at the Tennessee cabin, July, 1950. *"Oh, things couldn't be that bad."*

Mozelle, Ramona, early '70s

July 23, 1953, their 15th wedding anniversary

Me leaning into my mother, she leaning away from me. Maybe the most beautiful photograph I have of my sister. Our little brother defending his women from our father.

We start over. Our house in Ramona, the 1953 Ford before it was repainted two-tone light blue so as not to show the dust.

"Dear Jesus, don't let him know how much I hate it...I'm the blue fairy queen."

La Noche de Las Velas: November 2, 1956, El Año, *"You can see how much we love each other. I broke up with Ramon the next morning."*

Edens' Heavenly Hamburgers, Ramona, California

Gae, Gene, Suzi, Sergei and me on La Jolla. *"Blood sisters"*

"There's a photograph of the three of us during the last year of slow motion family dissolution. It's.... a basketball game... Clarke and Bridget are on separate ends of the front row, and Gae is sitting there too. I'm one of the cheerleaders... about to begin a cheer...."

Like verifying a dream:

"Police Captain Wayne W..... quit the North Las Vegas police department...for personal reasons..." Monday, June 27, 1955, Las Vegas Sun

"Jail Police Capt. as Wife Tells of Threat on Life..." June 28, 1955, Las Vegas Sun

Above: In the
dressing room,
Congregational
Church, Ramona,
June 26, 1959.

Left: Coming down
the aisle. Giving
away the bride.

Mr. and Mrs. Doubiago coming back up

Book III

Mama

and straight way the damsel arose,
and walked;
for she was of the age of twelve years.
                                    Mark 5: 42

"The lachrymose
cities of the plain weeping in the sulphurous smog; Anaheim
South Gate (smell of decaying dreams in the dead air.)"
                    Thomas MacGrath, *Letter to an Imaginary Friend*

Twenty-Four

Thursday, June 11, 53- ...I guess Marion's family is in Texas tonight. I saw Alice out at Audrey's tonight. Both were tired.

Friday, June 12, 53- Cecil had an automobile accident as he went to work today. No one was hurt.

Saturday, June 13, 53- Cecil bought a new car and we all went riding in it. It's green. He mashed his finger today.

The girl sits on the carpet before the House Committee on UnAmerican Activities, her mother above her on the sofa, petting the tummy of her black cocker spaniel whose brilliant red penis is sliding more and more out of its shaft. Her eyes are glued to the television, to the men accusing other men, and the woman, to the men demanding the couple be put to death, as she strokes nearer and nearer the hard, exposed genital because—well, because her beloved dog, sprawled on his back, all four legs hanging limp in the air, even though fixed, loves it so. She is aware her mother is watching. She pretends she isn't aware her mother is watching.

She is stroking near the base of her dog's penis in the rhythm her father strokes his, her fingers moving closer and closer to the raw, shiny, skinless thing. She is thinking about touching it. She's trying to snap her mother out of her silence. She is trying to force a conversation. Maybe she would say Daddy loves this too. Or Daddy strokes his thing just like this.

Her mother is staring at her. The girl pretends that she's mindlessly doing what she's doing, that she doesn't realize what she's doing or that her mother is watching her. Her mother has the look she has when seeing with her Third Eye.

"Sha-ron!"

And then Sharon cannot imagine, cannot explain, will never be able to explain to herself even, whatever it was she was doing.

There are two brief flashes of her father that survive this moment. He's pulling into the driveway—new car? old car? no matter, he's coming in the back door. She is on the sofa with her sister. There's dread, there's suffocation when he enters the kitchen, when he passes through the living room, flat-faced staring at her.

The family's at the dining room table. The deep brown polished mahogany table with the pressed white linen table cloth. It's the Sunday afternoon dinner, maybe the grandmother is here. The father, her son, standing at the head with the carving knife, explodes at her at the other end, facing him.

The execution of the Rosenbergs is set for June 19. This man and woman, this husband and wife, this father and mother, are traitors of their own country. Her brother testified against her, they gave the secret of the atom bomb to the Russians, they must die, even though they have two little boys. There are last minute appeals. There are efforts from all over the world to save them. They're Jewish. They're Communists. What do these things mean? Like Ethel Rosenberg's brother I've testified against my own flesh and blood.

Perhaps I'd complained, wanting to see something on television that all the kids at school watch but which was after our bedtime. Suddenly she relents. "You can stay up as late as you want, Sharon. It's clear you're no longer a child." Something stabs at my heart. Bridget has a crying fit, she wants to stay up too, but Mama whispers to her and suddenly she's pleased as punch and off the three of them go to the bedroom.

I'm all alone on the couch, me and the stupid television. Daddy's working night shift. Mama's in there talking and laughing with them. I want to be a child again, I want to go to bed with my brother and sister, I want to be in my bed I've always hated, I want my mother's loving mothering. I keep trying to watch the program. Everything just pixelates and echoes. When does Daddy get home? Will I still be up? When do I go to bed when I'm too old to be told to go to bed? The electric chair is in Sing Sing. Their little boys are crying. But they betrayed America. When she turns out the bedroom light she comes down the hall, goes to their bedroom, shuts the door. She seems mad at me. I don't ask again to stay up late. Rapists should be castrated. We do it to dogs, why not men? When was the first time I heard her say that?

Sharon May and I come up the lawn, Mama's on the porch, her arms crossed under her bosom. We're discussing, philosophically, the nature of each of our families. In Sharon May's house it's her father who's easy, her mother the hard one. I'm saying as we come around the Henka's storm fence in my family it's my mother who's the easy one.

Mama is standing on the porch. I look up and she's looking at me. Her eyes drill into mine. She doesn't like it that I think she's easy. She thinks I mean this in disrespect, not the wild deep love, gratitude and awe that I mean.

Her sack lunches have always been various and wonderful because she enjoys making them. But now for the rest of the year she makes only canned crushed olive sandwiches but without mayonnaise or celery or salt as before. We must not be able to afford those condiments. When I try to swallow the dry bite I see the old man's face mouthing *"Fuck."* All year she has actually bought packages of six-by-nine brown paper lunch bags but now my lunch bags are crumpled-up used ones and one day I carry my lunch to school in the Langendorf's Bread blue and white sack, so embarrassing.

She washes my hair every Friday afternoon in the kitchen sink. By Monday, the third day and the start of the school week, my hair is at its shiniest from the natural oils. It's too fly-ey, out of control at first. Your hair's so thick, Sharon, you'll always need me to wash it, you couldn't possibly get all the soap out. I love her bending over me from behind, I love feeling her body the whole side of mine, her fingers with the water moving through my hair, applying the shampoo twice, sudsing up, scrubbing my scalp, then rinsing. I love feeling her wrap my head in the towel, my whole head in her hands. I love sitting in the chair, her wrapping the towel around my shoulders and combing out my long wet tangled hair. I love to feel the knock of the side of her hand down my head, pushing in the furrows. She says this needs to be done for the natural waves to come out right. I'm so lucky to have naturally wavy hair. Her own hair has only the slightest curl.

But she didn't wash it last Friday and now it's Friday again and my blond hair is dark with oil and smog. My hair really needs washing! I can't do it myself. She's always said I'll always need help with my hair. Graduation is almost here and my hair hasn't been washed in ages.

Mrs. Ritchie notices. Your mother must be feeling bad, dear, come in, I'll wash your hair. This was hard, to let go to her, this most intimate ritual with my mother. But I'm in the Ritchie's kitchen and she's hurting me combing out my tangles. When I get home all Mama says is she didn't put the waves in right.

Monday, June 15, 53- Marion & his family arrived today, tired but looking fine. It was so good to see them after so many years.

Wednesday, June 17, Jack has a rising on his right shoulder. Marion got it treated at S. Francis Hospital....

Thurs. June 18, 53- Marion, Eliz & Alex went to LA. Jack lay around and watched T.V. I went with Fred & Audrey to see Sharon's class graduate from 6th grade. The program was interesting. I showed the family some keepsakes and papers in Avon's trunk.

She didn't finish the dress. She pinned the unsewed parts together with safety pins. A white delivery truck brought the corsage that had been on order. Grandma said she'd keep it for me in her ice box. She was the one who pinned it on me. I didn't know about the custom of corsages. It surprised me, it was too extravagant, I didn't need such an expensive thing. The smell under my nose was too strong.

Mama collapsed in bed so I walked to the school to graduate. When she was fitting me to this dress she told me I was beautiful, the first and only time she ever told me that (except when explaining Daddy's deeper-than-daughter love for me), everyone would see this at graduation, she would be so proud I was her daughter, the most beautiful girl on the stage. But she didn't get the dress finished, she pinned it on me with safety pins. It was the first time Daddy ever attended a school function, see, I'm a good father. I don't remember my graduation, the gardenia smell too strong, its waxy white petals. But just now writing this I saw my mother's face in the audience, a large, devastated face.

Both Jack and Alex could still wiggle their ears like they did that picnic at the cabin, an Edens' trait, they claimed again, but none of us could do it. Alex and Jack sitting around the television watching the Korean negotiations, their ears wiggling on their own. This was so weird we all laughed. And that was wonderful.

The house was still clean then.

Then Syngman Rhee suddenly released thousands of the North Korean anti-Communists prisoners in defiance of the United Nations. The Communists broke off negotiations and the war resumed.

Sun, June 21, 53- Father's Day. We took 2 pots of flowers to Avon's grave. Marion's family & I went to Gloria Gardens to church. Billie & Shirlie went too. Later we all took dinner which Audrey & Alice prepared to Bixby Park in Long Beach. I ate heartedly and enjoyed the day.

That it was Father's Day! I've always hated the photographs. Here we all are, the Edens, but I want never to come out of the water, I want to drown, I'm so ugly and self-conscious it's like I'm naked amongst them, I can't bear their eyes, their cameras. Every move is an effort. My terrible, ashamed posture, my little round shoulders, my little protruding tummy. Folding in, making myself less here. "You're not smiling, Sharon," he snarls passing me in the sand. My sister is all smiles. I don't look as bad as I've always remembered but long ago I cut myself out of the group photo. Alex is falling in love with Billie and Aunt Alice is saying it's okay, they're not really blood cousins, it's not incest. I love that Alex is falling in love with Billie Jean who I love too and Jack and Shirlie. I love my Uncle Marion too and I love my father (for a week I'd been sleeping in the house with the two men!), I love my mother, my sister and brother and grandmother. In the one photograph of my mother she's smiling. She won't smile again for years. Daddy and Marion both are smoking, looking into the sun grimacing. Daddy is still skinny. When he confessed the rape just before he died he told of seeing his oldest brother's big hands on my little nine year old breasts. He remembered that because when Mama confronted him, right then, his big brother showed up. His role model who'd fingered me too. He got so upset he wrecked the '49 Ford—I never knew that, that that's why we got the new '53 Ford (and to appease Mama and to impress Marion and Elizabeth). I remember his mashed index finger, the one that always circled my nipples, he hit it instead of the nail building our new garage, I remember feeling sick for him, dying for the big bandaged thing bleeding through the white gauze, he hit that nail so hard it split the bone in two, and the nail too, it's like I remember being present when he did it, maybe I was, yes, I think I was, and sleeping that night beneath Jesus' hands in the heart shaped frame above me, all night the hammer pounding nails into Jesus' hands, and Daddy never working on the new garage again.

Monday, June 22, 53- Marion's family left this morning for home in Tennessee. I hope to meet them again, somewhere, sometime. Didn't get to hear Alex play the piano while they were here. Heard him sing "Just a Closer Walk With Thee."

Sitting in the new Ford with Mama at Douglas' back parking lot, waiting for Daddy to get off work. A full grown boy is walking toward us, coming across the landing field. He floats across the white cement toward me, smiling, his eyes, he walks with clouds behind him, staring at me watching him. I want to say something to him, the angles of my body move out toward him, I want to touch him, a plane is taking off in the far field, I sit here with my mother and I don't understand why I feel so excited and confused, but I know that she does. I've already fallen and she knows it of me, as she has always feared, and the boy knows too, I'm the worst kind of girl.

After school was out, after Uncle Marion and our cousins left—I can hear clear as a bell *Just A Closer Walk With Thee* in Alex's voice though I can't remember him singing it—Daddy went back on day shift. I went at least twice with her to get him from work at 3:30. I wasn't wanted but I didn't allow that thought. I was proving my loyalty to both of them. I was proving I loved Daddy by getting him from work. In the grown beautiful boy I was showing her my interest in other men, not Daddy, being sexually aroused for the first time as demonstration to my mother that I wasn't after her man.

He comes across the field behind the boy. He's unhappy when he sees me in the passenger seat. I jump in the back like I couldn't be happier to see him. I ride home with them like everything couldn't be more normal. I remember the sun that day was too bright, the landing field too white. Chicken Little, the sky is falling, the sky is falling.

"Once I had a secret love" is playing in the kitchen. The pain in my mother's heart is separated from the pain in mine by the wall. She's in there looking out the window, looking down Industrial, Doris Day singing from the radio. School's out. I'm graduated. I'm frozen in the middle of the living room, I don't know where to be, where to look, where to go. I think my secret love is Ronnie, she thinks hers is Santa Baby.

It's hot. Daddy ordered me out here to weed along the property line between the apartments and the back fence on Industrial. I haven't been back here since the maniac came through. Thick, itchy, bramble bushes with stickers. The old men are walking by. *"Fuck."* The young ones are too, driving by and taking breaks from the factories. I'm trying to pull the weeds. It's too hot. Mama and Daddy are in the house together, watching the Hearings and discussing me. She woke the whole house last night with one of her nightmares. I'm terrified but to admit that would be to admit defeat, would be proof I'm bad, would be negative thinking. Would be to admit to myself that my mother is not acting right. It will never happen again. Sharon, he couldn't help it. I know that, Mama. I'm in my shorts and halter top she made me, with a red and white checkered sash through the waist loops that matches the inlets of the top, which is all the fashion. I couldn't survive in any more clothing, it's so hot, but I feel naked out here on Industrial and I can't go back inside the house. The men yelling and whistling and snarling. Mama received wolf whistles even after I was born, how good they made her feel. I feel the man driving by with the knife, I feel the twenty foot high foundry fire across the street. She made me promise I'd always come to her. I could depend on her for anything. She told me over and over in the bathtub of her unconditional love for me.

When I walk in they're arguing about Sharon. Daddy's screaming but Mama's taking care of it. I believe this like I believe in God. It's over for the Rosenbergs. They're dead. Albert Einstein and Pope Pius XII urged clemency. Extraordinary measures were taken by Justice Douglas. Oh, I just love that man, Mama always says. Joe McCarthy looks like my father. But the Rosenbergs stole the secret of the atom bomb, gave it to Russia. Her very own brother testified against her, that's how bad she was. They lost the argument so they died. The gray men won. I look at Daddy carrying on against me, see that he's turning gray. But what if they were innocent? What about their children? How could you kill them for their belief? I thought this was a democracy. Now they're showing old reruns of dropping the bomb on Japan.

I think I remember the photographs of Mr. and Mrs. Rosenberg sitting in the electric chair on the front page of the LA Times. He went first. She was so small it took five minutes to get the straps on right before the plume of smoke rose out of her head. They were waiting for the last minute reprieve. Eisenhower wouldn't give it to them. That sweet smiley know-nothing man. Daddy snarling and screaming and lunging toward me when I come in the door for my reprieve. Mama sitting there, just staring at me. Dust everywhere. She hasn't dusted since I told. I'm dissolving in dirt outside my grandmother's apartment and inside my mother's house. I stand on the Fifth, Mama. Do I say that or does Daddy? Why don't they just answer the question? Guilty or not, yes or no? How could her own brother do that? When they lie about you, Sharon, and they will, remember: you know the truth.

Yes, but they will still execute your parents.

What happened to my mother in the bath after I ran out? To write that would be to write fiction. To imagine the scene that for certain, however it took place, did take place in actual time, makes tears well. To imagine what I've never imagined, me with my vivid imagination and enormous empathy for my father. I flew off the front porch putting everything out of my mind. Mama will take care of it. I never gave it another thought. As her instructions went, I thought only of the positive. As my Sunday School preached, I forgave, I forgot.

He began courting her again, he started immediately with the new Ford, to win her back, using this new attention from her to build his case of innocence, or helplessness, using his attraction to me to make her jealous. He had always been jealous of her attention to me.

A man and a woman alone in a house together will have sex. That's why she made me promise that I would tell if it ever happened again. I thought she made me promise out of concern for me.

I don't think it ever happened again, telling her saved me from that, but she never asked.

What would have happened if I hadn't told?

I remember a woman once, jumping up in defense of my mother, snapping at me with the familiar hate in her eyes. We're in a writing tent somewhere.

"She couldn't handle it!"

I know that. Still, for some reason I've always been grateful for that woman's reaction. Perhaps just for the simple but awful words coming out.

In 1990 Gae told me that of course she always felt distant from her oldest daughter because she feared the father would love the daughter over her. "How could I not feel that?" she said, "given what happened to me with my father and mother." I found it astonishing that she understood this of herself, and deeply despairing that then she submitted to it. I reacted just the opposite. No man will ever come between me and my daughter. This has always been true. If it came to that, my daughter could have any man of mine she wants. *"I'll make the bed,"* I say in a poem. Impossible— impossible blackmail, impossibly evil—to love a man more than my daughter.

In 1992 my mother told me for the first and only time that when she was thirteen her Aunt Henrietta's husband, on a visit to the School, "pressed himself" on her. Henrietta was Guy's much younger half-sister, her Cherokee grandmother's youngest child by John Hammett, the junk dealer. It was the first time she was ever called into the office. It was terrible—Henrietta and the School blamed her.

How could my mother have had that experience and not been more concerned and careful, in her huge acclaim of maternal instinct, about my innocence?

What does "pressed himself" on her mean? Why did I assume it to be just like Daddy dancing with me? Why did I not think rape? Why didn't I ask? Thirteen's when she started rebelling. And got sick again.

Did my mother's heart ever break for me?

Mine breaks for her writing this, again and again. Mine has always been broken for her. Still I have to ask, especially now: did my mother's heart ever break for me?

Sideways, but continuously, to the end of her life. There was always a huge underlying river of sympathy and worry for me. Against the other river, the dammed reservoir of anger, rage, blame, jealousy, suspicion. Hate. Of being trapped. Of primal need. Of survival of the fittest.

"You are just like your father, Sharon."

She said this always, but especially, I see now, afterwards.

We were both her enemy.

It takes two. She was washing her hands of both of us. She never took sides. One of her lies! She stood by her man. Bridget was right. She did love one more than the other.

The real mother lets her child go to the one who will chop it in two. Anything to survive.

§

Twenty-Five

*Thursday, July 2, 53- Frederick & Audrey and children are loading up
the trailer & car to start on their vacation to Yellowstone Park and other
doings. Wish I were able to go....*

*Friday July 3, 53- Puppy George spent the night with me and moaned
all night. I slept very little myself. I hope I can hold up until they return.
This is the 47th anniversary of mine and Avon's marriage. I was not very
husky then.*

How odd that last sentence, how out of character. I've come to think
that's what he said to her on their wedding night.

There's nothing in Mama's vacation scrapbook—the fanciest of all her
scrapbooks—about this trip: no map of the route, no photographs, nothing
glued in, no dates, no title. There's one loose post card of Milwaukee,
Wisconsin, mailed to Grandma. There are a few loose photos of us there at
Aunt Giny's, and one booklet of photos at Uncle Kenneth's in Alabama—
not glued in or a part of a narrative of the trip. She was just following
through on the motions of a trip already planned; she didn't know what
else to do.

George lifted his head and howled when we pulled out. Daddy drove
all night to get across the desert. Mama fell asleep against the window,
little gasps of breath, little cries coming from her open mouth, her scarred
lungs. It felt like betrayal of her to witness her little snores. I tried to
pretend I was asleep.

"Sharon's sitting back there thinking up ways to trap me," he starts in
at sunrise. And continues all the way across the United States. "Sharon and
the imaginary things in her head." "Sharon hears things that aren't said,
isn't that right Sharon?" "The problem with Sharon is you can't believe
anything she says." "Her mind lies to her and it's making her miserable."
Mama not speaking, not even to defend the desert as beautiful. "Sharon
doesn't care about anyone but herself."

A moment on a particular stretch of highway, of pale gray-green scrub,
a very particular horizon I'll never be able to find again though I fought
there with my whole being to prove I love him, our whole family. Bridget
will always say she couldn't believe my bravery in arguing back to him.

We slept in the new trailer. They slept in the double bed in the back.
The front seats around the table pulled down to make a double bed.
Bridget and Clarke slept in it, I slept on the floor.

The fish aren't biting this year from Fisherman's Bridge. We move our campsite down on the Lake. A forest ranger is coming out of the trees. He smiles at me. Everything in me goes back to him, the way he smiles, my teeth to his teeth. I've never felt anything like it, my lips just going up for him in joy. Daddy sees, glares steaming crazy mad at me. My period starts. I want to cry for the dreaded blood again, for the cramps. For the bears that are sniffing me out. For the Kotex Mama lovingly packed for us. I write *Sharon Edens loves Ronnie Dowell* on the green bathroom stall door. I buy my first tube of lipstick at the Lake Yellowstone store. I go back and kiss those words on the swinging, moldy-tasting door, leaving my lips, *July 1953*. All the rest of our camping on Yellowstone Lake I'm looking for the forest ranger, my teeth aching. I'm almost a teenager now, I'm almost crazy.

Northeast into Montana, through the burnt forests to Custer's Battle-field.

Driving out Daddy says, you know, it wasn't right what we did to the Indians. I love my father for that. We pass an old farm house with old Indians gathered on the porch. Two women are standing by the front door, their hands on their wide aproned hips, the men in rocking chairs, big chins in their hands. Indians that old could remember Wounded Knee, even the Battle of the Little Big Horn. They watch us move along in our new, two-tone green Ford pulling our matching two-tone green trailer. Maybe this is when the nightmare changes and it's no longer Indians attacking. It's about here that I start becoming the Indian in me.

"You kids should know," Daddy says. "Your grandmother is not going to live forever."

I love his mother.

In Milwaukee our cousin Helen is six and we have a new boy cousin, Rick. Mama and Aunt Giny talk the whole time about the horrible thing that's happened to Aunt Myrtle. Her daughter Pearl stole her boyfriend, she's married him, breaking her mother's heart. Mama stares across the room at me. How could a daughter do that to her own mother?

I pick up Uncle Strick's heavy steel razor from the back of the toilet. *When super shaved/ Remember, pard./ You'll still get slapped./ But not so hard./ Burma Shave!* I just shave the thick blond hair from under both my arms. The relief is so immense I know that whatever happens now will be worth it.

We leave early the next morning. I trade places with Bridget who's thrilled to have the seat behind Daddy. I'm happy to be behind Mama. We drive out of Milwaukee, past the smoke-belching breweries. We're heading south now to Uncle Kenneth's in Alabama. My newly freed arm is up along the sweltering plastic, behind my brother's sweltering head. Daddy glances back, his eyes a bee-line to my underarm. He likes to look there. But he doesn't like what he sees now. He swerves to the side of the highway, slams on the brakes. Pulls me out of the car. Trees like you see only in the east. The rest of the family sitting quietly in the new Ford, staring down the road, the traffic whizzing by, Mama writing a postcard. I can't remember anything else, but the post card she sent to Grandma was written right then.

7:30 a.m. Wednesday morning, July 15, 1953: Dear Ma, We just left Mozelle's- From here we are headed for Kenneth's. We don't have the money to go to East Tenn. We will be home next week. Love Audrey.

We slept that night on the Ohio River in Southern Illinois. I don't know that I believe in past lives but when the subject comes up this particular spot, on the north bank of the Ohio before it empties into the Mississippi, always comes to mind as a place one of my old bodies is buried. A sandy beach surrounded by thick Eastern woods, something about the feel of the air, the haunting sad sound of the water flowing by. Recently I learned that this was the 1839 winter campground of the Cherokee on the Trail of Tears, that thousands died there of cold, starvation and grief. Maybe it's just that I—something in me—died there too that night, July 15, 1953.

Somewhere, coming back, after Uncle Kenneth's where I had a similar experience with my boy cousin Jim Edens as with the forest ranger—see Mama and Daddy, there's nothing wrong with incest—maybe Albuquerque, we had to wire for money. I remember being depressed on a side street in a hot depressing city, maybe Little Rock, on empty, waiting for the money to come.

We ran out of money before we got home! She was letting him sink, which of course he did, we all did without her. I remember a long humid afternoon in the car in front of a telegraph office, a cracked cement sidewalk, waiting for the money to come, Bridget studying the *Learn To Be A Magician!* ads in our comic books. *How To Vaporize Humans!* "There's no krypton left!" she screamed at Clarke Kent, our poor little brother.

July 21, 1953- Fred & Audrey & children reached home last night after midnight.

Two days later we celebrated their fifteenth wedding anniversary. A whole roll of film was taken.

Bridget is in her standard poses, that is, so posed she's cartoonish. In one both her arms are folded tight behind her back, her head twisted exaggeratedly down to peer at Clarke: my, what-a-curiosity-you-are, little brother. Her big-kneed, bare legs stand planted like two young tree trunks in white socks and beaded moccasins. She's the one who watches, who keeps posing to the camera the question about the family, what on Earth is going on? In one that Daddy's taking, Clarke, in belted-up levis, is facing him in a pugilist's stance, a little man glaring as big as he's smiling when Mama's behind the camera. Maybe he's being protective of us, his big women. My right arm is held spastically tight behind me, as it is in all of these photos, and Mama's left, alongside my right, is shot stiffly down her side. Bridget, her right hand in her left hand crossed under her stomach, looks this time directly at the camera, quizzically, in petition. This is as beautiful as any photo I have of my sister from childhood. Her fuzzy head is slightly bowed down posing the question, to Daddy, now to us, what is going on? Can anyone out there please tell me? She's plaintive, close to prayer, frowning, but on the verge, she could erupt into playing, into the coquettish, into the manipulator. Mama's just looking at Daddy, just holding her dead-serious look.

I've seen this photograph many times since but suddenly it is very startling.

Facing him behind the camera, I'm leaning into her at an angle that could not be increased without falling over.

Facing him, she's leaning just as exaggeratedly away from me.

There are three photographs of just her. My mother posing for my father, being attractive, coquettish, even sexual to him.

The final photo is of the two of them. I took it. Facing me, he stands in front of the white oleanders, hands behind his back, baggy khakis, narrow black belt around his slight paunch. How to say what his pose is? Here I am, daughter. He's comfortable in his body. He enjoys being fought over.

They're both posing for me. She's showing me her loyalty to him. She's fighting for her man. She's standing stiff next to his casual sexy insouciance, her big arms straight down her sides. And again, the exaggerated lean. Facing me she's leaning way over into him, exactly as I leaned way over into her.

July 24, 1953- I went to Cecil's tonight... Peace seems imminent.
July 27, 1953- The Armistice has been signed at Panmunjom and fighting has ceased for the time being. I thank the Lord and pray that peace may continue...

An agreement was reached on how to divide Korea. The 38th Parallel won out, creating The Demilitarized Zone at Panmunjom, a United Nations no man's land. Hundreds of thousands of families were separated. At The Bridge of No Return hundreds of thousands of Korean prisoners of war made their irrevocable choice of where to restart their lives. Some went south over the bridge, most went north. Over the footage Marilyn Monroe sashayed her big hindend down the banks of the River of No Return.

It wasn't a peace treaty. Solomon ordered the baby cut in two. No real mother came to the rescue.

July 29, 53- I've had an aching in my chest a lot today.
July 30, 53- Had a cramping in my chest after each meal today. ...Cecil's and Dee's families went to the beach.
July 31, 53- ...Letter from Kermit in Korea. Late this evening I had a more painful attack of cramps in stomach & chest than usual. Fred, Audrey, & children are gone to a show tonight.
Aug 1, 53- I was very sick all night, cramping through chest & back. Lovely day. ... Bridget came and cleaned house.
Aug 3, 53- ... I had another attack of chest cramps after lunch, which I fear is my heart.
Tuesday, Aug 4, 53- I washed a few pieces at Audrey's. Sharon came and I helped her a little on her Bible lessons. She is in Vacation Bible School.
Aug 7, 53- I had a light heart attack this evening after supper. Dr. Graham came. Audrey & Sharon & Alice came in. It was the worst since August 16, 1948.
Saturday, Aug 8, 53- ...Walked out to Cecil's this P.M. Sharon did my shopping.
Monday, Aug 10, 53- ...I had to take a pill for my heart. Audrey came and read to me the book on the bible that Mr. & Mrs. Payne sent, The Coming Kingdom of Christ....

Thurs. Aug 13, 53- I've lain around today to see if rest will help me. I've been quite sick one week and have to take tablets to ease me. Clarke went to the market for me.

Aug 24, 53- Alice got a letter from Kermit in Korea . Said it was awful hot there. I can't get shut of chest pains.

Aug 27, 53- Audrey drove me down to see Dr. Graham. He prescribed whisky! for those chest pains. I had two attacks after supper between 7 and 9 PM. Audrey came and helped me. ...Sharon went to market for me...

By the end of summer there was no denying that our mother, the immaculate housekeeper, had stopped cleaning house. I did deny having any inkling as to why.

The sun is setting. I'm on the front porch steps reading the evening Huntington Park Signal George has fetched for me. I'm sitting out here in agony because our house is dirty. I'm sitting out here at twilight because Mama is no longer interested in reading the paper and seems uncomfortable with me inside with her. I'm in constant torment, trying to figure what I can do. Spitwads are lining the kitchen wall. Amazingly, I read of my exact situation.

Dear Abby, Something has happened to my mother. Our once immaculate house is filthy. It even smells. I can't have friends over. When relatives or friends come I'm so embarrassed. What can I do?

Dear Embarrassed, Pitch in and clean it yourself! Your mother will get the idea. After all, children should help their mothers with the housekeeping.

That sounds so reasonable, more than reasonable. Children should help with the chores. But I can't do this. To do so would acknowledge that I see something is wrong with my mother. It would be acknowledging everything that has happened.

My mother didn't speak to me for years. Not of it, not of anything, really. But again, I did not know this. I remembered the bathtub lectures. I trusted her as she had lectured I must. Mama will take care of it.

But she didn't. She couldn't handle it. I was her rival, the other woman living right in her house.

There was a big dime store on Imperial Boulevard in Lynwood on the way to South Gate. I started walking up there, no one knowing. Up Industrial past the foundries, cross McKinley Avenue, down which on the far corner of Arizona is Ronnie's house, maybe he will see me, always I pray that we will run into each other, just by accident, I am not a forward girl but maybe that's what happened, I was too forward, on up to Gardendale and turn left, dip down in the eucalyptus gulch there in front of the County Farm gates, go up over the tracks and down, through the low stretch that always smells of sulfur, or at least what I think is sulfur, like it's gotten caught in some sort of air trap beneath the tracks and eucalyptus and the odd left-over dark-nothing land there, up to the dog pound, the dogs yelping and barking not to be gassed, turn right and walk a couple of miles through heavy traffic to the bridge and cross the Los Angeles River. This was a dangerous walk, especially the lonely sulfuric Gardendale stretch up to Garfield, but once up on the boulevards, for all the whooping and whistling and honking and gawking of the drivers it felt relatively okay, they were trapped in their cars, they were speeding by in traffic. They didn't know me, they didn't know where I lived, they'd never see me again. It was always hot, in the nineties and hundreds, the murky burning sun on my arms, smog pressing down on the top of my head, I wore what everyone wore, shorts and halter tops, my hair pulled back in a French fall, or up in a pony tail. This walk was like hers and Daddy's escape to freedom in the west, how when she smelled the orange blossoms crossing Cajon Pass she knew everything she'd done to get here was worth it. I got over the long concrete bridge and down the cracked concrete slabs of Imperial Highway, to the wonderful, cavernous, air-conditioned dime store that had, among other treasures, the tangerine colored lipstick I looked so good in. I had started with *Touch Me Pink* but when I found this shade I was astounded by how much better I looked. I wish I could remember the name of it. Not *Persian Melon* which I used later through high school. The old woman at the cash register wore the tangerine lipstick too. She comes back to me now in her knitted orange afghan tunic, an old woman still working, though probably born in the last century like my grandmother, though lipstick never touched my grandmother's lips, and so beautiful in ease and freedom, no one paying attention to her either. She always smiled at me, hello dear, find everything you were looking for? I loved her. I was grateful for her.

And then, out the door to the big difficult noisy hot world again to make the return journey. The sun is going down as I cross the river mirroring the blood and the golden streets of heaven. One by one the headlights come on the cars zooming down to Long Beach where I was born and the LA runs to the sea, how I ache for Gae, how I ache for Ronnie. I say my prayer to Jesus for safe passage home. And though it was at least a half mile further I usually went all the way home on Garfield into Hollydale, then turned on Main. To come down through Gardendale that late would have been really asking for it. And I wasn't.

Tangerine Kiss?

§

Twenty-Six

Sunday, Aug 30, 1953- ...Fred, Audrey, & children left for Capistrano Beach...

Monday, Aug 31, 1953- ...Clarke's 9ᵗʰ- I gave him a dollar. C. & A. got home before 10 PM last night.

Wednesday, September 2, 53- ... Sharon & Bridget are visiting Gae and Dotty at Capistrano Beach. 19 men drowned at Ft. Bragg N. Carolina today. Others died in a plane in Washington. Others died in plane crash from Ft. Ord to a point in Washington.

Monday, September 7, 53- Labor Day. I washed today. Took chest pains and rested one hr. Went back and finished and lay abed the rest of the day. .... I hope the loved ones are safe. I heard Geo Meany Pres of A.F. L. speak on Labor Unions from Washington. It was fine. Avon was a strong union man. I am proud he was.

Tuesday, Sept 8- ...Frederick, Audrey & family returned from Doheny State Park where they spent Labor Day holidays.

I remember the fact: ten days at the Walkers'. Mrs. Walker was scary, some of the time still wearing only a bikini top. I remember Mr. Walker barbecuing lobster he'd caught in a dive, his skin-tight rubbery suit, his tan crack showing, his bulge in front like octopus curled between his muscular thighs.

We renewed our blood sister ritual. She had little breasts now. She was certain that she didn't but I recognized that first pink swelling of the circles around the nipples. She was dark everywhere, no tan lines. She had dark pubic hair. Or did. She'd shaved it off. She said she didn't want to ever grow up.

We sleep on the sun roof beneath the night sky splattered with stars and planets.

When they first moved here, at the end of the fourth grade, they lived in a small trailer out back with the others. Her parents fucked every night, all night.

"Open it!"

Her mother would not open it, or could not open it. Or maybe it was that she was waiting for the right dilating wave when she would experience the ultimate pleasure. Suddenly she'd gasp, "Now! Hurry! Hurry!"

"One night my mother came to me and took me to him."

The infinite stars flash and contract in the iodiney seasalt black, the ocean thumps against the earth and she is saying "I want to fuck you, Sharon, let's do it, something happens to you when you do it."

Her mounds are black bristly quarter inch hairs like my father's cheeks when he needs a shave. She rubs against my mounds for hours until I'm sure I must be bleeding.

"Something happens," she keeps whispering above me. "If you do it long enough something happens."

The roaring ocean and all the world is whispering it with her. Something happens. Something happens. The gunshot snapcrack explosion of a wave. Then another. The heavy pounding of water onto the beach. Hours, all night, but nothing happens. This is devastating. Something happens to our parents. We so need to understand what happens to them. We love our parents.

"Do you remember Sharon, that my mother participated?" she reminded me in 1990, objecting to my feminism. "She got off on me with him. I can never forgive her for that."

There's a hideous middle-aged blond woman I awaken to, straddling me, riding me, raping me. She'll first come sometime in the next seven months, before we leave Hollydale, and in the not too distant future, in Ramona, she'll awaken me in orgasm—she'll be one of the things that happens. "Purely and inexplicably," Freud wrote in his study of the nightmares of traumatized soldiers, "the literal return of the event against the will of the one it inhabits." But maybe she's just Mary Jane that he threw on top of my face to keep me from screaming when he straddled me. Maybe she's just Mrs. Ritchie straddling Susan to cut her hair against her pleas. Maybe she's just Bridget sleeping next to me not in complete ignorance and innocence. Maybe she's Gae from this night, conflated with her mother, what she told me. Maybe she's just myself

...my archetype
the straw-bleached, boozy matron
the desert hag
who rode on top of me
those first nights of puberty
pulling from my sleeping girlbody
orgasm after orgasm ...

From menarche to menopause, I say of her elsewhere, making her a symbol of the menses. My early resistance as a poet to metaphor—for a long time to poetry itself—was the unconscious fear of using my imagery as shields against knowing what really happened to me, as blinds to the deeper facts and memory. Maybe—and this is still the hardest possibility for me to allow—she's a representation of my mother's simultaneous psychic control and abandonment of me.

Our parents come down for the Labor Day weekend. The news is full of awful accidents. Nineteen marines drowned in the swamps of North Carolina and thousands are dead in plane crashes and car wrecks. For the last two days of the three day weekend the headlines of the LA Times is just the number of accidental deaths so far.

We're sleeping in the fifteen foot trailer, parked on the asphalt, being covered with blowing sand. They're having sexual intercourse and the something that happens is happening to Mama, there's gratefulness in her strange moans and sobs and rhythms and rushes of breath. She's so glad that Daddy is loving her. It feels strange, I feel far away, but too close at the same time. The pounding of the surf, the cry of the gulls, the cries of my mother in joy of what my father is doing to her. My mother gasping in the joy of letting me know that my father loves her.

It's early in the morning. I'm still awake, on my back on the floor. Mama is starting to go into those sounds again, convulsive, hypnotic, undeniable waves. She said there's a point when a man can't stop it, this is the climax. She didn't tell me about the woman and her climax.

She was telling me what happens. She was telling me he's mine. She knew I was awake. They both did.

Wed, Sept 9, 53- I suffered the worst attack of chest pain for sometime... I hate to be alone so sick. Audrey's faithful to come. I get up in the morning and do a little work. Audrey helped me to get to bed.

Friday, September 11, 53- This is Bess' birthday. Born Sept 11, 1888. Willie wrote her name in the bible in red ink. I wrote Laura's name with a pencil. Mother wrote Charles with a pen and I believe blue ink. I do not remember the other 4. I mean who or how written. I called sister Bess....

Saturday, Sept 26, 53- Sharon helped clean my house. Audrey did my shopping –Alice, Gae & Bridget were in. Alice had letters from Kermit today. Clarke came in. We return to Pacific Time tomorrow. Turned on my heat tonight, first time this season.

Monday, Sept 28, 53- I dreamed about an ugly snake last night and was trying to call Avon; also Lucile.

Twenty-Seven

I find among Mama's things another letter from the Professional Screen Guild of Hollywood, this one dated September 11, 1953, requesting that "you bring your girl, Sharon" in for a screen test.

A few days go by and he erupts again. Sharon doesn't love me. Sharon is out to get me. Sharon just wants to torment me.

"That's not true, Daddy!" I scream, really setting him off.

We fight all the time now.

On our drives now we often cruise the Mexican side of Paramount, checking out the kids who'll also enter Junior High. Mama is silent, stone still, but Daddy sneers. "Look how they live in cow pastures, how their television antennas and cars are bigger than their shacks.

"Watch out Sharon Edens," he says. "Pachucos love blondes."

It's the first day, the mid-morning twenty minute break. I'm looking for my locker, my eyes ever alert for Ronnie when I'm caught in a gridlock of hundreds of kids jammed into the central hallway all looking for their lockers. We're inching down en masse when a finger jabs up my vagina. The gasp is involuntarily, the shock takes my breath, the humiliation my knees. I can't let anyone know, especially whoever it is, it's the only control I have. He has to still be right here behind me or beside me, but it can't be any of these guys, they are too small, too sweet. Even through the gathered folds of my skirt, the finger sheathed in cotton print, slip and panties, his aim was swift and accurate.

Sept 26 - Gae and Bridget were in tonight....

Oct 2, 53- Had that pain again after lunch...Sharon mopped my kitchen....

Oct 7, 53-...The kidnapped boy, Bobby Greenlease, was reported found today. He was dead. Such a horrid crime!

Oct 9, 53- Watched for the meteor shower tonight but failed to see it. Clarke came in.

Oct 10, 53- Gary, age 3, came in to tell me he saw me at the park on the teeter totter, the merry go round, the swing. Went up on the slide and didn't come down. Ha! he dreamed it. Audrey shopped for me. Sharon cleaned house. Bridget hid under the bed and helped move furniture.

Oct 12, 53- I dreamed last night Avon came home unexpected from hospital looking reasonably well and so very nice and handsome. Was wearing a brown wool shirt, open at neck and dark trousers. I was happy and so was he. Cecil returned safely home from fishing.

Oct 18, 53- Audrey drove me to town and drugstore where I bought pain tablets. I asked the druggist what those pain tablets were. He said nitro-glycerin. I was shocked, but I can't bear the pain I get in my chest.

Thurs, Oct 22, 53- In a pleasant dream last night, I was digging and working some rich soil in a lovely garden. Found potatoes. I was preparing to set a young peach tree, and felt able to work. Went to stay with Sharon while the others were gone, but she preferred to stay alone; so I came home.

By now I was unable to be at ease with even Grandma—I told on her son!—with almost anyone. Nothing I ever did was right. Everyone looked at me like they wanted something, or they hated me for something. I just wanted to disappear from people. I just wanted to be alone where I'm okay.

Sat., Oct 24, 53- I had head ache last night. Dee & Bertie moved today. I hated to see them and the sweet little boys go. Sharon & Clovis came. Sharon cleaned house.

Monday, Oct 26, 53- Dee, Bertie, & children came in. Dee's brother committed suicide yesterday. I am so sorry for all the family. Been sick this Eve.

The first two sentences of this last entry are parenthesized in pencil, the only such markings in the whole diary. I recognize my mother's hand. She was checking to see what Grandma said about Dee's brother.

Oct 28, 53- I rested very well last night. I ordered a spray of flowers for Harry Rupp's funeral, given in the names, Mrs. & Mrs. Fred Edens, Mrs. Nina Gepe and Mrs. Maude Edens....

Oct 29, 53- Audrey & I took some bronze geraniums to dear Avon's grave. The sun shone warm and bright, birds sang. I hope to see him in the great beyond. We also saw Harry Rupp's lonely, new grave.

I can't remember Harry Rupp but his suicide is clearly another factor in this strange, painful time.

Oct 31, 53- Audrey did my shopping. I did my house cleaning. A dozen spooks came this Halloween. I gave each candy and enjoyed seeing them.

There are two photographs of this Halloween. I asked Mama to take them. I'm wearing the elaborate colonial girl dress she made me last year. I'm under the elm tree, petting George. I go as the aristocratic Virginia girl she so wants me to be. I'm begging her please Mama look at me. Please.

He goes out of his way to pick fights with me, then accuses me of going out of my way to pick fights with him. But when I try to avoid the fight, which means avoiding him, he accuses me of avoiding him, of not loving him.

November 5, 53- In dreams last night I wandered to our Windy Ridge Ducktown home, stood on the back porch looked across the hills and saw Eva Bryson, slender & girlish, walking over the trails. Realized, faintly, that Avon was there. How wonderful are dreams! I walked out to Audrey's tonight.

November 6, 53- ...Sharon helped me today. ...Talked to O'Zella Yoakum...

Nov 14, 53- Our first good rain of the season. The streets are like little rivers. Bridget helped me clean today. Frederick came in awhile.

Nov 15, 53- I went to S. School and church. I really was sick with chest pains but took two tablets and went because I love the house of God and the gospel. Brother Johnstone brought a fine message. Two were baptized. I was sick most of the P.M. Audrey came in. So did the children.

Mon Nov 16, 53- I am very sick with my heart. Dr. Graham came. Alice came.

Tues Nov 17, 53- Frederick & Audrey are faithful. Mrs. Yoakum came.

Mama's been staying with Grandma at night. Tonight she tells me to sit with her for awhile so she can have a little break. I stay in the living room, frozen tight in the corner of the maroon couch, doing my Bible lesson and homework. I turn the pages loudly so she'll hear I'm busy, praying to Jesus don't let her call me. The house smells like an old person who never opens a window, stale oatmeal, boiled rhubarb, the drippy ice box. Her old Bible lies on the coffee table, different colored ribbons spilling from it. How many years have I sat here with her telling me stories about her girlhood before cars, telephones, radios and televisions. Mama says she's entered second childhood the way she keeps remembering horses, buggies, farms, the pupils of her one-room school, writing poetry, swimming in the copperhead infested Elk River, prayer meetings on Wednesday. Hard as I try, for all the stories, I can't imagine her as a girl, or me ever being as old as her.

"Sharon Lura?" she calls weakly. "Would you shut the crack in my curtain, please? The light is hurting my eyes."

The bed is in the corner. I practice entering before I enter. I stand facing the door, plastering a smile on my face. I enter, keeping my eyes on the window. I pretend that closing off the light is all my grandmother wants. On her trunk beneath the window lies a post card, "Overseas Highway," from Aunt Lucile, of a long modern bridge stretching across the Florida keys. She's burning her eyes into me, please Sharon Lura, sit here with me awhile, I'm so lonely and afraid, stand by me. I turn from the window to the left so I won't have to look at her. I'm hurrying out, when I do look, just once. Her white hair has never been cut, it flows in waves to both sides of her knees. I've never seen it down before. Her eyes meet mine. Above her bed is the photograph of me at ten months, a piece of graham cracker held in my fat hand. I'm chewing the bite.

At last Mama relieves me.

"Bye Grandma!" I shout as I run out the front door.

An old man drinking whiskey hisses as I run across the lawns around to our house. "Fuck. Blondie, come here." Inside, Bridget and Clarke are asleep and Daddy is naked in bed, the white sheet over his lap, reading the paper and I can't speak.

In the morning he fixes our breakfast; Mama is still over there.

At school we're learning how to use the library. I find a book of fantastic horse paintings down through the ages. I fall into one of them, a golden stallion rising on his hind legs, the clouds and sunset proclaiming the glory of life, of God. I fall into the painting as into the ocean, as into prayer. I want to take the stallion into my arms. I want to take everything in my arms.

I get off the bus with Clovis. Sharon May is coming down Gardendale from her new school, Pius X. Something very funny happens to the three of us on the four block walk down Arizona to Roosevelt but even the next day I couldn't remember what it was. When we turn the corner I see the Ford with Mama and Grandma coming up the street. Oh, Grandma I knew you'd get well. The three of us can't stop laughing. I want to take them in my arms like I wanted to the stallion.

But as the car approaches I see that the person in the passenger seat is not Grandma but Billie Jean. "I thought you were Grandma," I laugh, ducking my head in past Mama at the wheel. "For a minute you looked just like her."

Billie sits there like a ghost, not moving, not speaking. Just staring out the front window.

"Grandma died last night, Sharon," my mother is saying over the steering wheel. She's looking at me like she's disgusted and angry with me.

And Billie. Billie Jean Edens. I saw her as Grandma. How could I have made such a mistake? The hollow ringing sound is engulfing my whole head like being in the train tunnel. I can't stop laughing. I'm trying to tell my mother and my cousin of the funny thing that just happened to us after we got off the bus. Remember Mama you laughed when you were told your mother died. I'm wearing my blue circular skirt she made me last year with the matching reversible redlined bolero vest and a bolo string tie. The echo, the hollow sound is roaring down my ears to my stomach. Grandma is dead.

"I'm taking Billie Jean home," Mama says. She puts it in first and drives away. I say goodbye to Clovis and Sharon and walk down the block to our house, the sidewalk too far down there for my feet to reach. I go around to the back yard and sit in the swing, afraid to go in the house. Is Daddy in there? Oh dear Jesus don't let him hurt. Don't let me be alone with him now. Back and forth swinging to Grandma dead, to my grandmother in Heaven who knows everything now and understands. Even why I told. Her son can't help it and see, Grandma, I forgive him his trespasses.

That night is so silent. All of us in our separate bodies and our separate beds, thinking about death behind our faces. She'll never come back. We won't ever see her again. The whole house the hollow tunnel. She's disappeared forever. I feel my father the most, oh, to lose your mother.

"Why aren't you sad?" Susan asks behind me in the P.E. line. "I could never come to school if my grandmother died yesterday, I'd be too sad." I still don't know how to answer that question. Susan's grandmother won't die for another forty years.

That night we go to the drive-in. Mama says don't tell, the neighbors wouldn't understand but this is the healthy thing to do, to get away and forget. Mama's had so much experience with death, she knows all this.

We're going down Cherry. She's talking, just like the old days. "There is good in everything, even death." She explains that a man's mother is oppressive to him. "Daddy is free now. A son can't become a man until his mother dies."

When Grandpa died she wouldn't allow us to go to the funeral. "I just saw so much death when I was a girl I didn't want to expose you kids to it. But I guess you're old enough now. The big decision is whether to have an open coffin or not. I don't believe in the open coffin, it's morbid, but your grandmother did."

What did we see that night at the drive-in?

Probably a Laurel and Hardy movie. Daddy loves Laurel and Hardy. That was all he wanted to see at the end of his own life. He just wanted to laugh rather than cry.

You're supposed to wear black but we don't have any black clothes and we certainly can't afford to go out and buy some for this one occasion. "Besides this is Southern California," Mama laughs, "there aren't any black clothes in the stores, not even for funerals."

"I can wear my lavender dress, Mama, I haven't worn it since graduation. Pretty soon I'll outgrow it."

"Alright," she snaps, like what is she going to do with a daughter that wants to wear such a dress to a funeral?

The dried-up white corsage is still pinned to the shoulder and I have grown since June. I have to let out some of the safety pinned seams, but I don't unpin the dried gardenia because Grandma pinned it there. Sometimes through the rest of this day I think I get a whiff of it.

She's in her coffin right beneath the pulpit before us in the front pew of Gloria Gardens Missionary Baptist Church, an old-fashioned, one room, white-painted church with a cross on top, much smaller than Trinity Bible Church. There's lots of flowers. Smelling too strong.

The pew is not long enough for all of us so Uncle K.D., Aunt Alice and Billie and Shirlie are sitting in the second row. Uncle K.D., who barely made it in time from Japan, is right behind me, both of us on the end. Bridget 's next to me, then Clarke, then Mama and Daddy. I can hear Uncle K.D.'s heavy breathing that's just like Daddy's. It's his mother too, he came out of her body like Daddy did.

The pastor begins. Sister Lura Maude Chitwood Edens was the granddaughter of Tennessee pioneers and a graduate of Winchester Normal College, formerly Mary Sharp College. She taught school in a one room school house for a number of years before marrying Avon Marion Edens in Winchester Tennessee on July 3, 1906.

The too-sweet flower smells keep penetrating the room like from a machine gun. Mrs. Yoakum sits at the piano. *"Mrs. Yoakum came."* The last sentence in Grandma's sixty-four year diary. From my end place in the pew I can see the familiar whiff of her white hair sticking up over the baby blue satin-lined casket, the way she always combed it up and off her wide forehead. O'Zella Yoakum starts playing and everyone sings *Amazing Grace*, Grandma's favorite song. I control the sudden gush of tears to my eyes by watching her familiar hair through the flowers. Hard as I pray I can't understand death, how you can die. Most of all I must not let anyone see me cry, especially Bridget.

Then, sudden chords of the next tune, we all rise. Starting with the back row we come forward and file by for the viewing. The wooden floor boards creak. When the men get to Grandma they nod their heads slightly to her, hurry on. Some of the women rush by in their high heels making a big point of not looking at all. The open coffin is against their belief. As we shuffle along to Mrs. Yoakum's twanging piano I'm becoming aware that I'm the last person in the line. This can't be, there's some mistake, surely someone will catch it, this isn't right, it shouldn't be me, it should be Daddy and Uncle K.D. Or Mama who's always quoted Ruth in the Bible about her husband's mother, whither thou goest I will go, your people are my people now. The whole family is shuffling by, Daddy's face too big, lost and clammy in his tie. By some weird accident I'm going to be the last human on the earth to see Lura Maude Chitwood Edens. And she's going to be the first dead person I've ever seen.

I come up from her feet. She's on her back just as she was in her bed the other night when I wouldn't look at her. Except she's wearing her purple iris silk dress, not her nightgown, and her hair is bunned. Wouldn't sit and read to her. Wouldn't sit and just be with her. Wouldn't allow her last words. Something awful's been done to her. She's wearing makeup. Eyebrow pencil, lipstick, powder and rouge. Her white fly-ey hair that I've been concentrating on is actually powdered blue, is caught in a blue crisscross net like waitresses wear. I stand there longer than the others to control the shock and because I am the last one. It'll be sad when no one can see you. Maybe that's what being alive is: others seeing you. Everyone's watching me, waiting. Bye Grandma, and in the instant I turn away the lid of the coffin comes down over her.

Then Daddy and Uncle K.D. and Dee Rupp and other men I don't know lift my grandmother in her coffin to their dark padded shoulders, carry her down the aisle behind me coming down in my lavender satin and lace, bows and ruffles and safety pins and the corsage she pinned on me, down the creaking wood plank aisle to Mrs. Yoakum's piano, and he walks with me and he talks with me and he tells me I am his own, and out the wooden doors into the blinding sunlight to find my place with the others lining both sides of the dirt path under the palms, and they come out to us

and tip down the steep steps, eight men crunched into suits, with Grandma
on their shoulders, like they're the Chosen Children carrying the Ark of
Covenant. She looks too big, too big for everything. It looks like they'll
drop her. But this is the way we do it, this is the way it's done. This is how
Maude would want it. She carried them into life. Now they carry her to the
grave.

They line her head up with the open back door, they move in carefully,
all of them together, they slide her all the way into the black car with pink
satin curtains. The palm trees swish as if in relief and the birds in them
start chirping.

"Sharon," Mama orders coldly. "You sit in the front seat with your
father."

Obediently, mindlessly, I slide down the front seat to the driver.
Daddy gets in beside me. She and Bridget and Clarke get in the back seat.

Everyone else gets in their cars, line up behind us. Uncle K.D. and
Aunt Alice and Billie and Shirlie in the second one, their lights on.

Motors running, headlights turning on. This is called a funeral
procession.

The stiff black-suited driver takes us up to Paramount Boulevard,
Daddy close beside me, frozen stiff in his tie, just staring. We stop for the
traffic, right where the eucalyptus trees circle the County Farm. Daddy
breathing heavily, Mama behind us just staring.

Lonnie Hicks from seventh grade is crossing in the intersection before
us. His hands are shoved deep into his pockets. My hand goes up to the
windshield from Daddy's suited side to wave, but then just drops, before
Mama sees it. He would not know me in this black car, head of the
procession. He doesn't know me at all, though inside him is death too.

That night, all night long, I carry my grandmother in my arms. I walk the
streets and highways and stores and towns carrying her dead body the way
you carry a bride across the threshold, the way Daddy carried Grandpa the
last time I saw him. I come to a bridge and start across the water. I struggle
to contain her, her long thin arms and legs that flop everywhere like pickup sticks, rigor mortis having set in. I have to hurry before she starts smelling, she would not like that. I struggle with the rhythm of carrying her, like
you have to struggle to walk railroad tracks, her big head flopping off my
shoulders, hurting my breasts. She is so big, she died just as I got as tall as
her. I keep encountering members of the family and neighbors and other
people we know and have to duck from them. I hide us beneath the street,

watch them passing by from the gutter slit. I keep searching for the right place to bury her. I'm walking all the way down Cherry Avenue to Long Beach. I'm taking her to Gae's. I'm taking her back to her parents in Tennessee. I'm proceeding into the unknown, we are pioneers. It's November 22, the Linga Sharira, the ancient holy Cosmos Crossroads day. The universe is aligned as it was the moment I was born. Sometimes I'm trying to bury her under my parents' window with my bag of bloody pajamas and underwear but then Daddy sees me and I have to run with her. She gets heavier and heavier, so heavy she's really smelling now. The burden of her body is askew all over mine. But I will not let her go.

I still wake sometimes carrying my dead grandmother. She knows now what her son did to me, and being dead can bear it. She knows everything, knows why. She's the book I've carried ever since, this one, my father's love. She's our family, the only future. This is why I've carried her.

"When Grandma died I was shocked to realize she wasn't my mother. It actually hurt me to realize that," Mama told me in the nineties.

She ordered me into the front seat with him, head of the procession. I was the winner by blood. I was her rival, his coveted, most legitimate woman. She was acknowledging this. No doubt he got it. I didn't. Except in dream.

§

Twenty-Eight

We didn't have Thanksgiving the following week. With the four days off Daddy went on a hunting trip out by Lake Elsinore. Mama told the story of what happened to him for the rest of her life.

> *He was climbing a hill and when he came to the crest the sky*
> *went inside him*
> *Time blew around like a cloud*
> *and he saw the earth for the first time....*

He got separated from the guys, then lost. The guys would have been Dee Rupp, Bill Hogan, Mr. Shoemaker, who else? Is Odie still around? Has Sam come into the picture yet? He had to spend the long night alone, out in the hills. My books say it was the Sierras but she corrected me at the end, it was the hills above Lake Elsinore and it was rabbit hunting, not fishing. He hadn't seen the stars since Ducktown, he couldn't believe how bright they were, how many. He hadn't been able to breathe climbing those dry hills. He vowed never to smoke again.

His mother is dead. How can the bough breathe, Mary Austin asks of the death of the mother, if the root is dead? His best friend, Dee Rupp's brother has committed suicide. His wife has confronted him with his rape of his daughter—this is what he assumes I've told—and won't let him forget it. Now he's lost, he doesn't know where he is. The cold indifferent hills. The stars. His mother and father up there knowing what he has done. Knowing who their baby boy really is.

It is astounding to realize now that my mother never told this most important, oft-repeated story in the context of it being the week following his mother's death, three weeks after the suicide of his best friend's brother, and certainly not six months after my telling her about him, and the crisis we'd been living in ever since.

Mama said at the end of her life that his mother's opinion mattered to him. This surprised me and my surprise surprised her. She said his mother mattered very much to him. She may have said he was a Mama's boy.

It was not like my father to get lost. Maybe he got lost because he'd lost his way, as his mother would put it, meaning his soul. Maybe there was some crises with the guys, maybe something to do with Harry Rupp.

"Did you know that Dee Rupp's brother committed suicide because he was a homosexual?" she asked me out of the blue twice in the mid nineties. No, I did not know this. And I don't think because of denial. I think it was a closely guarded secret, one involving my father that she tried unsuccessfully to tell at the end. I think now that the poker ring, the stag parties as my grandmother calls them in the diary, and the fishing and hunting gang were probably gay. I think there was a major crisis involving Daddy, Dee, Odie, Mr. Hogan and Harry, that this was why Dee and his family moved out of the apartments just as Harry killed himself and Mr. and Mrs. Hogan divorced. On the sixtieth anniversary of their library meeting, five months before her death, my mother shocked me with that new detail to the oft-told story, that he was living with a male lover and was desperate to be turned on to a woman. I think now that my father was bisexual, that he led an active homosexual life, and that my mother, who knew of his homosexuality from the beginning, protected him in this secret, that this was part of her role as his wife.

All his life, she always said, he'd been unhappy. The Elsinore night was always told as his awakening to the wonders of life, as his coming to his senses, as the big change in him. At first I was blind, but now I see, amazing grace, for a wretch like me. She was announcing this change in him to me, to him, to herself. She had to have this change to go on with him. She was telling me he's changed, it will never happen again.

Back home safe, he put the open pack of Camels in his top drawer with his cherished arrowheads and deck of naked women, left it right there on top to test his will power. He told her he was ready to move to the country as she'd always wanted.

He never smoked again. What a great man he is, what will power. There aren't many men who could do that—quit smoking with the open pack in the dresser drawer. She pointed this out again and again. His strength, his depth of character.

I never questioned her beautiful story. To write in narrative is to put the fragments together. This was code talk for his vow to keep from being sexual with me, and maybe with men. But it doesn't all pan out. As with cigarettes he may have never touched me again—he certainly continued to rub up against me and my sister—but he didn't change with me, for the better anyway. He grew, steadily, worse. He grew to hate me. And I grew more and more oblivious.

"When Daddy learned the Mexican gang girls were fighting, challenging you in the showers," she said another day out of the blue on Jennifer, "that's when he said we have to move."

She was fighting for her man, for her marriage. She fought for him, her marriage, up until the last twenty minutes of her life.

I haven't heard from Gae, even for my letters about Grandma. I don't hear from her at Christmas. I know not to worry. To worry is to give energy to the problem.

A letter finally comes in January. She doesn't explain why she hasn't written but she's very sorry to hear about the death of my grandmother. "I loved your grandmother, Sharon." She includes three of her most recent drawings as her late Christmas gift. But though they're a gift that's not an excuse to get out of critiquing them for her. We can't just say we like something, we promised to always find something to criticize so that we can keep growing as artists.

The drawings are really really good, better than any she's ever done or I could ever hope to do. They're so good they're almost disturbing. They're of two stallions fighting, one black, one white, both raised on their hind legs, their front legs and bared teeth tearing into each other for the females who circle behind them, trying to kill each other to be leader of the herd. The three drawings are of the same scene from different perspectives. We've studied the anatomy of horses. She's got all the muscles in, even the small ones. Her shadowing makes them ripple, the skin perspire. The air, the energy crackles off the page.

I tape them on the wall over my bed with Jesus, the females circling the two stallions like a harem. I fall asleep, have the nightmare of the two men coming for me. I wake to the moon's shaft on them, they are so lifelike, their knife-sharp hooves flashing, their screams and sweat and blood beneath their flying manes. At last I get my critique. It takes me awhile to write the letter, carefully, so that my criticism will be positive.

Dear Gae, your two stallions are incredible! Better than you've ever done! The only thing I can come up with is that they look more like two naked men fighting than two horses. There's something about their haunches and loins, their things, even their faces, that are almost human, they're that good. They are so good they almost look obscene.

Our drives now are searching for a place in the country. When we were little we would go north to Lancaster, to Taft, east to Yucaipa, Mama daydreaming out loud about living in the desert. Now since Daddy's hunting trip and his change-of-life vision that we need to move to the country we're focusing on the Southland. Oh that we could move to Capistrano Beach! But I would not dream of saying that because Mama can't stand the damp weather at the beach. She needs the hills, she needs the sun.

This Saturday we head straight down One to Capistrano Beach. **Marilyn Monroe Marries Joe Dimaggio!** the headlines scream. We pull into the pink and green and white trailer court down in the half moon dip between the bluffs, the Pacific churning in white rows of waves. Daddy goes up to the door, knocks.

A grey-haired old woman in an apron opens the door.

"They left in the middle of the night. No one knows where they went."

Mama turns instantly to me. "You must keep your hopes up, Sharon. We will find them, if it is meant to be."

My mother still loves me. She just spoke to me in concern for the first time in I can't remember when.

The next week we check the trailer park again. Still, no one's heard a word. We head inland. From San Juan Capistrano you take Poncho's canyon east to Lake Elsinore, Mama saying the Cisco Kid's sidekick is really the actor Leo Carrillo, descendent of the oldest family in California. Then you keep going, northeast toward Perris, toward Hemet, toward Mt. San Jacinto, the Ramona Reservation. It seems like hours. The land and weather changes so much, see how the San Bernardinos and the San Jacintos wall it all in. It's January but glarey, humid, murky, LA smog all the way out here, warm but everything is the color of ice. We're looking for our home, to start our lives over in this stuff. If only Sharon would cooperate.

For once the accusation is true. I don't want to move. The thought is horrifying.

"I'm on your side, Mama and Daddy," Bridget chimes. "Yes, Sir-ee! I can't wait to move!"

Where is Gae? I'm so depressed I'm the same as the Ford's metal. I'm the same as the land, the color of ice, the grey rocks. Grandma's dead, we're free now, we get to move to the country now. I don't dare know that I'm afraid to move out in the tules, to be so isolated with my father, that so much of my wild reaction to the thought of moving is fear. I just think I hate the land, that I'm a city person. They left no forwarding address. Surprising, even my parents are curious, almost concerned about the Walkers.

We pull into an old gas station. A dark strapless blonde is pulling out in a topless red jeep, speeds down the two lane.

"That's Gae's mother!" Mama gasps, leaping out while the man pumps gas into our Ford.

No, it can't be.

"That woman's a close friend, Dorothy Walker, and her children, Gae and Dottie are our girls' closest friends, we've been looking everywhere for them. His name is Merrill Wayne Walker. Do you know where they live?"

"Owner, inside, knows."

It's a million miles down the broken white line of the asphalt. Then we turn right up a dirt fire road. Go seven miles up that, turn right onto a smaller dirt road. Once or twice, around a turn, up and around the grey sage brush and boulders, we catch up with her dust. We're escorted by a bird from the cartoons, a roadrunner with a bunch of smaller birds following. "I think they're quail," Mama says. "A covey of quail... Oh!" she says. "Quail is my favorite bird."

We turn right onto the smaller dirt road. THE SUN RANCH. NO TRESPASSING! Daddy gets out, unlatches and swings open the rod iron gate. We laugh about the unstoppable nature of the Edens. We gear up and around three or four more dust choking miles, the KEEP OUT! signs ever more frequent, KEEP OUT! KEEP OUT! KEEP OUT! pulling ever greater peals of laughter from us. How good it feels to laugh together as a family again.

We come through a last gate, pull up on top to a dusty white dirt clearing. All of Southern California wavers below us in the smog. And so does Mr. Walker! He's behind a pink cinder block wall of a little square house he's building with two other men, all shirtless. He waves his mortar spatula at the five of us Edens like he's been expecting us. Daddy pulls up beside the red jeep parked in front of a little white trailer, bouganvillia and fuchsia blooms hanging off it, and thick tall saguaros standing either side like sentinels. Beyond, up the hill, is a swimming pool under palm trees with people lying around it.

Daddy turns off the engine. There's a long moment when nothing happens, a stillness, everything is very quiet and still like no one knows what to do. Mr. Walker just stands there behind the pink wall staring at us.

"Did you hear that?" Mama says. "Chicago. Quail sound like they're saying Chi ca Go!"

Mrs. Walker comes out of the white trailer, wearing just Mr. Walker's big white dress shirt. Then Gae comes out. My thrill in seeing her is cut short by the way she's holding herself. She is not happy to see me.

"How did you find us?"

She's grown, is changed again. Her tee shirt is too small across her breasts, the stripes too tight up around her hairy underarms.

"I'm sorry about your grandmother," she says far away, her pale gold eyes looking out to the Basin. "Do you understand where you are?"

With you! I've found you. Gae Elaine Walker is standing right there in the frame of my backseat window.

But she keeps whispering, sort of hissing "Do you know where you are?"

My parents are talking with Mrs. Walker. Mr. Walker signals again he'll be right over. Dottie comes out of the trailer and comes around to Bridget's side, tells her to come in the house, she has something to tell her. Clarke jumps out, heads up to the swimming pool. Mrs. Walker stands there talking above Daddy, mainly across the seat to my stiff mother who's becoming stiffer. A palm tree sways behind her platinum, red-lipped head but I don't hear a word she's saying.

Mr. Walker doesn't come from behind the pink cement. Daddy gets out, goes over to talk with him. "You don't know where you are," Gae says. "Let's go for a walk."

She is leading me around the trailer and up a steep hillside thick with cactus.

"Do you know what this place is?"

I feel stupid, like a pickaninny, a dumb Okie up against inpenetrable hedges of prickly pear.

"This is where you live? Sun Ranch, near Hemet, California?"

"Sun Ranch, stupid, is a nudist colony."

Pixelating prickly pears. Fog colored dirt, silver gleaming boulders.

"What's a nudist colony?"

My question floats out of our solar system, has time to return before the answer.

"A year round community where people don't wear clothes."

The nun appears. Right then. In her black robes standing on the Compton downtown corner. I'm twelve. I've found Gae. She'll be twelve next week. I try to take in the impossible. Oh Gae. I panic to be nonchalant, she's so embarrassed. I can't imagine. I love you Gae. I try to be blasé. How interesting.

"What do you do when it's your period?"

The hills start around, the cactus apples shoot their thorns toward Gae's little nipples, the pubic hair she's grown out. Everything's in 3-D, too deep. I see blood running down the insides of her legs. I see a colony of erect penises rising year round from the dark hairy Daddy crotches. I want to run away forever. I have to help her escape. But how? It is not possible to take this in.

"We can wear our clothes then. Course the whole place knows it's your period, that you're bleeding.

"My father's building that room for us to all sleep in together. It will be our sleeping hut."

"Sharon, Bridget, Clarke?" Mama calls. "Time to go… Now!"

I'm back in the car, and Daddy and Bridget are too. Mrs. Walker is standing at Mama's window telling her all about the benefits of living in a nudist colony. It's so natural and healthy, so much vitamin D from the sun. The girls will grow up without the puritanical shame of the culture down there. We'll save two hundred and fifty dollars a year in clothes alone.

Clarke comes runnning back from the pool, jumps in the back seat, gasping, "There's a naked woman up there! There's a naked woman up there!"

Gae and I do not take our eyes from each other. She's a zombie. I love you. Wild horses. Mustang. I love you. I make our blood sister wrist rubbing sign just as I used to make to her across the playground when we were forbidden to play together in the fourth grade. She can barely get hers together but finally just as we're backing out she manages, in slow motion, her left palm turning up to the sky, a slight turning back and forth of the right one over it.

Forever.

Fast and falling around the curves to the land below, into the blinding sunset Dear Jesus protect Gae, protect Gae, protect Gae. I'm seeing all four naked Walkers sleeping side by side in the cement block hut. I'm seeing her father turn over on top of her. I'm praying Dear Grandma lie down by her side, be a shield, set the Lord before her, protect her, through the dust flying through the car, dear Jesus show me what to do.

You must act as if nothing has happened. You must assure her everything is the same between you. You must pretend it's perfectly normal that she lives in a colony where no one wears clothes. After all, God made us naked.

I see the letter I wrote so carefully all last week stamped and sealed, propped up on the bookcase waiting for Monday's mail. My critique of her drawings is the perfect solution, the answer to my prayer. Objective and impersonal. I wrote it before. I'll mail it as if nothing's happened.

Mama is saying right then, around a curve, out over the bleeding iodiney sunset, "The best thing, Sharon, is to pretend nothing has happened. So Gae won't feel rejected. So she knows you still love her."

"Yes. Yes, Mama, I know. I'm thinking the exact same thing. Yes. Exactly."

Soon as we get home I erase the Capistrano Beach address and pencil in the new Sun Ranch, Hemet one. I don't open it, reread it. I clothespin it to the mail slot on our porch for Max the mailman in the morning, a little comforted with the wisdom of my love. I love you, I love you Gae Elaine especially now. I will love you forever. Your blood sister, Sharon Lura.

It's Sunday night, February 7, Gae's twelfth birthday. I'm standing in my parents' bedroom, a place I'm never allowed, except when Daddy summons me. I've been summoned here by both of them. I love them so much I could die.

I'm standing before them in front of the dark stained, waist high double dresser with the three monkeys who hear no evil, see no evil, think no evil, and the curlicue gold handles to the drawer that holds the open pack of Camels he hasn't touched since Elsinore, the Cherokee arrowheads and tomahawks he picked up as a boy, the pack of naked women, and his white linen hankerchiefs I sometimes even now have to sneak to stop the hiccups. My long back is to the big round mirror. They are seeing themselves beyond me, each in their separate bed, staring at me.

The air in the room is not breathable. I'm too big. I can't hold my shoulders up.

"Mr. Walker intercepted your letter to Gae."

"Is it true, Sharon, you said her drawings of horses were obscene, like naked men trying to kill each other?"

It takes forever.

"Well... Yes. I did. But...."

"How could you, Sharon?"

"I was so hoping it wasn't true." My mother's Third Eye is drilling me to nothing.

"Mr. Walker says you're warped."

"What does warped mean?"

"Sick. A pervert."

"Unnatural," Mama says.

"He says you're the most warped human being he's ever known, that you would write that to his daughter. He says you can never see or write to Gae again. You are bad for his daughter."

"I'm so ashamed of you Sharon," Mama is saying.

"But I wrote that letter before we drove into the nudist colony. Before we knew...."

My words are bouncing off them like rain bouncing off asphalt. Whatever sinks in is sinking in wrong.

"Sharon just can't admit when she's lying!" Daddy explodes. "You're warped Sharon Edens."

Warp is a four letter word. Warp comes from worm. I'm bent, a worm, cut in two. That butterfly I swallowed, now a worm that won't come out. I saw the naked horses. I've lost Gae. Forever.

§

Twenty-Nine

You can't ever believe a word Sharon says. Sharon thinks too much. Sharon's mind works overtime. Sharon hears words that aren't there. Sharon sees only what she wants to see. Sharon's mind lies to her. Sharon has a twisted mind. Sharon's mind runs away with her. Sharon can imagine something to be true and it becomes true for her. Sharon builds up cases in her mind until they become truth. Sharon makes up stories and then sticks by them. Quit stretching the truth, Sharon. Sharon and her sheer inventions from start to finish. Don't you tell a story to me, don't you lie, Sharon Lura. Sharon can spin a yarn a mile long. Sharon's mind lies to her and it's making her miserable. It's all in Sharon's head. There's no explaining Sharon. Sharon just wants to prove she's right. Sharon always has to be right. Sharon needs to keep her anger alive. Sharon just loves to fight. Sharon waiting for her day in court. Sharon just waiting to spill the beans. Sharon always has to win. Sharon thinks she's Clarence Darrow for the Defense. Sharon doesn't care about anyone but herself. Sharon's the only one that matters. Sharon always has to win. You can't tell Sharon a thing. Sharon sees only one side of an argument. Sharon sees only in black and white. Sharon's an extremist. It always takes two, Sharon. Why can't you be more succinct, Sharon? Get to the point, Sharon. Say what you mean, Sharon. Can't you make yourself clear, Sharon? No one knows what you're talking about, Sharon. Just because you say it's so, Sharon, doesn't mean it's so. Sharon jumps to conclusions. Sharon's just looking for a fight. Sharon rebels just for the sake of rebelling. Sharon's just like her fifth great-grandfather John Hancock, the first to sign the Declaration of Independence. Sharon's just like her great-great-grandfather John Chitwood who was such a rebel he rebelled against the Rebels and lost everything. Sharon thinks she's better than everyone else. Come off your high horse, Sharon Edens. Quit putting on the style, Sharon Lura. Better get back to where you belong, Sharon. Sharon and her swollen head. Sharon slants the truth. Sharon fudges the truth. Sharon stretches the truth. Sharon's truth is the only truth. Sharon wouldn't know the truth if it were standing in front of her. You're not smiling, Sharon. Sharon and her big head. Sharon and her thick skull. Sharon and her big ears. Sharon can't talk unless she yells. Sharon screams so loud she can't be heard. Hold your head up, Sharon. Hold your shoulders up, Sharon. What are you hiding, Sharon? Sharon has a persecution complex. Sharon's always frowning. Sharon's warped. Sharon's a hypochondriac. Sharon and her vivid imagination. Sharon's stuck in the past. Sharon's so gullible.

Sharon's so naïve. Sharon's bought the whole hog. Sharon's a sheep
following the herd. Join the real world, Sharon. Sharon's just like her
father. There's no explaining the two of them. Sharon and the law of the
jungle. Sharon's so stubborn. Sharon thinks she knows everything. Sharon
knows no rhyme or reason. Sharon knows no shame. Sharon has a mind of
her own. Sharon believes only what she wants to believe. Sharon hears
only what she wants to hear. Not everyone believes what you're saying,
Sharon. It's all in your mind, Sharon. No one knows what you're talking
about Sharon. Sharon's mind lies to her and is making her miserable.
You're not smiling, Sharon.

Because we're moving and our beds are dismantled Bridget and I are
sleeping in Mama and Daddy's room. I'm staring at the rows of spitwads
on the wall above Daddy's bed. Bridget, in Mama's bed, is demanding that
I tell her who my favorite is, Billie Jean or Shirlie. I don't have a favorite. I
keep trying to get out of answering, she keeps demanding an answer,
lunging and looming over me from Mama's side, "Say it, Sharon Lura!
Say who's your favorite!" Comparisons are odious like comparing apples
and oranges; they're stupid. I stop myself from saying that.
    "Say it, Sharon!"
    Billie Jean is blond and glamorous. She's almost six feet tall, has what
everyone calls a striking personality. She's a bundle of energy and the life
of the party. I love her smile most of all, her big white slightly protruding
teeth from thumb-sucking, which Bridget says she still does in her sleep.
Billie's the oldest like me and we have the same color hair. Shirlie at
sixteen is as tall as Billie but in all other ways her opposite. She has a
square face, short brown hair and the olive complexion of her Navajo great
grandmother. Shirlie is quiet, philosophical, introverted, though very witty
when she does speak up. Everyone knows her IQ is at least as high as
Bridget's. "She's the genius," Mama always says.
    Bridget's unrelenting. Finally I give up.
    "Shirlie."
    I say Shirlie's my favorite because she's more like Bridget than me. I
say Shirlie because she's the less obvious choice. Sharon always chooses
the underdog.
    "Liar, liar!" Bridget leaps up. "This proves you're a liar. Everyone
knows that Billie Jean is the best one."

And then she says, lying back on Mama's bed, something really strange. "Uncle K.D. treats Billie just like Daddy treats you, but even worse."

I can't remember seeing Uncle K.D.'s angry side, but I keep hearing about it.

"I saw the worst fight, worse than you and Daddy, it was before you and Daddy started fighting. Billie Jean stood up to him like you do Daddy. She wouldn't back down so Uncle K.D. threw her through the sliding glass door and we had to take her to the hospital. That's when she painted her room black."

There is a bridge I've always dreamed. The bridge is white, ultra modern, and crosses the Pacific Ocean, Los Angeles to Japan. How impressive that humanity has advanced to building a bridge over the Pacific Ocean. My father is driving. We're speeding across, we're half way across when I see up ahead that the bridge is not finished, it gives out. For some reason Daddy doesn't notice, he doesn't let up on the gas, doesn't put on the brakes, we're headed for the plunge into the ocean.

§

Book IV

Ramona

*In me (the worm) clearly
is not righteousness, but this –*

persistence. H.D.

*How strong the attachment can be for kids who have been abused by their
parents! They try even harder to please, hoping this time they will do it
right and their parents will love them.*
Martha Wakenshaw, *This Child of Mine*

*Even Hitler is loved by Jesus. Even Hitler is born good. Even Hitler was
once a baby boy lifting up his arms to his parents in joy, squealing,
jumping up and down, thrilled to be alive. Even the murderer of six million
people is understood by Jesus, even forgiven by our Lord Jesus, the Son.*
Sharon Lura Edens, a childhood prayer

Thirty

We found the Ramona house in northeast San Diego County on February 13, the eve of Daddy's thirty-eighth birthday and moved at the beginning of April, three weeks before my thirteenth, "to start over." The first night was terrifying. A Santa Ana Wind blew, scraping the branches of the giant pepper tree across the roof, causing the whole house to creak and moan. A man entered the back door, crept through the kitchen, the living room, the hallway and approached our bedroom door. All night I listened to him coming. And coming. When he got to the closed door he just stood there, breathing heavily, waiting for the right moment. Sometimes he was in the tree, he was Lobo, the long-haired, bearded wild man we'd been warned about who lived down the road. When I dozed off my head fell off. It rolled down the aisle of the Hollydale dime store and under the art supplies counter where it could not be retrieved. Then I was across the street hidden behind a storefront wall watching Mama, Bridget, Clarke and myself come out of the dime store, walk down the street toward Main, me headless in the loving arms of my family. An older house creaks, sighs and resettles, Mama explained. My nightmare, one of the worst ones, still explains: to move to Ramona meant to lose my head. To forget.

On that Valentine's Eve my father came out of the real estate office having signed the contract for the house and fourteen acres, to us three in the back seat and slung his arm as hard as he could across the back of the front seat, his hand blinding across my face. *On my thirteenth birthday, three weeks after moving to Ramona, he hits me, a blow that throws me across the garden space he is ploughing.[11]* He accused me of not loving him. He accused me of sitting around thinking up ways to hurt him. He accused me of not liking Ramona because I didn't like him. He blamed me for the move.

I did hate Ramona. Everything pixelated, the sage, the granite slabs, the shacks under the burning sun. The collective negative attitude. But mostly the boys. The boys in the seventh grade came to school drunk, they whispered obscenities at me from their desks, the same obscenities as the County Farm men. They yelled and whooped "stacked!" "Cadillac bumper!" when I was called to the front to give my reports, the teacher saying nothing. I wrote I love Ronnie Dowell on everything. The first day, the girl in the seat in front of me, Judy McDonald, said "I'll be your body guard." Every recess and lunch she went before me down the hall, leading me through the throngs of whistling, jeering, hissing, wildly gesturing kids onto the playground.

But Mama loved "Ramona, the Valley of the Sun." Every morning of the year the sun rises from a different place behind the eastern mountains; every sunrise a new beginning. She worshipped the sun. Born the minute it ascended the North Carolina horizon in early spring, she was a double Aries. Guy ran to town for the doctor. Susie birthed her all alone, cut the cord herself.

The sunsets out the western window were spectacular, but nights, for all the unbelievable stars, made my mother sad.

Before school was out for the summer, Clarke and I almost drowned. Pamo is clumps of giant white boulders and granite slabs in the Santa Ysabel Creek. He slipped from an underwater boulder into a deep hole and panicked, grabbed onto the top of my head and held on, holding me down. I was coming up for more than the third time, gasping for air, trying to deflect his flailing limbs but not endanger him more, extraordinarily aware that we were about to die, and our parents didn't even realize it. Daddy, Mama and Bridget stood on shore, just feet away, their arms across their chests, unmoving, just watching us, when a middle-aged man and two high school boys on the other bank jumped in and rescued us.

Daddy went berserk on the steep drive out of Pamo, screaming stupid Clarke, phony Sharon! Anything to get attention, anything to get him in trouble. I still could hardly breathe, the shock and agony of suffocation, how painful death is. At Santa Maria Creek on Montezuma he suddenly stopped the car and flung himself out for a walk. Mama started her lecture about understanding him and three words I had not dreamed spewed out of me. "I hate him."

The following winter, the man who rescued us, Judy McDonald's father, died on Pamo grade. He hit something climbing up out of there in the middle of the night, probably a mountain lion, and was thrown from the car. Initially, his injuries weren't serious but there was no one around to rescue him as he had rescued us. He bled to death.

The next Saturday we were on the water again. We three and Daddy, floating around on Lake San Vicente in a little boat, fishing. It was over a hundred, Daddy had on a fishing cap and long pants, but we were in our shorts and tops. The glare off the water fractured the boulder and sage mountains surrounding us, the dead fish staring up at us, the old highway to San Diego disappearing beneath the water. "Eat dog doo-doo," Clarke kept snarling to Bridget. Daddy loved it, "Here ya go Doo-Doo," baiting her line. Doo-Doo and Lulu and Clarke Frederick were getting redder and redder. Mama was gone to town to grocery shop. It'd been six months since he'd had a cigarette, he'd gained twenty pounds and didn't look like Jesus now. He laughed about the sundogs behind the peaks. I still see us, the Edens, out there in the middle, turning in circles, stranded in a boiling caldron, trusting our father no matter what. We got the worst sunburns ever. Beet red, still burning up in the middle of the night, layers blistering and peeling for weeks. Mama doused us in vinegar, told again of their sunburns on Myrtle Beach.

Another day Bridget and I climbed the steep ridge behind our house, the southwestern rim of the valley. The Santa Maria Valley is strewn in enormous boulders looking as if they exploded from a volcano. There are enormous silver granite slabs everywhere too. On the ridge behind our house the batholith thrusts straight up. From our bedroom window it actually looked negotiable next to the brush, the weird thorny chest-high shrub with sticky orange webs growing across the tops. I remember climbing up, thinking as I placed each foot, this might be the very first time a human being has set foot on this particular piece of rock. We didn't know then that the long horizontal, mortero-pockmarked slab at the foot of the rise, adjacent to our fourteen acres, had been for eons a major village site. When we crested there was a breathtaking view of dark green wilderness, canyons and mountain tops all the way to the ocean. It was a stunningly different landscape than our rocky brown valley. The memory of this sudden contrasting sight—I didn't see it again until we were spreading our parents' ashes from the air forty-five years later—was important to me ever after: reality is a lot bigger than what's before our eyes.

Climbing up was a fun challenge, finding the fissures and crevices to make the next step, but I got stuck coming down. Descending backwards, I lost the momentum of rhythm and panicked, suddenly knowing the next step down would be fatal, I would fall. Bridget was descending on my right. I couldn't go up or down or over to her. My face against the burning rock which was cream white with gold streaks, the stage before marble. It was hard to ask her for help, but I had to.

It was a long wait, the sun baking me again to infrared, my heart drowning in the fear in my chest. Ramona below like rocky Golgotha. Did I wonder if my sister would really get help for me? Did I wonder if my father would really rescue me?

They did. I can still see Daddy way down there, and another man and Bridget behind him, running and shouting for me to hang on.

He climbed up, told me where to put my right moccasined foot. Then the left. Both he and Bridget seemed glad I didn't fall and were proud of themselves for rescuing me. But this moment will forever repeat itself in the images of nightmare with, oddly, Bridget in a cobwebbed window frame, coldly staring at me stuck.

By midsummer we were hiding the Ford on dirt roads behind the house-size boulders so the credit company couldn't repossess it. We lived on tomatoes and corn from the garden. Mama raved about Daddy's Ramona tomatoes and it was true, they were the best we'd ever eaten. We walked the two and a half miles to town every other day to the public swimming pool in Collier Park, that's how we bore the heat. She wouldn't let us go every day, chlorine isn't good for you, you'll get overly tired. I hated the commotion from the boys and the men who came by the pool on their lunch breaks to ogle. I stayed in the deep end, sometimes peeing right in it, so much was my dread of climbing out to their whistles and yelps. Daddy was living in the trailer somewhere in South Gate, still working at Douglas. All summer giant red and black flying ants waged war against each other on the mortero slab beneath the kitchen window. On weekends when he came home he'd make us come out and view the latest battle. He'd laugh in glee and quote Darwin again. In September he got on at Convair in San Diego.

Ramon lived in the adobe ranch house on the corner of Olive and Highway 78. He greeted us on the walk to town, started going with us to the pool. He was an Indian, a ward of San Diego County, and a foster child of the Reeves, the old couple who farmed that corner.

We were the same size and he was very kind to me, and funny and witty and so interesting. I felt my whole being, on the walk to town and back, and in the pool, being drawn to him. I loved his laugh, I loved his stories, his puns and jokes, I loved his face, I was mesmerized by the golden brown of his skin, his beautiful long-fingered hands with oval white nails, his perfect white teeth, his big bones like mine. I loved his drawings, even though they were mostly of battlefields which made me wonder what was going on inside him, and I loved his knowledge of the land, the Santa Maria Valley. Probably I loved most of all the deep unspoken river of sorrow that was in him, that matched my own.

One day, after swimming together all afternoon, we were descending the park when he said let's sit down under this oleander awhile. It wasn't our first kiss but it was the first time he touched my breasts.

"We lie in the deep cool grass," I wrote in my second story "Ramon/Ramona," breaking the five year vow not to write, *"within a half-circle of pink and white oleander bushes. We are talking, words we don't hear. I am lying on my belly. His hand is moving between my breasts and the grass. My surprise is deep, real, both in that he has done this and in the way it feels. I have prepared for years not to be seduced but this isn't what I thought it would be.... This is different. This is my body. His fingers on my breasts feel like rivets, the reverberations cutting deep down through me. The nipple grows like a small tower...until the green of the park has become the color of the sun setting, corals and pinks, streaks of violent red and my pounding insisting heart trying to reach through to his fingers, to push the tower the blood the trees myself through to him, Ramon, Ramon, trying to drown with my blood forever the enormous and boring time of childhood."*

I orgasmed.

I used to joke to myself that it must have been all those years of Daddy's foreplay, but deeper, I knew, even then, that sudden, surprising and very great opening as a claiming of my own sexuality. Miraculously I wasn't frigid—I'd always been totally numb—well, nauseous with fear—to Daddy's touch. *"This is different. This is* my *body."*

For the next two years Ramon and I were in love, finding passionate relief together from the loneliness, fear and danger, the traumatic objectification of us by everyone, he for being Indian. He said that in my arms he could feel his mother from whom he was taken at age two by the courts. I felt my grandmother watching from the All-seeing, All-knowing Heaven, and approving. Escape, sanctuary, sanity, meaning and joy—fantastic restorative joy. Fantastic physical therapy. And how we talked, in between making love. I wanted to be with him every minute, I wanted never to leave his arms. I understood in my soul the expression: "I've died and gone to heaven."

"Ramon climbs the pepper tree to my window.
My father is in the next room. He puts his tongue between my teeth.
He makes circles on my belly with his hands,
whispers I love you. I love you.
I see the earth for the first time as if I have left.
Tidal waves of ocean

come into the desert. I leap
from childhood's impotency to his dark hand on my breast. "

Opening to the power of sex within myself was still another way, too, of understanding and redeeming my father. And claiming my equality with him; I remember thinking this, with ferociousness. My "sexuality" is equal to his, a girl's "sexuality" is equal to a man's. (I didn't have the word "sexuality;" I had few words for what was happening to me.) It was, also, from that first orgasm in Collier Park, a claiming of a kind of morality in my body. The sexual force is controllable (Daddy!), is not an excuse (Daddy!). Even for the passion and awesome orgasmic life Ramon opened me to I remained a "virgin." I did not let him penetrate me.

My first orgasm in the park: I see now a public aspect of our lovemaking that I certainly wasn't conscious of then. Ramon and I made-out—helplessly, I thought—in the presence, or potential presence, of others. The memories are so contrary to my usual shyness, my inordinate lifelong need for privacy. There was the school bus journey home from the Ramona Pageant in Hemet, April of the eighth grade, in which I kept orgasming, silently, perfectly still, but right there seated among everyone. A couple of times he came through the window to my bed at night with Bridget sleeping three feet away. There were Saturdays when suddenly Mama or Daddy would return from town unexpected and Ramon would have to hide in the closet, sometimes for hours—me carrying on with them, Ramon right there, sometimes carrying on with him, they right there. A kind of exhibitionism, but not so much for the arousal of others seeing us. I think we were demonstrating our triumphant love in the midst of their small hatreds. I think we were being "political activists." I think I was coming from my secret history, trying to legitimize our love by not being secretive. Perhaps, as with petting George's penis in front of my mother, I was trying to crash through the barriers, bring the secret out, into language. With my sister in the bed three feet away I was repeating the scene with Daddy in the second grade—but which this time wasn't rape, but fantastically, miraculously, consensual. In some sense I guess I was testing her. Are you really asleep, sister? Were you that night? I was testing all of us.

But now to the ammunition with which my father attacked me was added still another accusation. He just knew I was having sex with Ramon. He knew I wasn't a virgin anymore. "Isn't that right, Sharon?"

I'm on the phone with Ramon. The timer is going. We've got ten minutes. One second over and all hell will break loose. I'm lying on the dining room floor, under the table, he's telling me how much he loves me, and I'm watching, not for the first time, Daddy, who's come home from the Turkey Inn, pull Bridget up from the sofa, shifting with his left hand his Big Cecil inside his pants, ha! and dance her around the room, demonstratively rubbing his chest against her blossoming breasts, giggling triumphantly. It's still happening to her, I think from the sad distance. Poor, poor sister.

Now I see that it was in part a show to me, that he was trying to make me jealous, as he made Mama with me, as he was of Ramon. And Bridget ate it up, showing me too. We were all showing each other what couldn't be said.

In September Mozelle was diagnosed with early tuberculosis. Milwaukee County wanted to put six year old Helen and baby Rick in foster homes, so Mama had them come live with us. We picked them up at the LA Airport.

"Get your cotton-pickin hands off me!" Helen screamed at Clarke as we were loading their luggage into the trunk. Everyone gasped. Her mother whispered something in her ear and she calmed down.

We're coming down the coast, Mozelle in the front passenger window sobbing to her baby. I'm in my seat behind Daddy, and Helen, small, dark, and very contentious, is next to me. Bridget's given up her window to Clarke to protect her from him. But it's Daddy who's picking on her, all the way. "*Hell—on!*" he roars emphasizing the first syllable, a forbidden word in our family. "Isn't she full of herself?"

"My goodness," Mama exclaims, "already an ego thing going on between them."

"On the day my mother returned to Milwaukee to heal the TB," Helen responded to the questionnaire I sent, while writing this book, to all the children in my father's life asking if he'd molested them too, *"I was on my little bed crying and Uncle Fred came in the room to comfort me. He laid down beside me which made me uncomfortable but did not stay long because I would not be comforted. It was in the middle of the day and there were people in the house, we were not alone. Even though I was fearful of Uncle Fred, I remember he told great stories and let me watch him chop the chickens' heads off so I could see 'a chicken run around with its head cut off' until your mother shooed me away (however, chuckling....)*

"I remember the smell of the sage brush enhanced by the heat, the swimming pool, the school, Olive Street, the lady with the goats, Clarke's dog Collie, the pepper tree, rattlesnakes, the garden gophers, chickens, being afraid of Uncle Fred, the gentle softness of Aunt Audrey, Tinker Bell, wishing upon a star, tumble weeds, pie on Sunday and asking why Uncle Fred always got to choose which kind first, Clarke hating my guts and wanting me gone!! Bridget protecting me. And your cold indifference. I remember Uncle Fred slamming you into a big recliner/rocking chair and making you get up, stand so he could do it over and over again until you cried. He wanted to break you and thought that with the tears came his triumph. Not so, I saw the steely determination in your face. I wonder if it frightened him. It frightened me. You let me lightly hug you one time, it felt obligatory so I don't think I tried again."

I remember the early morning walks down to the bus stop, almost a mile, I remember being so outside myself I was really the boulders and slabs spilling down the sage hillside watching the children go by. Me and Bridget and Clarke and Helen and Suzanne Elmer, whose mother, Mrs. Baldwin, had the goats. I'd climb aboard the bus behind feisty little Helen, so devastated, so separated from my body, I didn't know if I could make my legs make the steps, and the driver would greet us, "Good morning Helen. How are you today?" Then into the jeering obscene boys, the hissing girls, to the back, Helen staying up front with the first graders, Bridget and Clarke somewhere in the middle, Clarke's "Eat dog doo doo, Doo-Doo!" lingering in the aisle behind me. The driver, Glen, played jazz on the bus from San Diego's jazz station. Miles Davis, Stan Kenton, Lester Young, Art Tatum, Cal Tjader, Dave Brubeck blowing out over the Ramona landscape. That music was as strange as everything else, as disembodied as I was. Louie Armstrong crying down Rue Morgue Avenue one for my baby. Ramon was the last person on the route, and in him, I found myself back in my body.

After Aunt Giny and Uncle Strick came for Helen and Rick in March—Rick had begun to call our mother Mama, how terrible she felt about that—the bus driver still greeted me with those warm beautiful words. "Good morning Helen. How are you today?" I didn't correct him. At the end of the day, he'd swing open the door, I'd climb down from Billie Holiday and Glen would say, "Good afternoon Helen, sweet dreams."

Glen called me Helen to the day I graduated from high school and left Ramona. He was also the high school janitor, he called me Helen in the crowded halls. Did he know what he was doing? Everyone knew who I was. To continue to call me Helen was either like jazz, that kind of mentality, or he really did believe I was Helen. I worried about what to do. I dreaded the joy of his good morning Helen, good afternoon Helen turning into junk. Again and again, every good thing turning to junk.

And when Daddy lay down beside Helen I imagine that he came to his senses, he realized she was dangerous. "Get your cotton-pickin hands off me!" She'd been warned, taught to resist, conceivably, specifically him by her mother, and, no doubt, to tell.

And perhaps too my having told protected her, gave him second thoughts.

"You can't go outside," Mama announces to me and Bridget. "Daddy's taking Clarke down to the rabbits to watch them mate, to teach him the facts of life."

Out the kitchen door they go, Clarke obediently following Daddy. Inside, a start, a slight panic—the whirling red-streaked linoleum—for my baby brother. Some part of me is still down there at the rabbit hutch with them. It's dark. Very cold, very dark.

In our second Ramona summer we opened Edens' Heavenly Hamburgers, a drive-in restaurant, the first in the desert-mountain town. Daddy designed and built it, all by himself, of redwood. Daddy and Mama cooked. Mama, Bridget and I waitressed and Clarke was the janitor. We were a wild success.

Before we opened we visited drive-ins throughout Southern California in search of the best hamburger recipe. We visited McDonald's in Downey several times. Even then it had the arch and sign announcing the number of hamburgers they'd served.

On one of those trips, Mama driving, Billie Jean and Aunt Alice in front, Shirlie in back with us, we pulled onto that tree-lined Pasadena street on which we used to have our car picnics. We would eat our Bob's Big Boys here. I was so startled I actually said something.

"Penny lives on this street," Mama explained, nonchalantly. "Your cousin Penny lives in that house, right there."

The flowering tree canopy wavered like a blanket over the house of Penny. We had been watching her house all those times.

"We were always hoping to get a glimpse of her," Mama said, "but we never did. Strange, but she never came out of her house."

And it was not going to be different today. After our Bobs', after Mama told the story to Billie and Shirlie of what happened to Mozelle, that sailor's phony marriage to her, we gave up. She drove to a little market on the corner to get Aunt Alice some cigarettes. We were sitting there on the slanted asphalt, Mama still talking about Penny when a girl about ten or eleven pulled up alongside us on her bike.

It was as if Bridget's twin had ridden up on the blue and white Schwinn. I could have reached out and touched her. But no one said a thing. We just sat there, frozen.

The Pepsi man is at my feet fixing the carbonation under the sink, staring up at me in my waitress uniform trying to make drinks for the long line of customers waiting in the August heat. He wants to take me out Friday night. He's wearing a wedding band.

"Hey, man!" Daddy explodes, flipping hamburgers on the grill. "She's only fourteen."

"Hey, man," the Pepsi man snarls back. "I'm only twenty-six!"

I'm only fourteen but I make the vow right then and there that I have kept all my life: *I will never go out with a married man, I will never do that to a wife.*

But I didn't understand then that this vow stemmed from what I was forced to do to my father's wife.

Emmett Till was fourteen, same as me and Ramon. He was fished out of the Tallahatchie River in Mississippi that August, one of his ears missing, and an eye gouged out, a bullet hole in his head. He'd gone on school vacation from Chicago to visit his grandparents in Money, Mississippi. Someone dared him to flirt with the white girl working behind the counter in the general store. He called her "baby."

I lie on the floor alone in the house, waiting for Ramon to come. Emmett Till is all the news can talk of. I lie beneath the bookcase that Daddy made and Mama's so proud of. Then, for some reason, I reach up for the book that's always been there, *Wuthering Heights* by Emily Bronte, and begin to read. *"1801—I have just returned from a visit to my landlord—the solitary neighbor that I shall be troubled with."* Everything sort of dissolves and I'm Emily Bronte writing as Heathcliff wandering the English Moors to her bedroom window, I'm Emily Bronte writing as Emmett Till, I'm Ramon wandering the oak strewn canyons and hills of Ramona's starry nights to my window under the ancient pepper tree.

One day after an awful fight with Daddy, Mama came into our bedroom, handed me *The Call of the Wild*, by Jack London. She read it in the School. Bridget on her bed just watched. Then it was like I was Jack London writing as his dog Buck, plunging *"Into the Primitive."* Then I pulled from the bookcase a Book of the Month Club's biography of Mary Todd, Abraham Lincoln's wife. I loved learning about Abraham Lincoln through his wife's eyes, like knowing my father through Mama's.

For most of my fourteenth year I had a piercing, sometimes debilitating pain in my lower right side. Finally my mother took me to Dr. deCock on Main Street. She gave me her doctor lecture—when a man is being a doctor he has no sexual feelings. I lay on the table and he examined me anally. She stood over me to make sure he didn't examine me vaginally, to make sure he didn't break my hymen. He diagnosed a spastic colon, put me on a diet of Gerber's baby food. I did this for awhile until it felt so stupid the pain went away. Twenty-five years later Dr. deCock—that was his actual name—out on bail awaiting trial for sexually molesting his grandson, killed himself.

A late Sunday night in March, the five of us exhausted from working all weekend, from Friday night party madness to the Sunday night tourists returning to San Diego from the desert wild flowers. Daddy pulls up the long drive, the weighted silence typical. Soon as we hit the parking flat the three of us start scrambling out.

"No." Mama sighs. "Wait. There's something we have to tell you."

Her narrow Cherokee head in the front window, the giant moonlit tear-shaped boulder beyond.

"Billie Jean was killed yesterday."

There are moments of pixelation which actually save you.

"In a head-on collision on Imperial Highway.

"She and her fiancé were on their way to Shirlie's and Willie's in Borrego to deliver presents for their expected baby. They passed a slow-moving car but right then Imperial dipped down into ground fog. They never saw the diesel."

That I'd seen Billie Jean as Grandma two years before on the day she died came to me instantly, the only digestible thing of the news pouring over and through me.

And that moment with Bridget the last week in Hollydale when she forced me to choose between the two, and I stupidly chose, just to appease her, Shirlie, which then felt like and will forever feel like I abandoned Billie to her fate.

We closed Edens', went up for the funeral. Mama made a sign. I can still see her handwriting that I so loved: *Closed Due To Death In The Family*.

The shock of Billie Jean's violent, total disappearance is one of my roots as a poet—the insistence on staying conscious of the mystery and suffocating nearness of death. Billie Jean Edens is enormous in me. I can almost, if I try, remember her voice. But I don't remember a single word in that voice, much less a conversation, and barely a real scene. There's one moment, which must have been before the enforced nudity of the seventh grade, when I'm in the back seat of a car picking her up from a day on Huntington Beach—yes, it's the week after I've told because our Tennessee cousins are visiting, because Alex, who's falling in love with her, is back here too—and as she reaches over the backseat smelling of suntan oil, to set down her beachbag, the strap of her cotton elastic suit gets caught, pulling the top down and one beautiful, blue veined untanned blond girl breast is exposed. "Whoops!" And there is beautiful laughter all around. The laughter all around and the sight of her breast, verifying that my breasts were normal, was like salvation.

"Do you remember that Billie had gonorrhea when she was little?" Bridget asked me excitedly. In 1989 she was still feeding me things like this.

"Remember Aunt Alice and Mama said she got it from a public toilet seat?"

That gas station bathroom flushed through me, all of us in there, the warning and demonstrating how we must always use protection from the VD germs.

"Of course now I know you *can't* get gonorrhea from a toilet seat," she went on. "You can only get gonorrhea from sexual contact!"

"Funny how Mama and Aunt Alice didn't know."

We looked at each other.

"Or did they?"

"Of course Uncle K.D...." My sister shook her head, put her upper teeth over her lower lip, said how often she went over there when they lived in Bellflower.

"I was really into them, you know, they were teenagers. Remember Billie Jean painted her bedroom black! I saw the worst fight, worse than you and Daddy.

"Billie was everything to me. I felt about her as I felt about you. That she stood up to this huge man. She wouldn't back down. Then I was there at the kitchen table with all of them after the accident when Uncle K.D. received the birthday card and letter she'd mailed minutes before she died telling him she loved this man. And that's when I first thought: what does this mean? This grief, when he beat her so?"

I remember being at that kitchen table too, being overwhelmed by Uncle K.D.'s grief, his red eyes spilling endless tears, the newspaper story opened on the second page of the B section. Until we got there it was the sudden violent disappearance of Billie, the trying to digest that, but when we walked into the Bellflower tract house it was her parents' grief, the shock was palpable, like slamming into a diesel or falling into Pamo, you could feel the grief as an entity in itself. I don't remember knowing he beat her but if I knew—Bridget had told me—I wouldn't have experienced the contradiction that my sister claims she experienced. I'd been well-honed in that exact contradiction being love.

I told her then of Aunt Lucile kicking K.D. out of her house for molesting her children. It was after Billie Jean's death, they were trying to cope, they visited Ducktown, then his sister in Georgia.

"She kicked him out in the middle of the night, accusing him of molesting Nancy and Jim."

Mama told me this back then, very pointedly, I see now. She wrote a letter to Lucile defending Kermit as being grief-crazed and fiercely shaming her. She read this letter to me.

Ten years later, soon after Mama died, I spoke again to my sister about the Aunt Lucile-Uncle K.D. incident.

"I can't *believe*," Bridget said this time, "Mama told you *that*. She never told *me* anything like that."

"She told me that, Bridget, because I had told her of Daddy."

My mother never spoke directly again of what I told her at the end of the sixth grade about Daddy, but I see now that she spoke of it in code, indirectly, disingenuously continuing her bathtub lectures, instructing me in what my attitude must be.

She told me of Lucile and K.D., reading me her shaming letter to Lucile. She told me repeatedly of Joal and her stepfather. She told me repeatedly of Pearl and Myrtle, of how Pearl stole her mother's boyfriend. She told me of Helen being molested by a neighbor when she got home to Milwaukee from Ramona, reading me Mozelle's letter, the details about it across the dark mahogany dining room table. A stucco wall, a corner, the old guy in wait between the mobile homes. Four years later she read me another letter from Mozelle, this time across the new table, of Helen's once-rich paternal grandfather molesting her, explaining again the 1929 crash. The poor men jumped out of skyscrapers; they molested their children. This is common, this is normal, this is the way men are, your father is simply like all men, as a woman you must have compassion and understanding, this is a fact of life.

In my mind my father never touched me again after I told her. But Bridget remembers seeing me in my underwear with him under the Ramona house. She was just walking by and saw us through the window. Oh, well, she thought, same old thing.

I think it was Ramon she saw me with. I remember a time under the house with him, in my white bra and panties, and, possibly, Bridget coming down the hill from the kitchen, looking in the small cobwebbed window. I never told my sister I doubted her memory, which she used to tell repeatedly, I didn't want to shut her up, I wanted to know what more she could tell me, it was amazing to hear the confirmation, even if I suspected this particular memory askew, a conflation with earlier memories. Most of all I wanted us to go on pooling such memories.

Long before Billie died Daddy began my driving lessons. These miserable, grueling sessions lasted two solid years, Daddy sitting next to me in my shorts heckling me until I ground the gears, the car lurching and stalling when I missed the connection with the clutch. Usually the rest of the family was with us. Now I see he was flaunting his thing with me to Mama in the back seat, who never gave me a lesson, who was silent, just staring as she did in Grandma's funeral procession. (She learned from him in one lesson, coming down Atlantic from Mt. Wilson with me six weeks old in a basket in the back seat.) He did stress safety and the danger—after Billie Jean the images were graphic; the dip into ground fog, the smile to him still on her face when they pried them out—and taught me little tricks and emergency strategies I've always used. But in the same breath he accused me of wanting to kill him there in the suicide seat. He accused me of wanting to kill all of us, of wanting to drive us off Clevenger Canyon. "Isn't that right, Sharon?"

He, Mama, and Bridget, separately and at different times, recalled to me one fight, the same fight, as being the worst, "the worst anyone ever saw him." I remember it vaguely, but not what the fight was about, or that it was the worst. The difference with this fight was that Mama tried to defend me. We are at the dining room table. I have my back to the window, Daddy is across the table, toward the valley end, then Mama, then Bridget. Clarke is on my left. He's screaming at me, I can't remember, it isn't anything new, but she actually blurts out something on my behalf.

"*You!*" the contempt in his voice is still not bearable. "*You* shut up." He rises from the chair, lunges toward her.

Afterwards, he was sitting in the Ford over on Baldwin's hill, just sitting at the wheel, brooding. Bridget remembers this too. And the guilt she always felt about not defending me, it's just that she felt so sorry for him. I was shocked the first time she said that, I never expected her or Mama to defend me, the obvious reason borne out that day. But lately I've wondered about our all remembering him sitting over there. Olive Street made a ninety degree turn on top of Baldwin's hill, he parked right there in full view of all our windows. Maybe he was remembering his own father striking his brothers and sister, maybe even his mother, though never him, never Cecil. Lately I've wondered if perhaps he was in that other state, maybe along with remorse, the one that leads to one of the most common crimes, **Man Shoots Whole Family, Then Self.**

Why didn't I ask Mama what the argument was that night? She brought it up several times on Jennifer Street in Ashland. "Remember the time I tried to defend you?" Nor did I ever ask Bridget what the argument was in her many references to the incident. He remembered the incident in a 1985 letter as being the only time he ever "*hit or beat*" me. "*Your mother rightly took up for you and of course that ended that.*" I hear again his resentment of her power, but at least I never saw him hit her. I like to believe he never hit her. But then I don't remember him hitting me in this incident that he actually confessed, and they all remembered.

All my life has been veiled in the denial but twice in my teenage years the whole thing almost cracked. Twice my mother slapped me. My father's regular hitting me was nothing to those two slaps that threatened my clung-to belief that she was on my side, at least understood my side. They threatened my clung-to sanity.

One Saturday morning in my bedroom Ramon is depressed and angry. He says his foster parents are going to get rid of him. I can hardly believe him, he's been with them since he was eight. Then suddenly my mother is home and he flees through the window and down the pepper tree. My mother and I are in the living room when I look out the window and see him walking down the driveway in plain view. Luckily my mother doesn't look up, but I'm greatly alarmed and don't understand. When I ask him about it he says he just doesn't care anymore. I'm shocked. What about me? If my mother had seen. My father would have killed me, but it is my mother I cannot bear to know. My sense of betrayal is a sickening panic.

And then he is moving. He sobs in my arms. "You are the only good thing that has ever happened to me."

It'll take me years just to think the most obvious: Ramon and I were intentionally separated. His foster parents got him out of Ramona as a favor to my parents.

He was in a foster home in San Diego. He kept breaking the rules, hitchhiking back up the forty mountain miles. For the first time I experienced a feeling of shame in our sex. He'd betrayed me like my family always betrayed me; he'd forgotten to protect me. I no longer trusted him. I wrote him a letter, *"Please, Ramon, we must not do that anymore."* I left this letter unfinished on my bed.

I'm ironing a blouse in my bedroom, wearing only my bra and panties. Mama comes in. She found the letter. She doesn't even give me credit for this proof of my effort to do right, just this writing as proof of my sinfulness, she who has always said that no one, not even a parent, has the right to read another's mail. Suddenly she slaps me hard across the face. She who has always said she doesn't believe in hitting a child.

This is so shocking and hurting I forget it. I forgive it. It was just a bad mistake.

There's a photo of me and Ramon in our yearbook, *El Año,* November 2, 1956. It's Sadie Hawkins Day at Ramona High School and La Noche de Las Velas up on the reservations. We're Sophomores. You can see how much we love each other. We're sitting on a bale of hay and he is telling me that he received my letter. Unbeknownst to me, my mother mailed it, along with one of her own. "She called me every name in the book, told me I'd better never see her daughter again."

He hitchhiked straight to the drive-in. He told her that we may have done some things that were wrong but that we had never gone all the way. Her daughter was still a virgin.

I broke up with him the next day.

This was extremely painful. We went to the park. He started crying. When he saw that I actually meant it, he begged me to go one last time to our secret make-out place at the elementary school. The idea was repulsive but for his sake I finally agreed, promising myself that I wouldn't allow the explosions to happen. But for all my resistance they came, four, then five times. I felt vulgar. I knew immense shame.

I've never understood why I broke up with Ramon. I so loved him!

I broke up with him to demonstrate my fidelity to my mother over him (and Daddy), to demonstrate my fidelity to her sexual code. I couldn't allow myself to know this, but just as she slapped me to reinforce her contrived notions of me, I engraved loss of love of him into my body. I experienced shame and disgust to align myself with her, to go numb to him.

And then I really broke with him. My soul began to deny his existence. (My head fell off, rolled to a place where it couldn't be retrieved.)

Six weeks later she introduced me to Sergei Doubiago, a "lonely" nineteen year old Miramar sailor hanging out at Edens' late nights during the holiday season. She invited him and his buddies up to the house on Christmas Eve! Her encouragement of the relationship felt wonderful after the disapproval of Ramon. Doubi was a White Russian from Long Island, New York, six feet four and a half inches tall, intelligent, witty, humorous, too, but in a very different way than Ramon. A New Yorker! His grandfather had been a General Chief of Staff in the Czar's Army, his great grandfather the publisher of the great Russian literature of the 19th Century. He was lonely because his father had disappeared when he was five and he was subsequently raised in a school like Mama, in Yonkers. We had our first date January 2; twenty days later he shipped out on the USS Hornet for the seven month tour of duty in Southeast Asia. We wrote daily. When he returned at the end of July and was transferred to China Lake in the Mojave desert, two hundred and thirty-two miles north, we became secretly engaged, our wedding date set for two weeks after my high school graduation.

I've gotten off work after school, have taken my bath, am in my duster, sewing last-minute blue sequins to my white majorette uniform. I have to get back to town by half-time to lead the girls in our Indian routine.

It can't be, but I hear his car gearing up the hill.

"I couldn't stay away," he says, taking me in his arms. "I love you."

To drive all that distance for just two days!

We fall in laughter and passionate kissing to the living room floor.

Then Daddy and his friend Sam are above us. In the slow motion of nightmare we unscramble from each other, from them. Sergei runs out the kitchen door. They run after him.

I get to the bathroom, lock the door, my heart pounding in my mouth. I've never known what happened to Sergei that night. Probably the same thing that happened to Ronnie. He's running down the hill into the brush. They corner him, they threaten to kill him if he ever comes near me again.

Then my raging father is banging on the door.

"Open up, Sharon!"

"No!"

He's going to break down the door.

"Did he come, Sharon, did he come inside you?"

This is the first time I hear that expression. But I know what it means. "No!"

Then my mother is at the door. "Did he come Sharon, did he come inside you?"

"No, no, no! We've never gone all the way, Mama. I'm a virgin."

But even my mother doesn't believe me.

"It's none of your business, it's none of your business."

I almost throw up in the knowledge that it's none of their business.

This fight is the worst ever. (They remember the other because she was threatened.) Sam drove up alone, saw us through the window, drove back to the drive-in, got my father. They watched for awhile to be sure of what we were doing. The hideous sneering accusations of my father about what a sick, warped immoral person I am, he's going to ship me to Uncle Marion in Tennessee who'll straighten me out, that's for sure, my mother so ashamed of me, just passively watching, like always. "There's nothing more important than a high school degree," she cries.

He slung me down the room into the sliding glass door. Crashing into it, Mama screamed "oh, no!" We all held our breaths, frozen, waiting for the glass to shatter. It didn't. I stood up, turned around, faced him.

"Go ahead, do it again."

Then, it just came out of me.

"We're engaged to be married."

They seemed surprised, and they seemed to honor this. I brought out our rings from the hiding place. They said I could wear the engagement ring.

But we were forbidden to see each other for as long as I lived under his roof. I was grounded for six weeks. In two weeks I'd be allowed to go back to school but only to attend classes.

They were waiting to see if I was pregnant. I have no memory of how they knew when my period started, right on time as always. But if I'd been pregnant I would have been shipped to Tennessee. Daddy's Ducktown girl swung from the rafters before my eyes.

Four long months later my mother slapped me across the face again. We were outside between the three cars and the ping pong table. It was night. I don't remember why she slapped me, except that whatever it was I was telling the truth.

"Liar!"

My jaw wrenched, tears exploded out, the stinging went on forever.

"Twisted. Warped! I'm so ashamed of you, Sharon."

I bolted down the hill.

"You come back here! Right this minute, Sharon Lura."

I did. I love and honor my mother to infinity.

"I'm so disappointed in you Sharon."

I was in the hole again with the big boys of the block. "*Sha-ron!*" She was pacing the rim, the blue sky behind her.

I ran down the hill. Even as I did, I was still searching for the place I could obey her, some fragment of fairness and love coming from her.

"*Sharon Edens ....*"

Her tonal assessment of the warped Sharon Edens rained down on me until I dropped below the hill out of sight.

"You come back here this very minute!"

I didn't. I couldn't. I'd tried everything. I'd never disobeyed her. I'd never considered disobeying her, had never wanted to. But suddenly there was no alternative. I'd tried everything. I'd told the truth. She didn't believe me. This was sickening, terrifying. My brain, the organ itself, spun. I felt it spinning within my skull.

I fled into the impenetrable brush, the standing cactus weighted in apples. Across the moonlit slabs of granite, the silver night, away from her screams, the inside of my head whirling, an exploding galaxy of stars. Into the acrid smell of sage. Only stars, only the moonlit shadows of eucalyptus wavering, only my brain flying to their tops, *caw! caw!* Black bird, buzzard, hoot owl. Past El Paso, the rows of turkeys in their cages. *Gobble, gobble.* The heavy feathery flocking sound of the caged running from me. Blackmail, whirlpool, maelstrom of mind, the danger of going to the place of full understanding. Mama who climbed into the empty swimming pool in winter to escort the trapped tarantulas and snakes out, who so proudly was making our fourteen acres a quail refuge from hunters—she told stories of facing down their guns—who had always instructed me in the sacred identification with the Other, that it always has a side—that my mother had forgotten that I have a side was the most unbearable thing that had ever happened to me.

I walked most of that night, my eyes on the unlit house on the hill. I walked until my brain wasn't spinning anymore. Then I went back.

I went back for the fifteen months. I could stand it. I would finish high school. I was going to do it right, by their rules and codes. I would prove my fidelity to them, that I do love them, but I wouldn't let them drive me insane. I loved the world too much for that. Nor would I let them destroy my love for Sergei as they had succeeded in doing with Ramon.

I went back. I couldn't think my mother was trying to drive me away, that she'd set me up with Sergei, that my departure from the house would be the best thing for all of us. But now I hear again her voice from the sixth grade bathtub: "A man and a woman left alone in a house will always come to sex." I hear her saying again my father loved me in a deep, special way, deeper than normal father love. She herself ran away at fifteen.

And now, only now, the most unbearable, never allowed before thought: I was a constant sexual threat to her in her home.

She taught me to forgive. But my forgiveness of him confused her, fed her paranoia that I was a competitor for his love. Fed the deepest paranoia of all, that our sex continued. (Well, his attraction to me would have, just by my presence, no matter what didn't take place, or how oblivious I was—this realization has taken me longer to get than any other, though that is exactly how I was always treated by them, and by Bridget still: *my very being is the problem*.) How else to explain why I didn't act normally? Why did I stay, not run off and marry Sergei? "Rapists should be castrated," she will say a number of times at the end of her life. Oh Mama, I will say to myself, my head against her bedroom door, oh, Mama, you are talking about your husband, our father. You taught me as a little girl that Jesus came to correct the sin of an eye for an eye, a tooth for a tooth. You taught me to forgive. I didn't want him castrated. I wanted him to get it, to confess, to apologize, to repent, to be redeemed in asking for forgiveness, to know happiness and salvation in amending his ways. I wanted him to know my love and forgiveness and I wanted to be believed and most of all I wanted to love her, to be faithful to her, and she to me.

I went back, thanks to denial again, this time that I wasn't wanted there.

I came close to losing my mind that night rather than face that. And then I found again the escape hatch. I burrowed ever deeper into unknowing. Into amnesia.

§

Thirty-One

I came home from school one afternoon not long after the slap to find two women sitting in the long living room with my mother. It was unusual for my mother to be home at that time, she worked round the clock at the drive-in. I noticed right off that something was very odd about her.

"Do you recognize who this is Sharon?"

They stared at me. I looked from the one to the other. A middle-aged, brown haired, mousey woman with a big stomach, and the other, about thirty, not much brighter.

"No. I don't."

There was a long silence. All three stared at me.

"Are you sure, Sharon, you don't recognize who this is?" my mother asked again in her most reserved tone, indicating the younger woman.

I looked into the face, trying to see who it was.

"No, I'm sorry, but I don't."

"It's Gae Walker."

The sound of *Gae*, the name so long unsaid, so forbidden was the first shock. Then, to get from that, to the actual woman sitting on our couch, to Gae Elaine Walker, fifteen, sitting in our living room. *Gae.* I couldn't believe my eyes, that it was her.

I couldn't believe my heart either. I felt nothing, just pixelating weirdness. Mama was stiff and cold too in her new blue leather love seat, her legs properly entwined over her new wall-to-wall carpeting, the 180 degree view of the Santa Maria Valley in the glass walls behind her, the native acacia in yellow wafting bloom, our new swimming pool in front reflecting all of this. I stared at them like Palomar's telescope flashing in the sun atop the mountain behind us, working to keep my brain from spinning, working to come to the moment. They could not have been more altered.

Something was wrong with Gae; she was somehow messed up. I could see that it was going to be difficult. Difficult to respect her. Messed up, the great Gae was an embarrassment. But how could I think such? I did, just like that. Blink of the eyes, the zombie that I was for my mother by that point dismissed her; the assaulted slope head slammed the Gae door shut before it opened any more. All I could grasp then was the devastation I was looking at.

"I would have recognized you, Sharon, anywhere," she said.

The three of them looked at me so piercingly I remember what I was wearing. The greenish-brown and gold cross-stitched rayon tight skirt that

I'd made had tiny pleats defining it from waist to hips, a deep kick pleat in back. My top was a beige batwinged cashmere sweater. I was holding my books and baton. "I would have recognized you anywhere," she will say for the rest of our lives of this moment. "You acted so blasé, so nonchalant."

They left the nudist colony, Mrs. Walker explained, when Mr. Walker was hired by the North Las Vegas Police Department, and became the police captain. Physical transformation? Mrs. Walker explained it. Gae had been pregnant by her father. She took him to court on criminal charges of rape and incest, got him arrested and fired. It was a huge scandal. Amazingly, they won. Most amazingly, Mrs. Walker told the whole story, right there in our Ramona living room, in my mother's presence.

My mother didn't move. She sat there ramrod straight.

"I made my mother find you," Gae said. "Everything would be okay if I found Sharon." She slouched deeper in the sunset window corner of the divan. "I guess I didn't mean the same to you as you did to me. I would have recognized you anywhere."

I hated her whining. I wanted to scream "Quit feeling sorry for yourself!"

Mrs. Walker had had an operation, she almost died. He forced her to have a hysterectomy so they could have sex at all times, so she wouldn't get pregnant again. Her stomach muscles were severed and now she had a huge stomach.

"I'm only thirty," she said, standing up to show us. "But I feel and look like an old woman.

"Merrill kept threatening to kill us. He laughed at me when I tried to divorce him in Las Vegas. It was not possible. Then my little girl was pregnant by him, her father!"

In all my memories of this period my mother is holding herself stiffly, removed, but she is especially in this one. These two represented Hollydale: everything we'd escaped "to start over," especially the story we did not tell. Scandalous Dorothy Walker had her husband arrested for what he did to her daughter, while my mother, the proper and good mother, had done nothing or little to protect hers. (Imagine—as my mother must have imagined—pregnancy!) Everything in this moment threatened the code and truce between me and my mother. But much more basic, it threatened my sanity.

It took weeks that long spring before I could see that it really was Gae. Her coloring was still gold, but now closer to the unpolished bronze end of the gold spectrum. Her strange eyes, which are probably Missouri Indian in a Caucasian face, were the same. Her personality still would not allow her to lie, especially to herself. But as a woman, this was now more problematic than attractive. She was without veils, guile, social ease or the deceit of manners. I wanted to scream refuse to be a victim! But Gae was refusing to lie.

By summer she was living with us, and though kind, my heart stayed perfectly numb, my brain did not spin. I did not know this. I thought there was something wrong with her. I introduced her to Gene, one of Sergei's best friends. In September they were married. He shipped out for the seven month tour of duty. She enrolled in Ramona High School. She worked at the drive-in. She had an affair with one of the wild boys of the town, much of it taking place in his car behind the drive-in. She may have had affairs with some of his brothers too. I remember her wrapping cheeseburgers and saying "you know sometimes I just wish Gene would, you know, die somehow; I don't really want to be married. Isn't that awful of me?" Then she was kicked out of the school for being married. When he returned from Asia, they left for Southern Illinois, his family's farm. In five years she had four children. In this way we maintain our blood sisterhood for eternity: I introduced her to their father.

And I did desert her, I, the ever-faithful Taurus, just as she always charged and I always denied. Gae was everything I was struggling to forget, and of the present not to know, a huge threat to my carefully constructed amnesia. I left my head in Hollydale. If I had "recognized" her, if I had gotten it, I would have been hauled off—to Juvenile Hall, to Tennessee, to the insane asylum, or worse. As with Ramon, though completely unconscious of this, I chose my mother over her. I sacrificed them both to prove my fedelilty to my mother (over my father).

In January 2002, I drove to Las Vegas and found the newspaper stories. It was like verifying a nightmare. I found a front page photograph of Mr. Walker in his police uniform, handcuffed! Merill Wayne Walker was initially arrested for threatening to murder Dorothy after she filed for divorce. He was involved with a police dispatcher, Mary Lou Renteria, 23, who was living in their home. He was later charged with statutory rape, brutal treatment of prisoners, destroying police records, use of narcotics, and excessive use of firearms (firing at a couple on a motorcycle running a traffic stop in a residential area). He found himself in the same cell as a man he'd arrested, interrogated and beaten the week before. (The papers delighted in this.) The scandal precipitated a full scale investigation of the whole department—for narcotics, murder and international racketeering. Eventually the North Las Vegas Police Department was found to be in the control of organized crime.

The papers did not tell of the incest charges but it was hard not to read between the lines. Walker's "family troubles" are always cited. Statutory rape is one of the charges. Gae, age 13, is always mentioned, with other child rape stories laid out around their story and stories of the town's uproar against him.

Her father impregnated her. What happened to the baby? Maybe she had an abortion. Maybe she gave it up for adoption. I don't think she knows. In 1990, she said "I was never pregnant. You have such a vivid imagination, Sharon." But I remember her fifteen year old body. Her hips, stomach and breasts were striated and loose. Imagine being pregnant at thirteen by your father, imagine his use of drugs and hypnotism on you, imagine your mother's ongoing participation, imagine at puberty a year in a nudist colony, and the public trial and headlines, your father the police captain in jail because of your testimony, imagine pregnancy at thirteen and it's end, however and whenever. Imagine losing your mind.

I found an old sex manual based on the Kinsey Reports of 1948 and 1953. I learned for the first time the term female orgasm, something that had been happening to me regularly since I was thirteen, something I called explosions and earthquakes. This little blue book was clinical and scholarly, but it pressed the fact that only two percent of all women have multiple orgasms, and that most women are frigid altogether. Some part of me enjoyed my special status, as did Sergei to whom I gave the book, who then kept count, but the deeper truth was I didn't believe it. Some part of me was already skeptical of scientific man and his "data."

We meet in the night hills, down deserted dirt roads, in his '54 Olds, in my '53 two-tone, newly-painted baby blue Ford. Boulders, moonlit hills and coyote-prowled roads the places of our rendezvous, our beautiful, restorative, non-coital sex. I make secret trips to China Lake the weekends he has duty, sometimes for his Thursday night basketball games. Eight hour roundtrip journeys into unknown territory, triumphantly alone, unseen, unknown, the incredible and terrifying rapture of escape, of the night, of flight, of finding the way, following the map, of learning the land, of the great differences in places, the canyons west and north of Escondido, the dropping down into the long valley, the San Andreas fault, skirting the eastern boundaries of the Los Angeles Basin, San Jacinto and

Mt. Baldy ten thousand feet above, climbing Cajon Pass, dropping into the desert, ever going north, just a girl and her car across the night beneath the dazzling stars, one hundred thousand watts of power, rock and roll from Salt Lake City, from Tijuana, finding her fiancé on the base, coming and coming, then heading back, *faith,* sitting back in her World History desk by eight-thirty in the morning, no one imagining where she's been, journeys in which she finds herself, and survives.

Susan and her younger sister Dana, who was now Bridget's best friend, visited us regularly from Hollydale.

"Whenever I visited the Edens home," Dana responded to my questionnaire, Did Fred Edens Ever Molest You? *"I always slept in Bridget and Sharon's bedroom. On one occasion I awoke early and went to the kitchen for something to drink. While I stood at the sink that a.m. Mr. Edens came up behind me – put his hand on my shoulder & kind of giggled pulling me toward him. I quickly ducked out & under his arm saying "I'm going back to bed." After that, I always made certain I wasn't alone with him anywhere in the home. Once, while I was working at the drive-in, he moved his body up behind and against me in the hallway & when I quickly moved away and glared back at him, he tried to make some little joke about it. I was always careful not to ride alone with him in the car & it always seemed that no one (not Bridget, Mrs. Edens, or Sharon) ever put me in that position because it seemed to me that they were all a little leery about how he might get around me or any young girls. There always seemed to be an uneasy feeling about Mr. Edens within his own family & within his own home. Mr. Edens also made remarks occasionally about Bridget and her bouncing breasts which he tried to make jokingly but I always thought was disgusting that a father would even think (much less joke) about his own daughter's body and or make any type of sexually suggestive remarks about her."*

Dana was part of my mother's code talk too. She repeatedly charged that thirteen year old Dana was an example of a girl who had grown up too fast, who'd lost her innocence too soon and therefore was headed for a life of failure and unhappiness. She would be old before she reached adulthood. It's astounding to discover now why Dana was pinpointed for this charge from the bevy of beautiful, precocious girls in our life. My father, I know now, always chose one from a group and then worked that group to distrust and blame her in case she ever told on him.

Dana, shocked and hurt now to learn of our mother's portrayal of her, *"a stab in the heart,"* asked me if she said these things about her to Bridget. I have the sense that she lectured about Dana as regularly to Bridget as to me, but now I don't know. Maybe Bridget didn't hear them because Mama's words were directed just to me, a girl like Dana.

How insidious is the ecology of abuse. I have carried my mother's attitude about Dana, beautiful, innocent thirteen year old Dana, in some part of me all my life.

It's January of my senior year. Mama is sick. The bedroom where she lies feels like a cold dark hole at the center of the house. A heart attack, then walking pneumonia, then galloping tuberculosis to both lungs, she can't breathe. She's worked too hard. She's worked from 11 a.m. to 11 p.m. since the day we opened the drive-in. She prayed for a waitress a year ago. When cute and vivacious twenty-three year old Voncille came it was an answer to her prayer. Still it wasn't enough help, or soon enough.

Fifteen years later, in our first talk about our childhoods, Bridget will inform me that our father was having an affair with Voncille when our mother had the heart attack. She encountered all three of them in the walk-in refrigerator, Mama having caught them in the act, screaming "I'm so ashamed of you, Voncille!" Voncille was crying, Daddy just looking on.

She was hospitalized in the TB terminal ward in San Diego. Voncille was committed to the mental ward of the same hospital, and underwent electric shock treatment. Mama will always say of this time she had no reason to live.

I must have been afraid but I didn't admit it. We were alone in the house again with our father but I didn't allow this thought either. I began working every night to closing, usually midnight. I remember visiting my mother in the San Diego sanitarium feeling like an adult woman, driving to the city in the '53 Ford which I owned now, thirty eight dollars a month for two years, turning up the road to the bluff of the terminally ill, nodding to Voncille's building of the mentally ill, coming down the hall in my high heels and fuchsia floral sheath dress I'd designed and made, feeling beautiful, independent and strong, soon to be married. To my mother thin and pale in the bed. I'm in the chair beside her bed. All around us are the other dying mothers. She's assuring me she's not afraid of death, she wouldn't mind it. But last week Clarke visited her. Clarke's fourteen now. She woke to him sitting by her bed, she noticed his hands were becoming a man's hands. They were her father's hands hanging down between his legs. And suddenly, she wanted to live.

There's a photograph of the three of us during this last year of slow-motion family dissolution. It's in the *Año*, 1959, a snapshot taken at a basketball game, blown up to full page. Clarke and Bridget are on separate ends of the front row, and Gae is sitting there too. I'm one of the cheerleaders, my back to the camera, about to begin a cheer. Clarke's in the eighth grade. His mouth is opened with a slight scab on his long upper lip, a cold sore, or maybe where Daddy hit him, or maybe from a first shave, and his white hair is greased up in a long flattop that I taught him to comb. He's wearing the cool shirt that I made him for Christmas. Getting dressed for this game I couldn't find my best bra. Bridget is in her song leader uniform. I notice instantly.

"Bridget!" I communicate from out on the floor. "You're wearing my bra!"

And she laughs, and I laugh, we laugh the wonderful knowing laughter of sisters amidst the unknowing crowd. I'm a little stunned that she took it without asking me, that she went through my things. That she can fit into my 34D.

In the remote future (in writing this memoir) I will be forced to understand that much of my sister's soul intent has always been, will always be, to fill all my places, until she completely replaces me.

(But now having written this I'm forced to see that it's a conflation with an earlier event. Bridget's breasts reached my size by the time she was in the ninth grade. So I'm in the tenth. I'm the head majorette about to lead the girls out onto the gym floor for halftime entertainment. Bridget's sitting three tiers up in a pale blue cashmere sweater. I recognize the shape of my own breasts, that is, my Maidenform, that's how I know. And it is across *that* crowd that we are laughing.)

§

Thirty-Two

Sometime that last spring of my senior year Sergei sent me a photograph of a *Playboy* blonde stepping out of the shower. He bet I looked like her. He loved my breasts in the moonlight of the car, he longed to see me stepping out of the shower, walking around nude in sunlight. I couldn't wait to walk around naked for him.

But I was having nightmares now of not being able to have sexual intercourse. In these dreams, for all my effort and desire I could not open myself, or be opened. It was impossible to penetrate me, there was no opening there. Moments of panic, pure dread in day consciousness too. *How will I ever be able to do that?* I so prided myself on my will power in staying a virgin through all the necking but I was beginning to know a secret part of me was grateful for the rules. There was the sense of staving off an inevitable disaster.

A month before the wedding I arranged to have the pre-marital examination required by the State of California. I'd also obtain birth control. I'd just turned eighteen, Mama was still in the sanitarium. I drove down to a clinic in El Cajon rather than have Dr. deCock or Dr. Pilgrim do it. Though the new pill was all the rage I chose to be fitted for a diaphragm.

"Have you ever tried to have sexual intercourse?" the doctor asked, a dark dignified young man looking up from between my spread-opened, sheet-draped legs.

I didn't know how to answer. What was he seeing? Maybe it was important to what he was seeing that I tell the truth. But what was the truth? Maybe he could tell if I lied. Maybe my health, my life, my fiancé, my marriage, my future kids were at stake. I was proud of my sexuality. I was one of the two percent. I sort of stammered around.

"Well, it's a good thing, because only a brute could penetrate you," he said. "You have the thickest hymen I've ever seen. You will need surgery to cut it."

In the recurring nightmare my body was sealed shut, there was no opening but a wall of flesh there like a man. No man could penetrate that. Never with such a delicate thing as a penis. I'd never examined myself, never put my fingers there, nowhere near my vagina. Tampons were unthinkable. Despite my mother's reminders and demonstrations, I never even washed myself there. I let the nightly bath water do that. I was in my mid-thirties before I masturbated, other than in sleep. I didn't touch myself so as not to remember what happened to me there.

"You're lucky to have found this out before the wedding." He told of women with hymens like mine married years, their husbands unable to penetrate them. He told of a woman who was brutally raped by her husband after two years. And of another, where penetration took two years too, but by then the marriage was ruined.

He would give me sodium pentothal, also known as "the truth serum," to perform the surgery that would enable me to have sexual intercourse.

I headed straight for the drive-in, thirty miles back up the mountain. See Daddy, you misjudged your girl. See, I was telling the truth, I am a virgin. The truth will out. I walked into Edens, a busy Friday afternoon in May. My father was standing over the hot dog machine, near the telephone.

"I have to have surgery to have my hymen cut. It's too thick for me to have sexual intercourse. I have to have the money," the last thing he'll ever have to pay for me. I was trying to be funny. He'd be pleased to learn that his daughter was still, after all, a virgin. I was on the left side of him, a little forward of him, his big head, and I was telling him.

But the look on my father's face was so strange, his face over the steaming oven, something incredulous, something not discernible. The way he jerked to me. Startled.

He nodded. He'd inform the insurance company.

Aunt Alice drove me to the clinic. I was curious about the truth serum. What is the truth? The doctor stood again between my legs, injecting the needle. Dear Jesus may the truth come out. I was being cut open. I was losing my virginity to a knife.

I woke in a small narrow room with a red Navajo blanket covering me, crying. I woke curled around myself, semi-foetal, crying uncontrollably, Mama, Mama. Tears were spilling out. The blanket seemed mysteriously incongruous in the sterile all-white room. It made me cry harder, I was so grateful for it. My aunt came in but even then, so unlike me, I couldn't stop crying.

"There, there, honey, it'll be okay."

I remember the car ride back up the mountains to Ramona, my head against the sill, my aunt driving. Overwhelming sorrow across the land, this is the truth, the Earth is crying. Tears, endless tears.

I returned to the clinic three more times to be stretched. Even after surgery I was too tight for intercourse. This stretching was excruciatingly painful. I didn't know what he was doing, how he was stretching me, my feet in the stirrups, the white sheet between us, his hands and cold metal instruments inside me, but I've never forgotten the nature of the pain. A deep *aching*, wrenching waves like vomiting, not like the sharp penetration of a knife, or other piercing cut. I felt it again when Sergei first entered me, and again and again the first weeks of our intercourse. It hurt like an earthquake hurts the earth.

Why did I have to be stretched if my hymen was cut?

At the last stretching he fitted me to a diaphragm, size 85m, the second largest size, the size I would always use. My cervix is large, my entrance small? It was all so confusing. And though the tears had quit falling out of me, so inexplicably sad.

Until my father confessed that he raped me I marveled that I must have grown my hymen so I could not be penetrated. Between my mother's lectures on staying a virgin, my father's regular messing with me, and the powerful orgasmic sex life I'd had since thirteen I figured I must have toughened my hymen by will power. What exactly did the doctor cut? Could he tell I'd been raped? In 1997 a friend suggested it was scar tissue. (A friend had to suggest it, I couldn't think it, even then.) What is the nature of scar tissue in the vagina? What happens to the vagina of a raped seven year old? In what condition is it eleven years later? Is this why those women the doctor told me of couldn't have intercourse? I remember the rape now (on the conscious level, not just the dream one; I remembered the instant my father told me). I never forgot the bleeding that went on for three days.

I tried to research the hymen then, but learned very little. I petitioned a woman gynecologist who was also a lesbian-feminist poet acquaintance. She said she couldn't help me, she knew nothing. No one seemed to know anything about the hymen beyond the standard myths. In the 1994 *Hite Report on the Family, Growing Up Under Patriarchy,* Shere Hite reported:

Research for this study demonstrates quite surprisingly that most girls do not experience pain or bleeding on first coitus; the percentage of those who do is quite low. In fact, even more surprisingly, it may not be anatomically 'normal' for girls to have a painful-to-break 'hymen'. Those who are 'supposed' to know—gynaecologists or pediatricians—in fact have not particular expertise in this, since (1) gynaecologists usually do not see very young girls, and (2) pediatricians usually don't do in-depth or detailed vaginal examinations. Therefore, is the assumption that 'normal girls' have hymens, simply based on hearsay, or 'learned' in medical textbooks? On what body of knowledge and investigation, if any, are these texts based?[12]

Perhaps in part because of Hite's *Report*, there is now nascent research by the medical profession. "*Congenital frequency of imperforate hymen is low, estimated to be approximately 0.1% in female population.*" "*An imperforate hymen can be acquired from sexual abuse as documented by Berkowitz et al.*" "*An imperforate hymen most likely is caused by scar tissue from sexual abuse.*"[13]

There's the moment with my father in Edens'. It's also taken me a lifetime to understand it, to live in its terrible meanings. I think I am proving at long last that I'm a virgin, about which he has regularly accused me of lying. I don't dream that he's trying to figure this. I don't dream his fear that the truth is out. Nor do I nightmare that my need for this surgery will be used as evidence against me to my mother that I lied in the sixth grade about his sex with me, that it will be evidence she will covet, use, and mutely weave against me all the rest of her life. But he knows the truth, that's why the startled look on his face—*he* stole my virginity. And I know the truth, that's why the moment has lived in my nightmares.

Then my father was sick. His appendix ruptured but Dr. Pilgrim misdiagnosed it as kidney stones. He almost died. He spent a week in Palomar Hospital.

Both my parents almost died in my last six months at home. Voncille was in the nut house having electric shock treatments and I had the weirdest surgery imaginable. Maybe his appendix burst because of the stress. That he survived what would have killed the ordinary man was ever after part of his hero status.

When he came home, though he could barely walk, he took each of us for a walk, and a talk.

We climb the hill behind the house, up to the squeaky water pump beside the boulder on top. Tears stream his silver granite face, boulder tears, mica flecks onto the granitic ground.

"How could you have not visited your father when he was dying?"

Something about his being the father, something about no one teaching him how to be a father, something about how could I?

We get back down, we're outside Clarke's sun porch, his face reflected in the glass, the one I dream as God, the one I nightmare, telling me this is the way it is, Lu. You should be ashamed Lu. I'm sorry Daddy. I love you so much. I'm deep in the graduation and wedding plans. All I can think is how to escape.

I never hated my father. I hated what he did to me, to my mother, to my brother and to my sister, blocking natural love, making them incapable of love, of being responsible to me and therefore to themselves. I hate what he did to himself. To us as a family. To his mother. To the grandchildren. I hate what he did to the great grandchildren through us. The sins of the father: I hate what he did to the world through us.

I loved and accepted my sister by not looking closely—by not thinking, not knowing. She's raged ever since that I didn't see her, that I didn't see that she was hurt. That I didn't see that opposite of me she was the ugly duckling. That's how they treated her, she says, as Sadie Hawkins, a girl, Daddy told her in the presence of others, who would have to trap a man into marrying her. It's true, I saw the sister our mother ordered me to see, and she enthusiastically projected: the great and brilliant and wonderful and happy, smiley, selfless, loving, untroubled, visionary magical child whose personality could transform the world.

She has always maintained, also with vehemence, that he did not molest her and despite the demonstrative casual stuff that I witnessed so that I assumed all the rest was happening to her too (another reason we could not talk to each other) I have always tried to accept her denial. Most recently in a letter she triumphs "I'll accept the hugs, thank you. I *liked* dancing with daddy. I'm thinking of writing my own book about him."

My fierce fidelity was to my mother, who I was made to betray—by her husband, my father. My fierce fidelity was to who she said she was, no doubt to who she wanted to be. I clung to her bathtub wisdom not unlike the way humanity has always clung to religious beliefs right in the face of overwhelming contradictions. This is called Faith.

Late Sunday night before our wedding the following Friday, just before he starts his last drive back alone to China Lake, Sergei is out at the incinerators, silhouetted by high leaping flames. I'm cooking hamburgers for the hordes of tourists returning to San Diego from the mountains and desert.

Then he's at the back door.
"What were you doing?"
"Burning your letters."

He's standing there telling me a story of someone on his block on Long Island who found his parents' love letters. The whole gang gathered up in the attic and read them aloud. Something really embarrassing, their sex before marriage, maybe. Maybe just their words of love to each other.
   "We wouldn't want our children to find them."

§

Book V

Poet

One recent study looks at a hundred women who were seen in an emergency room as children. Doctors recorded then that these girls had been sexually abused. Researchers went back fifteen years later and asked these women if they had been abused as children.... Forty percent of them said no. Sue A. Meier

I do not think the rape affected me as profoundly as my adherence to those laws of concealment and secrecy my mother put into effect—silence could be the most eloquent form of lying. Pat Conroy, *The Prince of Tides*

I want to write like I dream, how
the mind in sleep
puts things together
it won't awake—(Journal, 1974)

"Nelly, I am Heathcliff!" Emily Bronte

Thirty-Three

Poet

I am twenty. Thinner. Becoming
smaller. Darker. Twenty

two. Pregnant
for the second time but for the first time
against the father's wishes. I make
this girl
for our boy.

It hurts. I'm mature
on top of things. The most
miserable nine months of my life.
I am not
angry

but she is.
She wakes up inside me, turns over and over
through the mute amnesiac ancestors.
My will, my beautiful
choice

growing my
Third Eye

She will be
unto herself

I'm twenty-three. I begin to break the vow. I start with the word
damn. Damn this and damn that. It's painful, like pulling teeth,
like a mouth full of rotting teeth. I'm such a phony. I pray to Jesus
to help me to say damn with abandon, with dignity, the word with
wings, as it once, in a pure moment, flew from me

I was formally introduced to poetry in Mr. Mikkelson's Basic Ideas in
Literature at Palomar Junior College in San Marcos. He gave us two
poems, a "good poem and a bad poem." Both were about mothers. The

assignment was to compare the two poems showing which was which and why.

I didn't know. The sentiment expressed in what turned out to be the bad poem was love. The language was the way everyone I knew talked, the way I talked; certainly, the way I express love. Profusely, directly. *I love you!* But Mr. Mikkelson said the poem was sentimental, feminine, nostalgic, cliché-ish, and Hallmark Card writing. He ridiculed the poet, and the poet's so-called love for his mother.

The good poem was "Sonnet to My Mother" by George Barker. His mother is sitting *"huge as Asia"* under a window drinking gin. *"She will not glance up at the bomber or condescend/To drop her gin and scuttle to a cellar."* Again and again Mr. Mikkelson returned to that image of the mother being huge as Asia and to the magnificent language—*"that she will move from mourning to morning."* The poem with its dense images and language, strange mother and severe syllabic and line count, the thing that made it a sonnet, felt artificial to me, and not of love.

I understand now that the major difficulty I experienced was from what felt like an attack—on my psyche, my language, my roots, my class, my ethics (gin!), my mother, my gender, on the way I love: my basic identity. I couldn't exactly think this. My mother raised me to loathe such thoughts, to believe in an egalitarian America. To identify with a class, for instance, was to contribute to a class structure.

Three months after the wedding I'd started working my husband through college. I needed secretarial skills. The first night of my first class at Palomar, where he was enrolled fulltime, walking up the campus of higher learning, a campus named for the world's largest telescope, to the World War II quonset hut that was the classroom, suddenly, the big night sky and all the world around and beneath cracked slightly in the brilliant starlight. It may have been an earthquake but in that opening I experienced instant and ecstatic release. *I saw my road to freedom.* I would follow through with the lowly, humiliating secretary class, hidden in the boulders behind the main campus and, most significantly, I would become pregnant before the end of the semester, but from that moment, even before I entered my first college classroom, I knew I had finally found the way to fulfill the promise of my own birth—to find, to know, to be myself in exchange with the miraculous world I so loved. This was a place in which such exchange would be honored and respected, not blocked and denigrated as it had been in my every endeavor, including now my love of my husband.

After Basic Ideas I took Creative Writing from Mr. Mikkelson. Every week of that summer session we wrote in a different genre. Poetry week: again, what is a poem? Everyone else seemed to know. One guy called himself a poet. He sat in the last row of the crowded class, in the corner up against the two walls, so hip, so cool, maybe angry in his white surfer mid-calf pants and thongs and sun-streaked strings of hair. I sat in the last row too, on the opposite end, polite, fashionable, married, a mother: pretty.

Mr. Mikkelson explained that a poem doesn't have to be about something pretty, or romantic. Poetry doesn't have to rhyme. He spoke about memory and the images we carry from memory, as in our dreams, about letting them come out through the pen on the natural rhythm of the breath. He read a famous poem about a street full of garbage. I saw the old men from Rancho Los Amigos hobbling and wheeling their chairs down Industrial Avenue, skirting Trinity Bible Church on the corner, disappearing up Main. I'd forgotten about those guys. He spoke of the importance of specific detail and I saw their handicaps from polio, Parkinson's, multiple sclerosis, birth deformities, the wars, accidents, indigency and alcohol. I saw that one guy in particular, unbelievably spastic, his pinched head bobbing up and down like a seapalm in a rising surf. The kids mimicked him and I hated that. It was unnatural for me to remember those old guys at all, but it felt perverse to try to write of their handicaps. To write the specific details felt like I was doing what the kids did, mimicking them.

But I was a compulsive straight A student. I began by describing my beloved church on the corner, the Sunday marquee that welcomed all in the name of Jesus. Then,

The evil old men who daily tread
The walk that cornered God's good church.
Down the street they came, one at a time
(as if they scared each other, too)
From the county farm four blocks away,
Braces that scraped,
Wheels that creaked,
Canes that prodded,
They turned the corner...,
And climbed the hill in conflicting lines,
Out of sight,
Maimed and mangled, as if
Disfigured by choice—

We thought so, anyway
As we came out of hiding, snickering.
We thought so,
We still lived in God's good world.

I had a long way to go, mainly in consciousness and language, but *"Pharisaism,"* my first poem, is similar to what will always come out of me when I can allow the tapping. Writing will take me to what is regularly denied, by myself, and everyone. Everyone's a poet. But finding the wherewithal to give voice to the self's inner knowledge is one of the great difficulties.

I'll have to work longest of all not to lie about myself for fear of the charges of ego. Until that moment of writing I had not seen that my church did not welcome, much less reach out to those men, but I'd always seen the unChristian cruelty of the neighborhood kids. I had never thought the old men were maimed and mangled by choice (and therefore sinners who deserved their exile from the church). My placing myself in that snickering "we" was untrue. We're awash in false humility but deeper, we are self-censored, we are disempowered from knowing and giving ourselves. I was realizing this as a new mother. I'd always been told by my parents who I was; more than anything I knew I must protect and encourage my son's true self. Becoming a mother and becoming a poet was similar psychic work.

The images of their exposing themselves from the tumbleweeds, and other frightening occurrences with them, rose too, but I couldn't say that yet either. Specific details? The specific penises to me from the specific tumbleweeds? The specific ejaculations and where I am on the walk to the store for our daily bread? The pantless man clutching a knife behind the wheel at Dakota and Main? The leering bloody eyes and broken mouth hissing *"Fuck! Fuck!"* in the bathroom window when I climb out of the bath? To tell these specifics would be like coating the crib bars with my own excrement (a word I don't think I knew then), as my baby boy had just done in exuberant "creativity." Of course I knew better. My story could not yet be carried in language—it can barely be carried now—much less in full consciousness. What I needed to say first about my childhood was that I saw their humanity, the old men were victims, this is the teaching of Jesus, we are to forgive and love and by this our neighbors will be healed; to not do so is to be pharisaic, a Christian hypocrite; more seriously, a contributor to their continuing decline, a perpetuator of their suffering. If in writing my first poem, when my professor instructed let the images inside come through your pen like breath and I saw my father at my breasts, as I did, right across the blackboard behind his butch blond head, and in the hills driving home that day, I knew, of course, beyond the fundamental theme of forgiveness, not to allow those details into language, not to go that much up against the temple, not even inside myself.

But my self is deeply in the vision of this poem. How good it felt to finally be able to say, if inadequately, what I knew on my twelfth birthday when Nancy Meir went spastic mimicking that poor man struggling by and all the kids convulsed in laughter. How that man bore it, kept proceeding down Industrial, I still don't know.

I got the word "Pharisaism" from my Grandmother's 1928 Bible Encyclopedia, a source I still use. I remember a kind of breathlessness in using a new word I wasn't sure of, a kind of dread for being a fake, of making a mistake, but also a kind of magic. The Pharisees *were intolerant of those who differed from them.* They were the moneychangers that Jesus threw out of the temple, a story my mother cited from the bathtub as proof that Jesus was not a wimp, afraid of confrontation. My concern about that word as the title of my first poem continues to this day. Are the Pharisees a people I'm being intolerant of?

At the end of poetry week Mr. Mikkelson called me and the poet, the one who pressed himself into the back corner, so funky in his beach clothes, his burnt aura, so rhymey and feral and intellectual and contemptuous and experienced in poetry, and with whom I was shyly, weirdly fascinated, to stand before the class and read our poems. It was like being in the last week of the first grade when the teacher called me and my secret boyfriend Raymond to the front of the class and awarded the two of us for being the best behaved boy and girl of the year. Dear Jesus—to whom I rarely prayed now—don't let my mouth open up like then!

My mother kept mine in her Bible for the rest of her life, the one I gave her for her birthday that same year, 1962. "When I read it I knew that Sharon was a poet."

I also wrote a short story for this class which Mr. Mikkelson said didn't work. It was based on Susan's secret pregnancy the year before and then her search for the couple who adopted her son at birth. Mr. Mikkelson said the story was cliché-ish "like a Tijuana soap opera." Again, I felt mortification and confusion. I couldn't say then that my teacher, who wrote on proper subjects like fishing and hunting, was being, however well-meaning, sexist and racist. Write what you know, he had lectured. I didn't know what a Tijuana soap opera was. I knew Suzi and her lost son, a true story that I had lived. What is literature?

He praised one line about the sounds of children playing down the street as she approaches the woman's house. Somehow I knew it was the best line too, but felt a suspicion that it was simply the most easily identifiable. The street was the one we'd spent so many Sunday afternoons on in Pasadena when I was a girl, watching (unbeknownst to me) the house of my long ago given-up-for-adoption first cousin. And the street would be like the one on which I would later find Suzi's son in LA. Eating my lunch, doing my homework, watching his door, hoping to get a glimpse of him for her.

Let the images rise on the natural rhythm of your breath as your dreams do in sleep. But, professor, what would happen if I allowed my images to rise? What would happen to my father? To my mother? What would happen to my parents' marriage? What would happen to my marriage? What would happen to my son? What would happen to our country if we allowed the images, if we wrote poetry? Marilyn Monroe died that summer, her diary stolen from her house the same night. Everyone said she was murdered because she was about to tell what she knew about Cuba, President Kennedy and the Mafia. And Ernest Hemingway died that summer too. One morning Mr. Mikkelson announced his suicide. He said the same thing my parents always said, you get so smart you go insane. "Hemingway suffered from his intelligence." *"I wouldn't be alive today if I hadn't learned to control my thoughts,"* my mother will write me on the publication of my first book, *Hard Country.* *"What frightens me is that poets commit suicide."*

My sister, Bridget, was at Palomar too. She was writing her big paper for English on Princess Margaret, Queen Elizabeth's younger sister, and her scandalous love affairs. We hardly ever saw each other now, but sometimes, suddenly encountering her on the walk to a class, it would seem like waking to her far away on the other side of our small childhood bedrooms.

In Ceramics I made a magical bird of clay. He was "abstract," in his lack of detail (as hard to let go of as using them in writing), and mounted on a platform with black clothes hanger legs. Part of his magic was that the clay was deeply buffed with Johnson's floor wax which when fired looked like wood. I gave him to my father for his 46th birthday, thinking he would be especially intrigued with the wax-trick technique. "Your father's meditation is sanding," Mama always said. The hours I put into waxing my bird made me think of him. In another life my father would have been a sculptor.

When he opened my present he laughed. Then he became insulted, then enraged that I would give him "modern art." He may have thrown it against the wall. I have remembered it that way. Once again my son was standing in the living room of the Ramona house with all the rest of the family witnessing his grandfather's contempt for his mother. On TV Jacqueline Kennedy was giving her celebrated tour of the White House. I never saw the magic bird again.

I didn't exactly remember then my clay elephant and Dalmatian/ prehistoric monster I'd made for him in the second grade and how offended he was by the dog. "Sharon's modern art" that looked more like a penis than anything. But now I think that's what my father reacted to that Valentine birthday thirteen years later when I gave him the abstract bird, about the same size and, though beautiful, to my eyes anyway, of a similar shape as the dog. I think my father saw his rape of me coming out of me via a kind of Rorschach art. That he could have seen his penis in his eight-year-old's clay sculpture is rather stunning in its sophistication. His hatred for all things Freud was up there with his hatred for modern art and Richard Nixon. My father may have been just a good old Southern boy, as Mrs. Ritchie described him when I visited her after Mama died to ask why the neighborhood committee thought we should be put in foster homes, why they ran off our caretaker and if she knew he'd raped me, to thank her for her concern, but he was no dummy. Mrs. Ritchie said she didn't remember. I fully anticipated that but not the other thing she kept saying: "You understand, I loved your mother." She would not betray her.

In the last years of his life there was a bird in his Florence, Oregon home that he made himself, a bird very similar to the one I made him for his Valentine birthday in 1962. I was newly married to a sculptor which triggered the memory. "I thought you hated abstract art, Daddy. Do you remember the bird I made you?" He just nodded, looking at me with his heavy-lidded, sad eyes.

Later, heavily medicated and gone into his pain, he cursed me again for the prehistoric monster I gave him in the second grade.

The night before we married Sergei quit speaking to me and did not speak to me again in our seven years and two children, though he carried on exuberantly with all others.

The hurt was devastating, the kind of shock from which you never fully recover. I deduced that suddenly, at the altar, he became afraid, suddenly he couldn't trust me. His father deserted his mother and him when he was five, his mother broke down, took him home to her parents, went into her old bedroom and did not come out for years. His beloved grandmother promised she would never leave him in the Yonkers school. But his grandfather was jealous of him, threatened either he goes or I do. From eight to fifteen he lived in Yonkers School. There were Christmases only he and another kid were there, and a janitor he feared and hated.

For better or for worse, that's the vow. Until death do us part. Divorce, in our world, was still unacceptable and carried the stigma of failure—in our case, a failure prophesied by everyone. I didn't believe in divorce. Emotional withdrawal from intimacy was common with men of my generation. This is the way men are and I am still turned off by whiny, nagging women. That could not be my fate. Everyone had argued that I was too young to marry. I was not, my love for him was not. I would not fail marriage. Or him, whom my father detested.

And then we had children, Daniel Clarke and Shawn Colleen. Sergei was a good father, enthralled and happily involved with them. He was a good father except in his not relating to me, a factor hard for me to consider given that it wasn't much different from my pariah role in my birth family.

I remember my whole being responding to Nathaniel Hawthorne's short story, *The Great Stone Face.* My husband the Great Stone Face. I was haunted by Henry James's ghost story, *The Turn of the Screw,* in the voice of an emotionally remote man like my husband. When Nikita Khrushchev visited Disneyland and warned Americans they didn't understand the Oblomovian personality of Russians, I found the Russian novel *Oblomov.* I became a literature major in the same spirit I'd poured myself into the Bible as a girl, to understand, to make my life, now my marriage-for-life, meaningful. Bearable.

What I mainly remember of our seven years is the heartache, my constantly breaking heart. A loneliness unlike any pain I will ever know again, that this was to be my life forever, that no one knew what my life was or who I was with the great bon vivant, Sergei Doubiago. That he wouldn't even say to me "pass the salt." I remember that my lips literally ached to be kissed. I found myself fantasizing turning away from a man trying to kiss me. It was my only fantasy.

But we made love every night. How to explain this? How to explain our two children?

He'd turn over to me around three or four, after he'd gotten home from his midnight shift as an electronics engineer at General Dynamics working on our secret space shuttle to the moon, the race against Russia, his lost father's country. From sleep, from dark, from the anonymity of the blankets and the suburbs, from time and in time Danny and Shawn, his face buried in my long hair and the pillow. There was vulnerableness in our lovemaking akin to tenderness which created great gratitude in me. I'd have orgasms in rapid succession, his pelvic bone against my pelvic bone, little imageless clitoral poems coming on the breath from deep inside telling him *I love you.* Telling him *thank you.* Telling him *it's okay that you can't talk to me.* Then he'd come, and withdraw back into sleep.

For better or for worse: I assumed that somehow (I wracked my brain trying to figure how) his behavior had to be half my fault, because it takes two and marriage is about compromise and it's forever, that's what we vowed, and I loved him. In fact it was half my fault, but so opposite all my thought and belief patterns and so of my denial ones, it would take me years to glimpse it. I couldn't allow the most obvious, that despite the two passionate years of our engagement, suddenly he didn't want to get married and then, passively aggressive, he wanted me to leave him. That then he experienced my fidelity as being to the marriage vow, not to him, and this angrily propelled him to ever continuing coldness in order to communicate who he really was, not who I was relating to, claiming to love, a pattern not unlike my mother and father, and not unlike me with my parents; actually not unlike nearly all couples I've known through the years. The Lover seems in love with a dream, not the reality of the mate. The Beloved feels unseen, not loved, must challenge the Lover, must fly in the face of the insult and trap called, maddeningly, love, must keep trying to pierce the dream. And the Lover must meet this. My mother did not respond to my father's cruelty, she dismissed his stupid abuse in the name of love, in the name of it not being the real him. As I did, with my father, and then with my husband.

When I told my mother, staying with us the month Shawn was born, November 1963—it was probably also the shock of the assassination that released the secret, that he hadn't spoken to me since the wedding—her reaction was sorrow for me.

"He can't help it," she said.

"I know that, Mama."

It was an enormous psychic journey to leave Sergei, as large as any I've ever undertaken. It included examining and leaving all my early religion too. It was going against my whole life and identity, and certainly my family's. He can't help it, is how I explained him to our children, five and two, when it was finally over, how I explained him to them through their childhoods. So that they are condemned to the same pattern, chronically rushing in to the vacuum he perpetually creates, to understand, to love and forgive him. "You've always wanted something from me," he hissed recently.

I left him. He found the letters of the lover I had then—only then after all those young years of heartbreak and loneliness amidst constant outside male attention. He became emotional, broke down and actually talked to me. He called my mother and told her I was having an affair, knowing what I steadfastly refused to know, how it works in my family. I returned to him, instantly, painfully agreeing that he could have a lover to make up for mine. But not even that appeased his jealous agony. One day in one of the arguments he slugged me in the face, the right cheekbone and eye, Daddy's old target. The second time he hit me, a year after my return, he left; he cried he had to, he couldn't take the chance of doing it again, he'd hated his stepfather for hitting his mother. I loved him for that.

Now as a single mother I had to get my degree. Now I had an excuse to go to college seriously; even to graduate school.

Before he found the letters, he took his vacation time to keep the kids during the week while I attended summer school at San Diego State. I stayed with Bridget, who was pregnant with her first child, in Pacific Beach. One afternoon, bereft, I went up to Ramona the back way from the college to spend the night with my parents. My geology class was as intriguing as it was difficult. I wanted to see if I could grasp the origin of the giant boulders of the Santa Maria Valley. The news on the radio was that Adlai Stevenson had died. My mother would be sad. She loved that man.

The old barn-red house on Olive Hill was being remodeled, expanding ranchstyle spectacular with lots of glass and decks. I missed its former mountain cabin look but I was happy for my mother.

They had moved into the bedroom Bridget and I had shared, bigger and more pleasant with the huge pepper tree in the window. Their old room was now the guest room with a crib for Shawn, my daughter, and Chelli, Clarke's daughter.

It felt strange to be alone. No kids, no husband. To be alone with my parents in the old house. Alone in bed in their old bedroom. I could hear my heart, breath, and blood echoing off the walls of the universe. (That's the way I wrote it in my first journal.)

A beautiful, familiar young man entered the room, came up the narrow space between the bed and the crib. He bent over me, touched the inside of my thigh, was coming down on me. I struggled to scream through the paralysis of sleep. I fought him, his overwhelming physical strength, the engulfing darkness of his Goliath chest. I struggled to reach the nightstand light, to turn it on. If I could turn on the light he'd disappear. I wrestled with him, his forearms, my arms against his arms, pushing them away, my arms twisting and tangling in his. The fast slapping of his skin on my skin, the smell of his flesh. I screamed, managed to get to my feet, was fully out of the bed fighting him off, banging against the crib, beating him away trying to keep me from turning on the light. When I finally got the light on and he disappeared, I realized I'd screamed at least three times loud enough to wake my parents.

I stood stranded between the bed and crib. My whole body, arms and legs but especially my heart, hurt from the terror and the effort to scream out of my sleep; then, more and more awake, in confusion and humiliation. How could I lose control like that? How will I ever explain those screams? I'd surely awakened my parents.

But no one came. And then I fell into grief, overwhelming sorrow for the disappeared man.

A few weeks or months later I was again sleeping in my parents' old bedroom. This time Shawn was sleeping in the crib. The man came in the room again. The terror was so great it felt like I was having a heart attack. Again, no one responded to my screams except Shawn, who started crying. I grabbed her, rocked her back to sleep in bed with me. I remember waking to my mother's nightmare screams when I was little. The sorrow and regret, the feel and smell of his flesh, the sense that I'd failed him. Whatever did he want?

The next evening I was down at their closed office, Edens Real Estate, studying. Mama was taking care of Danny and Shawn. Suddenly, in the middle of a paragraph I was reading, I remembered the nightmare and then the terrible sorrow that came with it. Then I remembered that it had happened before, the first time I slept in that room. I remembered what

I've never been able to forget, the man from the very first night we slept in that house, who walked through the kitchen and living room and then stood at our door, one of my all-time worst nightmares. I called them up, excited. "Did you hear me screaming last night?" "Well, yes, we did," Mama said, "was something wrong?"

"There's a ghost in that house!"

How thrilling to think this. Our very own ghost.

He was handsome, young, in an exquisite gray suit. Or a white dress shirt, jacketless. He wanted me to go with him. He pleaded with me not to turn on the light, he fought to keep me from it. I kept seeing him leave through the door, fleeing back down the hallway, his shoulders hunched around his chest, screaming no! no! no! The nausea I was wracked with for having failed him rises as bile even as I write this. My ghost haunted me. I told of him to my family, to my new love, Max, to my girlfriends, to my sister (who to this day argues it was a real ghost, not a dream hallucination of our father; she saw him a number of times too in the Ramona house). I told our new neighbor when we moved to LA. Esther conducted Ouija board séances, came up with a story about a man in 1913 who died in a Victorian garden on the spot where the Ramona house was now, a story of a woman he loved. Maybe he killed her. She brought back instructions that I am to release him, that he's stuck in the Ramona house, that only through me can he get free. All this was even more mystifying. I was fairly certain there was nothing on that hill in 1913, that by then it was already a long-abandoned Indian village site, just metates left in the morteros y ollas of the granite slabs. Any true ghost of the place would not be wearing a white man's suit.

I determined that the next time I slept in the room I would not fight him no matter how great the terror. I would try to meet him. I would try and go with him. This would be a spiritual task. His soul needed release. I needed to know who he was.

But he comes only when I'm not waiting for him. He comes to have his way with me, not me with him. After Ramona he came in all my places, he haunted all my beds. In all the years I called him "my ghost" I pondered the realness of his flesh, the feel and sound and smell of his flesh slapping my flesh.

I was home, in my parents' former bedroom. I was on my father's side of the bed, in the space he slept in for years. I was sleeping alone for the first time since I left their house as a bride, actually for the first time since Bridget's birth, with whom I'd been living again. Family restirred. Being married had been a shield to the memories. I was beginning to write. Let the images rise. It was the crib over me like Clarke's in Hollydale.

And the ghost came too that first time because my first lover's wife found us in bed that summer, me in orgasm. I opened my eyes to screams not mine, to a woman over us. Until that moment I hadn't known Milton Foster was married. (You can keep your vow never to be with a married man only if you know he's married.) How memory and the mind work. That horrible experience of her over us, the shocking revelation in orgasm of his betrayal of her with me, of me with her and however innocent, of my betrayal of her, awakened the memory of my father over me, his betrayal of my mother with me. But mostly the memory started because we had dissolved the marriage, the structure that was held together by not thinking many many things.

For years I said I'd recognize my ghost anywhere. I looked for him in crowds and on the street. The mind is a natural riddle maker; this is how it works both to inform and to fool itself. Of course you would recognize him, Sharon Lura, you know damn well who he is, but you keep turning on the light. You keep struggling to stay in day consciousness that's allowed you to forget.

What did my father think about my screaming, the ghost/haunted-house theory? "I've never forgotten what I did to you for a single day of my life," he said when he confessed. Did it fill him with terror, the fear of exposure, as did my modern art, my getting an education? Was it at such times that he redoubled his campaign to vilify and demonize me to the rest of the family so that no one would believe me if I told? If I did become a writer like Mama kept prophesying?

When I got home the early evening after the second appearance I limped in pain as I came from the car. My old arthritis, or whatever it was, had flared up in my ankle for the first time since high school. He was standing, hidden, under the front pepper tree, watching me. "Hypochondriac," he hissed, just like he did that first time in the second grade. I could hardly breathe for the sharp cut through my chest, the ankle-collapsing hurt. But something else too—almost consciousness of his conscious cruelty. I never had "arthritis" again.

§

Thirty-Four
Carry No Purse, No Bag, No Sandals, Nor Two Tunics

I'm twenty-eight.
I wear a thrift store yellow silk lace lingerie top
and hip hugger bell bottoms
every day for three years
When it's over a hundred
I rinse the top, put it on wet
In minutes I'm cool, dry, clean, finally
Beautiful

I stop writing
so as not to remember more

So as to forgive

I try to remember the moment. I do, but it is outside time and place, though I know it was on Topanga Beach in September 1969. The white churning waves are coming in to that extraordinary place of light and motion, and across the sky along the ocean horizon Daddy's fingers are delicately twisting my right nipple.

After a six month adventure around the country in our Falcon station wagon, we returned to LA and found the magical beach cabin. Danny started fourth grade and Shawn first. I hadn't anticipated what this would mean, that I would have a few hours alone each day. Max urged me to write. We would get food stamps, which he regarded as a political act, and he'd bring in the money.

First I had to finish my Master's. I had an Incomplete in Creative Writing and one week left to make it up. There was this story I'd been writing all through college that I hadn't been able to finish, about the anguished love between a father and a daughter, who, inexplicably, could not, for all the longing in both, communicate. The problem was it wasn't a story, there was no plot, there wasn't an ending, and I wanted it thus. I couldn't bring myself to make up something. My professors were Aristotelian New Formalists who demanded plot—character, crisis, climax and closure—a far cry from the experimentalists I was reading on my own and loving. I wrote endlessly around one haunting image, which probably had its origin in dream.

My father is outside the house at the sliding glass door on the side deck begging me to let him in. Behind him the night land is cold, alive and thinking. The full moon is coming up over the rolling blue-gold hills and purple peaks of the Santa Maria Valley. The pregnant lady of granite lies on her back, the southern horizon. Someday she will birth, the Indians say, she will sit up, she will stand up, and when that happens, the land will be theirs again. Sometimes a band of coyotes runs behind my father, howling, sometimes he moves to the front glass door so that the moon is behind his big head like a halo. I'm right behind the glass, inside the house, warm and secure. Our faces are separated only by the glass. His eyes, which my mother always said are my eyes, are large with tears. So are mine. He begs me to let him in. He is hurt to tears that I won't open the door. I cannot understand why I won't. But I can't. I die a thousand deaths in our tears running down the same stream, almost the same face, my face to his face, but I am on the inside of impenetrable glass and I can't, I won't open the door.

But then, under the deadline pressure—I had to have my Master's Degree—on the Wednesday before it was due Friday morning, the mysterious glass shattered. I put into words for the first time what those sickening, harrowing years, between nine and twelve, as I remembered then, had been. I wrote *"California Daughter/1950."* I'd never heard or read such a thing. No one was writing or telling this kind of story then.

This revelatory moment. My father's hands at my girl breasts, my father making me look at his penis in his hands had lain across everything, conversations with others, across their faces, strangers coming down the street, across the landscapes and towns we traveled, the classrooms, the blackboards, across my dates and lovers (I went blind to those images to find sexual pleasure), and yet without language the images were somehow inaccessible, not knowable. Nothing has ever informed me more about the nature of language and the mind.

And yet I remembered in language at other times, or almost. I undertook the father-daughter story when I learned that incest is a theme in Southern literature. I remember the moment I first learned this, the desk I was sitting in, thinking, oh, that's why! Daddy's Southern. I remember a lecture by a prominent visiting professor on the misanthropic, "naturally murderous," father-son theme that runs through Western literature. Hatred steamed from the so-called objective scholar, a bitter, ironic malaise identical to my father's with me, Mama, and Clarke. I remember thinking if Father/Son is an important literary theme, so then is Father/Daughter.

Bang! The images exploded from the biggest wave at the exact moment of high tide, leaving words on the page.

I was blown away most of all by just the stunning fact of what my father had done with me. To say it, to grasp what saying it meant. I was blown away by the fact that it wasn't that I had forgotten, I just hadn't had it in words.

That night in bed I told Max. He was astonished too, and he praised me, then and for our remaining five years, for not being angry at my father. He loved me for that. Then we made love and I knew he was seeing my father at me. In recent history I've asked him to tell me his memory of this moment. He gets defensive, annoyed, says we didn't know then what we know now about molestation. That's true, but I never got off on it sexually as he did, I knew that much, and it was a hurting turn-off that he did. I know he came close to introducing the fact into our sex acts, but always abandoned that, sensing my objection. I was grateful he was at least that sensitive and I'm grateful he's never pretended this didn't happen.

Bang! One moment. I see the images coming in on the waves to Topanga. Most of the molestation memories I've written here came in one giant flash, and most are in the sixteen page *California Daughter* story I wrote then. It's possible I've remembered all the important incidences, though the fact that I didn't remember the rape at seven (except in nightmares) until he told me, despite meditating on (and continuing to nightmare) his molestations regularly afterwards, makes this highly suspect. I didn't remember Uncle Marion. I didn't remember the two men who stalked me for a week until their numerous appearances in my journal of nightmares and poems were enough to motivate me to ask my mother a second time about their possibility. (I didn't recognize Gae. I quit loving her and Ramon.)

I was in shock about what I had written but the excited attention I then received turned the shock into aversion and panic. My Creative Writing professor, a successful novelist and a man who had let me know through my entire career on campus of his sexual desire for me, said my story was brilliant. He passed it around the English department. I was offered a full scholarship to the Ph.D program at the University of Iowa, and another, if for some reason I was unable to leave California, to the University of California at Irvine. But I was certain the brilliance of my story was its sensational subject matter, not my writing; I was certain they were just interested in working with a girl who'd had sex with her father and dared to write about it. I was certain I had no other story in me though no telling what else would come out if I kept writing. I certainly did not want to move south again, to conservative Orange County; it'd taken me years to get back to LA, and Iowa, to a Southern California girl, was unfathomable. I turned down the fellowships. I took a vow never to be a creative writer. I dropped out completely, began a critical book on the structure of the Molly Bloom soliloquy in James Joyce's *Ulysses,* and began with Max to develop a counter culture hippie life in which to raise our children in a more healthy, loving, life-affirming way than we had been raised.

Then, in 1972, after three years on Topanga Beach, we were looking for another big adventure. Many of our friends in protest to the Vietnam War were leaving the country, but I was still drawn to America. The East Coast seemed as foreign to us, all Southern California natives, as we could imagine and still be in America. Somehow not intending to break my vow, I applied to the Provincetown Fine Arts Work Center on Cape Cod in Massachusetts and had to submit a work sample. I had only one thing that could possibly win a full fellowship—all living expenses, plus a stipend for nine months for my family of four. Mindlessly, I submitted *California Daughter*, thinking I'd handle it later in the unlikelihood I got in. I was chosen as one of two alternates, and told that the odds of one of the ten writers in front of me dropping out was significant. Provincetown, Massachusetts became our goal and destination. We'd arrive opening day and I'd be ready to take my place if the opening was there.

Two poets on the faculty were Howard Moss and Louise Glück. I found Louise's *First Born* along with Galway Kinnel's *Book of Nightmares* in the downtown Los Angeles Public Library, on a little wooden bookshelf labeled Contemporary Small Press Poetry Publications. Checking these out became my first encounter with the notion that one could be a poet in the contemporary world.

But when we arrived in Provincetown I could not knock on the door. They just want to lay their eyes on the girl who wrote that story. I sat paralyzed and mute in the suicide seat. I want to continue with James Joyce. The kids grabbed the map of New England, found the state with the most ski symbols. We want Vermont! And off we went in search of Vermont, me greatly relieved. We lived in Plainfield, Vermont for the next two years, with, coincidentally, Louise Glück as a near neighbor. Plainfield, the village of Goddard College, just happened to be a town of poets.

In 1976, living on Albion Ridge just south of Mendocino, California, *California Daughter/1950* was published by the New York feminist magazine, *Aphra*, under the initials D.S. The consciousness-raising groups had come up with the revelatory commonness of incest—*"one of the more spectacular revelations of modern women—that a quarter of us and more are raped as children."[14]* —and the search was on for the writing. Someone in Provincetown had told *Aphra* of my story. After some pressure by mail and phone—I needed to do this for my sisters—and the promise of anonymity, I relented. It was chosen for Martha Foley's *One Hundred Distinguished American Short Stories of 1976.* For a brief period after the publication I was hounded by New York literary agents despite the editor's promise. My mother, who was contacted in the search for me, stirring the old panic, would say I know Sharon's going to write a bestseller someday, I have her first poem in my Bible. I would think, Oh Mama, the only bestseller in me is about you and Daddy.

California Daughter/1950: I always said it started at nine when my mother was in the sanitarium. I didn't remember then the rape, but the story centers mainly in February 1949 when she was gone. I was in the second grade, I was still seven. The pre MA writing goes back earlier than that:

Coming up the deck stairs was Judy Clare, just the same as in kindergarten, but bigger. She still had the mannerism of holding her head in an arrogant tilt.

What is a father, what is a daughter, what is wrong between us? I looked at my father, my head tilted, a Judy Clare smile curling my face and went over to open the door. Judy Clare knew how to be a daughter. Judy Clare knew how to show her love for her father. But as I approached mine his face was blank and he looked past me, not recognizing me.

My mother is worried that I don't know my own self.

On my son's eleventh birthday, September 25, 1971, my father had a near-fatal heart attack in Portland, Oregon while visiting his brother K.D., himself recuperating from a heart attack. The news came three days later as a post card from my mother. Later Aunt Alice told me she had to admonish her, "Audrey, you *have* to tell them, he's their father." I took it then to mean she couldn't bear to tell us, not that she didn't want to share him in this. I remember driving into Santa Monica, finding Max at a construction site and then being completely mute, unable to say the words though his time clock was ticking: *my father has had a heart attack.* I've read since that incest victims have a greater than normal fear of the death of a parent perpetrator because the full story can never be told then, there'll never be resolution. But of course it's far more than that, it's the complexity of the emotions the crisis stirs. Muteness—alexytemia, the inability to verbalize the trauma—is a primary characteristic of incest victims.

I borrowed the money from our drug dealer neighbors and flew to Portland. To do this I managed to stutter and stammer, my left eyelid ticking in a similar rhythm, and a sore place spreading deep under my left breast. On the plane, my second flight ever, I went mute again, a great panic in itself. More than anything I was terrified that I might have to be alone with him, a fear that filled me with guilt, but whatever would I say? Desperate for words I began to write to him, a kind of prayer to him to live, a prayer to the many businessmen of his generation on the plane who all reeked of incest to me. Or was that odor coming from me? *Fly me back to before, Daddy. To before, before, Daddy.* Mama picked me up. She said it was the odor of fear, she had it too. For years she had sworn "if your father dies so will I." On St. Vincent's high floor I still couldn't speak. Bridget says I put on lipstick for the first time since I'd become a hippie. "'For Daddy,' you stammered, 'to make him feel better.'" It was instinctual acupressure, to open my mouth, to release the words. I entered Intensive Care, my head tilted like Judy Clare's. He saw my panic, my frozen dumbness, and though his heart had stopped seven times already, was alive only because of the electric paddle, he took over. He talked of my cousin Joal. What was wrong with Joal was her stepfather had molested her as a girl. My ears rang. I was going to faint. He continued, directly into my distress, past the wires plugged into him and the machine showing his heart beat above him, about how terrible and wrong that was for Joal. It felt like he was fathering me, it felt like it was the first time my father had ever fathered me. Then as I was leaving his heart stopped for the eighth time. On the other side of the bridge waiting to greet him was his old childhood friend who drowned, Stanley Payne welcoming him with open arms, and *amazing grace*, forgiveness. The alarms went off. Nurses and doctors rushed past me through the swinging doors. When they shocked him back this time he pleaded that they not use the paddle again, no matter what his wife demanded. He was ready to go.

His heart attack was diagnosed as being caused by a potassium deficiency from the Stillman Water Diet he'd been on. We were all instructed to get an electrocardiogram. Potassium deficiency is hereditary. I had mine later that month in Santa Monica. The electrocardiogram showed that one of the two main arteries in my heart was completely gone—dissolved is the word I remember—that my heart had formed parallel blood vessels to accommodate this loss. He said if it had been the other artery it would have killed me. He said I had had a heart attack when I was around seven.

Bridget had a similar test result in San Diego. She had the heart of a very old woman, the result of potassium deficiency from years of diuretics and laxatives, and from having had a heart attack at age five. She denies this now—she triumphs "this shows how Sharon makes things up!"—but that is what she wrote me then, and that is what was told to me repeatedly by our mother in her last decade. Bridget says in her book she had a heart attack when young.

That Christmas, our father miraculously still alive, but still in Oregon, I pulled my plane prayer from the journal, and honed and edited it into a two page poetic piece, *Carry Me Back Taddy*. I was three years into daily work with James Joyce's Molly Bloom soliloquy. *Carry Me Back Taddy* is a line out of *Finnegans Wake*. To speak like that, in Joyce's free association/ automatic/preverbal/the images-on-your breath/dream language, to be in the air flying to my dying father, opened me to language I'd been unable to access since the news, words I could, and somehow did, write. They swirled around free of grammar and spelling and the other demanded constraints. I managed to say carry me back Taddy to when I was a wee girl before it got all fucked up. Carry me to that Daddy before we died. Carry me back Taddy before you die.

And he did.

It is hard to know the boundaries. Both my parents will use those words when he tells of raping me at seven. But I wasn't confused about the boundaries. I was expressing in that writing, *Carry Me Back Taddy*, my love of him though *he* broke the boundaries, I was going right to the broken boundary lines and past in my prayer that he not die, or die of a guilty broken heart, to know before it's too late that I forgive him, that I love him despite his trespasses. I was expressing my love of his body out of which I came, that boundary-less source, which was in great peril. *Let me waltz with you still Taddy, let me climb on your toes again Taddy, give me a horsy ride around the room Daddy.*

Incest is not a taboo, the famous saying went, but telling of it is. The feminists, those raw, hysterical women, were insisting that we confront our abusers. The advice, the articles, the instructions on how to do this seem to be everywhere, even in *Dear Abby*. I longed to tell my father directly that I forgave him for what he did to me, I so feared he suffered guilt. I wanted to explore it with him—had he been molested as a boy? I

wanted to tell him I understood our culture's contribution to this, that he
was a victim too, rapist being close to its definition of the male. But I
wasn't sure that he remembered. And the danger that such a confrontation
would kill him, as it almost did in the hospital, and my mother too—well, I
always decided it was not my place to do the confronting, it was theirs.
They should come to me.

My denials, my forgiveness, were many things, certainly a survival
technique. But my denials: I never worried for my children about the
common danger of sexual molestation and assault, nor for the five children
of my sister and brother with whom I was close—not with neighbors, with
my men, with the world, with my father. I was overly lax in all things
sexual with them. I was unable to even warn them, or to suggest anything
negative about sex, because that would be revealing and informing myself
about what had happened to me. I know now it's characteristic of incest
victims to believe they are the only ones—because it is so horrible, so
outrageous, so taboo, so unspeakable, so impossible to compute, such an
aberration, such a sin—but my blankness with my children is almost un-
forgiveable, is the thing I cannot forgive in myself.

And now I find the Christmas version of *Carry Me Back Taddy* I sent him
among her things and read it with my new understanding of my mother,
her sense that I was her rival for him, and I want to die again. I read it now
succumbing to the powerful taboo I was always fighting, that I must not
articulate love of my father from the truth of our relationship, that I must
not address the issue even as he's dying. *Carry Me Back Taddy* sounds
sexual, seductive, it sounds like my love for him was sexual. (No, but our
relationship was sexual.) It could read like I'm trying to fuck him back
from death. I finally allow now that it read that way to her.

St. Vincent's Hospital employed the youngest, most attractive nurses
in Intensive Care. This was explained to us, his wife and daughters and
granddaughters, by the hospital staff, as being part of the cure. There's a
photograph Bridget took of Daddy and a nurse flirting; there's a first poem
I wrote *"how placing your hand on the nurse's behind, Daddy/as she took
your blood pressure/is what saved you./Even as the Germans placed/naked
female Jews on their dying soldiers."* The first thing he told me when I
walked into the room was of the prostitute in Regina, Canada who had
propositioned him a few days before. "I'm like you two," he kept saying,
meaning Bridget and me, meaning "the river of life" he mumbled,
meaning, I think, sexuality, or maybe the free spirit. Monique and Simone,

Bridget's daughters celebrating their sixth and third birthdays that week, performed exotic/erotic dances for him. Anything and everything to make our father want to live.

The brush with death changed him, Mama and Bridget exclaimed forever afterwards. Many times I heard Bridget tell "First he was up near the ceiling and he could see the medical team trying to resuscitate him. He heard the doctor say 'he's had it!' Daddy yelled back 'whatever it is, I don't want it!' but nobody heard him. Suddenly he was walking over a bridge with a dry river bed underneath. Walking to greet him was Stanley Payne, his best friend who drowned. He was overjoyed to see Stanley who greeted him warmly, told him to observe everything because he had to go back. 'Why?' 'Because you haven't learned a damned thing, Fred. You haven't learned how to love.' Right then my father opened his eyes into the startled gaze of a nurse. The words 'I love you' came out of his mouth. Then he said I love you to each nurse and doctor in the room."

Daddy knew love now, he knew the value, the joy of life. He was on Portland's Six O'clock News. He and the sexy nurse, not he and Mama. Ninety-five percent of all men with myocardial infarction the severity of his do not survive. The surviving five percent are dead in five years.

He survived and that became one of the miracles of love in the Edens' mythology. He survived because of our mother's nursing, her research into all aspects of his disease, her studied dismissal of much of the doctors' advice, especially their medication, her undertaking the radical change in his diet, red meat, bacon and potatoes being a culprit. She rebuilt his heart. She even quit drinking coffee, "my greatest vice," because he had to. Aunt Alice did not quit smoking though Uncle K.D. had to. This is why Kermit David Edens did not survive. Alice Edens didn't love him enough.

"For the remaining sixteen years of my father's life," Bridget expounded at the Celebration of our father's life, *Amazing Grace* playing triumphantly behind her, "Daddy was making up for lost time. He learned to listen, to really hear others, to take great interest in all aspects of the lives of others. He traveled extensively with Mama to various parts of the world trying to understand people from different cultures, making amends for the past with all the family members, and immensely enjoying the company of his grandchildren.

"Knowing there was a limited time to get all that he could out of the life he so loved, as well as give all he could to all of us, he went as far as I think a human being can go. He seemed like a Master at the end. He opened! I've never known a human being to open so completely. It takes such a great love, I think, to open that much and let us all in.

"Daddy grew so much in his illness. He had said that no one had ever coached him on dying, and so that's what we did. For those last three and a half hours, we stood around his bed, laughing, crying and cheering him on. We felt so a part of his birthing experience, for that's what it was like for us, a birthing. It was very beautiful, and Daddy healed us all. It was the finest gift of my life. We were all left with the deepest bonding, the most profound fulfillment and an extraordinary joy. As I said, Daddy healed us all."

Not only did he survive another sixteen years—his rebuilt heart wouldn't stop beating when everything else had shut down—but he survived to molest at least one of his grandchildren, Clarke's daughter, Chelli Dawn.

§

NOTES

[1] (Author's Notes) The "memory wars" have been conducted by a political, right-wing, fundamentalist Christian think tank, The False Memory Syndrome Foundation; much academic and journalistic research has revealed this now, including its blocking of publications and reviews. See for instance: *Trauma and Recovery,* Judith Lewis Herman, M.D., Basic Books, 1992, 1997; *Telling Incest, Narratives of Dangerous Remembering from Stein to Sapphire,* Janice Haaken and Devon L. Hodges, The University of Michigan Press, 2002; *The Limits of Autobiography,* Leigh Gilmore, Cornell University Press, 2001, pp 28-30; *The Writer's Chronicle, Special Commemorative Issue,* AWP, George Mason University, 2002.

[2] (Chapter 1) from *Hard Country,* Minneapolis, West End Press, 1982, 1999. All poem citations are from *Hard Country* unless otherwise noted.

[3] (Chapter 1) Sarah Susie Simmons Clarke died a few minutes after midnight, April 21, 1924, but Easter Sunday, April 20, 1924, the last time my mother saw her mother alive, was always the mourned date. My mother hated Easter Sundays.

[4] (Chapter 3) The Diary of Maude Lura Chitwood Edens, 1889-1953. And all subsequent entries.

[5] (Chapter 4) from "Lady Godiva," a first poem.

[6] (Chapter 8) "Santas," *Body and Soul,* Sharon Doubiago, Cedar Hill Publications, 2000.

[7] (Chapter 8) Ibid.

[8] There are conflicting birth and death dates for Christopher Columbus Simmons. In her *Memoir* his daughter Luella says that he died at 51, and that her grandfather, John Simmons, was still alive. This conflicts with my mother's accounts.

[9] (Chapter 9) The historical events of the era must be a part of this analysis: "In England during the 1630s a long and tangled series of events was slowly coming to a head.The process was throwing off refugees by the hundreds and thousands who were coming to the New World to escape the conflict in the Old, which we call the Puritan Revolution.The beginning of the end, so to speak, may be designated by the infamous 'Star Chamber' of 1637, a sort of English Inquisition in which men were forced to voice their loyalty to the Church of England, or face the loss of property and freedom. Immediately, thousands of English Catholics and Puritans left their homeland, and came to America." *A Witness for Eleanor Dare, The Final Chapter in a 400 Year Old Mystery,* Robert W. White, Lexikos, San Francisco, 1991. p. 205. Both Catholics and Puritans were on the Baltimore.

[10] (Chapter 21) "Letter To My Father on his 65th Birthday," *Psyche Drives The Coast,* Empty Bowl, 1990.

[11] (Chapter 30) "Ramon/Ramona," *The Book of Seeing With One's Own Eyes,* Graywolf, 1988, p.5.) And all subsequent prose quotes in this chapter.

[12] Hite, Shire, *The Hite Report on the Family, Growing Up Under Patriarchy,* Grove Press, 1995, c. 1994, p. 104.

[13] (Chapter 32) "Imperforate Hymen: Congenital or Acquired from Sexual Abuse," http://pediatrics.aappublications.org/cgi/content/full/108/3/e53.

[14] (Chapter 34) Judy Grahn, blurb, *The Obsidian Mirror,* Louise M. Wisechild, Seal Press, 1988.

THE FAMILIES
Paternal: Hancock-Corn-Chitwood-Edens

John Hancock, a decorated Revolutionary War soldier, but evidently—despite what I was told all my childhood—not the one who was the first to sign the Declaration of Independence, built his plantation on land bordering Thomas Jefferson's Monticello in today's Charlottesville, Virginia. (The land survey was done by Peter Jefferson, Thomas Jefferson's father.) The records show that John Hancock, unlike Thomas Jefferson, did not own slaves. His daughter Nancy Hancock married Jesse Corn, also a decorated Revolutionary War soldier; he was at Valley Forge with George Washington, and in the Battle of Guilford Courthouse, South Carolina, March 15, 1781; after the Revolution he was a pioneer farmer, land speculator, member of the Virginia House of Delegates, store owner in Goblintown, Patrick County, Virginia, and a Primitive Baptist traveling elder. Jesse and Nancy had ten children, the fifth being Mary Corn Sharp, born August 8, 1789, the eighth being my great-great-great grandmother, Nancy Ann Corn Chitwood, born April 1, 1797. When her son, my great-great-grandfather, John Chitwood, born August 10, 1815, was three years old, the entire Hancock-Corn family (except for Jesse Corn Jr.), and the Chitwoods, McCutcheons, and Sharps, (husbands of the Corn daughters) and apparently Martins and Stovalls, migrated to the Elk River in Tennessee, and pioneered Estill Springs and Winchester. (But James Sharp, Mary Corn's husband, appears on the 1812 Franklin County tax list so they may have been there that early.) On the death of James Sharp in 1848, Mary Corn Sharp endowed the first academic college in the U.S. for women, the Mary Sharp College—"Latin and Greek are *sine qua non* for graduation, mathematics, science and logic are prominent"[1]— and in 1852 emancipated her slaves, giving them the choice of going anywhere they wanted with her financial aid and protection, or staying in Winchester with the same terms. She paid passage for 82 former slaves to Liberia, Africa, her nephew-secretary, my great-great grandfather, John Chitwood, making the arrangements.[2] This Estill Springs-Winchester family, consisting of four separate households, the males being preachers, justices-of-the-peace, educators and, some (the Sharps), cotton plantation slave owners, are the four families of the area that sided with the North during the Civil War, incurring much loss, infamy, ostracism, death and still-lingering psychological wounds. ("Franklin County was directly on the line of the contending armies, and consequently her citizens suffered greatly from the ravages of war. ...Estill Springs was almost entirely destroyed during the war..."[3])

Mary Sharp died May 9, 1864, her college during the four years of the War staging ground and hospital for both armies. My grandmother, Maude Lura Chitwood (daughter of John Chitwood's son George Washington Chitwood), whose diary is quoted throughout *My Father's Love*, was born on the Elk River, April 26, 1880, in a homestead given to her mother, Nancy, from her parents, Jane Winn Goodloe and Mikajah P. Reagan, the Estill Springs church founder and minister. Maude Lura married my grandfather Marion Avon Edens, on July 3, 1906, in the Baptist Parsonage in Winchester, Tennessee.

Although there is evidence that there were Edens in Tennessee as early as 1558,[4] the first official Edens were on the *Baltimore* which landed at what is today Baltimore, Maryland, "the second English ship, after the Mayflower, to America" (Maude Edens). The Edens also were Revolutionary War soldiers, and as with the Chitwoods, brothers fought and died on both sides. (The name was originally Eden; those for Independence added an *s* to distinguish themselves from those who remained loyal to England, such as Sir John Eden, the governor of Maryland in 1776.) Male ancestors were also in the Battle of New Orleans (the War of 1812), and at the Alamo. Avon Edens' mother was Phoebe Stovall Overby whose weavings are in Tennessee museums and history books; his father was Francis Marion Edens, one of the few survivors of "Turney's Men," the 1,200 Tennessee volunteers who organized on the grounds of Mary Sharp College and went off to the first battle at Bull Run in Virginia before Tennessee declared secession; later, during the Battle of Chickamauga near Chattanooga (estimated casualties, 34,624), he walked away with his older brother, Samuel. They walked home to Lynchburg where upon arrival their mother, Nancy Franks Edens, had them arrested for desertion. In 1867 Francis Marion Edens built a farmhouse at Beech Hill outside of Lynchburg, still in residential use today. My grandfather Marion Avon was born February 15, 1878, the seventh of eight children. (His brother, born in 1854, was the well-known physician of the era/area, Dr. William M. Edens; he was the Chitwood's physician). Athena, the youngest, died at one year, leaving Avon the baby of the family.) This family was also Primitive Baptist.

Avon and Maude Lura Edens had five children, Lucile, Marion, the twins Kermit David (K.D.) and Kenneth, and the youngest, my father, Cecil Frederick, who was born February 14, 1916, in the copper mining town of Ducktown, Tennessee.

Maternal: Reynolds-Swain-Willits-Simmons-Jackson-Clarke
The Reynolds and Swains were Quakers (from which the profound family
heritage of survival through love is surely partially rooted) who settled on
the Cape Fear River of North Carolina (possibly as early as 1650). As with
the Corn-Chitwoods, most of this family, though loyal soldiers of the
Confederacy, were anti-slavery—North Carolina was the last state to
secede, consistently voting anti-slavery—and thus similarly incurred
infamy, loss and danger. Five sons of Mary Ann Swain Simmons—the
father, Stephen A. Simmons born January 10, 1806, is otherwise
"Unknown;" possibly he was Indian—fought in the Civil War, four of
whom died; the Town Creek plantation on which my great-grandfather,
Christopher Columbus Simmons (born March 2, 1868) was raised—son of
the lone survivor, John Burrows Simmons (born April 24, 1847)—was
finally lost in 1902 after years of resistance to the infamous Wilmington-
based carpetbagger/white supremacist terrorism.

My great-grandmother, Elizabeth Reynolds (born October 2, 1869) of
Town Creek, had a child, Olive, "out of wedlock" between the ages of
thirteen to fifteen by her German piano teacher. She married Christopher
Columbus Simmons about ten years later and had ten more children, seven
of whom survived to adulthood—Ernest, Dewey, Sarah Susie, Myrtle,
Maybelle, Luella and Bessie. Sarah Susie Simmons was my mother's
mother. Elizabeth Reynolds Simmons died September 14, 1935 in
Lynchburg, Virginia. Cause of death: rape and murder.

Christopher Columbus Simmons' Native American heritage is mostly
unknown, but it has been deduced that his mother was Eahnee, a Chero-
kee/ Lumbee woman buried at Black Mountain, North Carolina; when I
was a child my mother always said we were Cherokee, Seminole and
Choctaw. CC's youngest sister Belle (d. 1979), of whom I have three
photos, looked, according to my mother, "just like him;" she looks full-
blooded Indian.

Susie Simmons (born June 12, 1899) married Guy Henry Clarke (born
December 9, 1896) in 1916 and had three children, Lawrence (b. 1917),
Garnet Audrey (my mother, b. March 27, 1920), and Mozelle Virginia (b.
September 26, 1922). She died at the age of 24 of tuberculosis in Danville,
Virginia, April 21, 1924 when my mother was four years and three weeks
old, and is buried in the Mt. Carmel Church cemetery on Oregon Road,
northeast of Reidsville, North Carolina.

My other maternal great-grandmother, Guy Henry Clarke's mother, was Nancy Jackson of Spartanburg, South Carolina, Asheville and Roan Mountain, North Carolina, Danville and Lynchburg, Virginia. Nancy and her mother, Hester Andrews Clark, and two sisters are listed on the Cherokee Rolls of 1900, and though the two sisters are on the 1924 Final Rolls, my great-grandmother Nancy is not. However, her genealogy records go back to the Cherokee territory, 1793, with the first US census, in which Ca-tal-sta Catalst and her son, Saloli (Fox Squirrel), born in 1791, are listed. (The Cherokee/Native American heritage is surely also part of my family's survival-by-love heritage.) Guy Clarke, "that redheaded Irish Cherokee," was raised in Asheville, Roan Mountain and, from about twelve, in Juvenile Detention in Richmond, Virginia. The persistent family lore has always been that Guy's father was the grandson of William Rogers Clark of the Lewis and Clark expedition, but no records of Charles Rogers Clark have been found. (Records for the 1890 U.S. census were destroyed in a fire in 1921. Several accounts say Charles Rogers Clark came from St. Louis, longtime home of William Rogers Clark. Given the insistence of the telling, and other factors, I continue to regard it.)

Guy Henry Clarke, my mother's father, died in Danville, Virginia, January 25, 1936 from complications of lung surgery. She was fifteen. His death occurred four months after her maternal grandmother's rape and murder.

My Great-Grandparents on My Father's Paternal Side:
Francis Marion Edens: b. September 9, 1832; d. Dec 25, 1912, Franklyn, County, Tennessee. (His father: Samuel G. Edens. His mother: Nancy Franks. They migrated into Tennessee from New Market, Alabama in (___)

Phoebe Stovall Overby Edens: b. 1839; d 1895. (In my 1988 journal there's a rubbing I made of her gravestone at Marble Plains Methodist Church and Cemetery, suggesting she was Methodist, not Primitive Baptist. Interesting, Jesse Corn Sr. is buried in the Corn-Stovall Cemetary of Goblintown, Patrick County, Virigina (1809), suggesting that her family, the Stovalls, also came from Patrick County, Virginia.)

My Great-Grandparents on My Father's Maternal side:
George Washington Chitwood: b. November 17, 1847; d. March 11, 1915 in Estill Springs, Tennessee. Maude Lura's father, the third son of

John Chitwood and Francis Martin. In her diary there is an account of him at twelve encountering the Union army on the Elk, the implications being that he never fully recovered psychologically.

Nancy Goodloe Reagan (Reagin) Chitwood: b. July 7, 1859 ; d. Sunday, September 20, 1914, Estill Springs, Tennnessee. Her father: Mikajah P. Reagan (d. Jan 3, 1902), known as Kaj, "founded the church in Estill Springs." Her mother was Jane Winn Goodloe of Virginia. "Jane Winn Goodloe was fifteen when she was sent from Virginia to marry Kaj. She charmed everyone." Audrey Garnet Edens.

My Paternal Grandparents:
Edens, Maude Lura Chitwood, b. April 26, 1880, Estill Springs, Tennessee; died November 18, 1953, Hollydale, California.
Edens, Marion Avon, b. February 15, 1878, near Lynchburg, Tennessee; died May 27, 1948, Los Angeles, California.
The children of Maude and Avon Edens:
Nancy Lucile Edens (Aunt Lucile): b. August 14, 1907, Ducktown Tennessee; d. November 27, 1978, Georgia. Mother of cousins Nancy Walton Cook and Jimmy Walton.

Marion Chitwood Edens (Uncle Marion): b. July 15, 1909; d. March 3, 1992. Husband of Aunt Elizabeth.

Kermit David Edens: b. March 19, 1912, Ducktown, Tennessee. Kermit David (Uncle K.D.) d. November 28, 1977 in Aumsville, Oregon. Husband of "**Aunt Alice,**" father of cousins Billie and Shirlie Edens.

James Kenneth (Uncle Kenneth) b. March 19, 1912; d. August 28, 1994 in Georgia. Husband of "**Aunt Mary**, father of James, Bob, and Joseph Edens, Georgia.

Cecil Frederick Edens: b. February 14, 1916, Ducktown, Tennessee; d. September 18, 1987, Florence, Oregon. Husband of **Audrey Garnet Clarke.**

My Great-Grandparents on My Mother's Paternal Side:
Nancy Clark Jackson, b. 1870, Spartanburg, South Carolina; d. Danville (Lynchburg?), Virginia, February 7, 1940. (She's buried in Lynchburg but my recollection, from Harold, is that she died in Danville. Her parents were Andrew Jackson and Hester Andrews.)

Charles Rogers Clark—Unknown. ("Died 1903 in a forest fire on Roan Mountain, or of smallpox in the Ivy Poor House outside of Asheville, North Carolina.")

> **The Children of Nancy Jackson and Charles Rogers Clark:**
> **Dora Clark Spain:** b. May 3, 1890; d. March 6, 1967, Danville, Virginia. "Here's a picture of Dora, an exact picture," my mother said in 1997, handing me a picture of the English actress, Glenda Jackson.
> **Walter Clark,** the father of Myrtle's children (Dewey Harold, Pearl, Hugh, Ina, Harley). WWI wounded veteran who never fully recovered, died age 50 during WWII. Buried in the Oteen Veteran's Cemetery, Ashville, North Carolina.
> **Guy Henry Clarke,** my grandfather: b. December 9, 1896, Asheville, North Carolina; d. January 25, 1936, Danville, Virginia.
> **(Henrietta Hammet,** half-sister born of the union of Nancy Jackson and John Hammet.)

My Great-Grandparents on My Mother's Maternal Side:
Simmons, Christopher Columbus (CC), b. March 2, 1868, Town Creek, North Carolina, d. April or December 1927, Schoolfield, Danville, Virginia. Son of John Burrows Simmons, Civil War veteran, and Eahnee, Cherokee/Lumbee. (The Lumbee legally changed their name from Cherokee in 1952.)
Simmons, Elizabeth Reynolds (Lizzy), b. October 2, 1869, Town Creek, North Carolina; died September 14, 1935. Lynchburg, Virginia.
The Children of Christopher Columbus Simmons and Elizabeth Reynolds Simmons:

> **Ernest Carl,** b. November 20, 1896; d. March 5, 1935. (Father of Lyn Simmons who was the father of Lala Simmons Strader, b. 1939 Danville, Virginia, died September, 2005. Also a son, b. April 26, 1941, the same day I was born; murdered early 1980s.)
> **Sarah Susie Simmons Clarke,** my grandmother: b. June 12, 1899, Town Creek, North Carolina; died April 20-21, 1924, Danville, Virginia. Buried in Mt. Carmel Church Cemetary, Reidsville, North Carolina.
> **Dewey Hobson,** b. February 19, 1901; d. June 18, 1926. ("The one Lizzie depended on. He's buried next to Susie.")

Myrtle Simmons Clark, b. June 6, 1902, died 1967?, mother of
Dewey Harold, Pearl, Hugh, Ina, and Harley. (Hugh's son was
murdered also.)
Maybelle, b. July 16, 1904; d. January 10, 1927.
Sadie Luella Kilmer Simmons Sperry(Aunt Luella), b. January
26, 1908, Wilmington, North Carolina; died May 29, 1990,
Danville Virginia, mother of Seifert and Hallie Sperry.
Bessie Lee: b. September 25, 1911; d.March 13, 1932.

My Maternal Grandparents
Sarah Susie and Guy Henry Clarke (See above.)
Their children:
Lawrence Clarke, b. 1916.
Audrey Garnet Clarke Edens, b. March 27, 1920, Sanford, North
Carolina; d. August 14, 1998, Bandon, Oregon.
Mozelle Virginia Clarke Strickland, b. September 26, 1922; d. April 18,
1999, Green Bay, Wisconsin.

The Double First Cousins :
Dewey Harold, Pearl, Hugh, Ina, Harley Clark, the children of
Walter Clark and Myrtle Simmons
          and **Lawrence, Audrey Garnet, Mozelle Virginia Clark,** the
children of Guy Henry Clarke and Susie Simmons Clarke.
                                        *
My parents Cecil Frederick Edens and Audrey Garnet Clarke
married July 23, 1938, Charlotte, North Carolina (actually, Rock Hill,
South Carolina. "We went over the line to get married.")
                                        *
Other Ancestors mentioned in *My Father's Love*:
The Edens/Chitwood side:
Jesse Corn, b. October 13, 1753, Albermarle County, Virginia; d. March
5, 1809, Patrick County, Virginia.
Nancy Elizabeth Hancock Corn, b. January 17, 1763, Fluvanna County,
Virginia, d. June 17, 1848, Winchester, Tennesee.
Mary Corn Sharp, b. August 8, 1789, Henry County, Virginia; d. May 9,
1864, Winchester, Tennessee. The Sharp plantation was cotton.
Nancy Ann Corn Chitwood McCutcheon, April 1, 1797, Patrick
County, Virginia; d. June 17, 1848, Winchester, Tennessee.

John Chitwood, my great-great-grandfather, my grandmother Maude Lura's grandfather, b. August 10, 1815, Goblintown, Patrick County, Virginia, "died about 1887," Estill Springs, Tennesee. He was the Justice-of-the-Peace, minister and school master, and Mary Sharp's legal secretary. When he sided with the North (or probably more correctly, opposed secession from the Union), "he lost everything, land, congregation, jobs, standing in the community, and his family. His wife wouldn't let him back in the house. So he took up with the housekeeper and had ten (three?) more children by her. When Maude was a girl she wasn't allowed to speak to those cousins." John Chitwood married the housekeeper and mother of his second family, Elizabeth F. Rhew, July 31, 1871. "She was born about 1839." Though he was the main Franklin County recorder from the 1830s-1860s—he married many couples—the records, history and accounts of him and this important Estill Springs family—the Corns, Chitwoods, Sharps—from the Civil War era on, have vanished; I assume in ostracism still.

Frances Louise Martin Chitwood, my great-great-grandmother, my grandmother Maude Lura's grandmother, b. 1820 in Tennessee, daughter of Edward Martin and Unknown. She married John Chitwood, December 25, 1835 in Franklin County, Tennessee.

Ida Belle Chitwood, Maude Lura's sister: b. November 13, 1882; d. June 2, 1904. Poet, school teacher, she died at 22 of probably cholera. Every June 2 Maude Lura wrote in her diary that she and Ida went for a ride in the buggy, Maude at the reins. On the way home Ida became sick and died about 10:00 p.m. the next evening. "My first great sorrow." Her brother Will got home from Arkansas, where he was on a construction crew building a railroad bridge across the Arkansas River, a few hours late for the burial in the Estill Springs Cemetery. Four months later he himself was dead.

John William Chitwood (Willie, Will): Maude Lura's older brother, born Nov 20, 1877, died October 15, 1904, 20 miles west of Cotter, Arkansas

> *"and your brother on the trestle siding*
> *of the bridge they were building*
> *across the Arkansas*
> *when the first train came through*
>
> *who fell into the river when the bridge collapsed*
> *breaking his neck between two rocks"* (*Hard Country*, p. 15.)

The newspaper account of this accident is in my grandmother's trunk.
Their mother, Nancy,

> *"who never recovered.*
> *Ida and Will*
> *dead from the rivers.*
>
> *She used to sit and rock*
> *seeing way off*
> *never acknowledge nothing"* (*Hard Country*, p. 15).

Fred Leonard Chitwood: Maude Lura's youngest sibling, b. March 6,
1886, Estill Springs, Tennessee; d. December 21, 1948. *"My murdered
Great Uncle Fred."* The accounts of his death are in the trunk.
Bess Louise Chitwood (Aunt Bess): Maude Lura's sister, b. September
11, 1888, Estill Springs, Tennessee; died 1970. Chattanooga, Tennessee.
m. (1) J.G. Schaeffer, April 17, 1918; m. (2) Stoke Rogers, 1940.
Laura May Chitwood: Maude Lura's sister, b. May 4, 1891, Estill
Springs; d. March 8, 1953, Detroit, Michigan. Mother of Bobby, George,
and Albert Krotzer.

---

[1] Goodspeed's History of Franklin County, Tennessee,
http://freepages.history.rootsweb.ancestry.com., p. 15.

[2] 1930s Tennessee newspaper accounts in Maude Lura Edens' trunk.

[3] Goodspeed's History, pp. 10, 13.

[4]   *Eden Stone*
The broad human head
and shoulders rise from the forest floor.
The nose, the mouth, the eyes
look from the ridge out over the land
that has disappeared beneath the waters
of Dale Hollow Lake on the mid-
Tennessee-Kentucky line

and the words

E.Edens, age 94, English
died
1558.

(*Hard Country*, p. 7.) This headstone is now at Vanderbilt University and
has tested as authentic.

§

A NOTE ON SOURCES

The Jesse Corn Web Site, "Sketches of the Life and Times of Jesse Corn, Sr, 1753-1809," By Larry and Becky Christiansen and Tom Melton. 2004.

Maude Lura Chitwood Edens' Diary, 1889-1953.

Luella Simmons Sperry's autobiography, "*Childhood Recollections of Sadie Luella Simmons Sperry, Born 26 January 1908, Wilmington, North Carolina.*" Self-published, Danville, Virginia, 1976.

Audrey Garnet Clarke Edens' Diary, 1987-1998; letters (1960 to 1998), journals, baby books, scrapbooks, photo albums, oral stories, conversations, interviews, and memory.

Mozelle Clarke Strickland: letters, journals, photographs, conversations, interviews, and memory.

Cecil Frederick Edens: US Army Records, letters, journals, conversations, interviews, photographs, tapes and memory.

Family members and friends: extensive correspondences, 1960-to present. Interviews.

Cousins Lala Simmons Strader, Dewey Harold Clark, Seifert Sperry, Nancy Walton Cook: letters, conversations and stories.

Genealogy records. Historical records. Newspaper accounts. Google.

Did Fred Edens Ever Molest You? Questionnaire sent to the children in my father's life.

Many books on child sexual abuse, including *All of Our Secrets Exposed, Southern Oregon Women Writing on Abuse and Molestation,* 1993, Macha Press, (ed by Ni Aodagain and Tee Corinne), but probably the most instructive to me during the writing was *Because I Love You, The Silent Shadow of Child Sexual Abuse,* Joyce Allan, Virginia Foundation for the Humanities Press, 2002.

ACKNOWLEGEMENTS

Grateful acknowledgment is made to these arts organizations whose financial and other support enabled me to write:

The Oregon Cultural Heritage Commission; The Oregon Institute of Literary Arts; The Modern Language Association; The California Arts Council; The Espy Foundation; The Vermont Studio Center; The Virginia Center for Creative Arts; The Djerassi Foundation; The Kentucky Foundation for Women; Poets and Writers; Ucross Foundation, Wyoming; Split Rock (University of Minnesota); California Poets In the Schools.

To those who provided me shelter (housesitting) during the writing: Lynn Jeffress, David and Cary Goheen, Dan Read, Charlotte Mills, George Doubiago, Lydia and Charles Rand, Bill Bradd and Judy Sterling, Christy Wagoner, Dawn Hofberg and Bob Schlosser, Susan Hofberg, Colleen Williams (Michele Earle), Rick Gallagher and Shawn Doubiago, Jack Hirschman and Agneta Falk.

Special thanks to these friends and family members who have been particularly supportive during this decade of work: Tom Chamberlin, Alan Scouten, Lynn Jeffress, Amy Kohut, David Meltzer, Charles Potts, Karla Andersdatter, Robert Rasmussen, Michael Tuggle, Ken Eckstein, Gordon Black, John Griffith, Ernie Rivera, Bruce Dahl, Devreaux Baker, Jack Retasket, Neeli Cherkovski, Colleen Williams, Joseph Semudio, Robert Yoder. And Danny, Shawn and Ryan.

Enormous thanks to my readers, Julia Doughty, Michael Sheehan, Gerald Nicosia, Lenore Weiss, Carolyn Casey, and especially, Robert Yoder.

Thank you for the profoundly generous technical and soul help at the last minute, Theresa Whitehill (cover design), Charles Deemer (technical support), Eduardo Smissen (logo), and Charles Francis (holy scanner).

And to Gaea, her holy places in which I wrote *My Father's Love,* from November 2000 to the present, chronologically:

Oysterville, Washington; The Presidio and North Beach San Francisco; Newport, Marylhurst, Silverton, Oregon; Taos, New Mexico; the headlands, Mendocino, Westport, California; Duluth, Minnesota; Berkeley, Sea Ranch, Nevada City, Lake Minden, Miramar-San Diego, Borrego Springs, California; Las Vegas, Nevada; Oakland, The Sea Ranch, California; Port Townsend, Washington; The South Jetty, Florence, Yachats, Oregon; Boulder, Colorado; Portland, Oregon; Grand

Forks, North Dakota; Ashland, Oregon; Bolinas, California; Johnson, Vermont; Highway One; I-5; Caspar Campground; Noyo River Campground; Ten Mile River; Middle Ridge, Albion; North Beach, The Marina, Bernal Heights, NOPA, San Francisco; Petaluma; Gualala, Mendocino, Fort Bragg, California. Antigua, Guatemala. The Mission, Russian Hill, North Beach, the Sunset, San Francisco, California.

And last but hardly least, Valentine, my mother's 1987 conversion Ford 350 Econoline van that she bequeathed me. And to Isis too. (Thank you again, Alan Scouten.)

§

ABOUT THE AUTHOR

Sharon Doubiago's *Love on the Streets, Selected and New Poems,* was published by the University of Pittsburgh, November 2008. She has written two dozen books of poetry and prose, most notably the epic poem *Hard Country* (West End Press), the booklength poem *South America Mi Hija* (University of Pittsburgh) nominated twice for the National Book Award, and the story collections, *El Niño* (Lost Roads Press), and *The Book of Seeing With One's Own Eyes* (Graywolf Press), selected to the Oregon Culture Heritage list: *Literary Oregon, 100 Books, 1800-2000.* She holds three Pushcart Prizes for poetry and fiction and the Oregon Book Award for Poetry for *Psyche Drives the Coast.* She's an online mentor in Creative Writing for the University of Minnesota (Split Rock) and a board member of PENOakland. For two decades she has been writing *Son,* a mother-son memoir, for which she has received two Oregon Institute of Literary Art Fellowships. She lives in San Francisco.

5964477R0

Made in the USA
Lexington, KY
02 July 2010